This Business of™
SONGWRITING

Jason Blume

Jonathan —
I hope you sign
every contract in this
book!

Jason Blum
11/7/09

BILLBOARD BOOKS
an imprint of Watson-Guptill Publications
New York

First published In he United States in 2006 by Billboard Books,
an imprint of Watson-Guptill Publications,
a division of Crown Publishing Group,
Random House, Inc., New York
www.crownpublishing.com
www.watsonguptill.com

Library of Congress Control Number: 2005933954

ISBN: 0-8230-7759-4

ISBN 978-0-8230-7759-5

Printed in the United States of America

First printing, 2006

  2 3 4 5 6 7 8 9/14 13 12 11 10 09 08

Executive Editor: Bob Nirkind
Editor: Meryl Greenblatt
Design: Jay Anning, Thumb Print
Senior Production Manager: Ellen Greene

Contents

Part I

UNDERSTANDING MUSIC PUBLISHING   1

Part II

HOW SONGS GENERATE INCOME   123

Part III
HOW TO PROTECT YOUR SONGS 247

Acknowledgments

I'd like to acknowledge several people who played enormous roles in the writing and publication of this book. First and foremost, I'd like to thank C. Stephen Weaver, Esq., who served as legal consultant for this book, helping me to acquire, understand, and translate the legal agreements and licenses. Steve, I hope you know how much I appreciate your contribution. I could not have written this book without you.

Neil Rice: thank you for your tireless work as research assistant and editor, and for your never-ending support throughout this project. Bob Nirkind: thank you for believing in me and offering me this opportunity. I continue to be in awe of your talent. Meryl Greenblatt: thank you for being such an excellent editor, making me look good, and for being such a pleasure to work with. Rita Rosenkranz: you're the best literary agent I could hope for.

I'd like to acknowledge the contributions of the many music industry professionals who shared their contracts, expertise, and knowledge about the workings of their respective fields. They truly went above and beyond the call of duty: Geoff Mayfield and Silvio Pietroluongo of *Billboard*; *Radio & Records*' Julie Nakahara Kertes, Josh Bennett, and Cyndee Maxwell; ASCAP's Cindy Braun; BMI's Mark Mason, Jean Banks, and Jerry Bailey; SESAC's Tim Fink; songwriter/producer Chris Pelcer; Drew Cohen of Music Theatre International; David Powell, President of The Music Bridge LLC; Ralph Sevush of the Dramatists Guild; Michael Alltop of TheatreWorks USA; publishing administrator Carol Vincent; Justin Wilde, Publisher of Christmas and Holiday Songs; and, for their assistance in the field of children's music, Jill Person, Jessica Harper, Elly Tucker, James Coffey of Blue Vision Music, Jim Moore of the Animal Band, and multiple Grammy–winning songwriter Cathy Fink.

I'd also like to thank Ritch Esra of the Music Business Registry, the Gospel Music Association's Michelle Nipp, the Harry Fox Agency, Gary Christensen of CCLI, Convergent Entertainment's Todd M. Fay, Ted Lowe of ChoiceTracks, Brian DiDomenico of G.A.N.G., Attorneys Howard Lieb and Dave Maddox, Darla Crain and Wayne Coleman for sharing their expertise regarding audits, and Jane Garton of MIDEM.

Preface

> I wish there was one grand artistic depot where the artist
> need only hand in his artwork. As things stand now, one must
> be half a businessman, and I don't know if I can endure this.
>
> LUDWIG VAN BEETHOVEN

When teaching songwriting business workshops I sometimes begin by asking for a show of hands. "Who writes songs because your favorite aspects of being a songwriter are typing cover letters and lyric sheets; making copies of and pitching your songs; pursuing publishers, managers, and A&R representatives; deciphering publishing and licensing agreements; and dealing with rejection?"

Invariably, no hands get raised. Instead, I typically hear, "I *hate* doing the business part. The contracts might as well be written in Greek—and I get knots in my stomach when I have to call a publisher. I just want to write songs, hear them on the radio, make lots of money, and quit my day job."

Most of the writers who achieve success in the music business are those who accept that in order to accomplish their goals, they must understand and excel at both the creative *and* the business sides of their chosen field. By learning about the contracts and licensing agreements you may encounter as a writer, your potential sources of income, and how to conduct business in a professional manner, you will gain a much better chance of having your creativity acknowledged and rewarded. It is my hope that this book will help demystify the business of songwriting and be a resource for you throughout your career.

JASON BLUME

PART I

UNDERSTANDING MUSIC PUBLISHING

CHAPTER ONE

Grasping the Basics of Music Publishing

When studying the business of songwriting, there's no better place to start than with the concept of music publishing. Understanding a music publisher's various functions and responsibilities, the benefits of working with a publisher, as well as how income is allocated between you—the writer—and the publisher is essential for successfully navigating the road to songwriting success.

What Music Publishing Really Means

There are widespread misconceptions about what it means to have a song published. Among them are the notions that publishing a song will make you rich, that it involves the printing of sheet music, and that it is synonymous with the song being recorded and/or played on the radio. While it is possible that these events might occur as a result of a song being published, it is not typically the case.

Music publishing can best be defined as the act of assigning all, or a portion of, ownership, particular legal rights, and a percentage of any income a song or musical composition might generate to an individual or a company, for a specified period of time. Any income a song derives can be conceptualized as being divided into two approximately equal components: the *writer's share* and the *publisher's share.*

The term publisher is used interchangeably to refer both to a music publishing company and to an individual who acquires and promotes songs and writers for a music publishing company. If you have signed a publishing agreement with Jim Smith of Universal Music, you might say, "Universal Music is my publisher." You might also state, "My publisher at Universal is Jim Smith."

By signing a contract granting a company or individual the right to publish your song, you are typically giving away half of any money the song might earn, as well as many of your rights. Why would a songwriter willingly do such a thing? The simple answer is that 50 percent of what might amount to a substantial amount of money (and the credibility and opportunities that come along with success) is better than 100 percent of nothing.

The expectation is that a publisher will use his or her expertise and connections to cause the songs he or she represents to generate income. This is often referred to as *exploiting the copyright.* While the term "exploitation" tends to have a negative connotation, in this context, it's quite desirable. Exploiting the copyright means developing and using a song to its fullest potential: getting the composition recorded and released by an artist (or on your own album, if you are a recording artist as well as a songwriter); generating *print fees* (for sales of, or Internet access to, sheet music, as well as licensing for inclusion in books and magazines); or having a song licensed for inclusion in a film, television show, commercial, or other medium that will produce income. Unless this occurs (and it does not for the majority of published songs), you and your song, along with your publisher, earn nothing. While for many aspiring songwriters publishing a song seems synonymous with success, it is in actuality only the first step in the journey.

What a Music Publisher Really Does

A publisher's responsibilities can be divided into two categories: creative and administrative. This section examines the various tasks and functions that each of these categories encompasses.

Creative Responsibilities

One of the primary creative aspects of a publisher's job is the acquisition of songs for his or her company's *catalog* (the total collection of songs published by any given publisher). Songs are acquired either one at a time or by signing songwriters to exclusive songwriting agreements typically referred to as *staff-writing deals*.

Publishers can help nurture your development by critiquing and honing your songs, providing constructive criticism, suggesting revisions, and serving as a coach, encouraging you to do your very best work. They also oversee the *demo* (demonstration recording) process, sometimes offering suggestions regarding the musical arrangement and production of the demo, and may recommend studios, engineers, musicians, and vocalists.

Yet another important responsibility of publishers is to advance your career by setting up collaborations, both with other songwriters and with recording artists who cowrite their songs. Collaborations—especially those with successful artists—often result in garnering more recordings than those generated as a result of a publisher pitching songs to record label executives and music producers.

In addition to acquiring and pitching songs, publishers sometimes sign aspiring recording artists who are songwriters as well. In these instances, publishers contribute to the development of the artist's songs, musical identity, and image; set up collaborations; finance and produce demos; and use their contacts and connections to try to secure a recording contract. They might also help the artist select a production and management team.

In the event that a publisher secures a recording contract for the writer/artist, the publishing company will likely reap the benefit of publishing many, if not all, of the songs included on the artist's album. Macy Gray, Melissa Etheridge, and Gretchen Wilson are among the many writer/artists who were signed and developed by publishers as they pursued recording contracts.

Another important responsibility is the pitching of songs from the publisher's catalog to recording artists and their managers and producers, as well as to record label executives and those in charge of selecting songs for inclusion in television shows, films, and commercials. In this aspect, publishers act essentially as your agent. They decide which songs from their company's catalog they believe are the most appropriate for a given project. This process is called *casting*.

Casting involves a variety of tasks. To determine which songs might be most appealing and appropriate for a particular artist, publishers typically begin by studying the artist's most recent recordings. If the artist who is seeking songs has not previously released any recordings, a publisher might request demos from the act's record label or producer. The publisher assesses the style of music, the artist's vocal range, the kinds of lyrics he or she typically sings, the image being promoted, and the instrumentation. Then, reviewing the songs he or she represents, the publisher makes a subjective determination of which songs from his or her catalog might be the best fit for the artist. The publisher then submits the songs (either at face-to-face meetings or via mail or e-mail) and does his or her best to persuade those in charge of making the decisions to select their songwriters' material.

Having the right connections is crucial in the music business, and a substantial part of a successful publisher's job is the development and nurturing of close business relationships with music producers, recording artists, artists' managers, and others. Established publishers are likely to have direct access to one or more of the decision makers at every major record label, as well as to the majority of producers.

The individuals at a publishing company who are primarily responsible for pitching songs are often referred to as *songpluggers*. By maintaining regular contact with artists and repertoire (A&R) representatives, artists' managers, and record producers these pluggers stay up to date regarding those artists who are looking for songs and/or collaborators.

In the event that you are signed as a staff-writer at a large music publishing company, you will likely be assigned to work with a specific songplugger. This individual, known as your *point person*, takes primary responsibility for your development, pitching your catalog, making others at the company aware of your strongest songs, scheduling collaborations, and providing you with access to information. At smaller companies, writers might work equally with the entire staff.

In order to pitch their catalogs successfully, publishers need to be aware of which artists are seeking material at any given time. Therefore, at each music publishing company, one or more publishers typically compile this information by contacting record label executives, artists' managers, and producers at least once each month. They may also glean information from publications such as *RowFax, SongQuarters, SongLink International,* and *New On The Charts,* which are available for purchase (for more about these publications, see Chapter 5). This information is assembled into a *pitch sheet* that is shared with their staff and writers. The pitch sheet, sometimes referred to as a *tip sheet* or *casting list,* provides essential information including which artists and film projects are currently seeking songs; the kinds of songs they are looking for; the name of the producer; the A&R person primarily responsible for the project; and the date the artist is scheduled to record.

Large publishing companies typically hire one or more individuals who focus their song pitching efforts primarily toward film and television projects. These individuals maintain regular contact with *music supervisors*, those responsible for the selection of songs for films and television shows. These pluggers search their catalogs for appropriate songs to pitch for films and TV shows, as well as suggest that their company's writers create songs geared specifically to these projects. In many instances, publishers and their writers are granted access to scripts or synopses of television and film projects for which songs are needed.

Administrative Responsibilities

High on the list of a publisher's administrative responsibilities is the collection of *mechanical royalties* (often referred to as mechanicals; these are royalties paid for sales of tangible products, such as CDs and DVDs, as well as digital downloading) and licensing fees, the sending of royalty statements (typically twice per year, as stipulated in the song publishing agreement), and the distribution of the writer's share of those royalties.

Publishers are typically paid mechanical royalties from record labels on a quarterly basis (four times per year). In theory, the collection of royalties appears to be as simple as opening envelopes that contain checks. In actuality, it may involve much more, including monitoring statements to ensure that proper payments have been made, auditing record labels and other licensees when errors are suspected, and negotiating deals with subpublishers in foreign territories to collect royalties on the publishing company's behalf.

Publishers earn their income from the *publisher's share* of royalties paid for the sales of products such as CDs and DVDs; from payments made to *download* songs digitally (purchasing a song electronically over the Internet for future use); from the sale of sheet music; from licensing fees paid for inclusion of their songs in television, films, and commercials; and from royalties generated when songs from their catalogs are broadcast on radio or television. (A detailed explanation of royalties is included in Part II.)

When you sign a song publishing agreement, your publisher performs a myriad of additional organizational and clerical functions on your behalf. Protecting your songs by securing a copyright is among them. This entails completing paperwork, providing a copy of the song, and paying the required fee to the U.S. Copyright Office before the material is distributed to the public. (For more about copyrights, see Chapter 16.)

When a song is considered for inclusion in a television show, film, or commercial, it's the publisher's job to negotiate the fees and issue the *synchronization license*. The *sync* (pronounced "sink") *fee* (the amount paid for the right to synchronize a song or piece of music to a film or TV show) and the preparation of the sync license are typically handled by a publishing company's business affairs or legal department. (See Chapter 11 for additional information about sync licenses.)

The issuing of licenses for audio recordings, print, and *digital print rights* (the right to distribute and sell sheet music via the Internet) is also among a publisher's responsibilities, as is the registration of songs with the *performing rights orga-*

nization (also called a *performing rights society*), or PRO (a company that collects and distributes royalties earned for performances including radio and television airplay), with which the songwriter and publisher are affiliated. This is required to facilitate the collection of *performance royalties* (paid primarily for radio airplay, television broadcasts, Internet performances, and ringtones). (Performing rights organizations and performance royalties are discussed in Chapter 10.)

Depending on the contractual agreement, a publisher may be responsible for paying all or part of your expenses incurred for the production of demos. This may be as simple as cutting a few checks. However, in the U.S., if the players and singers performing on a demo are members of their respective unions, it is necessary for the publisher to prepare paperwork required by the musicians' union (the American Federation of Musicians, typically referred to as the AFM) and the vocalists' union (the American Federation of Television and Radio Artists, known as AFTRA). These contracts are often referred to as *the card* or *the union card*.

From many writers' points of view, a publisher's most important administrative function is providing monetary advances against future royalties so that the writer is free to create. It's rare for a publisher to pay an advance to publish a single song— unless the song has already been recorded by a recording artist and is likely to earn royalties. However, when writers sign exclusive songwriting agreements (staff-writing deals), they are typically advanced enough money to allow them to quit their "day jobs" and concentrate 100 percent of their energies on their songwriting. (You'll learn more about single song agreements and staff-writing deals in Chapters 3 and 4.)

The Difference Between a Music Publisher and a Record Label

The distinction between a music publisher and a record label is often misunderstood. The previous section outlined the responsibilities of music publishers. This section addresses the role of record labels. You will see that these two entities serve very different functions.

Record labels are in the business of signing and developing recording artists—not songs. They are also responsible for the promotion and distribution of their artists' works. Employees in various departments of a record label oversee virtually all budgetary and creative decisions involved in the recording and marketing of albums.

The *Artists and Repertoires Department* (almost always referred to as *A&R*) is responsible for the creative elements of the process. The A&R department's employees' responsibilities include scouting, signing, and developing artists; helping artists to find the ideal producer to best capture their sound; locating hit songs for those acts who do not write their own material; and overseeing song selection for those artists who are also songwriters. The A&R representative in charge of a given artist's album supervises all aspects of the project and serves as the artist's advocate to the other departments at the label, disseminating information and generating excitement about the artist's music.

Within the A&R department is a division called *A&R Administration* or *Recording Administration*. This division handles many of the administrative functions of the recording process, including monitoring recording budgets; approving payments for studios, vocalists, and musicians; and generating and proofreading *label copy*. Label copy is the technical name for the information printed on an album (such as the name of the artist and the album's title) as well as the information comprising the album's liner notes, which generally include the title and length of the songs; credits for musicians, vocalists, producers, engineers, and studios; acknowledgments; and the songwriters' and publishers' names and performing rights organization affiliations.

The A&R department also serves a "quality control" function. The A&R executive responsible for a particular artist listens closely to master recordings of his or her artist's albums and singles to be certain that there are no flaws. This person then checks to be sure that the sound is not distorted; the songs are sequenced in the desired order; there is a proper amount of space between songs; and that the overall sound level is correct. Final recordings must be approved by both an A&R representative and an artist's producer before being mass produced or made available to the public.

Additional departments at record labels include *Business Affairs*, responsible for contract negotiation and all legal concerns; *Art*, in charge of product packaging, including album cover design; *Accounting*, which tracks and pays royalties to recording artists and song publishers; *Marketing* or *Product Development*, responsible for developing advertising campaigns and additional ways to promote the label's artists; *Publicity*, which generates and coordinates media coverage, such as television appearances and magazine interviews; *Promotion*, which provides radio and video programmers with product and tries to persuade them to play it; *Sales*, responsible for product placement in stores, catalogs, and online Web sites that sell music, and for monitoring sales; and *Human Resources*, in charge of hiring employees and administering employee benefits.

A record label's income is generated primarily by the sale of music product (CDs, digital downloads, videos, and DVDs). Labels also collect licensing fees for placement of their master recordings in television, films, and commercials.

Record labels pay their artists a royalty for sales and downloads of singles, albums, and videos, as well as a share of money collected for *master use licenses* issued for additional uses of the artist's master recordings, for example, in a film or commercial. This royalty is negotiated when an artist signs a recording contract and constitutes a completely separate payment from any royalties paid for the use of the songs.

If a recording artist writes his or her own songs, he or she is paid separately as an artist— and as a songwriter.

For his or her role as a recording artist, a performer is entitled to royalties for sales, downloads, and licensing fees from the record label. In addition, in his or her capacity as a songwriter, the artist receives mechanical royalties and licensing fees from a publisher, as well as performance royalties from a PRO.

Similarly, when a recording is included in a film, television show, or commercial, two separate licensing fees are paid: the publisher is paid for the use of the song itself, while the record label is paid for the use of the master recording, encompassing the artist's performance.

In summation, music publishers and record labels serve very different functions. Publishers work with songwriters and song demos, the raw material of the music business. They deal primarily with the acquisition and promotion of songs. In contrast, record labels work with recording artists and their finished products—recorded versions of songs (referred to as *masters*)—and are responsible for the promotion and marketing of master recordings.

The Relationship Between a Songwriter and a Music Publisher

Successfully placing songs with recording artists and in television shows and films is typically a team effort, with a songwriter and a music publisher each contributing their expertise toward a common goal. Described simplistically, writers contribute songs while publishers attend to the business so the writer can be free to create.

As previously noted in this chapter, publishers are salesmen of sorts, pitching songs in the hopes of placing them in situations where they will earn income. The best thing that you as a writer can contribute to the process is exceptional songs. A good work ethic, a great attitude, and a personality that makes others eager to work with you are all important assets. But, without great songs, it is unlikely that even the best publisher will be able to generate income in this highly competitive business.

Once you have signed a song with a publisher, it is both appropriate and advisable to maintain contact with him or her on a regular basis (perhaps, once or twice per month). Remember that in addition to your songs, your publisher has hundreds, if not thousands, of others in his or her catalog; it's your job to remind him or her of how terrific your songs are. One way to accomplish this is by apprising your publisher of any positive feedback you receive. It can also be effective to send an e-mail periodically along the lines of: "Just wanted to put in a plug for 'If It Hadn't Rained.'"

Ask your publisher monthly for a list of those artists for which he or she is currently seeking songs and make suggestions. But remember that every song is not appropriate for every artist—and be prepared to accept that your suggestions will not always be acted upon. Publishers establish and maintain their credibility by presenting songs they deem to be the very best and most fitting songs for a given project—and it's likely that they have many good songs in addition to yours.

There are countless instances of writers securing their own recordings of songs about which their publisher may, or may not, have felt strongly. Many publishers expect writers to augment their songpluggers' efforts by pitching their own songs. However, it is always advisable to communicate with your publisher and formulate a game plan before pitching on your own.

The extent to which a publisher can contribute to the development of a songwriter's career cannot be overestimated, and it speaks volumes to note that only a handful of songwriters have ever achieved and sustained a lucrative career without benefit of having been affiliated with a music publisher.

Music Publishing Versus Work for Hire

Aspiring songwriters sometimes state that their goal is to "sell" a song. In actuality, most successful songwriters rarely, if ever, sell their songs outright. When you "sell" a song to a publisher (by signing a publishing agreement), you are granting specific rights to an individual or company. The expectation is that in exchange for ownership of your song, the publisher will use his or her efforts to cause the song to generate royalties by placing it with recording artists, or having it included in films, television shows, commercials, or in print. In the event that this occurs, you are compensated.

As you will learn in Chapter 4, in a typical publishing contract the music publisher agrees to pay the writer the *writer's share* (typically, 50 percent) of any royalties his or her song earns. The publisher also accepts responsibility for issuing the licenses necessary for recordings to be used in various media, distributed to the public, and made available for sale (often referred to as being *commercially released*) on a CD, video, DVD, or via digital downloading, and for providing an accounting of the sales. So, while a song publishing contract typically refers to a song being "sold" to the publisher, in actuality, the writer continues to be credited as the "composer" and is paid accordingly. The relatively rare instances in which songwriters actually do sell their work are designated by the copyright statute as "works made for hire."

As it applies to songwriting, a *work for hire* (as it is typically called) can be defined as a song, melody, or lyric specifically created on someone else's behalf in exchange for compensation. The individual or company commissioning the work is considered the owner.

The creator of a work for hire waives all rights of ownership, including the rights to copyright, sell, or publish the work. Depending upon the provisions of his or her contractual agreement, the creator may, or may not, relinquish all rights to any revenue the work might generate.

There are two categories of works made for hire. The first applies to works created by employees *within the scope of their employment*, meaning, works that an employee has been paid to create as part of his or her job. The staff of an advertising agency, a jingle production company employee, an in-house composer who scores training films, or a theme park employee hired to create background music are among those who might be included in this category. In these instances it is implicit that an employer owns what it has paid its employee to create.

As defined by the U.S. Supreme Court, a person is defined as an "employee" (for copyright purposes) if the company or individual who commissions the work has the right to control the manner and means by which the work is created. This legal definition applies regardless of how the parties describe their relationship. When contested, court rulings have established that two criteria weigh heavily in determining whether an individual is an employee:

- Whether the firm pays the worker's Social Security taxes and

- Whether the firm provides the worker with employee benefits (such as health insurance and paid sick days).

These criteria do not apply to staff-writers (as explained in Chapter 3) and the songs they write are not works made for hire.

The second type of work for hire applies to creations specifically ordered or *commissioned works*, meaning, created at someone's request. To be considered a work for hire these works must be created for one of nine specific uses delineated by copyright law. Below are the five of these criteria that might apply to songwriters:

- *Created for inclusion in a motion picture or other audiovisual work.* This is the category in which a songwriter, who is not employed to create music, would most likely produce work considered a work for hire. This category encompasses songs or musical scores written for films, television, or video games—provided that a written agreement is signed, acknowledging that the songs and/or music were indeed commissioned for the film (or other audiovisual work).

- *As part of a collective work.* A *collective work* can be defined as a collection comprised of individual works that are each eligible to be copyrighted, such as the songs on a CD.

- *As a compilation.* A *compilation* is similar to a collection, but has a broader definition. The material within a compilation includes groups of works, including collections, such as a boxed set of previously released albums. A compilation may include both works that are, and are not, copyrightable.

- *As a translation.* This applies to instances in which a translator is paid a one-time, flat fee to translate a lyric from one language to another. (However, it is more common for a translator to be regarded as a co-creator and, therefore, to share a percentage of copyright ownership and revenue.)

- *As a supplementary work.* A *supplementary work* is something that adds to another work, such as an album's liner notes or an introduction to a book.

The copyright statute states that, in addition to meeting one of the criteria previously listed, to fulfill the definition of a work made for hire, an agreement must be signed by both the composer and the party commissioning the work, documenting that both parties are aware that the specified work has been commissioned as a work for hire and that the creator understands that he or she retains no rights to the composition. A sample letter expressing this agreement is shown on page 11.

Salaried employees who create works within the scope of their employment are not required to sign this type of agreement because it is understood that they are being paid to create such works.

When a song is published, the rights to it are transferred from the creator to the publisher. The "termination of transfers" provision of the 1976 Copyright Act al-

Date _____

Name of hiring firm _____

Address of hiring firm _____

Dear _____ :

This letter will serve to confirm that ____name of hiring firm____ has commissioned you

to prepare the following work: _____description_____ to be completed

no later than _____date_____ .

You agree that this is being created as a "work made for hire," and that

_____name of hiring firm_____, for whom the work is being prepared, shall own all

rights, title, and interest in and to the work, including the copyright in the work.

You further agree that, if applicable, to whatever extent the work is not a "work

made for hire," you will assign to _____name of hiring firm_____ all rights of

ownership, including ownership of the entire copyright in the work.

You agree to participate in preparation of all documents necessary for

_____name of hiring firm_____ to protect ownership of the copyright of the work.

You represent and warrant that the work you create will be original, will not

infringe upon the rights of any third party, and will not have been previously

assigned, licensed, or otherwise encumbered.

As compensation for your services, _____name of hiring firm_____ will pay you the

following amount upon satisfactory completion of the

work:_____payment_____ .

The signatures below make this a binding contract between us. Please sign both

copies and return one to me. The other signed copy is for your records.

Sincerely,

_____name of hiring firm_____

By:_____signature_____

_____typed or printed name_____

Title:_____ Date:_____

I agree with the above understanding.

By:_____signature_____

_____typed or printed name_____

Sample work-for-hire agreement.

lows creators, or their heirs, to reclaim ownership of a song thirty-five years after the copyright has been transferred to the publisher. In contrast to a published song, the rights to a work made for hire never revert back to its creator because in the eyes of copyright law, the work was never owned by the creator.

The benefits of writing works for hire can include a steady source of income; access to "inside" information about what a film production company is seeking; and a guaranteed payment, instead of having to wait for royalties that may take a year or more to arrive, or may never materialize. But bear in mind that the way the music business is currently set up, it is extremely unusual for a songwriter to write a song that meets the definition of a work for hire, unless he or she is an employee of an advertising agency or is hired by a film production company.

Now that you understand what publishing a song really means; a publisher's functions; how publishers differ from record labels; and that songs are rarely sold, it's time to learn how to get a publisher.

CHAPTER TWO

Getting a Publisher to Represent Your Work

"How do you get to Carnegie Hall? Practice, practice, practice." How do you get a publisher to represent your work? Write exceptional songs that publishers can place successfully with recording artists and in films and on television shows—and take the steps necessary to ensure that your songs get their attention.

It All Starts with Writing Great Songs

Music publishers have a tough job. When they meet with A&R executives, record producers, or other individuals seeking hit songs, the songs they play must compete with those written by the most successful current hit-makers in the business. Songpluggers work hard to cultivate their business relationships and sustain them by consistently bringing in material of the highest caliber. Therefore, publishers require a constant influx of exceptional songs—material that can beat out the stiffest competition.

A&R representatives and music publishers listen to hundreds of songs each week. One more well-crafted tune is unlikely to capture their attention. As Lynn Gann (Vice President of Full Circle Music Publishing) said, "When you go to a record label to play songs, you have to slap them out of their A&R trance."

To get you and your work on their radar screen, it's necessary to go beyond what is expected and include original, fresh elements. Once you've mastered the songwriting basics you've got to go a step further and craft melodies, rhythms, lyrical concepts, and imagery that will compel an artist, an A&R executive, or a music supervisor to say, "Wow. This is what I've been looking for!" and a publisher to think, "I've got to get this writer under contract."

. . . But You Also Need to Consider the Market

It's self-evident that publishers need outstanding songs to work with—but there's an additional element to consider. Not all artists record *outside songs*, that is, songs not written or cowritten by the artist, producer, or band members. In fact, in many genres of music, such as hard rock, Americana, alternative, hip-hop, and R&B it's rare for an artist to record material that is not self-penned or cowritten.

When pitching songs for recording artists, publishers need an arsenal of material that is appropriate for artists who do not write their own material. If the songs you write are perfect for U2, Green Day, Sting, Ani DiFranco, Beyoncé, Jay-Z, Dido, Hoobastank, or any of the countless other *performing songwriters* and bands who exclusively record their own or cowritten work, publishers may have few, if any, places to go with them.

If you write exceptional songs that are of the ilk best suited for artists who write their own songs, a savvy publisher may be able to arrange for you to collaborate with artists and producers who are also songwriters. When contacting publishers, let them know whether you are interested in pursuing such collaborations. Bear in mind that it is easier for songwriters who have not yet established a track record of hits to work with artists who are on their way up, as opposed to trying to write with established superstars.

Getting Feedback About Your Work

It's difficult, if not impossible, to remain objective about your songs; you know what the lyrics mean and, presumably, the melodies move you. But only by receiving impartial input can you ascertain whether your songs are successfully communicating the emotions and meanings that you intend to convey—and are measuring up to professional standards. Some doors may open only once so it's important that your work be ready prior to pitching it. You can accomplish this by securing both professional and peer critiques.

Supportive friends and family are likely to offer comments such as, "Your songs are as good as anything on the radio." Unfortunately, they are probably not qualified to offer objective input regarding the construction of your work, how it might be improved, or its commercial potential. These are tasks best left to professionals and to those who have studied the craft of songwriting.

Where to Go to Get Your Songs Critiqued

Professional song critiques are available from a variety of sources. In Nashville, New York, and Los Angeles, qualified songwriting teachers offer private consultations. If you are not in close proximity to these cities, many of the instructors offer their services via telephone, Internet, or mail. You can find these instructors online and by referrals.

You can also get critiques from other songwriters by joining any of the hundreds of songwriting groups and associations throughout the U.S. and internationally. Typically, at monthly meetings members have opportunities to present works in progress and benefit from numerous sources of feedback. Additionally, members of the Nashville Songwriters Association International (NSAI), SongU, and Taxi can avail themselves of critiques provided by these organizations. An extensive listing of songwriting organizations and instructors can be found in the Appendix of this author's book *6 Steps to Songwriting Success: The Comprehensive Guide to Writing and Marketing Hit Songs* (revised and expanded edition) (Billboard Books).

How to Get the Most from a Song Critique—and What Not to Do

Ideally, the critiques you receive will address the strengths and weaknesses of your songs' structures, melodies, chords, rhythms, lyrics, and commercial potential in the current marketplace. As opposed to simply expressing what is wrong, the most effective critiques offer specific constructive suggestions for improvement.

If the feedback from a critique resonates and you think, "What a great idea! Why didn't I think of that?" it's likely you will want to go back to the drawing board and institute changes. But what if you disagree with the input you receive? What if you think it's off the mark or simply wrong? It is neither appropriate nor beneficial to argue or become defensive about a critique. Nor does it help to clarify what your song *really* means; the listener should be able to discern this from listening to the song—without explanation.

If you feel the criticism and suggestions you receive are not valid, seek additional input from other sources; not all those who critique are equally skilled, nor do they necessarily see things in the same way. But if you consistently receive the same feedback (for example, "The story is confusing. I didn't understand the second verse. . ." or "The chorus melody is complicated and difficult to sing and remember. . ."), you would be wise to accept that a rewrite is in order.

Remember that you have nothing to lose by instituting changes; if you don't prefer the rewritten version you can go back to your original draft. Ultimately, you need to please yourself before you will have the confidence to attempt to please others with your work.

Getting Your Foot in the Door

Taking the steps necessary to getting your songs heard may be as important a part of your songwriting career as is writing great songs. Regardless of how good your work is, you must knock on the proverbial doors if your talent is to be recognized and rewarded. These doors rarely open without effort, but there are actions you can take to encourage the process.

Why Referrals Are Useful in Attracting a Publisher's Attention

A publisher's limited time is best spent by listening to songs by hit writers, not by weeding through piles of *unsolicited songs*, material which has been neither requested nor submitted by an established writer, an entertainment attorney, or another reputable music business professional. Although it is certainly conceivable that a gem may be hidden among those songs submitted by unpublished writers, the likelihood is that a publisher or A&R person stands a much better chance of finding that elusive hit if his or her time is spent listening to material from established hit-makers.

Unless requested, material mailed to publishers and record labels is typically either returned unopened or is relegated to the "unsolicited" pile, where it joins countless other submissions that will likely go unheard. The best way to avoid this is to secure a referral from someone the publisher knows and trusts. If a music industry professional feels strongly enough about your work to recommend that a publisher listen, the publisher can be relatively certain that his or her valuable time will not be wasted.

How to Get Referrals That Attract Attention

Wouldn't it be wonderful if the formula for attracting a publisher's attention were as simple as buying a book with a listing of publishers, making some introductory phone calls, and mailing out your songs? Then all you would need to do is sign a contract and cash the royalty checks that overflow from your mailbox. Unfortunately, in the real world it doesn't work that way.

The keys to getting the attention you need are:

- Obtaining referrals from other songwriters and industry professionals and

- Interacting with publishers and other professionals at music industry events.

The number one way to get a publisher's ear is by securing a referral from a source that he or she respects, for example, a writer with whom the publisher works, an entertainment attorney, or a staff member of one of the performing rights organizations.

Each of the PROs—the American Society of Composers, Authors, and Publishers (ASCAP), Broadcast Music International (BMI), and SESAC (formerly known as the Society of European Stage Authors and Composers)—employs a staff whose jobs include meeting with and advising developing writers. (For a detailed explanation of PROs, see Chapter 10.) If one of these representatives hears material that he or she deems exceptional, it's likely that you will be referred to one or more publishers. Be aware, however, that PRO representatives are inundated with requests for appointments, and as a result it is typically necessary to schedule a meeting far in advance.

In addition, BMI and ASCAP both offer free songwriting workshops that provide excellent educational, as well as networking, opportunities that sometimes lead to referrals, as well as opportunities to play your songs for publishers. For information about upcoming PRO workshops visit www.bmi.com and www.ascap.com.

Writing with published songwriters, and with those who have established business relationships at music publishing companies, typically provides your best source of introductions to publishers. Most publishers are happy to listen to material from someone who is writing with and/or referred by one of their writers.

An effective way to meet and network with writers and, in some instances, publishers and other music industry professionals who might provide referrals, is by attending classes at local colleges and at song camps, such as those presented by NSAI (www.nashvillesongwriters.com), SummerSongs (www.summersongs.com), Paul Reisler's Songwriting Camp (www.kitheatre.org), NashCamp (www.nashcamp.com), and Breckenridge Educational and Music Seminars (BEAMS; www.beamsonline.com), as well as by taking classes given online by SongU (www.songu.com).

Local songwriting organizations offer camaraderie and educational opportunities, as well as a chance for members to interact and share information and contacts. An extensive listing of national and local songwriting organizations as well as songwriting camps can be found in the Appendix of *6 Steps to Songwriting Success*.

There are also opportunities to meet and play songs for publishers at music industry events such as BMI's Songwriters' and Artists' Workshops (www.bmi.com), the Taxi Road Rally (www.taxi.com), the West Coast Songwriters' "Creation:Craft: Connection" (www.westcoastsongwriters.org), NSAI's Spring Symposium and Song-posium (www.nashvillesongwriters.com), the Texas Songwriters Cruise (www. txsongwriterscruise.com), the Kauai Music Festival (www.kauaimusicfestival.com), and the Durango Songwriter's Expo (www.durangosong.com).

For writers of folk and Americana music, festivals such as those held annually at Kerrville (www.kerrville-music.com), the Swannanoa Gathering (swangathering.org), SummerSongs/WinterSongs (www.summersongs.com), the Philadelphia Folk Festival (www.folkfest.org), the Frank Brown Song Festival (www.fbisf.com), and the Amer-icana Music Conference (www.americanamusic.org) present excellent networking opportunities.

Writers focusing on the Christian music market can meet publishers and like-minded writers at events such as those listed on the following Web sites: www.christianmusic.about.com/od/festivals, www.christianteens.about.com/od/festivals, and www.christianmusic.about.com/od/forsongwriters. NSAI also offers a monthly workshop in Nashville geared to writers of Christian music.

What about finding a publisher by reading books and magazines that include lists of publishers and/or posting your songs on Internet Web sites? Successful publish-ers typically represent hundreds, if not thousands, of songs, and have a vested in-terest in the success of their staff-writers, many of whom have track records of writ-ing hits. The majority of a publisher's time is spent pitching songs that are already in his or her company's catalog, as well as working with the company's staff-writ-ers. It is highly unlikely that these publishers will take the time to meet with or re-view songs mailed in by unknown writers. It's even less likely that they will spend their time surfing the Internet to listen to songs posted on Web sites. Nor will le-gitimate publishers spend money running ads in magazines to find songs.

Preparing to Interest a Publisher with a Presentation Package

Because, as previously stated, few legitimate publishers will listen to unsolicited material that arrives by mail or via the Internet, it is imperative that you secure a referral or permission prior to sending your songs. Some publishers and other music industry professionals may require you to include a *submission code*, a pre-determined word or series of numbers, on the outside of your package. This code, which publishers will furnish if necessary, alerts them that this is indeed requested material. Writing "Requested Material" on your mailing label will not do the trick if your submission was not actually solicited.

At the time of this book's printing, compact discs (CDs) are the format being used to present songs by mail and at meetings. However, technology advances quickly and CDs may soon be relegated to a place in history alongside vinyl records, 8-track tapes, digital audio tapes (DATs), and audiocassettes. Regardless of which recording formats come into vogue at any given time, prior to preparing your submission, your job is to ascertain how your listener prefers to receive your music—and then, present it as requested.

Be sure to address your package to a specific publisher at the company, as opposed to: "Moondream Music—Attn: Publishing Department." Protect your CD by placing it in a plastic CD case and mailing it in a padded envelope slightly larger than the materials you are sending. Mailing your CD in a box or an oversized envelope or padding it with paper or bubble wrap will have the same effect as writing "Amateur" on the outside of the package.

Presuming that you've networked, gotten referrals, and secured permission to submit your material—now what? Until you have established credits, it is likely that you will be asked to mail in your songs before a publisher or other industry professional will be willing to invest time in a meeting. The sections that follow explain the components of a successful song submission package.

Composing an Effective Cover Letter

Your cover letter is your emissary and, as your sole representative in your absence, it establishes the first impression you make. It should be succinct and typed on professional-looking letterhead. Adorning your letterhead with musical notes and/or other fancy embellishments, such as glitter or drawings, will classify you as an amateur. Save your creativity for your songs; let them be what sets you apart from the competition.

As you can see from the sample that is shown opposite, your cover letter should be brief, providing only the most pertinent information: the source of your referral, what you have enclosed, and your contact information. If you have major songwriting credits it is acceptable to include this information. For example, you might say, "My songs have been recorded by artists including Britney Spears, Clay Aiken, and Kenny Chesney" or "The first song on the CD ("Not the Way That I Loved You") won first prize in the U.S.A. Songwriting Competition." However, stating that your songs have been performed at high school talent shows and in local pageants does not help your cause.

It is not appropriate to include extraneous information such as the names of the singers, musicians, engineers, or demo recording studios. Nor should you mention your day job or describe the songs, such as: "The first song is a thoughtful, sensitive, positive love ballad; song number two is an up-tempo happy pop/rock song . . ." If the publisher can't tell by listening, you're in big trouble.

Including a lyric sheet is advisable, although not mandatory. (A sample lyric sheet can be found on page 23.) Do not, however, include a *lead sheet* (sheet music) or a chord chart unless specifically requested—and never send a lead sheet in lieu of a demo recording. Nor should you send a photo or bio unless you are an aspiring recording artist and are contacting the publisher in the hopes of achieving representation as such.

It is acceptable to follow up your submission with a phone call, e-mail, or fax a week or two after sending your package. If you do not receive a response, you might follow up a second time after several additional weeks have passed, but doing so more frequently can label you as a pest.

REBECCA ST. CLAIRE

123 Possumbush Rd., Mytown, NY 12345   (123) 456-7890
e-mail: hitsongs.com


```
Date
Publisher's Name
Company Name
Address
City, State   Zip Code
```

Dear (Publisher's first name):
As we discussed, I was referred to your company by
my collaborator, Neil Thurston.

As promised, I've enclosed a CD with two songs
I've written, as well as lyric sheets.

I feel strongly about these songs and I appreciate
your reviewing them. I look forward to speaking
with you when you've had a chance to listen.

Sincerely,

Rebecca St. Claire

Encl.

Sample songwriter's cover letter to a music publisher.

Bear in mind that most publishers do not keep a log of the songs submitted to them and their secretary may not be able to confirm that your package has arrived. It is not realistic to expect a response to your mailed submission. While some publishers may send a "form" rejection letter, most of them will not take the time to do so. If a publisher is interested in signing your songs or hearing additional material, you can be sure that he or she will contact you.

What to Include on Your CD

The only recordings on your CD should be your song demos. It is never appropriate to include a spoken introduction, description, or explanation.
Attach a typed label that lists the following information:

- The name of the individual to whom the CD is being pitched

- Your name

- The song titles

- Your contact information: address, phone number, fax (if applicable), and e-mail address.

Including the writers' names, the copyright symbol, and the year of copyright for each song is optional. The law only requires inclusion of the copyright symbol (©) on "visibly perceptible copies," meaning printed music, such as sheet music. It is not necessary to include the copyright notice on the CD itself.

When creating your CD label it's a good idea to print a duplicate to affix to the inside of the case (in the indented area where the CD rests) or type the information listed above onto the CD cover insert (see sample opposite). This allows your listener to reference song titles and track listings without removing the CD from its player. Note that it is not appropriate to include any additional information such as the length of the songs; the names of the singers, musicians, engineer, or recording studio; or descriptions of the songs.

How Many Songs to Include—and in What Order

When presenting your music (whether in person or via mail), begin with the songs you feel are strongest. If your songs fail to make an immediate positive impression, it's likely the publisher will not continue listening long enough to find the gem you've saved for last. Unless a publisher (or A&R person) has requested a compilation or collection of your work, when submitting by mail limit your submission to a maximum of three songs. Two or three outstanding songs create a better impression than ten or more well-crafted, but unexceptional, songs.

For many writers there is a powerful temptation to pitch more than the recommended number of songs: "What if the eighth song would have been the one they loved?" Even the most successful writers don't write a hit every time, and part of your responsibility as a writer is to discern which songs are your very best—and

TO: Mike Hollandsworth

JASON BLUME SONGS

1. ON ANGELS'
   WINGS

2. WHAT I NEED

JASON BLUME
222 2ND AVENUE, HITSVILLE, NY 12345
(123) 456-7890, myemail@aol.com

Sample songwriter's
CD label for a publisher.

then, pitch only those. By playing your work for family, friends, and other song-writers, you will learn which of your songs garner the strongest reactions. If you impress a publisher by sharing two or three excellent songs, you will likely be in-vited to submit additional songs. However, if you send a dozen less-than-stellar songs, you may not get that same opportunity.

Preparing for and Meeting with a Publisher Face-to-Face

It is always preferable to have a meeting, as opposed to mailing songs or dropping them off. By sitting face-to-face you'll have an opportunity to begin a relationship, learn which kinds of material appeal to the individual you're meeting with, and possibly gain valuable feedback about your work.

It's likely that you've worked hard on crafting your songs as well as networking in order to secure a meeting. When you get through the office doors, your job is to keep them open. The tips that follow will help ensure that you are prepared beforehand and present yourself in a professional manner when meeting with a publisher.

Preparing a Proper Lyric Sheet

Many publishers prefer not to look at lyric sheets while they listen to songs, instead reacting to them as they might if they were hearing the songs on the radio. Some music business professionals do like to be able to peruse a lyric sheet while listening, so to play it safe, it is always a good idea to have a typed copy of the lyric sheet available for each song you anticipate playing in case it is requested.

A lyric sheet (see sample opposite) should include only:

- The song's title
- The lyric
- The writers' names
- The copyright symbol followed by the year of copyright (*Tip*: To avoid the impression that you are pitching an old song you might omit the date if your song was copyrighted more than a year or two ago—or replace it with the current year.)
- Your contact information (including address, telephone and fax numbers, and e-mail address)
- Although it is not mandatory, it is acceptable to include the writers' PRO affiliations (BMI, ASCAP, or SESAC for writers and publishers in the U.S.), if applicable.

It is not appropriate to include:

- The singer's or musicians' names
- Chords
- The date of creation (other than the year of copyright registration)
- Any description of the song (for example, "pop/rock love song" or "builds from a ballad to high energy")
- The tempo
- The name of the demo recording studio or engineer
- Suggestions of artists for whom you would like the song to be considered.

Presenting Yourself Professionally

When a writer is hungry for recognition and validation (not to mention hoping to quit his or her day job), it's only natural to place enormous expectations on each meeting and opportunity to pitch songs. "If this publisher would only say 'yes' it would change my entire life." With this mindset, some writers become nervous and overly solicitous, but appearing desperate will not help your cause.

It may take some of the pressure off if you keep in mind that, presuming you are talented, attentive to business, and persistent, your career will not be contingent on what any one individual feels about your work. Publishers need great songs; without them they cannot persuade the decision makers to choose songs from their catalogs.

Jason Blume

9 Music Square South, PMB 352, Nashville, TN 37203 • (615) 665-2381
JBSongdoc1@aol.com

TO BE LOVED BY YOU

We were strong—We were close
Ridin' on a one-way ticket to forever
Now we're just shadows of the past

And you say—I'd be okay
If these arms would learn how to forget you
I'd do anything for you—But that's too much to ask ('Cause)

> **You don't know how it feels inside**
> **To be loved by you—To be loved by you**
> **When I'm reaching out through the dead of night**
> **To be loved by you—To be loved by you**
> **I'd give my last breath away**
> **To hear you say it's not the end**
> **And be loved by you**
> **Loved by you again**

In the dark—In the night
Feel the whisper of a touch—A sweet sensation
I think what we could and should have been

But I can't—Make you feel
The way I feel if you just don't feel it
And the touch of your hand's something my heart can't forget (No)

(repeat chorus)

And again I'm pounding my fist on a door
Can't take anymore—Wantcha back—Can't have you
And the pieces of my heart won't start to heal
And I know that you've never ever felt this deal
Now have you? Have you?
I've got to have you

(repeat chorus)

Jason Blume (BMI)
© 2006

Sample lyric sheet.

If you are writing the kinds of songs publishers seek, they need you as much as you need them—so don't grovel. But neither should you be arrogant. Few things put off a professional as quickly as statements such as, "I guarantee that this song will be a Number One and a Song of the Year Grammy winner." So, avoid hyping your songs; let the music speak for itself.

When preparing for a meeting, be aware that the music business tends to be less formal than most of the corporate world. It's far more likely that the publisher you meet will be wearing jeans or casual slacks and a sweater rather than a jacket and tie, so dress accordingly.

Arrive at your meeting on time. Being late instantly starts you off on the wrong foot. Allow extra time for parking, getting lost, other unexpected delays, and the traffic that is synonymous with major music centers. Organize your CDs and lyrics and carry them in a briefcase or portfolio—and be sure to bring a notepad and pen so that you can jot down notes.

It's typically appropriate to address the individual with whom you are meeting by his or her first name. Unless you are meeting with a music industry icon (for example, Quincy Jones or Clive Davis), referring to a publisher as "Mr. Rice" or "Ms. Cook" may make you appear as a novice.

In the event that your work receives criticism, or a less-than-enthusiastic reception, resist the temptation to be defensive, even if the comments seem ridiculous—and at times they might. You will have the best chance of keeping the proverbial door open by thanking your listener for the input and mentioning that you will carefully consider his or her feedback. Trying to justify your creative choices, or making comments such as, "Well, all the other publishers I played it for loved the song," will not help your case and may brand you as someone who is closed to constructive criticism.

Remember that your goal is not only to publish or place the songs you've brought to any given meeting, but to keep an open door and establish a long-term business relationship. Even if your songs are not yet at the level where they can compete professionally, you'll contribute to accomplishing your goals by being perceived as pleasant, receptive to feedback, and easy to work with.

It's always a good idea to listen to your CDs (or whichever recorded format you are using) prior to a meeting to ensure that they are not defective. When preparing the CDs that you'll be bringing, it's best to compile your songs onto one or two discs so that valuable meeting time is not spent shuffling through stacks of recordings in search of specific songs.

Bringing an extra copy of the CDs that you plan to leave with the person with whom you are meeting not only saves you the time and expense of having to mail or drop off additional discs, it allows the listener immediate access to your songs and has the added benefit of providing a "backup" in the event that your CD doesn't play properly. It's a good idea to prepare a list of the songs you plan to play—as long as you remain flexible. Your listener may say, "I only want to hear up-tempo songs . . . " or "I only need female songs at the moment." As your meeting progresses you will get a sense of the kinds of songs to which your listener best responds.

First and foremost, make no apologies for either your songs or demos. If you don't believe your songs and demos meet industry standards, you should not yet be meeting with professionals.

Music publishers typically review only complete songs—words and music. Unless specifically requested, it is never acceptable to submit just a lyric, a melody, or a music track.

If you write only words or only music, you need to find a collaborator. However, it is perfectly acceptable to inform a publisher that you are interested in expanding your base of collaborators.

Don't expect a publisher to listen all the way through a song and don't express disappointment when he or she doesn't. Publishers can likely assess whether your song is something that interests them by listening to the first verse and chorus. It is not appropriate to make comments such as, "If you'd only waited until the last verse—it ties the story all together" or "But the modulation at the last chorus makes it sound so much better." If a song does not grab your listener's attention immediately and continue to sustain interest, he or she cannot be expected to continue listening.

Depending on the publisher's personality and skills, you may or may not receive any critique or feedback. Remember that unless you are signed as one of his or her staff-writers, a publisher's job is neither to teach you how to be a better songwriter nor to explain why he or she has decided to pass on a song. You may be lucky enough to find individuals who offer input, but don't count on it.

Finally, when meeting with a publisher it is not realistic to expect to be offered a contract on the spot. Presuming that the individual feels strongly about one or more of your songs, it's likely that he or she will request a copy before making a decision about how to proceed. He or she will probably want to listen to the song several more times before making a commitment and, depending on his or her rank on the corporate ladder, may need to have the song acquisition approved by his or her supervisor.

Asking the Right Questions

Asking the right questions will not make you appear as an amateur, but as a savvy professional. It's a good idea to research a company prior to meeting with one of its representatives. By visiting its Web site you can familiarize yourself with a firm's credits, writers, artists, and services. When meeting with an established publisher, the following questions may provide you with valuable information:

- What kinds of songs are you looking for?

- Do you offer single song agreements—or do you work primarily with staff-writers?

- Would you be willing to play me a song you've signed that you're excited about?

- Are you looking for material for specific artists?

- Do you have writers with whom I might collaborate?

- Are there specific artists to whom you would pitch my songs?

When meeting with a publisher who has not yet established major credits, the following additional questions are appropriate, provided that they are asked in a respectful manner:

- What genres of songs are you representing?
- Have you placed any songs yet with major label artists?
- Have you secured any "holds"?
- Are there specific artists for whom you think my songs would be appropriate? If so, how would you get the songs to these acts?

Also, be prepared to answer the following questions:

- What are your goals?
- Who are your collaborators?
- Have any of your songs been published or recorded?
- Which artists do you feel would be appropriate to record your songs?

Doing some research prior to the meeting will help you be able to suggest at least several artists who do not write their own material for whom each of your songs would be a good match.

If you are unable to think of anyone who might be an appropriate pitch for your song, or you suggest artists who consistently write their own songs, it will appear as if you are failing to address a crucial aspect of your business.

By studying the *Billboard* charts you might get ideas about which artists might be a good fit for your songs, as well as learn which acts wrote or cowrote their own current hits. If you are uncertain about whether an artist might be appropriate to sing your songs, in most instances you will be able to listen to excerpts of his or her work at the artist's Web site or by visiting online stores that sell music. But try to maintain some objectivity, bearing in mind that every song is not right for every artist.

When the person with whom you are meeting indicates that your meeting is winding down, take the hint and don't insist on playing "just a couple more songs." Express that you've appreciated and enjoyed the meeting and that you hope he or she will be willing to listen to additional songs in the future. Follow up your meeting with a brief thank you note. Mailing a note may be more effective in helping you create a lasting impression than sending an e-mail.

Now that you understand how to pursue a publisher, it's time to learn about staff-writing.

CHAPTER THREE

Working As a Staff-Writer

For many songwriters, earning enough money to allow them to quit their day job and devote 100 percent of their energies to their creative pursuit is the ultimate dream. This is most often accomplished by signing a staff-writing deal.

It's hard to imagine the music publishing industry without the concept of staff-writing. Every major music publishing company has staff-writers under contract and almost every song on the charts was written by a writer affiliated with a publishing company. Very few songwriters who are not also recording artists have ever achieved and sustained major success without being signed to a publishing company at some point in their careers.

What Staff-Writing Really Means

"Staff-writing" is a misnomer, as a *staff-writer* is neither an employee nor a staff member of a publishing company, but a songwriter who has entered into an agreement to publish all of his or her songs exclusively with one music publisher. Being a staff-writer essentially means that during the *term* of your contract (the length of time it will be in force) with a publisher, all songs, melodies, and lyrics that you create are automatically published by the company to which you are signed.

Being a staff-writer is synonymous with signing an *exclusive songwriting agreement*, a contract that defines the terms under which your songs are published by a given publishing company. While the agreement (sometimes called a *term songwriting agreement*) is in force, you are signed exclusively to one publisher, foregoing the right to publish your work elsewhere.

Staff-writers receive neither a salary nor employee fringe benefits, such as health insurance or a retirement plan, from the music publisher to whom they are signed. Any money they receive is considered an advance to be recouped against their future royalties. At the same time, they are not required to keep set hours or to work at their publisher's offices either.

Staff-writers, however, are required to deliver an agreed-upon quota of songs per year. The number of songs you are required to write and turn in to your publisher is referred to as the *delivery requirement* and is specified within the exclusive publishing agreement. It typically ranges from ten to fifteen songs annually. But this number only applies if you are the sole author of each song you write. To meet a twelve-song-per-year quota, if all of your songs are cowritten, twenty-four songs must be delivered. Likewise, songs that result from a three-way collaboration are counted as one third of a song.

A staff-writer's song delivery requirement is expressed within the exclusive songwriting agreement as the number of songs that must be turned in monthly, quarterly, or annually, for example, one song per month, three songs per quarter, or twelve songs per year.

How Staff-Writers Are Paid

Writers without established track records rarely command large advances when signing a staff-writing deal, but they typically earn enough to allow them to write songs full time. Writers who have had major hits, those also producing established artists, and those who cowrite with successful artists pose little financial risk to publishers. Therefore, these writers typically receive advances on the highest end of the spectrum.

In some instances, as part of an exclusive songwriting agreement, you may offer the publishing rights to one or more songs that have already been recorded by a successful artist and are either anticipated to, or are in the process of, generating significant income. In exchange, you would likely receive a higher advance. In these instances, again, the publisher incurs minimal risk by offering an advance equivalent to up to three quarters of the amount it anticipates receiving from the song. This money, which has already been earned, but has not yet been received, is often referred to as *pipeline money*, or royalties that are "in the pipeline."

Successful writers, as well as those with money in the proverbial pipeline, can receive advances exceeding $200,000 per year or more. But this money is essentially a loan of the writer's own future royalties and will be deducted when applicable payments are received by the publisher. No publisher would grant this large an advance unless there was a tremendous likelihood of it being recouped. Staff-writers who have not yet demonstrated their ability to generate income for a publisher should expect an advance in the range of $15,000 to $35,000 per year, with writers in Nashville (with its lower cost of living) typically receiving lower amounts than those signed to companies in New York and Los Angeles.

Depending on a publishing company's policy, advances are paid weekly, bi-weekly, monthly, quarterly, or annually. You are responsible for paying income taxes and social security contributions on your advances. Because you are not considered an employee, money is not withheld for any purpose.

In some instances, an attorney may be able to negotiate a *signing bonus*, a portion of the advance to be paid to you up front, upon the signing of the contract. Often, this is done to allow you to purchase equipment for a home studio. This money, as well as virtually all other sums advanced to you from your publisher, is typically recoupable, meaning that it must be repaid.

Options

Staff-writing agreements almost always cover a one-year period and include provisions for the publisher to extend the duration of the agreement for additional periods. These extensions are referred to as *options*. In most instances, an exclusive songwriting agreement grants a publisher two or three one-year options. By having the opportunity to continue the agreement, a publisher increases its chances of recouping the money and time invested in developing a staff-writer.

The decision whether to exercise an option is made exclusively by a publisher; you may or may not choose to remain with a particular publishing company, but if the publisher exercises its option, your contractual commitment is automatically extended. It's in your best interest to grant as few option periods as possible—while publishers try to negotiate as many option periods as they can get.

The amount of money to be advanced in the event that options are exercised is specified in the exclusive songwriting agreement. Increases for subsequent years are usually provided for. For instance:

- Initial advance: $25,000 a year

- Advance for 1st option period: $30,000

- Advance for 2nd option period: $40,000.

In some cases, advances for option periods are expressed in a range, such as:

- Option period 1: $25,000 to $35,000

- Option period 2: $30,000 to $50,000

- Option period 3: $45,000 to $85,000.

Whether your advance reflects the high or the low end of the range is based on factors such as whether the publisher has recouped its investment and the amount of money you have earned for the company.

If you become "hot," writing hits or collaborating with successful recording artists after your first year, the publisher benefits by having you locked in for additional years at specified advances. The prenegotiated amounts may be considerably lower than the money you might command elsewhere. In these situations, savvy publishers typically increase the advance for subsequent option periods, keeping you happy while incurring little risk, as the money advanced is likely to be recouped if you are having hits.

How a Publisher Recoups

The various sources of income from which a publisher may *recoup*, or get back money advanced to you, are delineated in your contractual agreement. Typically, publishers recoup from your share of money collected for mechanical royalties (for sales of tangible products, such as CDs and DVDs, as well as digital downloading); print fees (for sales of, and Internet access to, sheet music, as well as licensing for inclusion in books and magazines); and from synchronization licenses (for inclusion of songs in television, films, and commercials).

Publishers do not typically recoup from your share of performance royalties, which are paid directly to you by the performing rights organization with which you are affiliated. (As you will learn in Chapter 10, PROs collect and distribute money earned primarily for radio airplay, ringtones, television broadcasts, and Internet performances.) However, it is not unheard of for a publisher to request to recoup from these earnings as well. Specifying those royalties from which a publisher may recoup is a critical contractual negotiation point.

Determining which of its operating costs a publisher may recoup is another important, negotiable aspect of a publishing agreement. Recoupable costs may include a portion of or 100 percent of demo expenses, copyright fees, postage, printing costs, music duplicating costs, and even office supplies.

In the majority of instances, songwriters do not earn enough royalties for their publishers to recoup during the term of their exclusive agreement. This is because it sometimes takes many years for songs to be recorded—and then, additional time before the publisher receives the royalties they earn.

When an exclusive publishing deal ends, you are not required to pay back the money advanced to you. Should your songs generate income after the term of the agreement has concluded, this money will be applied toward recouping any amount that was advanced.

In the event that your songs eventually generate sufficient earnings for the publisher to recoup all money advanced, then your share of any royalties subsequently collected by the publisher will be distributed to you. This is the case both during the term of the agreement and afterward. However, the publisher's share of royalties belongs to the publisher and is not applied toward your recoupment. Publishers are entitled to this amount because they advance money and invest time, energy, and expertise in developing your skills—with no guarantee of ever recouping.

Let's look at a theoretical example that presumes that a publisher recoups only from a writer's mechanical royalties and licensing fees:

• A writer is advanced $30,000 for the first one-year term of his or her contract.

• An additional $10,000 is advanced throughout the year for demo expenses.

At the end of the first year, although the writer has not yet generated any royalties, there is the possibility of major recordings pending and the publisher, pleased with the writer's progress, exercises the option for a second one-year term:

• The writer is then advanced $30,000 for the second one-year term.

• An additional $10,000 is advanced to cover demo expenses.

In this example, at the end of the second year, the writer is still not generating income for the company, and the publisher decides not to exercise the remaining option period, thus ending the term of the agreement. The publishing rights to those songs written during the two years encompassed by the exclusive songwriting agreement remain with the publisher, who may continue to exploit these works in the hopes of recouping its investment.

The publisher is entitled to collect $80,000 (the total amount advanced during the writer's first and second terms in the example above) from the writer's share of recoupable royalties before paying the writer any royalties. Remember that the amount the publisher collects as the publisher's share does not apply toward re-couping for the writer.

At the royalty rate in effect January 1, 2006 through December 31, 2007, each unit sold (for example, each cut on a CD) generates 9.10 cents for songs up to and in-cluding five minutes or 1.75 cents per minute for songs longer than five minutes. The math below shows that if the writer's cuts are the result of a two-way collab-oration, he or she would need to have songs included on albums that sell 3,516,484 copies in order for his or her publisher to recoup the full amount advanced:

$$
\begin{array}{ll}
3,516,484 & \text{(units sold)} \\
\times \quad \$0.091 & \text{(U.S. mechanical royalty rate paid per unit)} \\
\hline
\$320,000.04 & \text{(total amount collected—to be split among writers} \\
& \text{and publishers)} \\
\$320,000.04 \div 2 = \$160,000.02 & \text{(total publishers' share)} \\
\$320,000.04 \div 2 = \$160,000.02 & \text{(total writers' share)} \\
\$\ 80,000.01 = \text{each writers' share.}
\end{array}
$$

This is the equivalent of having seven songs included on albums that are certi-fied "gold" for sales exceeding five hundred thousand units in the U.S.—not an easy task to accomplish. (A "platinum" certification is granted for sales over one million units, a "diamond" certification for ten million.) After the publishing com-pany has earned back its investment, the writer's portion of any subsequent roy-alties will be paid to the writer, while the publisher continues to retain the pub-lisher's share. This applies both during and after the term of the agreement.

Reversion

Reversion is the term for a clause that entitles you to reclaim your copyright in the event your song's publisher fails to meet specified criteria (for example, a record-ing and release of the song on a major record label) within a stipulated period of time. (For additional information about reversion clauses see Paragraph 9 of the Single Song Agreement analyzed in Chapter 4.)

It is extremely rare for an exclusive songwriting agreement to include a clause allowing for reversion of songs back to you. This is because a publisher will likely have invested considerable time, energy, and money in your development, pro-duction of demos, and exploitation of your songs. A publisher will want every op-portunity to make back its investment.

When your tenure with a publishing company is over, you may leave hundreds of songs behind as a permanent part of the publisher's catalog. In theory, these songs will still be pitched. In actuality, "out of sight, out of mind" is often the case. A songplugger is more likely to focus on exploiting songs recently turned in by writers he or she is currently working with than those written by a writer who is no longer affiliated with the company. In these instances, you would be wise to actively pitch the songs that may be collecting dust on your former publisher's shelf—or engage the services of an independent songplugger for this purpose. (For an in-depth discussion of independent songpluggers, see Chapter 17.) Under specified circumstances (discussed in Chapter 16), you may be able to reclaim ownership of your published songs. However, without a reversion clause, this will not occur until at least thirty-five years after your works' publication.

The Pros and Cons of Staff-Writing

For many writers, the biggest incentive to signing a staff-writing deal is the financial freedom it represents. In addition to the financial benefit, though, there are numerous other advantages to being signed as a staff-writer. In fact, in rare instances, to take advantage of the benefits that follow, a writer might even sign an exclusive songwriting agreement without receiving any monetary advance.

When you sign as a staff-writer, you reap the benefit of your publisher's strong motivation to promote your songs; your success or failure will reflect upon the publisher. You also have the benefit of receiving professional feedback from your publisher, who may provide valuable creative suggestions or contribute input regarding the kinds of songs he or she is currently having success pitching. In addition, you may gain access to information acquired by your publisher regarding which artists, record label executives, and producers are currently looking for songs and the types of songs they are seeking. You may choose to tailor your material to specific projects.

Another important benefit of staff-writing is that publishers will typically set up collaborations for their writers with recording artists and other songwriters, some of whom may also be signed to the same publisher. In many instances, these collaborations lead to your most significant successes. While writing with an artist or producer does not guarantee getting a cut on a given project, it is typically easier for you to get songs recorded by artists with whom you have written than it is to have a song recorded as a result of pitching material to A&R executives, producers, or artists' managers.

Staff-writers also reap the benefit of having a staff of songpluggers to promote their work. These pluggers typically maintain close working relationships with record label executives, music producers, recording artists, and additional industry professionals. Being represented by such well-connected individuals can be a big component of success.

Publishers may assist the writers with whom they work by recommending demo recording studios, engineers, musicians, and vocalists, and may even be willing to contribute their experience and expertise to the demo production process. Having your publisher creatively involved throughout the writing process and through the completion of the demo can be advantageous. A publisher who has contributed to the development of a song and/or demo may feel more invested in its success and is more likely to remember it when deciding which songs from his or her catalog to pitch.

Being a staff-writer at some companies, especially in Nashville, provides access to writing rooms and recording studios where you can work. In addition, you also have the assistance of support staff who handle administrative functions and make the copies necessary to pitch songs.

Being allied with a respected publishing company provides a benefit that should not be underestimated: it provides you with a level of credibility that can open up doors at record labels and with successful potential collaborators.

While there are numerous advantages to being a staff-writer, there are a number of potential disadvantages as well. For instance, staff-writers are required to deliver a specified quota of songs. For some writers, this added discipline is perceived as a "plus," while for others it may feel like excessive pressure. In deciding whether you are well suited to be a staff-writer it's a good idea to explore whether meeting the demands of a quota seems like a stimulating challenge—or a ball and chain that might stifle your creativity.

Another possible drawback to staff-writing is that you take the chance that the publisher who believes in your work strongly enough to initiate the deal may leave the company. A *key man* or *key person clause*, which states that the agreement remains in effect only as long as a specified individual is employed by the company, prevents this eventuality. But only the very top echelon of successful writers has the clout to demand the inclusion of this clause.

One more potential downside to staff-writing is the possibility that a publisher might cease to effectively promote specific songs or your entire catalog. In these instances, your only recourses are to pitch these songs yourself, or to hire an independent songplugger to serve this function. However, if one of these songs is recorded as the result of your efforts, the publisher still retains the publishing rights and the publisher's share of the royalties—typically, 50 percent of the song's income.

A staff-writer relinquishes the option of placing his or her songs with a variety of companies, based upon which publisher feels the strongest about a given song—or whether a different publisher may be better qualified to place that particular song or style of music. When a publisher offers a single song agreement to represent one particular song, it can be assumed that it feels very strongly about the potential of this song and plans to work hard to promote it. However, when a writer commits to an exclusive songwriting deal, the publisher controls the publishing rights to *all* songs written during the term of the agreement. It's unlikely that every song delivered as part of the agreement will be among a publisher's favorites and, therefore, some of the writer's songs may not be pitched or promoted at all.

Now that you understand the advantages and disadvantages of signing a staff-writing deal, it's time to learn how to get such a deal—if that is your goal.

How to Get a Staff-Writing Deal

In order to secure a staff-writing deal, you must give a publisher a compelling reason to believe that by signing you, the company stands an excellent chance of earning back its financial investment—and making a profit as well. There are various things you might do to lead a publisher to this conclusion.

The best thing you can do to induce a publisher to offer a staff-writing deal is to offer something of tangible value. For example, if a writer offers a publisher a portion of the publisher's share of a song that has already been recorded by an established artist, the publisher can safely assume it will recoup any money it advances to the writer. Of course, few writers find themselves in this enviable position, but it is an ideal way to secure a staff-writing position—and to negotiate the terms of your agreement from a position of power.

Developing writers can also be offered staff-writing agreements based upon a publisher's conviction that he or she has uncovered a diamond in the rough, a writer with tremendous potential, who is writing songs worthy of commercial recognition. Writers who show promise as producers or recording artists are especially appealing to publishers. If these writers become successful, it's likely that their publishers will reap the benefits of having many songs recorded.

We are often judged by the company we keep—and this certainly applies in the music business. A writer who collaborates with successful writers is attractive to publishers. The assumption is that if an individual's cowriters are getting major recordings, the songs he or she writes with them also stand a good chance of being recorded. In addition, the fact that high-profile writers choose to write with an individual indicates that the developing writer is likely contributing important elements to the collaborations.

Finally, writers with a track record of securing their own successful recordings are desirable to virtually any publisher. These writers have demonstrated their ability to cause their songs to generate income—and a publisher who signs them can assume it will reap the benefits of future recordings.

It's extremely unlikely that any publisher will enter into the financial and additional obligations inherent in signing a staff-writer without first becoming well acquainted with the writer and his or her work. Without a history of hits, it is unrealistic for a writer to schedule a meeting with a music publisher, play some strong songs, and expect to be offered an exclusive publishing agreement.

Analogous to dating, most writer–publisher relationships begin with a period of getting acquainted. During this time a publisher assesses the quality and quantity of your creative output, as well as your attitude and manner of conducting business. As the courtship progresses, the publisher might set up collaborations and evaluate the resulting songs. If the evaluation is positive, the publisher may offer one or more single song agreements and begin pitching your songs with a verbal agreement that if recordings are secured, you will sign a publishing agreement. This allows publishers to play the songs for record label executives and other industry professionals and to garner additional feedback regarding your work with the confidence that their efforts will not be in vain.

If there is considerable interest in the songs, or if the publisher secures a recording, it is likely that an offer of a staff-writing deal will be forthcoming, presuming that the publisher is pleased with how the relationship is developing. Of course, this is also contingent on the publisher's budgets and needs.

In the hopes of attracting a publisher's attention, many aspiring songwriters send compilations of their demos to a slew of publishers (for example, those listed in publications such as *The Songwriters Digest* or *The Publisher Registry* or, for writers of country music, in the annual "Publishers" issue of *Music Row* magazine). However, while these and similar publications can be beneficial in terms of providing names, addresses, and telephone numbers of publishing companies, sending an unsolicited demo rarely elicits the desired response. Reputable publishers hardly ever take the time to review material they have not requested from writers without established track records.

The best route to a staff-writing deal is to network and secure referrals to publishers who offer exclusive songwriting agreements. Then, maintain a great attitude and a solid work ethic—and deliver exceptional songs.

CHAPTER FOUR

Understanding Music Publishing Agreements

There are no "standard" music publishing agreements—despite the fact that many publishing contracts have "Standard Publishing Agreement" printed at the top of the first page. There are essentially two categories of song publishing agreements. A contract that transfers the publishing rights of one specific song is referred to as a "Single Song Agreement." A contract that encompasses all of the songs a writer creates during a specified period of time is called an "Exclusive Songwriting Agreement" and is typically referred to as a "Staff-Writing" deal. This chapter examines both kinds of agreements.

While some version of most of the clauses contained in these contracts appear in the majority of publishing agreements, each publisher typically develops contracts that include specific wording that reflects the company's priorities. The agreements presented and analyzed in this book are an aggregate of clauses included within contracts used by a variety of music publishers in the U.S. Individual agreements, however, can differ considerably.

Please note that the contracts that follow are presented as examples; the author is not licensed to practice law and is not rendering legal advice. It's crucial to secure the services of a skilled music business attorney to review and negotiate publishing contracts before you sign them.

Analyzing a Single Song Publishing Agreement

As the name implies, a *single song agreement* is the contract a writer and publisher enter into to publish one song. However, in some instances a single song agreement may encompass multiple songs that are subject to the same terms. In these cases, the song titles may be inserted into the body of the agreement or may be included as an attachment (or *exhibit*) known as an "Exhibit" or "Schedule A."

It's rare that a publisher will advance money for a single song agreement unless the song being published has already been recorded, is currently generating income, or has income in the pipeline. However, occasionally, a publisher of a single song will advance money to reimburse a writer's demo expenses or pay to have a demo produced. This money will typically be considered a recoupable expense.

As previously stated, it is always advisable to have your contracts reviewed and negotiated by a music business attorney. Nonetheless, by studying the sample agreement that follows and reading the explanations after each paragraph, you will better understand what it is that you are agreeing to when you sign a song publishing agreement—the rights that are granted, the assurances each party makes, and the compensation promised when publishing a song.

SINGLE SONG PUBLISHING AGREEMENT

THIS AGREEMENT, made and entered into this ___day of_____, _____
by and between _____ (referred to as "Publisher"),
whose address is _____ and
_____ (referred to as "Composer"), whose address is
_____.

> This paragraph establishes the date the contract takes effect and includes the names and addresses of the writer and publisher entering into it. It also states that throughout the remainder of the agreement, the writer will be referred to as "Composer" and the publisher as "Publisher."

In consideration of the mutual promises and covenants herein contained, Publisher and Composer agree as follows:

> To understand this sentence it's important to be aware that all contracts must have "consideration" to be binding, meaning that each of the parties benefits from entering into the agreement. The writer and publisher acknowledge that they will each benefit from signing the contract and agree to abide by its provisions.

1. Assignment of Work

The Composer hereby sells, assigns, transfers and delivers to the Publisher, its successors and assigns, a certain heretofore unpublished original musical composition (the "Composition"), written and/or composed in the following percentage _____ by the above named Composer and _____ (___%), now entitled: _____ including the title, words, and music, and all copyrights thereof, including but not limited to the copyright registration thereof Number _____ and all rights, claims and demands in anyway relating thereto, and the exclusive right to secure copyright therein throughout the world, and to have and to hold the said copyrights and all rights of whatsoever nature now and hereafter for and during the full terms of all of said copyrights. In consideration of the agreement to pay royalties herein contained and other good and valuable consideration in hand paid by Publisher to the Composer, receipt of which is hereby acknowledged, the Composer hereby sells, assigns, transfers and delivers to the Publisher, its successors and assigns, all renewal and extensions of the copyrights of the Composition to which the Composer may be entitled hereafter and all registrations thereof, and all rights of any and all nature now and hereinafter hereunder existing, for the full terms of all renewals and extensions of copyrights.

> This paragraph states that the portion of the song owned by the writer engaging in this contract is being sold and transferred to the publisher. Stating that the song is being "sold" may create a misunderstanding for writers who

confuse this with relinquishing all rights to a song—and any income it might generate, as is the case with a work for hire. (Work for hire is explained in Chapter 1.) When a song is published, the writer grants specified rights to the publisher, as well as an amount referred to as "the publisher's share" of any income the song might earn. The publisher's share typically equals 50 percent of any money the song generates. The writer benefits from the publisher's exploitation and administration of the song.

This paragraph also documents the title of the song being published; that the song will be referred to throughout this agreement as the "Composition"; the percentage that the writer owns; and the percentage(s) owned by any cowriters, if applicable. The writer affirms that the song is original and that his or her share has not previously been published. In addition, the writer grants the publisher all rights to the song, including the rights afforded by copyright throughout the world. Additionally, the paragraph has a place to list the copyright registration number.

The writer, in exchange for receiving royalty payments and other benefits, gives the publisher (and anyone who may acquire the song from the publisher) all rights during the initial term of the copyright and any renewals and extensions.

2. Compensation

Provided that Composer shall faithfully and completely perform the terms, covenants and conditions of this Agreement, Publisher hereby agrees to pay to Composer for the rights acquired hereunder the following compensation:

This paragraph establishes the amount the writer will be paid, provided that he or she abides by the terms of this contract.

(a) Fifty (50%) percent of any and all net sums (less any taxes, costs of collection and other expenses related to the Composition) actually received by Publisher in the United States from the exploitation in the United States by Publisher or by any licensees of Publisher of mechanical rights, electrical transcription and reproducing rights, motion picture and television synchronization rights, print rights, multi-media rights, and all other rights, now or hereafter known, (except public performance rights) therein.

Subparagraph (a) states that the writer will be paid half of all money the publisher receives from mechanical royalties (for sales), licenses to reproduce the song online, royalties generated by including the song in films or television shows, and licensing fees charged to include the song (or lyric) in books, magazines, sheet music, and all other usages, including those that might apply in the future. Also stated is that the publisher will deduct expenses, which include the cost of royalty collection and taxes. This paragraph does not apply to the writer's share of performance royalties (which are paid directly to the writer from the PROs: ASCAP, BMI, and SESAC).

(b) Fifty (50%) percent of any and all net sums (less any foreign and domestic taxes, costs of collection, and other expenses related to the Composition) actually received by Publisher in United States dollars in the United States from the exploitation of the Composition in countries outside of the United States (other than public performance royalties) either directly or from collection agents, subpublishers or other licensees of Publisher.

Subparagraph (b) states that the writer will be paid half of any money the publisher receives from companies outside the U.S. However, the publisher will deduct expenses, including taxes and costs incurred to collect the royalties. As in the previous paragraph, this does not apply to the writer's share of performance royalties.

(c) Notwithstanding any of the foregoing, Composer shall receive his/her public performance royalties throughout the universe directly from his/her own affiliated performing rights society and shall have no claim whatsoever against Publisher for any royalties received by Publisher from any performing rights society which makes payments directly or indirectly (other than through Publisher) to writers, authors and composers.

Subparagraph (c) declares that the publisher will not pay the writer performance royalties unless the writer's share is sent to the publisher. But, as previously stated in subparagraph (a), the writer's share of performance royalties is typically paid directly to the writer from the PROs (ASCAP, BMI, and SESAC).

(d) Publisher shall not be required to pay any royalties on professional or complimentary copies or derivatives of the Composition which are distributed gratuitously or at or below Publisher's costs or for promotional or similar purposes.

Subparagraph (d) indicates that the writer will not receive royalties for free promotional copies or for copies sold for less than the publisher's costs.

(e) Royalties as hereinabove specified shall be payable solely in instances where Composer is the sole author of the entire Composition, including the words and music thereof. However, if one or more other songwriters to whom Publisher is required to pay royalties are authors together with Composer of the Composition (including songwriters employed by Publisher to add, change or translate the words or to revise or change the music), then the foregoing royalties shall be divided equally among Composer and such other songwriters of the Composition unless another division of royalties is otherwise set forth herein. Further, without limiting the foregoing, Composer shall not be entitled to share in any income received by Publisher as a collection agent and/or administrator for another publisher and/or songwriter of the Composition.

Subparagraph (e) says that if a song is cowritten, and more than one of its writers are signed to this same publisher, the writer will be paid the portion of any royalties equal to the percentage of his or her authorship of the song. However, if the publisher handles the administrative function of collecting royalties for any other writer or publisher of the composition, the writer entering into this agreement is not entitled to any part of that money.

(f) Except as herein expressly provided, no other royalties or monies shall be paid to Composer. In no event shall Composer be entitled to share in advance payments, guarantee payments or minimum royalty payments which Publisher shall receive in connection with any subpublishing agreement, co-publishing agreement, collection agreement, licensing agreement or other agreement covering the Composition.

Subparagraph (f) notes that advances received by the publisher for subpublishing and other agreements are typically paid for the use of the publisher's entire catalog. This subparagraph also states that the writer will not receive a share of these advances. (For a detailed explanation of subpublishing see Chapter 14.)

(g) Composer agrees and acknowledges that Publisher shall have the right to withhold from royalties or other monies payable to Composer hereunder such amount, if any, as may be required to be withheld by Publisher under the applicable provisions of the Internal Revenue Code, and any applicable state or municipal tax laws, and Composer agrees to execute such forms and other documents as may be required in connection therewith.

Subparagraph (g) says that the publisher may withhold federal, state, or local taxes as required by law. The writer agrees to complete any forms required for this.

(h) Composer hereby acknowledges that Publisher shall have the right to apply for and collect, on Composer's behalf, all sums which may be payable to Composer pursuant to the provisions of the Audio Home Recording Act of 1992. Composer's share of all such sums shall be payable to Composer as royalties hereunder and shall be subject to all of the terms and conditions hereof.

Subparagraph (h) states that the publisher will collect payments due the writer as a result of the Audio Home Recording Act of 1992 (referred to as "AHRA"). The writer's share of these royalties will be paid by the publisher in the manner specified throughout this contract.

AHRA (also known as the "DART" bill) requires manufacturers and importers of digital audio recording equipment to pay a royalty intended to offset the anticipated loss of income to record labels, artists, writers, publishers, and musicians resulting from digital copying of their work. This royalty is imposed only on equipment that is used *solely* for the purpose of duplicating audio recordings (for example, DAT players and blank DAT tapes—which are rarely, if ever, used anymore). Computers and CD burners (which are capable of additional functions) are exempt from this royalty. A 1998 addition to the bill specifies that royalties also be paid for webcasts. However, this income is treated as performance royalties and is paid directly to writers and publishers. The royalties currently being generated from AHRA are minimal, typically comprising less than 1 percent of a successful song's income.

3. Royalties

Publisher agrees that it will render to Composer within sixty (60) days after the close of each regular semi-annual accounting period of Publisher in which royalties are accrued hereunder, a statement showing all sales and royalties earned by Composer during such accounting period, and will pay at the same time all sums shown thereon to be due to Composer provided that Publisher shall be obligated to pay royalties hereunder only with respect to sums actually received by Publisher.

This paragraph states that the publisher will send the writer a royalty statement twice each year, within sixty days after the close of its accounting period, if any royalties have accrued. This royalty statement will list all royalties earned by the writer during the six-month period and will include payment for any money due to the writer. The writer will be paid only his or her share of royalties that the publisher has actually received.

All royalty statements and other accounts rendered to Composer hereunder will be binding upon Composer unless specific objection in writing, stating the basis thereof, is received by Publisher within one (1) year from the date rendered, in which event such statement shall be binding in all respects except for those specifically stated in such written objection. Composer shall be barred from instituting or maintaining any action, audit or proceeding of any kind or nature with respect to any statement rendered hereunder unless same is commenced within one (1) year after delivery of such written objection by Composer to Publisher. Composer and any attorney, certified public accountant or other individual reasonably experienced in music industry audits designated by Composer shall have the right to examine and inspect Publisher's books and records with respect to the Composition at Publisher's principal office upon reasonable notice during normal business hours.

This portion of the clause states that if the writer disagrees with any information listed on royalty or accounting statements, his or her objection must be submitted in writing within one year of the date the statement was provided. The writer, at his or her own expense, may hire an attorney, accountant, or other qualified auditor to review the publisher's books and records. This audit must be scheduled with reasonable advance notice and take place at the publisher's main office during normal business hours.

4. Warranties and Representations

The Composer hereby warrants and represents that the Composition is his/her sole, exclusive and original work, of which the title, music and lyric was written and composed by him/her, that the Composition is new and original and does not infringe any other copyrighted works, that he/she has the full right and power to enter into this Agreement, that the Composition has not heretofore been published, that the Composition is original with the Composer and does not contain any matter which, if published or otherwise used, will be in violation of any proprietary right at common law or any statutory copyright or penal law, and that he/she will hold harmless and defend the Publisher against any suit, claim, demand, or recovery by reason of any violation of any of the representations, warranties or covenants, rights or copyrights or any injurious matter in the Composition, actual or alleged and the Publisher is hereby granted the right in event of any such claim or claims, to make such defense as may be advised by counsel and the costs and counsel fees therefore together with any damages sustained and amounts of any such settlements shall be charged to and paid for by the Composer.

In this paragraph, the writer affirms that the song is original, does not infringe on any other works, and has not been previously published. As this clause is worded, it is accurate if there is only one writer of the song. If the song is cowritten, all references to the writer being the "sole" creator of the song should be changed to include: "together with any cowriters of the composition."

The writer also promises that he or she has the right to sign this contract and that the publisher will not be held responsible if it is determined that the writer did not have the right to enter into this agreement. If the writer's representations and warranties are not true and as a result it costs the publisher any money, the writer must pay for the publisher's legal expenses, as well as any settlement amounts or damages awarded.

5. Assignment

Simultaneously with the execution of this Agreement, Composer shall execute a short form assignment as additional evidence of this transfer of rights. Composer does hereby appoint Publisher and its successors or assigns as Composer's attorney-in-fact to take such action to make, sign, execute, acknowledge and deliver such documents, in his name or its own name, as may from time to time be necessary to secure, transfer, assign (to itself or others), register a claim to, record or otherwise evidence Publisher's rights in the copyrights in the Composition and all other rights herein granted; said power shall be irrevocable and coupled with interest.

According to this paragraph, the writer agrees to sign an additional document transferring ownership of the song to the publisher. An example of this document, known as an Assignment of Copyright, can be found on page 46.

In addition, the writer grants the publisher (and any person or company to whom the publisher might assign the song) the right to act as the writer's attorney and execute and sign documents on the writer's behalf in order to protect the publisher's interest in the copyright. Additionally, the writer acknowledges that he or she is receiving benefits by entering into this agreement and that it is final and binding.

6. Terms Defined

Unless otherwise provided herein, all terms used herein shall to the extent applicable have the meaning set forth in Title 17, United States Code, Section 101 et seq. (Public Law 94-553), as amended. The term "Composer" as used herein shall include all the persons who have executed this Agreement in such capacity and the covenants herein contained shall be deemed to be both joint and several by each of such person. Where appropriate in context all references herein to the singular shall include the plural and to the masculine gender shall include the feminine.

All terms in this contract are used as defined in the U.S. Copyright Law in Title 17. All singular words (including "Composer") also refer to the plural. Masculine pronouns as used throughout are meant to include the feminine counterpart, as appropriate.

7. Correspondence

All notices given hereunder by either party to the other (excluding accounting statements) shall be transmitted in writing by United States Registered or Certified Mail, Return Receipt Requested, to the parties' addresses set forth above or to such other address as a party shall designate by notice to the other. All notices and accountings shall be deemed given upon the date of deposit thereof in the United States Mail.

This paragraph states that any correspondence between the writer and publisher (with the exception of royalty statements) must be sent in writing by registered or certified mail with a return receipt requested to the addresses included in the beginning of this document, or to another address specified by written notice. The date any correspondence is postmarked is considered to be the date that it was mailed—not the date on the letter or notice.

8. Legal Action

Publisher may take any legal action as it deems necessary, either in Composer's name or in its own name, against any person to protect its rights and interests in the Composition in Publisher's sole discretion and at the Publisher's sole expense. Composer will, at Publisher's request, cooperate fully with Publisher with respect to any such action, but Publisher shall have the right, in its sole discretion, to employ attorneys and to institute or defend any action or proceeding and to take any other steps to protect the right, title and interest of Publisher in and to the Com-

position and every portion thereof, and in that connection, to settle, compromise, or in any other manner dispose of such claim, action or proceeding and to satisfy any judgment that may be rendered in any manner as Publisher in its sole discretion may determine. Any recovery by Publisher as a result of such action, after deduction of the costs and expense of such recovery, including, without limitation, attorneys fees, court costs and any payments to any other owners of the copyright in and to the Composition, a sum equal to fifty (50%) percent of such net proceeds after payment to any other publishers of the Composition shall be paid collectively to the Composer and any other authors of the Composition to whom Publisher is obligated to pay a royalty. If a claim is presented against Publisher in respect of the Composition and because thereof Publisher is jeopardized, Publisher shall have the right thereafter, until said claim has been finally adjudicated or settled to hold any and all monies due Composer pursuant to this Agreement or any other agreement between the parties or their respective affiliates in trust pending the outcome of such claim. In the event of any recovery against Publisher, either by way of judgment or settlement, all costs, charges, disbursements, attorney fees and the amount of the judgment or settlement may be deducted by Publisher from any and all royalties or payments theretofore or thereafter payable to Composer by Publisher or any of its associated, affiliated or subsidiary companies pursuant to this or any other agreement between the parties or their respective affiliates. Notwithstanding Publisher's right to deduct such recovery from sums due Composer, Composer understands and agrees that same shall be a debt due and owing Publisher and agrees that Publisher shall be entitled to reimbursement of same from Composer upon demand.

This paragraph states that the publisher, at its own expense, may take legal action to protect its rights. The writer agrees to cooperate to defend the publisher's rights and interests in the song. It also establishes that the publisher has the sole right to accept or decline a settlement. In addition, the paragraph states that the publisher will pay the writer and his or her collaborators (if applicable) half of any money recovered after the publisher's legal fees and costs have been deducted. If the publisher receives notice of a claim against the song, it has the right to keep any money due to the writer until the claim is settled. If the publisher is required to pay either an award or a settlement regarding the song, this amount, as well as legal expenses, will be withheld from the writer's royalties and other payments. The paragraph concludes by stating that the publisher has the right to demand payment instead of waiting to recoup from the writer's royalties.

9. Reversion
If Publisher has not caused a commercial release of this Composition or fails to license the Composition for print, synchronization or mechanical use with a third party licensee at any time within eighteen (18) months following the date of execution of this Agreement, all rights to the Composition will revert back to Com-

poser. For reversion to become effective, Composer must reimburse Publisher for the costs of any demo made and Composer must notify Publisher in writing of Composer's intention to reacquire the copyright of the Composition at anytime within ninety (90) days thereafter, or Composer's reversionary rights shall therefore lapse. In the event that there may be considerable activity with the Composition at that time, Composer agrees to an extension of Agreement terms for a reasonable time period, not to exceed one hundred and twenty (120) days.

This paragraph is typically referred to as a *reversion clause*. It states that if the song has not been recorded and commercially released, licensed for print (for example, sheet music), or licensed for use in a television show or film, within eighteen months of the date of this contract, all rights will revert back to the writer. However, for this to occur, the writer must reimburse the publisher for any demo expenses and notify the publisher in writing within ninety days following the eighteen-month deadline. If the writer does not fulfill these two requirements, he or she relinquishes the right to reclaim ownership of the song. This paragraph further states that if there is "considerable activity" (for example, the song is placed on hold or there is a release pending) the writer agrees to extend this agreement for a maximum of one hundred twenty additional days.

Be aware that the length of time specified before the rights revert back to the writer will likely be an important negotiating point. Not all publishers are willing to include this clause, and some of those who do may request two, three, or as much as five years before the songs reverts. It is in the writer's best interest to further define the criteria the publisher must meet. For instance, instead of stating that there must be a commercially released recording, many attorneys include that the recording must be released on a major label or a label distributed by a major label. They might also specify that if the song is licensed for print, or for use in a film or television show, the licensing fee must meet or exceed a specific amount (for example, $1,000).

These additions protect the writer from being unable to reclaim the song in the event of scenarios such as the following: the song has been released on an artist's own independent record label and generates only a few dollars in royalties; the song is used in an educational film that pays a $50 licensing fee; or, a license is issued at no charge to include the song's lyric in a magazine. A reversion clause is a writer's primary protection against the many situations that may result in a song collecting dust on a publisher's shelf indefinitely, for example, if the publisher is sold; if the songplugger loses interest in the song; or, if the plugger who signed the song leaves the company.

10. Complete Terms of Agreement

This Agreement sets forth the entire agreement of the parties regarding the subject matter hereof and shall be construed in accordance with the laws of the State of _____ with respect to contracts executed and to be performed therein and shall be binding upon parties their respec-

tive successors, heirs and assigns. In the event of litigation, venue shall be
_____. In the event that any provision of this Agreement
shall, for any reason, be held invalid or unenforceable, all other provisions
herein shall continue in full force and effect. This Agreement may not be modified or amended except by written agreement signed by the parties hereto.

This paragraph states that this contract reflects the complete terms of the
agreement regarding the song, meaning that anything not stated in the contract is not part of the agreement. This contract is governed by the state that
will be written in the space provided. This will typically be the state where
the publisher's primary offices are located. In addition, the writer and publisher signing the agreement, as well as their heirs, or anyone else to whom
they assign the song, are legally obligated by the terms of this contract. This
paragraph also includes a space in which to list the county and state in which
any legal action will be decided. If any part of this contract is found to be illegal or unenforceable, the rest of the contract will still be binding. This contract may be changed only if the writer and publisher both agree in writing.

IN WITNESS WHEREOF, this Agreement has been executed on the date first
above written.

This specifies the date the writer and publisher signed the contract.

PUBLISHER: **COMPOSER:**

By:_____   _____

                                                  SS#:_____

                                                  PRO:_____

Date:_____   _____

The spaces provided above are for the signature of the writer and the publishing company's representative, as well as for the writer's social security
number and PRO affiliation (ASCAP, BMI, or SESAC).

Analyzing an Assignment of Copyright

The document that follows is used to transfer ownership of a writer's share of his
or her song to a publisher. This agreement is typically attached to a single song
agreement.

ASSIGNMENT OF COPYRIGHT

Assignment made as of this _____ day of _____, _____ between
_____ (the "Assignor") and _____
(the "Company"), for good and valuable consideration, the receipt of which

both parties hereby acknowledge, Assignor assigns, transfers, sets over and conveys to Company Assignor's entire right, title and interest to the following musical composition (the "Composition"):

> By signing this contract the writer (referred to as the "Assignor") transfers ownership of his or her share of the copyright to the publisher. This means that the writer will no longer have the right to issue licenses (for example, synchronization licenses for inclusion of the song in films and television shows and mechanical licenses for audio recordings), nor will the writer be permitted to collect royalties generated by the song (with the exception of performance royalties). These functions will be handled by the publisher, who will distribute the writer's share of royalties to the writer.

TITLE:_____

WRITER'S SHARE BEING ASSIGNED (%):_____

> This space is provided to write in the song title and the writer's name and percentage of ownership. If the song is the result of a two-way collaboration, the writer's and publisher's percentage would be listed as 50 percent. If the song is written solely by the writer entering into this agreement, the writer's and publisher's shares would be 100 percent.

Copyright Registration Number;_____
Date Of Creation;_____

The within assignment, transfer and conveyance includes, without limitation an undivided One Hundred percent (100%) of Assignor's right, title and interest in the lyrics, music and title of the Composition, any and all works derived therefrom, the United States and worldwide copyright therein, and any renewals or extensions thereof, and any and all other rights that Assignor now has or to which Assignor may become entitled whether existing or subsequently enacted under federal, state or foreign laws, including, without limitation, the following rights: to reproduce the Composition in copies or phonorecords, to prepare derivative works based upon the Composition, to distribute copies or phonorecords of the Composition, and to perform and display the Composition publicly. The within grant further includes the undivided interest in any and all causes of action for infringement of the Composition, past, present or future, and all of the proceeds from the foregoing accrued and unpaid and hereinafter accruing.

> This paragraph reiterates that the writer grants the publisher 100 percent of the writer's interest in the song and all worldwide rights (currently existing or enacted in the future) to every aspect of the song and any additional works derived from it (for example, parodies, translations, and samples of the song used in other recordings). These rights include, but are not limited to: reproducing, distributing, performing, and displaying the song. In addition, the

publisher has the right to protect the copyright and receive any money due as the result of settling an infringement case in the past, present, or future.

EXECUTED this ____ **day of** _____, _____
ASSIGNOR:
" _____ "

By:_____
STATE OF _____
COUNTY OF _____

Before me, a Notary Public of the State and County above, appeared Assignor, with whom I am personally acquainted or provided to person whose name is subscribed to the within instrument, and who acknowledged that he executed the foregoing Assignment of Copyright for the purposes therein contained. WITNESS my hand and official seal on this_____ day of_____, _____.

The signing of this assignment must be witnessed by a notary public. In this paragraph, the notary attests that the writer is indeed who he or she claims to be and that he or she signed the assignment.

My Commission Expires: **NOTARY PUBLIC**

_____   _____

Analyzing an Exclusive Songwriting Agreement

When a writer states that he or she is a staff-writer, it means that he or she has entered into an exclusive songwriting agreement. An exclusive songwriting agreement is the contract a writer and publisher sign establishing that all songs, melodies, and lyrics composed by the writer within a specified period of time will be acquired by the publisher.

An exclusive songwriting agreement is a binding, legal document that defines the terms of the agreement between the writer and publisher. It addresses issues including the length of the commitment, the number of songs to be delivered, the percentage of ownership and the specific rights being conveyed, the amount of money to be advanced to the writer, the circumstances under which the publisher can recoup its investment, and much more.

The agreement that follows is an example of the contract a writer and publisher sign when entering into an exclusive songwriting agreement. Each paragraph of the contract is followed by an explanation of what it means.

EXCLUSIVE SONGWRITING AGREEMENT

AGREEMENT made as of this _____ **day of** _____, **200__, by and between**_____ **("Writer") whose address is** _____ **and** _____ **("Publisher") whose address is** _____.

This paragraph establishes the date the agreement takes effect and states the names and addresses of the parties entering into it. Throughout the remainder of the agreement, the writer will be referred to as "Writer" and the publisher as "Publisher."

IN CONSIDERATION of the mutual promises hereinafter set forth and other good and valuable consideration, the receipt and sufficiency of which each party acknowledges, the parties do hereby agree as follows:

This paragraph establishes that the writer and publisher agree that in exchange for the benefits and/or compensation each is receiving, they will abide by the provisions in the agreement.

1. Engagement

Writer agrees to render Writer's exclusive services to Publisher as an author, composer, arranger and adaptor of musical compositions during the term hereof. Writer further agrees to devote the necessary time, attention, skill and energy to Writer's duties hereunder and to render Writer's services diligently and to the best of Writer's ability to the end that the intent and purposes of this Agreement may be fully realized and achieved.

In this paragraph, the writer agrees to use his or her best efforts to write and deliver songs of the highest professional quality. While it would be difficult to quantify whether a writer has indeed put forth his or her "best effort," the inclusion of this paragraph is intended to protect the publisher from a situation in which the writer quickly churns out a batch of substandard songs simply to fulfill the delivery requirement established in paragraph 8 of this agreement. This paragraph also reaffirms that all songs, melodies, lyrics, and titles created by the writer during the term covered by the agreement will be published exclusively by the publisher.

2. Term

The Initial Period of the Term of this Agreement shall commence as of the _____ day of _____, 200__, and shall continue through the _____ day of _____, 200__.

This paragraph defines the initial period covered by the agreement. It will typically be for one year.

Writer hereby grants to Publisher two (2) separate and irrevocable options, each to renew this Agreement for a one (1) year period, such Renewal Periods to run consecutively beginning at the expiration of the Initial Period hereof, all upon the same terms and conditions as are applicable to the Initial Period except as otherwise provided herein.

This paragraph establishes that by signing this agreement, the writer agrees that at the conclusion of the one-year period (the date of which is shown at the beginning of this paragraph) the publisher has the right to extend the contract for an additional year. The decision as to whether to exercise this option is made solely by the publisher—regardless of whether the writer wishes to continue the contractual arrangement or not.

In the event that the publisher chooses to invoke the option, thereby keeping the writer under contract for an additional year, the terms established in the initial contract apply to the option period. If the publisher does exercise the first option, at the conclusion of that option period (two years after the signing of this initial agreement), the publisher has the right to exercise an additional one-year option.

While staff-writers are rarely afforded the security of a contract period that extends beyond one year, publishers typically request two or three one-year options beyond the initial one-year term of the agreement. This protects the publisher's investment of time and money expended to develop the writer. If, at the end of the first year (or at the end of the second year in the event that the first option has been exercised), the publisher is pleased with the work being produced, he or she has the right to invoke the option period for a monetary amount that has been established in the initial agreement. In the event that the writer enjoys success, this allows the publisher to retain the writer for an additional period—without having to pay an exorbitant advance. However, if the writer is not generating significant income, the publisher can choose not to exercise the additional one-year options.

Note that the monetary advance the publisher must pay in order to exercise the additional option periods may be different from the amount paid for the first year. The advance typically increases for each of the options. The amount of these advances is specified in Paragraph 9.

The Initial Period plus all Renewal Periods, if any, are herein referred to as the "Term" of this Agreement. Each such option shall be deemed exercised by Publisher automatically by the expiration of the immediately preceding one-year period of the Term unless written notice is given to Writer (via certified mail) before the expiration thereof of Publisher's election to terminate this Agreement as of the end of the then current period of the Term.

Each additional option period will be considered invoked unless the writer is given written notification via certified mail that the publisher has chosen not to exercise the option. This notification must be received prior to the end of the term of the initial agreement, or the applicable option period, as the case may be.

3. Grant of Rights
(a) Writer hereby irrevocably and absolutely assigns, transfers, sets over and grants to Publisher, its successors and assigns, each and every and all rights and interests of every kind, nature and description in and to the results and proceeds of Writer's services hereunder, including, but not limited to, the titles,

words and music of any and all original musical compositions in any and all forms and original arrangements of musical compositions in the public domain in any and all forms, and/or all rights and interests existing under all agreements and licenses relating thereto, together with all worldwide and universe wide copyrights and renewals and extensions thereof, which compositions are listed on Schedule "A" which is attached hereto and made a part hereof by reference thereto, and which compositions may hereafter, during the Term hereof, be written, composed, created or conceived by Writer, in whole or in part, alone or in collaboration with another or others, including, without limitation, the title, words and music of each composition, and all worldwide and universe wide copyrights and renewals and extensions thereof, all of which Writer does hereby represent are and shall at all times be Publisher's sole and exclusive property as the sole owner thereof, free from any adverse claims or rights therein by any other person, firm or corporation. The foregoing compositions which are the subject hereof are sometimes hereinafter individually and collectively referred to as the "Composition" or the "Compositions".

Ownership of the writer's songs is granted to the publisher. If the publisher is bought or sold, all rights granted in the agreement transfer to the new owner. The agreement also applies to specified, previously written works. These works are to be listed on a form titled "Schedule A," which will be attached to this agreement.

In this subparagraph, the writer affirms that no other individual or company has any claims against or rights to the songs and/or other works included in the contract.

The paragraph also states that the works created by the writer during the term of this contract as well as the preexisting songs listed on Schedule A will be referred to as "Compositions."

(b) Writer acknowledges that included within the rights and interests hereinabove referred to, but without limiting the generality of the foregoing, is Writer's irrevocable grant to Publisher, its successors, licensees, sublicensees and assigns, of the sole and exclusive right, license, privilege and authority throughout the entire universe with respect to the Compositions and original arrangements of compositions in the public domain, whether now in existence or hereafter created during the Term hereof, as follows:

In this subparagraph, the writer permanently grants the publisher the rights that are specified in subsections (i) through (vi) of this paragraph. These rights also apply to any company or individual that buys or licenses the rights from the publisher.

(i) To perform the Compositions by means of public and private performance, radio broadcasting, television, or any and all other means, whether now known or which may hereafter come into existence.

This subparagraph declares that the publisher has the right to authorize performances of the writer's works. In this instance, "performance" refers not only to a live performance, but to broadcast on radio, television, or by forms of technology that may come into existence in the future.

(ii) To substitute a new title or titles for the Compositions and to make any arrangement, adaptation, translation, dramatization and transposition of the Compositions, in whole or in part, and in connection with any other musical, literary or dramatic material, and to add new lyrics to the music of the Compositions (including, without limitation, parody lyrics) or new music to the lyrics of the Compositions, all as Publisher may deem expedient or desirable.

This subparagraph states that the publisher may change the songs by giving them a new title, new lyrics (including parody lyrics or translation into another language), or new melody without consulting the writer. Note that depending on the amount of clout the writer has, this clause might specify that the writer's permission (not to be reasonably withheld) is required for the publisher to make these changes.

(iii) To secure copyright registration and protection of the Compositions in Publisher's name and at Publisher's cost and expense and at Publisher's election, including any and all renewals and extensions of copyrights, and to have and to hold said copyrights, renewals, extensions and all rights of whatsoever nature thereunder existing, for and during the full term of all said copyrights and all renewals and extensions thereof.

This subparagraph indicates that the publisher has the right to copyright the writer's works and to apply for copyright renewals and extensions. The publisher is responsible for any costs incurred to secure the copyright.

(iv) To make or cause to be made, master recordings, transcriptions, phonorecords, sound tracks, pressings, and any other mechanical, electrical or other reproductions of the Compositions, in whole or in part, in such form or manner and as frequently as Publisher's sole and uncontrolled discretion shall determine, including the right to synchronize the same with sound motion pictures and the right to manufacture, advertise, license or sell such reproductions for any and all purposes, including, but not limited to, private performances and public performances, by broadcasting, television, sound motion pictures, wired radio, cable, satellite and any and all other means or devices whether now known or which may hereafter come into existence.

This subparagraph notes that the publisher has the sole right to grant recording licenses (allowing master recordings to be produced and distributed); synchronization licenses (to include the works in television or motion pictures); and licenses for the works to be used in advertisements, as well as additional licenses for cable, satellite, and technologies that may later come into existence. Depending on the writer's clout, this paragraph may include specific limitations. For example, the writer may retain the right to deny usage of his or her songs in adult films and political advertisements without prior approval.

Note that if the writer is also a recording artist, his or her attorney might negotiate the right for the "first use" license, ensuring that the writer/artist has the option to be the first one to record and release his or her own songs.

(v) To print, publish and sell sheet music, orchestrations, arrangements and other editions of the Compositions in all forms, including the right to include any or all of the Compositions in song folios or lyric magazines with or without music, and the right to license others to include any and all of the Compositions in song folios or lyric magazines with or without music.

This subparagraph says that the publisher has the right to grant permission for the publication of sheet music, lyrics, orchestrations, and arrangements, and for inclusion in song folios and lyric magazines.

(vi) Any and all other rights of every and all nature now or hereafter existing under and by virtue of any common law rights and any copyrights and renewals and extensions thereof in any and all of the Compositions. Writer grants to Publisher, without any compensation other than as specified herein, the perpetual right to use and publish and to permit others to use and publish Writer's name (including any professional name heretofore or hereafter adopted by Writer), likenesses, voice and sound effects, and biographical material, or any reproduction or simulation thereof and titles of all Compositions in connection with the printing, sale, advertising, distribution and exploitation of music, folios, other printed editions, recordings, performances, phonorecords and otherwise concerning any of the Compositions, and for any other goodwill and promotional purpose related to the business of Publisher, its affiliated and related companies, or to refrain therefrom. This right shall be exclusive during the Term hereof and nonexclusive thereafter. Writer shall not authorize nor permit the use of Writer's name or likeness or biographical material concerning Writer, or other identification, or any reproduction or simulation thereof, for or in connection with any of the Compositions, other than by or for Publisher and its affiliated companies. Writer grants Publisher the right to refer to Writer as Publisher's "Exclusive Songwriter and Composer," or other similar appropriate appellation, during the Term hereof.

This subparagraph indicates that for compositions encompassed by this agreement, the publisher retains all legal rights that are granted by law and by ownership of the copyright. During the term of the contract, the publisher has the right to use the writer's name, likeness (photo or drawing), recordings, biography, and titles of that writer's songs to promote and exploit the writer's works or the business of the publisher. The writer will not be paid for such usage.

Also, the writer shall not grant permission to any other company to use or publish the items listed above (name, likeness, etc.) in connection with the compositions.

4. Prior Compositions

Attached hereto and marked Schedule A is a list of certain musical compositions written and composed by Writer individually or in collaboration with another or others prior to the Term hereof. With respect to each of such Schedule A Compositions, Writer warrants that Writer's interest has not been assigned to another person or entity. Writer hereby assigns to Publisher the Schedule A Compositions and grants to Publisher for the Territory all the same rights, and Publisher hereby assumes all of the same duties, as are set forth herein with respect to the Schedule A Compositions.

According to this paragraph, compositions listed on Schedule A are works the writer has written prior to the term of the agreement. These are compositions the writer and publisher have agreed to include as part of their agreement. The writer states that his or her portion of these songs has not been published by any other company or individual. The publisher has the same rights and duties with regard to these songs as for any works written during the term of the agreement.

5. Exclusivity

From the date hereof and during the Term of this Agreement, Writer will not write or compose, or furnish or dispose of, any musical compositions, titles, lyrics or music, or any rights or interests therein, whatsoever, nor participate in any manner with regard to the same for any person, firm or corporation other than Publisher, nor permit the use of Writer's name or likeness as the writer or co-writer of any musical composition by any person, firm or corporation other than Publisher.

This paragraph reaffirms the exclusive nature of the agreement, stating that the writer will neither publish nor grant any rights for songs written during the term of the agreement to anyone other than the publisher with whom he or she is contracting. The writer also agrees not to authorize any other person or company to use his or her name or likeness as the writer of any musical composition created during this term.

6. Warranties, Covenants and Representations
Writer warrants, covenants and represents:

The writer makes the following promises:

(a) The Compositions are or will be new and original and will not infringe upon or unfairly compete with any other works, compositions, arrangements or material, and will not violate, invade, infringe upon or interfere with the rights of any third party.

In this subparagraph, the writer affirms that the songs he or she submits to the publisher will be original and will not infringe on anyone else's work.

(b) Writer has the full right, power and authority to make this Agreement, perform its terms and conditions, grant the rights herein granted Publisher and furnish Writer's services hereunder, and to vest in Publisher all the rights as provided for in this Agreement free and clear of all other claims, rights, obligations, and encumbrances whatsoever.

This subparagraph declares that the writer is free to enter into the agreement with the publisher and provide the services promised. In other words, the writer is not under contract to any other company and there is nothing that would prohibit him or her from entering into this agreement.

(c) The exercise of Publisher's rights in and to each of the Compositions, including the copyright therein, will not violate, conflict with or unfairly compete with the rights of any third party, and there does not now and will not hereafter exist any claim by a third party in or to any of the Compositions and no third party has or will have any conflicting rights in and to any of the Compositions.

This subparagraph confirms that the writer, the songs he or she may deliver during the term of the agreement, and any songs listed in Schedule A are not currently and will not become legally bound to any other company or individual that might prevent the publisher from securing copyrights or exercising the rights granted by the agreement. This also protects the publisher from any third-party claim of infringement, slander, plagiarism, etc.

(d) Writer has heretofore executed, or shall promptly hereafter execute, an agreement with a performing rights organization with which Publisher or one of its subsidiaries or affiliates is affiliated. During the term of said agreement, said organization shall have rights of public performance of the Compositions. So long as Writer is eligible for affiliation with a performing rights organization which pays royalties directly to authors and composers, Writer shall not be entitled to any portion of the publisher's share of sums received by Publisher with respect to the public performance of the Compositions. Writer agrees to give written notification to Publisher of any termination, modification or extension of said agreement within sixty (60) days of any such event. In the event, however, Publisher licenses the public performance of any Composition directly to any third party and receives sums with regard thereto, Publisher shall pay to Writer, without regard to recoupment, fifty percent (50%) thereof at the same time in the same manner and subject to the same terms and conditions (other than recoupment) as other royalties payable to Writer hereunder.

This subparagraph confirms that the writer has joined, or will promptly join, one of the performing rights organizations (ASCAP, BMI, or SESAC). The writer agrees to choose an organization with which the publisher is affiliated.

(Most major publishers are affiliated with all three of these organizations.)

Note that all PROs within the U.S. pay the "writers' share" of performance royalties directly to the writers—and the "publishers' share" directly to the publishers. The writer shall not be entitled to any portion of the "publishers' share" of performance royalties.

If the writer changes or extends his or her PRO affiliation, the publisher is to be notified in writing within sixty days. (For an explanation of PROs see Chapter 10).

Finally, if the publisher issues a performing rights license directly to an individual or company, fifty percent (50%) of the monies received by the publisher for this license go to the writer, regardless of whether or not there are advances that the publisher has not yet recouped.

7. Power of Attorney

Writer does hereby irrevocably constitute, authorize, empower and appoint Publisher, or any of its officers, partners, owners and/or employees, Writer's true and lawful attorney (with full power of substitution and delegation) in Writer's name, and in Writer's place and stead, or in Publisher's name, to take and do such action, and to make, sign, execute, acknowledge and deliver any and all instruments or documents which Publisher, from time to time, may deem desirable or necessary to vest in Publisher, its successors, assigns, and licensees, any of the rights or interests granted by Writer hereunder, including, but not limited to, such documents required to secure to Publisher the renewals and extensions of copyrights throughout the world of the Compositions, and also such documents necessary to assign to Publisher, its successors and assigns, such renewals and extensions for the use and benefit of Publisher, its successors and assigns. The aforesaid power shall be irrevocable. Further, Publisher may request Writer to execute a separate agreement and/or assignment of copyright in Publisher's customary form with respect to each Composition hereunder. Upon such request, Writer will promptly execute such agreement and/or assignment. Publisher shall have the right, pursuant to the terms and conditions hereof, to execute such agreement and/or assignment on behalf of Writer hereunder. Such agreement and/or assignment shall supplement and not supersede this Agreement. In the event of any conflict between the provisions of such agreement and/or assignment and this Agreement, the provisions of this Agreement shall govern.

In this paragraph, the writer grants the publisher (and any person or company that might acquire the publisher in the future) the right to sign documents on his or her behalf if these documents help the publisher to secure its rights in the compositions. These documents include (but are not limited to) copyright forms, their extensions, and renewals. The writer acknowledges that this power of attorney is irrevocable and that the publisher has a financial stake in it. If the publisher requests it, the writer shall sign a separate agreement and/or complete a copyright assignment for any individual songs. The publisher has the right to complete these documents on the writer's behalf. These separate agreements and assignments do not override the provisions of the exclusive songwriting agreement.

8. Delivery Requirement

(a) During each month of the Term Writer will create and deliver to Publisher the equivalent of at least one (1) Composition meeting the requirements prescribed below (the "Delivery Commitment").

The delivery requirement establishes the writer's quota—the minimum number of songs that must be written and submitted in order for the writer to satisfy his or her contractual commitment. While this agreement sets the quota at twelve songs, to be turned in at a rate of at least one per month, it would not be unusual for the delivery requirement to be anywhere from ten to fifteen songs per year. Some publishers require that the songs be delivered within specific timeframes (for example, a minimum of three songs per quarter).

Note that the delivery requirement refers to the writer's minimum commitment. Many staff-writers write and turn in many more songs than they are contractually obligated to write.

In some instances the delivery commitment is expressed, not as a minimum number of songs to be delivered, but as a minimum number of songs to be recorded and released on a major label, or on a label affiliated with and/or distributed by a major label. This requirement is most often invoked when the writer is also a recording artist or producer, or when a well-established writer is given a very large advance. The definition of the minimum commitment as a number of songs recorded and released is found more often in contracts originating in New York and Los Angeles than in Nashville.

(b) No Composition will apply in fulfillment of Writer's Delivery Commitment unless it is accepted by Publisher, in Publisher's sole and unrestricted discretion, as satisfactory for commercial exploitation. Any unsatisfactory Composition will remain fully subject to Publisher's rights under this Agreement. If any Composition not accepted as satisfactory generates income during the Term it will apply in reduction of Writer's Delivery Commitment for the first month in which such income is earned.

This subparagraph states that in order to be considered part of the writer's delivery commitment, any given song must be deemed acceptable by the publisher. While the publisher does not expect every song to be a "hit," this clause protects the publisher by establishing that songs must meet a standard of professionalism. If a composition is considered unacceptable (and is not applied to the writer's quota), the publisher still retains the same rights set out in the agreement that would apply to a song that is accepted as part of the delivery commitment.

If a song that was deemed unacceptable (and therefore, was not applied to the writer's quota) generates income during the term of the agreement, it is considered acceptable and applies to the delivery commitment in the first month in which it earns income.

(c) No Composition will apply in fulfillment of Writer's Delivery Commitment unless it is entirely new, original and copyrightable. Further, it is specifically understood and agreed that the Compositions listed on Schedule "A" to this Agreement shall not apply in fulfillment of the Delivery Commitment.

This subparagraph indicates that only new, entirely original compositions count toward the writer's quota. Songs written prior to the agreement and included in Schedule A do not go toward fulfilling the quota.

(d) If Writer has less than One Hundred (100%) Percent creative interest in a Composition which is otherwise applicable in reduction of Writer's Delivery Commitment, then such Composition shall be treated as a fractional portion of a Composition under Paragraph 8(a), calculated on the same basis of the same proportionate relationship as that between the creative interest of Writer and the aggregate of the creative interest(s) of the other author(s) of the Composition. (For example: If creative interests of authors other than Writer amount in the aggregate to one-third, then, such Composition shall be treated as constituting two-thirds of a Composition for the purposes of Paragraph 8(a).

This subparagraph establishes that for songs that the writer has not written entirely on his or her own (in other words, collaborations) only the portion that belongs to the writer goes toward fulfilling the quota. For example, a song written with one other writer equals one half of a song.

(e) If Writer shall fail, refuse or be unable to fulfill the Delivery Commitment, Publisher shall have the right, in addition to all of its other rights and remedies at law or in equity, to suspend the Term of this Agreement and its obligations hereunder (including, without limitation, any obligation hereunder to make advance payments to Writer) by written notice to Writer, or, in the event such failure, refusal or inability shall continue for two (2) months or longer, to terminate this Agreement by written notice to Writer. Any such suspension shall continue for the duration of any such failure, refusal or inability, and, unless Publisher notifies Writer to the contrary in writing, the then current period of the Term hereof shall be automatically extended by the number of days which shall equal the total number of days of suspension. During any such suspension, Writer shall not render services as a songwriter and/or composer to any other party other than Publisher, or assign, license or convey any musical composition to any other party other than Publisher.

This subparagraph means that if, for any reason, the writer does not submit enough songs to meet his or her song quota, the publisher has the right to suspend the agreement and stop paying the writer until the commitment has been fulfilled. If this failure to deliver songs continues for two months or more, the publisher has the right to end the agreement by notifying the writer in writing.

In addition, any suspension of the agreement extends the term of the current contract equal to the length of suspension. For instance, if the writer goes three months without delivering songs, the agreement may be extended by three months. During any suspension, the writer cannot work as a songwriter or composer for anyone other than the publisher.

9. Advances

Conditioned upon Writer's full and faithful performance of all of the material terms and provisions of this Agreement, Publisher shall pay to Writer or on Writer's behalf the following amounts, all of which shall be recoupable by Publisher from any and all royalties payable to Writer hereunder:

This paragraph states that provided the writer fulfills his or her contractual obligations (such as delivery of acceptable songs) the publisher must pay the following amounts, which are recoupable from the writer's share of any mechanical (sales) royalties and licensing fees that his or her songs covered under this agreement might earn. Note that the publisher does not recoup from the writer's performance royalties, which are paid directly to the writer by the PRO with which he or she is affiliated.

(a) $_____ with respect to the Initial Period of the Term, payable (i) $_____ upon the execution hereof and (ii) the balance in twelve (12) equal monthly installments, one during each of the first twelve (12) calendar months of the Initial Period.

The advance agreed upon between the writer and the publisher is specified here. Also specified is how much of the advance is to be paid to the writer upon the signing of the agreement. The remainder is to be paid in twelve equal monthly installments.

Note that there are many other ways for the publisher to pay the advance. Some publishers pay weekly, others pay biweekly or quarterly, and yet others pay in one lump sum. The publisher may, or may not, provide an initial payment upon the signing of the agreement.

(b) $_____ with respect to each Renewal Period of the Term, if any, payable in twelve (12) equal monthly installments, one during each of the first twelve (12) calendar months of the applicable Renewal Period.

Specified here is the amount of the advance to be paid to the writer if the publisher chooses to pick up the writer's options. This amount is to be paid in twelve equal, monthly payments. Note that the advance(s) for the second (and/or third) option period(s) may be higher than the amount for the first option.

(c) For the avoidance of doubt, it is specifically understood and agreed that if any period of the Term shall last longer than twelve (12) months, the monthly installments payable to Writer during such Contract Period nevertheless shall discontinue after the twelfth such installment.

Noted here is that in the event that the term of this agreement is extended beyond twelve months (due to writer's failure to meet his or her quota, for example) there are to be no additional payments after the twelfth payment.

10. Royalties

(a) Subject to the rights reserved to Publisher herein, Publisher agrees to use reasonable efforts to exploit the Compositions in accordance with its customary business practices and to pay Writer as royalties with regard to each Composition an amount equal to fifty percent (50%) of any and all net sums actually received by Publisher or its agent in the United States after deduction of collection fees, if any, charged by any such agent or other collecting organization from all uses of the Composition, including, but not limited to, print, mechanical reproduction, digital broadcast or transmission rights, electrical transcription and synchronization, provided that Writer shall not be entitled to share in the so-called "Publisher's Share" of any sums received by Publisher with respect to public performance of any Composition from any performing rights organization which pays a share of performance fees directly to writers or composers. Without limiting the generality of the foregoing, Publisher shall pay to Writer fifty percent (50%) of net sums with respect to the Audio Home Recording Act of 1992 in the United States from the exploitation in the United States of digital audio recording technology ("DART"). In this respect, Writer hereby designates Publisher Writer's agent to collect on Writer's behalf one hundred percent (100%) of the income earned from the exploitation of DART.

In this paragraph, the publisher agrees to promote the writer's songs in such a way that they will hopefully generate income. The publisher agrees to pay the writer 50 percent of all income received by the publisher after the deduction of any fees it might have to pay to collection agencies or organizations. If the writer is paid the "writer's share" of performance royalties and the publisher is paid the "publisher's share" directly by a PRO, then the writer is not entitled to any portion of the "publisher's share" of these royalties. (Note that this is typically the case.)

In regard to money payable for digital audio recording technology (referred to as "DART"), the writer specifies that the publisher shall collect the total amount of any income—and subsequently pay 50 percent to the writer.

(b) In the event any Composition is co-written by Writer and another person or persons to whom Publisher is obligated to pay royalties, Publisher shall pay to Writer a share of the foregoing sums corresponding to Writer's proportionate authorship interest in relation to the entire authorship interest of all per-

sons to whom Publisher is obligated to pay royalties.

This subparagraph declares that if a song is cowritten and more than one of its writers are signed to the same publisher, the publisher shall pay the writer the portion of any royalties equal to the percentage of his or her authorship of the song.

(c) It is agreed that Publisher shall not be required to pay any royalties on professional or complimentary copies or any copies or phonorecords which are distributed or sold by or under Publisher's authority at or below Publisher's cost or for promotional or similar purposes.

This subparagraph states that the publisher will not pay royalties for free promotional copies or copies sold below the publisher's cost.

(d) Writer shall not be entitled to share or receive any portion of any advance payments, guarantee payments or minimum royalty payments which Publisher may receive in connection with any subpublishing agreement, collection agreement, licensing agreement, or other agreement with respect to the Compositions unless such payments are made solely for the use of a specific and separately identifiable Composition(s) and no other compositions, in which event such sums shall be deemed net sums actually received by Publisher for such uses.

This subparagraph indicates that advances typically received by the publisher for subpublishing and print agreements are paid for the use of the publisher's entire catalog. Individual writers do not participate in the publisher's advance because there is no way to anticipate how to allocate these monies among the various writers' compositions.

However, if an advance were given because a subpublisher wanted exclusive rights to an individual writer's catalog, that writer would be entitled to 50 percent of the monies advanced to the publisher for such rights.

(e) As used herein, the term "net sums" shall mean the gross sums actually received by Publisher or its agent in the United States, reduced by collection fees and costs charged by any collection agent or organization, legal fees, court costs and/or other direct costs incurred by Publisher in the collection of such sums and in the exploitation of the Compositions.

Here, "net sums" is defined as all monies received by the publisher after the deduction of fees and other direct costs paid to collect payments owed that publisher.

(f) As used herein, the terms "payments," "paid," "received," and other words of similar import shall be deemed to include final credit in reduction of an advance minimum royalty payment received by Publisher unless such sums have been credited to Writer pursuant to subparagraph (d) above.

This paragraph refers back to the terms of subparagraph (d) in which the publisher receives an advance that is not shared with the writer. Royalties credited to the publisher's account for the usage of the writer's works must be paid to the writer regardless of whether the publisher has paid back the monies it was advanced by the third party.

11. Accounting

(a) **Publisher shall compute the royalties earned by Writer pursuant to this Agreement and pursuant to any other agreement between Writer and Publisher or its affiliates, whether now in existence or entered into at any time subsequent hereto, on or before March 31st for the semiannual period ending the preceding December 31st and on or before September 30th for the semiannual period ending the preceding June 30th, and shall thereupon submit to Writer the royalty statement for each period together with the net amount of royalties, if any, which shall be payable after deducting any and all unrecouped advances and chargeable costs under this Agreement or under any separate agreement between Writer and Publisher for any individual Composition. Royalties payable pursuant to this Agreement to Writer shall be due and payable on payments actually received by Publisher in the United States in U.S. Dollars or credited to Publisher's account against an advance payment.**

This paragraph establishes that the writer will receive a royalty statement and any payment due, twice per year: on (or before) March 31st for the six-month period from July 1st through December 31st; and on or before September 30th for the preceding January 1st through June 30th. The writer's royalties are based on the money received by the publisher (in U.S. dollars) after the deduction of expenses (as provided in this agreement). Any advances paid to the writer will be recouped from his or her royalties before payment is made.

(b) **Each statement submitted by Publisher to Writer shall be binding upon Writer and not subject to any objection by Writer for any reason unless specific written objection, stating the basis thereof, is sent by Writer to Publisher within one (1) year after the date said statement is submitted. A certified public accountant on Writer's behalf may, at Writer's expense, at reasonable intervals (but not more frequently than once each year), examine Publisher's books and records insofar as same concern Writer, during Publisher's usual business hours, at the location where such books and records are normally kept, and upon no less than thirty (30) days written notice, for the purpose of verifying the accuracy of any statement submitted to Writer hereunder. Publisher's books and records relating to activities during any accounting period may only be examined as aforesaid during the two (2) year period following service by Publisher of the statement for said accounting period.**

This subparagraph states that if the writer disagrees with any information listed on the royalty statement, this objection must be submitted in writing within one year of receipt of the statement. The writer, at his or her own expense, may hire a certified public accountant (an auditor) to review the publisher's books and records. Any such audit must take place during the publisher's normal business hours and at the place where the records are kept. The publisher must receive written notice at least thirty days prior to any such audit. Audits of any given period must be completed within two years of receipt of the corresponding royalty statement.

12. Writer's Services; Demonstration Recordings

Writer shall perform his required services hereunder conscientiously, and solely and exclusively for Publisher. Writer shall duly comply with all requirements and requests made by Publisher in connection with its business as set forth herein. Writer shall deliver to Publisher a CD or tape "work copy" of each Composition immediately upon the completion or acquisition of such Composition. Publisher's failure to exploit any or all of said Compositions shall not be deemed a breach hereof. In this regard, Publisher shall have the right to produce demonstration recordings hereunder and Writer shall cooperate fully with Publisher in connection with such production. Writer shall not incur any liability for which Publisher shall be responsible in connection with any demonstration recording session without having obtained Publisher's prior approval as to the nature, extent and limit of such liability. In no event shall Writer incur any expense whatsoever on behalf of Publisher without having received prior written authorization from Publisher. Writer shall not be entitled to any compensation (except for such compensation as is otherwise provided for herein) with respect to services rendered in connection with any such demonstration recording sessions. Publisher shall advance the costs for the production of demonstration recordings, (not to exceed six hundred fifty ($650) dollars per recorded composition) subject to the foregoing, and one-half (1/2) of such costs shall be deemed additional advances to Writer hereunder and shall be recouped by Publisher from royalties payable to Writer by Publisher under this Agreement or any separate agreement between Writer and Publisher for any individual Composition. In the event that Writer has collaborated with any other person (who is not one of Publisher's exclusive songwriters or Writers) in the creation of a Composition, then Publisher shall only advance that portion of the costs for the production of demonstration recordings that is consistent with the percentage of the Composition which is owned by Publisher hereunder. All recordings and reproductions made at demonstration recording sessions hereunder shall become the sole and exclusive property of Publisher, free of any claims whatsoever by Writer or any person deriving any rights from Writer.

This paragraph states that the writer must deliver a rough recording (a "work tape") of each new song submitted. This recording may be on CD or tape. The publisher is not obligated to pitch or promote a song.

In addition, the publisher has the right under the agreement to produce a demo recording. If requested, the writer must help the publisher in the production of demos. (Note that in actuality, the writer is typically responsible for producing his or her own demos.)

The writer must also receive prior written consent before incurring or approving any demo costs and is not to be paid for his or her work (such as programming or singing) on the demo.

In addition, this paragraph establishes that the maximum the publisher is required to pay is $650 per demo recording. Note that in some instances (for example, when a writer owns his or her own recording studio), the writer might be expected to absorb the costs of demo production out of any advances he or she has received. This is typically the case outside the U.S. and is more commonly done in New York and Los Angeles than in Nashville. Note, too, that the money allocated for demo production costs will vary depending on the style of music and the location; musicians, vocalists, and production costs tend to be higher in New York and Los Angeles than they are in Nashville—and this sum (or the monies advanced to the writer) should be adequate for the writer to produce competitive, professional demos.

Finally, one half of the writer's demo costs shall be considered a recoupable advance against writer's future royalties. For collaborations, the publisher must pay a percentage of the demo costs equal to the writer's percentage of the song. (For instance, if a song is written with one other writer, the publisher would only be required to pay up to $325 for a demo.) All demo recordings become the sole property of the publisher.

13. Promotional Appearances

Writer shall, from time to time, at Publisher's reasonable request, and whenever same will not unreasonably interfere with prior professional engagements of Writer, appear for photography, artwork, and other similar purposes under the direction of Publisher or its duly authorized agent, appear for interviews and other promotional purposes, and confer and consult with Publisher regarding Writer's services hereunder. Writer shall also cooperate with Publisher in promoting, publicizing and exploiting the Compositions and for any other purpose related to the business of Publisher in his capacity as a songwriter. Writer shall not be entitled to any compensation (other than applicable union scale if appropriate) for rendering such services, but shall be entitled to reasonable transportation and living expenses if such expenses must be incurred in order to render such services.

According to this paragraph, the writer shall participate in the promotion of his or her songs and the publishing company within reason. The writer is not paid for these services, however, reasonable costs for expenses such as transportation, meals, and lodging, will be reimbursed.

14. Collaboration with Other Writers

Writer warrants and represents that prior to collaboration in the creation of any musical composition with any other person who is not signed to an exclusive writer's agreement with a bona-fide third-party publisher, such person shall be advised of this exclusive Agreement and that it is Publisher's desire that any such composition be published by Publisher. In the event of such collaboration with any other person, Writer shall notify Publisher of the extent of interest that such person may have in any such musical composition and Writer shall use reasonable efforts to cause such other person to execute a separate songwriter's or appropriate agreement with respect thereto, which agreement shall set forth the division of the writer's share of income between Writer and such other person.

Any songs written as a result of collaboration are covered by this paragraph of the agreement. In the event that a cowriter is not signed exclusively to a legitimate publishing company, the writer shall advise the collaborator(s) that the publisher wants to publish the cowriters' portion of the song. In the event of such a collaboration, the writer must notify the publisher of the cowriters' percentage of ownership of the song and request that the cowriter signs an agreement specifying each writer's share of ownership in the song.

15. Name and Likeness

Publisher shall have the right to use and to allow others to use Writer's legal and professional name and likeness, biographical material and facsimile signature in connection with Publisher's music publishing business and with the use, promotion and exploitation of the Compositions in particular, including, without limitation, personality folios.

Under the terms of this paragraph, the publisher has the right to allow others to use the writer's legal and professional name; photo or artist's rendering; bio; and representation of his or her signature to promote the writer's compositions and the publisher's business.

16. Separate Agreements

If Publisher so desires, Publisher may request Writer to execute a separate agreement in Publisher's customary form with respect to each Composition hereunder. Upon such request, Writer shall promptly execute and deliver such separate agreement, and upon Writer's failure to do so, Publisher shall have the right, pursuant to the terms and conditions hereof, to execute such separate agreement on behalf of Writer. Such separate agreement shall supplement and not supersede this Agreement. In the event of any conflict between the provisions of such separate agreement and this Agreement, the provisions of this Agreement shall govern. The failure of either of the parties hereto to execute such separate agreement, whether such execution is requested by Publisher or not, shall not affect the rights of each of the parties hereunder, including but not limited to the rights of Publisher to all of the Compositions

written, composed or acquired by Writer during the term hereof.

According to this paragraph, the publisher may request that a separate contract be signed for each song submitted. If the writer does not furnish these separate agreements, the publisher may sign the contract on the writer's behalf. Any future agreements may address additional issues but may not override anything agreed upon in the exclusive songwriting contract. Whether or not additional agreements are executed, the terms of this agreement remain in force.

A primary reason why many publishers request separate contracts for each song submitted as part of the exclusive agreement is that it makes it easier for them in the event that they should decide to sell or transfer the publishing rights to specific songs from their catalog. Requesting a separate agreement for each song also helps the publisher to keep track of those songs that have been turned in.

17. Actions

Publisher may take such action as it deems necessary, either in Writer's name or in its own name, against any person to protect all rights and interests acquired by Publisher hereunder. Writer will, at Publisher's request, cooperate fully with Publisher in any controversy which may arise or litigation which may be brought concerning Publisher's rights and interests obtained hereunder. Publisher shall have the right, in its absolute discretion, to employ attorneys and to institute or defend any action or proceeding and to take any other proper steps to protect the right, title and interest of Publisher in and to each Composition hereunder and every portion thereof, and in that connection, to settle, compromise or in any other manner dispose of any matter, claim, action or proceeding and to satisfy any judgment that may be rendered, in any manner as Publisher, in its sole discretion, may determine. Any legal action brought by Publisher against an alleged infringer of any Composition shall be initiated and prosecuted by Publisher, and if there is any recovery made by Publisher as a result thereof, after deduction of the expense of litigation, including, but not limited to, attorneys' fees and court costs, a sum equal to fifty percent (50%) of such net proceeds shall be deemed net sums hereunder.

This paragraph grants that the publisher has the right to take whatever action it deems necessary to protect its rights and establishes that the writer is required to cooperate in the publisher's effort to do so. The publisher may employ attorneys in this regard and has the sole right to decide whether or not to accept a settlement. Any monies received as a result of a settlement are to be divided between the publisher and the writer after legal and administrative fees are deducted.

18. Indemnity

Writer hereby indemnifies, saves and holds Publisher, its successors and assigns, harmless from any and all liability, claims, demands, loss and damage

(including counsel fees and court costs) arising out of or connected with any claim or action by a third party which is inconsistent with any of the warranties, representations or agreements made by Writer in this Agreement, and Writer shall reimburse Publisher, on demand, for any loss, cost, expense or damage to which said indemnity applies. Publisher shall give Writer prompt written notice of any claim or action covered by said indemnity, and Writer shall have the right, at Writer's expense, to participate in the defense of any such claim or action with counsel of Writer's choice, provided, however, that the final control and disposition of same shall remain with Publisher. Pending the disposition of any such claim or action, or the disposition of any claim or action by Publisher against Writer, Publisher shall have the right to withhold payment of such portion of any monies which may be payable by Publisher to Writer under this Agreement or under any other agreement between Publisher and Writer and/or either of their affiliates as shall be reasonably related to the amount of the claim and estimated counsel fees and costs.

If the publisher is sued by a party who claims that the writer has signed this agreement under false pretenses or makes agreements or representations that he or she does not have the legal right to do, then according to the terms of this paragraph the publisher will not be held responsible and any costs or damages will be paid by the writer. The writer must be notified in writing of any such claims and may participate in the lawsuit with his or her own attorney. However, the publisher has the right to control the lawsuit, including the right to settle any actions that result from the writer's misrepresentation, and may withhold any monies payable under this contract (and any other contract between the publisher and writer or their affiliates) to cover the publisher's legal and administrative fees in defending itself.

19. Post-Term Rights
The termination or expiration of the Term hereof shall in no way affect the respective rights and obligations of Writer and Publisher with respect to the Compositions. In such event, the relevant provisions of this Agreement (including without limitation the warranties, covenants and representations by Writer) shall continue in full force and effect with respect thereto.

This paragraph states that after the agreement ends, the ongoing rights granted to the compositions continue to remain in force.

20. Unique Services
Writer acknowledges that the services to be rendered by Writer hereunder are of a special, unique, unusual, extraordinary and intellectual character which gives them a peculiar value, the loss of which cannot be reasonably or adequately compensated in damages in an action at law, and that a breach by Writer of any of the provisions of this Agreement will cause Publisher great and irreparable injury and damage. Publisher shall be entitled to the remedies

of injunction and other equitable relief to prevent a breach of this Agreement or any provision hereof, which relief shall be in addition to any other remedies, for damages or otherwise, which may be available to Publisher.

Here the writer agrees that the services he or she is offering have unique value. Therefore, if the writer does not live up to his or her obligations, the publisher has the right to seek "equitable relief" (where the court orders a party to do, or not do, something) in addition to financial compensation, which is known as "damages."

21. Notices

All notices given to Writer hereunder and all statements and payments sent to Writer hereunder shall be addressed to Writer at the address set forth on Page 1 hereof, or at such other address as Writer shall designate in writing from time to time. All notices to Publisher given hereunder shall be addressed to Publisher at the address set forth on Page 1 hereof, or at such other address as Publisher shall designate in writing from time to time. All notices shall be in writing and (except for royalty statements) shall either be served by registered or certified mail, return receipt requested, all charges prepaid. Except as otherwise provided in this Agreement, such notices shall be deemed given when mailed, all charges prepaid. Notices of change of address shall be effective only after the actual receipt thereof.

This paragraph establishes that all correspondence between the publisher and the writer must be sent to the addresses listed on page one of the agreement. Changes in address and all notices (other than royalty statements) must be presented in writing and sent via prepaid certified or registered mail, with a return receipt requested.

22. Entire Agreement

This Agreement supersedes any and all prior negotiations, understandings and agreements between the parties hereto with respect to the subject matter hereof. Each of the parties acknowledges and agrees that neither party has made any representations or promises in connection with this Agreement or the subject matter hereof not contained herein.

According to this paragraph, regardless of what one or the other party might have discussed, promised, implied, or agreed to, the written contract constitutes the entire agreement.

23. Modification; Waiver; Enforceability

This Agreement may not be canceled, altered, modified, amended or waived, in whole or in part, in any way, except by an instrument in writing signed by both Publisher and Writer. The waiver by Publisher of any breach of this Agreement, in any one or more instances, shall in no way be construed as a waiver of any subsequent breach (whether or not of similar nature) of this Agreement by

Writer. If any part of this Agreement shall be held to be void, invalid or unenforceable, it shall not affect the validity of the balance of this Agreement.

This paragraph states that any changes to this agreement must be in writing and agreed upon by both publisher and writer. If the publisher agrees in writing to waive a particular breach of this contract this does not change the contract. Any subsequent breaches may or may not be permitted. If any part of the agreement is determined to be invalid or unenforceable it will not affect the remaining parts of the contract.

24. Assignment

Publisher may assign its rights under this Agreement in whole or in part to any person, firm, corporation or other party, without restriction and such rights may be assigned by any assignee. This Agreement shall inure to the benefit of and be binding upon each of the parties hereto and their respective successors, assigns, heirs, executors, administrators and legal and personal representatives. Any attempted assignment or delegation by Writer of all or any part of this Agreement and/or of any or all of Writer's rights and/or obligations hereunder shall be null and void and of no legal effect whatsoever.

The publisher may assign its rights to another individual or company according to this paragraph. For example, the writer's catalog may be sold to another publishing company. The writer may not sell or assign any of his or her rights or responsibilities granted by the contract. Any contract that might result from an attempt to do so shall be illegal. In the event that the rights specified in this contract should be passed on, the terms of this agreement will still be binding upon the writer's and publisher's successors.

25. Status of Parties

This Agreement shall not constitute a joint venture by or a partnership between Publisher and Writer, it being understood that Publisher is acting hereunder as an independent contractor.

This paragraph establishes that the writer is not an employee of the publisher. Writer and Publisher are considered to be independent contractors.

26. Notice of Breach

In order to eliminate misunderstandings between the parties, each party hereto agrees to advise the other in writing of the specific nature of any claimed breach of this Agreement, and the party alleged to be in breach shall have a period of thirty (30) days after the receipt of said notice in which to cure such claimed breach. The aforesaid written notice shall be deemed a condition precedent to the commencement of any legal proceedings by either party hereto against the other, and shall be sent by registered or certified mail, return receipt requested. Notwithstanding any of the foregoing, the cure provisions of this Paragraph 26 shall not be applicable to the exclusivity provisions

hereof nor to Writer's failure, refusal or inability to fulfill Writer's Delivery Commitment pursuant to the terms and provisions of this Agreement.

Under the terms of this paragraph, any claim of breach of contract must be provided in writing and sent via registered or certified mail, return receipt requested. The party accused of failure to live up to obligations has thirty days after receiving the written notice to remedy the alleged problem. No proceedings may begin until this has been done. However, the thirty-day provision does not apply to parts of the contract that specify the writer's being published exclusively by the publisher during the term of the agreement. Nor does the thirty-day provision apply in the event of the writer's failure to deliver the required number of songs.

27. Insurance

Publisher shall be entitled (but in no event shall be obligated) to secure, in Publisher's own name or otherwise and at Publisher's expense, life, accident, and/or other insurance covering Writer, with Publisher or any party Publisher designates being the sole beneficiary thereof and neither Writer nor Writer's estate shall have any right, title or interest in and to such insurance or any proceeds therefrom. Writer shall cooperate fully with Publisher in connection with the obtaining of such insurance, if any, including, without limitation, by timely submitting to medical examinations and by completing any and all documents necessary or desirable in respect thereof.

This paragraph states that the publisher may insure the writer at the publisher's expense with the publisher being the beneficiary. The writer agrees to cooperate if the publisher chooses to obtain insurance. The writer (and his or her estate) is not entitled to any proceeds of this insurance.

28. Legal Counsel

Writer hereby represents and warrants that writer has been advised of writer's right to retain independent legal counsel in connection with the negotiation of this agreement and that writer has either retained and been represented by such legal counsel or has knowingly and voluntarily waived writer's right to such legal counsel.

Here the writer acknowledges that he or she has been advised of his or her right to consult a lawyer before signing the agreement. If the writer chooses not to do so, he or she acknowledges that this decision has been made voluntarily.

29. Headings

The headings of paragraphs or other divisions hereof are inserted only for the purpose of convenient reference. Such headings shall not be deemed to govern, limit, modify or in any other manner affect the scope, meaning or intent of the provisions of this Agreement or any part thereof, nor shall they otherwise be given any legal effect.

This paragraph establishes that the headings used for each paragraph are provided for convenience. They do not affect the meaning of the text and have no legal consequence.

30. Controlling Law
This Agreement shall be deemed to have been made in the State of _____, the venue for any action or proceeding brought by either party hereto against the other shall be in the County of _____ in said State, and the validity, construction and legal effect of this Agreement shall be governed by the laws of the State of _____ applicable to contracts entered into and wholly performed therein.

According to this paragraph, the contract is governed by the laws of the state specified. Usually it will be the state where the publisher's main offices are located.

31. Attorneys' Fees
In the event of any action, suit or proceeding by either party against the other under this Agreement, the prevailing party shall be entitled to recover reasonable attorney's fees and costs of said action, suit or proceeding.

This paragraph states that if the publisher or writer takes legal action against the other, the winning party has the right to be reimbursed for legal fees from the other party.

IN WITNESS WHEREOF, the parties have executed this Agreement as of the day first written on page 1 hereof.

"Writer":   **"Publisher":**

By: _____
_____
Soc. Sec. No: _____

CHAPTER FIVE

Self-Publishing Your Work and Exploiting Your Copyrights

Songwriters who have not assigned their publishing rights to another individual or company own both the writer's share and the publisher's share of any income their songs earn. Writers in this category control 100 percent of the rights to their songs. In other words, if you don't *have* a publisher—you *are* a publisher. In addition, you control all creative and business decisions regarding your songs.

Self-publishing is ideal for songwriters who do not need the assistance of a publisher in order to generate income from their songs. This most often applies to performing songwriters who record their own material as well as to writers who collaborate with successful artists or producers, and therefore have a built-in outlet for their songs. Writers in these enviable positions do not need to relinquish large percentages of their income in order to get their songs recorded. They might opt instead for an *administration deal*, engaging the services of a company to collect income, issue licenses, and handle additional administrative functions in exchange for a small percentage of the writer's revenue. (More about administration deals in Chapter 8.)

Some songwriters self-publish without benefit of a specific outlet for their material in the hopes that they will be able to pitch their songs successfully—and retain 100 percent of their income. However, if the reason you choose to self-publish is because you have been unable to secure a publisher, despite earnest efforts, you might want to examine whether you are writing the kinds and caliber of songs that publishers are likely to place. But, presuming that your work has received excellent feedback, if you enjoy engaging in the business aspect of the music business and you are willing to invest the time, effort, and money to promote your songs, being your own publisher may be ideal for you. As you will learn in this chapter, establishing oneself as a publisher is relatively easy. The greater challenge is to be a successful publisher.

The Association of Independent Music Publishers (AIMP) can be a valuable networking and educational resource for independent music publishers. The organization has chapters in Los Angeles and New York and offers monthly meetings, forums, and workshops. Membership is available not only to independent music publishers, but also to songwriters, artist managers, publishers affiliated with record labels, film and television production companies, and other areas of the entertainment community. For additional information visit www.aimp.org.

Setting Up a Music Publishing Company

First and foremost, in order to be a publisher you need one or more songs or musical compositions to which you own the publishing rights. As previously explained, you own all rights to songs that you have written—provided you have not published them elsewhere—and you may open and operate a publishing company even if you retain only a small portion of the ownership of a copublished song.

In order to conduct business you will need letterhead, address labels, CD labels, business cards, and envelopes with your company name. If your artistic abilities extend beyond your songwriting, you may be able to generate these items on your computer; otherwise you can pay a nominal fee to have them created. A graphic artist can likely design a simple, yet eye-catching logo for $100–$250.

Be sure your design represents you as a professional by keeping it simple and avoiding embellishments such as musical notes. It's also a good idea to have a telephone line that can be answered (or transferred to voicemail) with the name of your business. A fax machine and access to e-mail are helpful, if not mandatory.

Affiliating with a Performing Rights Organization

While songwriters are permitted to be a member of only one performing rights organization (ASCAP, BMI, or SESAC) at any given time, a publisher must affiliate with each of those PROs to which his or her writers are signed. Therefore, a company that publishes songs written by various writers who belong to ASCAP, BMI, and SESAC must establish an ASCAP, a BMI, and a SESAC publishing company—each with different names.

> If you are your own publisher and are publishing only your own material, you need to affiliate as a publisher only with the PRO that you are a member of as a writer.

To qualify for affiliation as a publisher with BMI or ASCAP you must demonstrate that you are the publisher of one or more commercially released musical compositions (for example, a song available for sale on CD, DVD, or as a digital download); or material that is being broadcast, or is likely to be broadcast, on radio, television, film, or other electronic mediums such as cable, Internet, or pay-per-view; or work that is being performed in venues that are licensable by PROs (such as nightclubs, concerts, or symphonic recitals).

Unless these criteria are met, there is no benefit to affiliating as a publisher with any PRO. Nonetheless, you might still create letterhead with the name of your publishing company and pitch your own material. Songs that are sent by a publisher sometimes garner more attention and credibility than those being pitched by a writer.

There is no fee to join ASCAP as a publisher and no annual dues. BMI levies an initial charge of $150 for solely owned publishing companies and $250 for partnerships, corporations, and limited-liability companies. On a case-by-case basis this fee may be waived.

SESAC, the smallest of the three PROs in the U.S., is more selective about who may affiliate. Requests for affiliation as a writer and/or publisher are reviewed by SESAC's Writer/Publisher Relations staff.

As part of the publisher application process you are required to complete a form to register your songs with your PRO. This entails listing the songs' titles (including any alternate titles); the length of the songs; whether they have been released commercially (and if so, the label, date of release, recording number, and artist's name); the writers' names and PRO affiliations; and the percentage of each writer's and publisher's ownership. Songs written subsequent to your affiliation as a publisher can be registered with your PRO at its Web site.

Applications for affiliation can be downloaded at www.ASCAP.com and www.BMI.com. To affiliate with SESAC (www.SESAC.com), contact a member of their Writer/Publisher Relations staff. It typically takes four to six weeks for an application to be processed. The affiliation agreements automatically renew, continuing your association indefinitely, unless canceled by either party, as specified by the agreements.

Clearing a Name Through ASCAP, BMI, or SESAC

When applying to affiliate with a performing rights society you are requested to provide three potential names for your publishing company, listed in your order of preference. A PRO representative researches databases to determine whether the names you have chosen are available. This process, typically referred to as *clearing a name*, takes approximately two weeks and may be more challenging than expected.

To avoid administrative confusion and the possibility of wrong companies being paid, prospective publishers are neither permitted to register a name being used by any other publisher in the world, nor permitted to register one that is deemed similar to any previously registered publishing company's name. There are instances in which publishers have submitted twenty or more names before having one approved—so be creative in your selection. In addition to your company name being highly original, it's a good idea to include a word to identify it as a music publishing company, for example, Moondream Music, Moondream Publishing, Moondream Songs, Moondream Tunes, etc.

When your publishing company's name has been cleared, your next step is to complete the paperwork required by the state in which you reside, to legally establish yourself as a business. You may be able to learn what your state requires and to download the necessary forms by visiting the Web site of the Secretary of State's office or the County Clerk. It is likely that you will need to file either a "fictitious name statement" or a "d/b/a" ("doing business as") form. Depending upon the requirements in your location, you may also need to publish a statement of your intent to do business in a local newspaper.

In most locales, proof of completion of these forms is required in order to open a bank account in the name of your business. This is necessary in order to cash checks drafted to your business (such as performance and mechanical royalty checks).

What It Takes to Be a Successful Publisher

As you learned in Chapter 1, publishers are responsible for a myriad of creative and administrative tasks. When publishing your own work you shoulder all of these responsibilities—in addition to having to write great songs. Without exceptional songs it's unlikely that even the most talented, well-connected publisher will achieve success.

As previously explained, unless you have assigned your publishing rights elsewhere, you own 100 percent of the rights to your songs, as well as the writer's share and the publisher's share of any income they might earn. However, there is a world of difference between retaining your publishing rights and successfully exploiting your songs.

Successful publishers must develop persistence in the face of inevitable, repeated rejection. There are countless stories of songs that took five or more years to be recorded before soaring to the top of the charts. To do well as a publisher you need the kind of personality that can withstand being rejected seventy-five times or more—and still believe your songs are potential hits.

Being your own publisher also requires an ability to handle the business side of the music business—negotiating licensing fees and subpublishing deals, issuing recording licenses, and monitoring royalty statements. It requires registering your songs with the U.S. Copyright Office and with your PRO as well. But, you don't have to do everything yourself.

Many independent publishers contract individuals or companies to manage administrative chores such as copyright registration and issuing recording and synchronization licenses, and to collect royalties, allowing them to focus on the creative and pitching aspects of being a publisher. This is typically accomplished by entering into an Administration Agreement (discussed in Chapter 8). In the event that your songs generate income internationally you will likely need a *subpublisher*, a company that operates on your behalf in countries outside the U.S. and Canada. Subpublishing is addressed in Chapter 14. The tough part of being a music publisher is getting songs recorded and used in situations that generate royalties and licensing fees.

Exploiting Your Self-Published Work

A publisher's success, to a large extent, can be measured by the ability to generate income from the copyrights represented. This typically entails causing these songs to be recorded by artists who achieve significant sales and downloading; having songs played on the radio; placing material in films and on television shows; and/or having songs used in commercials. Accomplishing these goals is not an easy task and typically requires considerable time, expense, and effort. It also demands very strong songs—songs that can compete with material being written by established staff-writers and submitted by top music publishers.

One of the most important responsibilities for self-published songwriters who are not also recording artists is pitching their songs. *Pitching* can be defined as the process of submitting songs for consideration by decision makers—those who screen or select songs for recording artists and for inclusion in films, on television, and in commercials. Songs are pitched by mail, via the Internet, or at face-to-face meetings.

The importance of timing in the pitching process should not be underestimated. When an artist has recently finished recording an album, it's highly unlikely that his or her representatives will be seeking additional material. The majority of artists' albums are released eighteen or more months apart, with many acts waiting two years or more between album releases.

To time your pitches to your best advantage it will help to understand that in the country music genre, albums typically are recorded in two or three specified blocks of time. For instance, there may be a week in an artist's schedule allocated for recording music tracks in January, and another week scheduled in March. The *basic tracks* (the foundation of the musical arrangement—typically bass, drums, guitars, keyboards, fiddle, and pedal steel guitar) for an entire album are recorded at these sessions, with vocals and instrumental overdubs being added over extended periods. This is because country albums are recorded using live musicians (as opposed to synthesizers and computer-generated sounds).

Country musicians are booked for two, or three, three-hour blocks per day, allowing an album's producer to record ten or more songs in a given week. Therefore, in the two or three months leading up to the recording of a country album's basic tracks, the A&R staff intensifies its song search, meeting with publishers and established songwriters.

However, in other styles of music (pop, hip-hop, R&B/urban, dance, etc.) the basic tracks are typically recorded using computers and synthesizers. Instead of six or seven musicians convening in a studio to record at one time (as is typically the case in country music), a keyboard programmer is likely to work alone using a synthesizer or computer to create the drum, bass, and various keyboard sounds that will comprise the basic track. Because these tracks are crafted one at a time, artists and producers have the flexibility to record songs as they find them.

In many instances, songs pitched at the last minute bump other songs off the list, while songs submitted six or more months prior to an album's scheduled recording may not even get listened to. Regardless of the musical genre, an A&R executive's focus is likely to be on the next artists who are preparing to record.

As when sending packages to publishers, it is acceptable to follow up your submissions to record labels, producers, and artist managers with a phone call, e-mail, or fax a week or two after sending your package. But as stated by Tom Luteran, Director of Creative, EMI Music Publishing, "Usually no answer is a 'no' answer."

In the majority of instances you will not receive any response to your submission. Because of the volume of material they receive, most music industry professionals do not take the time to send rejection letters. If you have not been contacted within six to eight weeks, presume that your material has been listened to and not chosen. While the lack of feedback is frustrating, it's best to focus your energy on the next submission.

How to Know Who Is Looking for Songs—and How to Get to Them

As you learned in the previous section, having the right song for the right artist is only part of the equation—it also needs to be at the right time. To pitch songs effectively you need to know which artists who record outside songs are currently seeking material. There are several ways to accomplish this.

At many large publishing companies, individuals are assigned to maintain regular contact with A&R executives at various labels, as well as with artists' managers and producers. One songplugger might be responsible for keeping track of which artists are seeking songs at Warner Brothers, while another might be expected to monitor upcoming recording dates at Universal. This requires making phone calls and/or sending e-mails or faxes to individuals at various record labels.

Some A&R departments maintain a telephone hotline to provide this information via recording. This saves them the time and trouble of repeating this same information to multiple publishers. Other record labels routinely send the information to publishers via fax or e-mail. By introducing yourself as a publisher (with a telephone call or e-mail) and presenting yourself in a confident, professional manner, you should be able learn which artists are seeking material by calling the A&R department secretaries. You may also request to be added to the list of those who receive notifications via e-mail or fax. It's important to maintain this contact on a regular basis (for example, once a month) in order to keep track of ever-changing recording schedules and requirements for songs.

When contacting an A&R representative or artist's manager, it can be beneficial to ask the following:

- Can you describe the kinds of songs you're looking for?
- Are there specific tempos that you need—or don't need?
- And, if you are not familiar with the artist's work: Can you play me something this artist has recorded?

Sources that list contact information for record labels, artists' managers, and producers include *New On The Charts* (www.notc.com), the *A&R Registry* (www.musicregistry.com), the *Country Music Association Directory* (www.cmaworld.com), and the *Billboard International Talent and Touring Directory* (www.Billboard.com).

Using Tip Sheets Effectively

Phoning numerous record labels, record producers, and managers each month is quite time consuming and, depending on your location, may incur considerable long-distance telephone charges. One option is to pay someone else to do this research and compile it on your behalf. This is essentially what occurs when an individual subscribes to a tip sheet or pitch sheet.

As you learned in Chapter 1, a tip sheet is a publication (typically sent by e-mail unless otherwise requested) that lists recording artists who are seeking material. Some tip sheets are available only to publishers and published writers; others are sold to anyone who can write a check. These publications include mailing and e-mail addresses, as well as telephone and fax numbers for those in charge of screening songs for the projects listed. The artist's name, a brief description of the kinds of material requested, when recording is scheduled to begin, and the name of the producer and A&R person in charge are also typically provided.

Some of the most reputable and helpful tip sheets are *RowFax* (www.rowfax .com), *SongQuarters* (www.songquarters.com), and *SongLink International* (www.songlink.com). The various publications have different focuses. For example, *RowFax* primarily lists country music artists; *SongLink International* and *SongQuarters* do an excellent job of providing tips for acts outside of the U.S. Sample copies—available at the publications' Web sites—can help you evaluate which tip sheets will best serve your needs.

Using tip sheets can eliminate hours of research time and provide valuable information the subscriber might not otherwise be aware of, such as artists on small, independent labels; acts based outside the U.S.; and aspiring recording artists who are looking for songs to include on their demo, in the hopes of landing a recording contract.

The information gleaned from tip sheets is best used as a starting point to augment additional efforts, as opposed to replacing them. While these publications can be of great value, they cannot take the place of personal contact with individuals at record labels who may yield valuable information not provided in the tip sheets. Even by subscribing to all of the various tip sheets it's unlikely that a reader would be apprised of every major label artist who is looking for songs. This is because many A&R representatives and producers choose not to be listed. They prefer to receive material only from sources they've learned to rely upon, thereby avoiding being deluged with unsolicited material.

While those who research and compile tip sheet listings do their best to ensure the accuracy of their information, it is always advisable to initiate contact by e-mail or telephone prior to sending material. The type of songs requested, the recording schedule, mailing address, or other information may have changed or been listed incorrectly. By making contact you can confirm that you have the correct information as well as gain the added benefit of beginning a business relationship.

Joining Taxi

Taxi (www.taxi.com) describes itself as "The World's Leading Independent A&R Company." It provides its members with a tip sheet—and then takes the concept a step further. Members pay a yearly fee ($299.95 at the time of this book's publication), which entitles them to receive an extensive bimonthly e-mail listing of artists, films, and television projects seeking songs, as well as publishers and record labels soliciting songwriters and recording artists. There are approximately twelve hundred listings per year. However, the artists', record labels', television shows', and publishers' names remain anonymous. A listing seeking material for Celine Dion might request "Adult contemporary/pop songs for an international female superstar with an exceptionally powerful voice and great range."

For each song submitted for consideration the member pays an additional $5.00. The songs and artists are screened by a member of Taxi's staff, many of whom were formerly high-level record label or publishing company executives. Those submissions that the screeners deem both appropriate and up to the highest professional standards are forwarded to the A&R representative, artist's manager, or producer who placed the listing. The writers and artists of those submissions that are not forwarded have the option of receiving a brief assessment and critique of their work at no additional cost.

Taxi also provides its members with an excellent educational and networking opportunity at its annual Road Rally, held in Los Angeles each November. The Road Rally, one of the best events of its kind, features a smorgasbord of songwriting and music business classes; music industry panels; opportunities for songwriters to pitch songs to music publishers and for artists to submit their demos and press kits to record labels and producers; performance opportunities; and an unmatched chance to socialize and interact with aspiring songwriters and artists from around the world.

This is a legitimate organization that can be of great benefit to writers and artists with material that can compete with the top hit-makers and with those composing for television and film projects—but lack the connections necessary to get heard. The primary complaint lodged by Taxi members is that the organization fails to forward their material. Some songwriters have submitted songs for hundreds of Taxi listings without having any of their work forwarded. This is because Taxi maintains its credibility with record labels, music supervisors, and other industry professionals by passing along only material that their screeners believe is truly competitive with the songs and the hit-makers who are on the radio, at the top of the charts, and being featured in television and film projects.

Regardless of what they are paid, neither Taxi, independent songpluggers (discussed in Chapter 17), nor any other organization can secure legitimate recordings of songs that are less than exceptional. Like subscribing to tip sheets, Taxi can be an excellent resource, but is best used as one of many tools in your arsenal of pitching songs.

Preparing Your Song Submission Package

When pitching songs as a publisher, the packages you submit to record labels, artists, managers, music supervisors, and producers should be comprised of a cover letter, a CD, and a lyric sheet. Your presentation will identify you instantly as a legitimate professional—or as an aspiring amateur. By studying the sections that follow you will learn how to create and present these components in an effective manner.

Note that it is never appropriate to include a *lead sheet* (sheet music that includes a song's notes, words, and chords) or a *chord chart* (a listing of the chords to be played in each measure of the song) unless specifically requested. A photo or bio should be included only if you are submitting for consideration as an artist—as opposed to submitting songs in the hopes of your songs being recorded by other artists.

Cover Letter

Your publishing company's letterhead should include a distinctive, yet businesslike logo. As mentioned previously, an effective logo can be created inexpensively by a graphic designer. Similar to the personal letterhead you would use to contact publishers, your company's stationery should avoid any fancy decoration, such as musical notes or flowers. A good rule of thumb is to have your letterhead look comparable to the stationery used by a law office.

Your letterhead should include the following contact information: mailing address, telephone and fax numbers (if applicable), and your e-mail address. Note that if you are working from your home you might want to use a post office box to avoid providing your home address.

Always address your submission to a specific person; sending a package to a record label and marking it "Attention: A&R Department" will almost certainly earmark it for the "unsolicited" pile, to be returned unopened—or relegated to the trash bin. You can learn the names of a record label's A&R staff by reading the *A&R Registry* (www.musicregistry.com), tip sheets, and trade papers, or by calling the record label and requesting this information from the receptionist or A&R secretary.

When signing your letters, be sure to include your title. Publishers' titles are typically Professional Manager or Creative Director.

Your cover letter should be concise, similar to the sample shown on the next page. Analogous to the cover letter from a writer used to contact a publisher (described in Chapter 2), the cover letter you send as a publisher should not include information such as the names of the singers, musicians, engineers, or demo-recording studios. Nor should the songs be described or "hyped."

There is one primary difference between pitching songs as a writer to a publisher versus submitting to record labels, producers, or artists as a publisher. When pitching songs as a publisher it's important always to target one specific artist. For example, "Enclosed are two songs I feel strongly about for John Legend." In contrast, songs pitched to publishers are intended to be submitted to many different artists, so it is not appropriate to specify any particular artist.

Lyric Sheet

Including a lyric sheet is advisable, although not mandatory (see page 23). Note that the only difference between a lyric sheet being sent from a writer and one being sent by a publisher is that the one coming from the publisher should be typed on the publishing company's letterhead.

Compact Disc

When submitting material from your publishing company, the music on your CD and the information included on its label should adhere to the guidelines recommended in Chapter 2—but with several important differences. As shown on page 83, your CD label should include your publishing company's name and logo, the

DREAMER'S MOON MUSIC

222 HITSONG RD., GRAMMYTOWN, CA 12345 • (123) 456-7890
E-MAIL: HITSONGS.COM

Date

A&R Executive's Name
Record Label Name
Address
City, State Zip Code

Dear (use first name):

I've enclosed a CD with two songs for your consideration
for Carrie Underwood. I feel strongly about these songs
and I appreciate your reviewing them.

I look forward to speaking with you when you've had a
chance to listen.

Sincerely,

Jamie Elizabeth
Creative Director
Dreamer's Moon Music

Encl.

Sample publisher's cover letter.

A&R representative's (or manager's, or producer's) name, the name of the artist for whom the songs are being sent, and your name. All demos should be extremely well produced in order to convey your songs' hit potential, but demo recordings submitted to record labels, artists, producers, and artist's managers may be held to an even higher standard than those played for publishers.

It is never appropriate to include a spoken introduction, description, or explanation. Nor is it appropriate to list the writers' names, or any additional information, such as the length of the songs, vocalists, musicians, recording engineer, or studio, on the CD label. Likewise, including the copyright symbol, year of copyright, or PRO affiliation is not recommended.

Some writer/publishers believe that including their PRO affiliation on their CD labels, as well as on their letterhead and lyric sheets, lends credibility to their company. But this may actually have the opposite effect, because it is assumed that all major publishers are affiliated with BMI, ASCAP, and possibly SESAC. As discussed earlier in this chapter, publishers routinely represent writers who are members of various PROs. In order to collect the publisher's share of performance royalties generated by their writers the companies must be affiliated with performing rights organizations. Pointing out that you are an ASCAP (or BMI, or SESAC) publishing company draws attention to the fact that you are not affiliated with other PROs—and implies that you are likely to be a very small firm. A sample CD label is shown opposite.

When pitching songs, the concept of "less is more" applies. As discussed in Chapter 2, limit your submissions to a maximum of three songs and always lead off with the song you feel has the best shot for a particular pitch. If you fail to impress with the first song on your CD the listener may not listen further.

Casting Your Self-Published Songs

As you learned in Chapter 1, casting is the process of deciding which songs are potential hits—and are the best fit for a given artist. It's hard for anyone to discern a great song; careers have been built upon this ability. But it's even harder to be impartial about our own work.

To earn the respect of, and access to, record label executives and other music industry decision makers it's important to establish and maintain credibility, especially as a small, independent publisher. One of the toughest challenges facing individuals who publish their own material is being objective about whether their songs are indeed as competitive in the current marketplace as they hope.

Writers who publish and pitch their own songs need to avoid the trap of believing each of their songs is perfect—and suitable for a wide spectrum of artists. Failure to do so may result in the proverbial doors being closed and locked in the future. Remember that every song you write cannot be your best—and only those that are truly exceptional should represent you and your company. There are tools you can use and actions you can take to assess the strength of your songs and to determine for which artists they are most appropriate.

Sample publisher's CD label.

Getting Feedback

One way to gauge which songs are your strongest is to solicit input from individuals whose opinions you trust, such as your collaborators and other writers whose work you respect. Also, as you pitch your material it will become apparent which songs elicit the strongest positive responses—and which ones fail to do so.

You can also evaluate the strength of your songs by having them reviewed by professional critiquing services and in songwriting classes. These situations also offer opportunities to receive objective feedback regarding which artists might be a good match for specific songs.

When having a song critiqued you might ask, "Do you believe this song is competitive with songs on the radio? Do you think this song would work well for Keith Urban?" In the event that the answers you receive are not what you hope for, seek additional input. If the responses are consistently negative, it's likely that your songs or casting skills may be in need of some additional work.

Analyzing Artists' Work

By studying artists' ranges, vocal styles, the types of lyrics they typically sing, and the genres of music in which they are successful, you should be able to assess whether a given song might be a good fit for a particular artist. For example, by listening to an artist's most recent album you can determine the lowest and highest notes they sing.

Most artists are comfortable singing approximately ten notes, an octave and a third (for example, from a C to the E an octave and a third above). If your analysis reveals that the artist you're studying has a very limited range and never sings more than eight notes, it would not be appropriate to pitch an exceptionally "rangy" song that requires twelve or more notes. Conversely, an artist who is known for having exceptional vocal ability, such as Celine Dion, Andrea Bocelli, Martina McBride, or Clay Aiken, would be likely to seek material that showcases his or her range and talent.

Another element to examine in determining which of your songs to submit for a given artist is the style of music the artist sings. Some songs can work in more than one variety of music. For instance, "Buy Me a Rose," "I Swear," and "I Can Love You Like That" were recorded with great success by both country and pop/R&B artists. Recordings by artists such as Faith Hill, Keith Urban, Martina McBride, and Lonestar have enjoyed success on the country, pop, and adult contemporary charts. However, the majority of songs fit only one style of music.

To maintain credibility it's crucial to pitch songs that match an artist's style. Do your homework; you can listen to snippets of an artist's work by visiting his or her Web site or any of the Internet sites that sell albums and offer downloads. A&R representatives and other industry professionals will likely listen to a minute or less of your song. It's extremely improbable that they will be able to imagine how the song might sound if it were produced in a different style. If your demo is hip-hop, don't pitch it to a rock act. Likewise, if an artist records Euro-dance, your best country ballad will not work—regardless of how good it is. While this may seem self-evident, many writer/publishers are lured into this pitfall by the combination of unrealistic assessment of the quality of their own songs—and hunger for success.

When casting songs, analyzing the types of lyrics an artist tends to record can help in making the determination regarding whether a given song is appropriate for a particular artist. While it is rarely effective to rehash what a singer has already said in previous songs, if you note that he or she typically sings happy, positive lyrics this might help you choose which of your songs might be best suited for his or her sensibility. Likewise, depending on the image and persona an artist presents, he or she may regularly sing lyrics that are blatantly sexual, while others avoid this. Some artists, especially women in country music, consistently present themselves as strong and independent. A lyric that portrays them as weak and needy would not be consistent with the image they put forth.

When casting your songs it's important to maintain objectivity. Again, seek feedback to learn which of your songs are your best—and pitch only those songs that are the appropriate musical range, style, and lyric approach for the artist you are targeting.

Allowing Developing Artists to Record Your Songs

Every writer who is not writing exclusively for him- or herself dreams of having songs recorded by superstars. While a history of gold or platinum sales does not guarantee an artist's upcoming album will sell equally well, it is a good indicator. In addition, the credibility and prestige that comes with a recording by a major artist may have a powerful effect on a writer's career, leading to invaluable opportunities for collaborations and additional pitches.

While it is certainly appropriate to hope and aim to have songs recorded by established acts, in actuality, this is a goal many songwriters may never attain. While it is by no means easy to secure recordings with unknown artists, it is undoubtedly easier than having songs recorded by well-known celebrities. The downside to having songs recorded by new acts is that according to the Recording Industry Association of America (RIAA), approximately 90 percent of all new artists signed to major labels do not become successful. In fact, five out of six albums released in the U.S. sell fewer than a thousand copies.

When considering pitching your material to an artist who has not yet established a track record of hits, remember that when an artist decides to record a song, it is likely that the song will go on hold. (Holds are explained in Chapter 9.) It may be several months or more before the song is recorded. An additional year might pass before the artist's album is released. During this time the song is out of circulation and not available for any other artist to release. If the album ultimately fails to generate significant sales and the song does not receive considerable radio or television airplay, the writer and publisher earn little—or nothing.

In the time between when a song is placed on hold and when the album on which it appears is no longer promoted, musical styles may change, rendering the song dated and inappropriate for the current market. It's possible that when subsequent artists learn that a song has been previously recorded and released (without achieving success) they may not be willing to record it. An additional danger is that a song released as a single may peak low on the charts (for example, in the fifties or lower), but attain sufficient airplay and video exposure to discourage other artists from recording it.

Without benefit of a crystal ball it's impossible to know whether pitching to an unknown artist will lead to phenomenal success—or will simply tie up your song without ultimately generating any income. However, there are factors you can examine in order to make the best decision based on the information available.

In deciding whether to pitch a song to a new artist (or an act with an unimpressive track record) assess their record label's recent success in breaking new acts. It's likely that a label with new acts that are generating hits has the kind of promotion, budget, and clout to establish yet another successful new artist. Conversely, if a record label has consistently failed to generate sales or radio airplay for their artists, this may indicate a low probability that they will be successful promoting your song.

Similarly, evaluate the artist's management team. An act whose manager handles a stable of superstars is likely to have connections and influence that can be beneficial. A manager in this position may be able to encourage a record label to invest additional money in promotion and publicity. He or she may also have the savvy to help mold and guide an artist to great success.

Another factor to consider is how strongly you believe in the artist. If you hear a new artist's demo and are convinced you're listening to the next megasuperstar, you will obviously want this artist to record your material. But if listening leaves you scratching your head, wondering how this act ever landed a record deal, this may not be the best home for your song.

Aim high; pitch to the artists who are your top choices and wait at least four to six weeks to receive responses. If this doesn't lead to the song being recorded, it's time to send out the second batch, this time, to artists one tier down. Similarly, if this fails to yield a recording it may be time to target new and developing artists.

If the singer you most hope to record a particular song is not scheduled to record for six months or more you will have to make a difficult decision. It's probably too early to pitch your song. Are you willing to pass up other opportunities to submit the song? If another artist says "yes," you will forego the chance to pitch this song to the artist at the top of your list. There is no right or wrong answer. But when making your decision, remember that every superstar began as an aspiring artist. When Norah Jones, Toby Keith, Christina Aguilera, Brooks & Dunn, Joss Stone, and Lonestar searched for material to record for their debut albums they were each unknown acts.

Pitching Songs to Unsigned and Independent Artists

Many publishers and songwriters pitch songs from their catalogs to artists who are seeking, but have not yet secured, a recording contract. Singers need strong original material to demo in order to capture a record label's interest, and if they are not writing potential hits they need to find them. You often find these artists listed in tip sheets under the categories "deal shopping," "label pending," or "label to be determined."

In many instances, an artist's record label affiliation is listed on a tip sheet, but in actuality the label has been established by the artist for the sole purpose of distributing his or her own work. A bit of research on the Internet should reveal whether this is the case.

In the recent past, in order to garner significant sales, independent labels were required to have nationwide distribution. If their products were not available in local stores there were few ways for potential customers to purchase them. But, with the explosion of new technologies for selling music online, distribution is not as crucial as a record label's ability to promote their artists successfully and secure radio and video airplay.

Now, a music buyer needs only to click on the Internet to purchase or download music through an artist's Web site or online music sellers and subscription services. However, few people will buy or download music by an artist they have never heard of. The vast majority of tiny record labels have neither the financial backing nor the skills to publicize and promote their artists successfully—and without the benefit of widespread radio, video, or other media exposure, it is unlikely that many music buyers will be aware of the music released by such companies. Having your songs recorded by artists on such labels may not generate income.

There are, however, several benefits to having unsigned and independent artists recording your material. Having a song included in an artist's demo package may provide exposure for the song to industry professionals who might otherwise never get to hear it. There have been many instances when a record label executive liked a song—but not the artist who recorded it. In one notable case, John Ims' "She's in Love with the Boy" was pitched by an aspiring artist who sought a recording contract with MCA Records. Although the A&R executive did not sign the artist, he kept a copy of the song. It became the debut single for a new artist signed to the label, Trisha Yearwood. This song, which might otherwise have never been submitted to MCA Records, became a career-making hit, earning more than a million dollars in royalties.

Many songwriters and publishers pitch songs to artists who are signed to small, independent record labels, and to acts releasing their own self-produced albums. The negative aspect to this is that, lacking an established distributor and promotion team, as previously stated, more than five out of six of these releases sell less than one thousand copies and receive no appreciable radio airplay. They generate virtually no income for the writer and publisher. Yet, by granting a first recording license, the publisher relinquishes its right to control who may subsequently release the song. (See Chapter 9 for more information about first use, mechanical, and compulsory licenses.)

Of course, it's impossible to guess what may result from even the limited exposure an independently released song may receive. There have been instances of major, established artists recording songs they first heard being performed in a small venue. There have also been times when having a song included on an independently produced album has led to great success. For example, when a twelve-year old little girl with a huge voice recorded a song for an independently released album (produced by her father), the writer and publisher could never have anticipated that this singer would subsequently sign with Curb Records and include the recording on her major-label album—and that the album would sell more than six million copies. The song was "Good Lookin' Man" (written by Joyce Harrison) and the artist was LeAnn Rimes.

As in so many areas of the music business, there are no hard and fast rules regarding whether to pitch songs to new and developing artists. Nor is there a right or wrong answer as to whether to provide demo tracks to aspiring artists, and if so, whether to charge for this service. These decisions are best made on a case-by-case basis by weighing factors that might be indicative of an artist's likelihood of achieving success: an assessment of artists' talent; their image; the clout and skill of their management team; whether they are affiliated with established producers and songwriters; and the manner in which they conduct business.

Providing Track Mixes

Artists sometimes request instrumental tracks from a publisher so that they can add their own vocals. This saves the artist the considerable expense of hiring musicians and producing a full demo. Instrumental tracks can be provided two different ways. One option is *unmixed individual files*, computer files that contain all of a demo's individual recorded sounds, such as the kick drum, snare, each cymbal, bass, acoustic guitar, electric guitar, etc. In this case, after an artist adds their vocals, a recording engineer needs to mix all of the sounds, balancing and adjusting the volume levels and adding effects to make each individual instrument and vocal track sound its best. The other alternative is a *premixed two-track recording*, a stereo recording including all of the instruments already mixed onto two tracks, the left and the right sides. With a two-track mix, the only thing an artist needs to do is add his or her vocal and background vocals, eliminating the time and expense of mixing the individual instrumental tracks.

While some publishers are willing to share recording files, premixed instrumental tracks, and *TV track mixes* (essentially a karaoke version of a song; premixed instrumental tracks with background and harmony vocals—but no lead vocal), others choose not to essentially finance artists' careers—unless they feel the artist has great potential of achieving success. Some publishers charge a nominal fee (such as $100 to $200) to provide an artist with demo tracks.

Of course, if an artist is already signed to a major recording contract and wants the instrumental tracks in order to assess how he or she sounds singing a particular song, your answer should be a resounding "Yes!" Artists such as Britney Spears and Garth Brooks have recorded their vocals onto writers' demo tracks before including these songs on albums that sold more than ten million copies each.

The Pros and Cons of Self-Publishing

The biggest advantage to self-publishing is that you keep both the writer's and publisher's shares of any royalties your songs earn. You also retain all rights and control the usages of your material. In addition, it's unlikely that any other publisher would be as familiar with your catalog, or be as motivated to exploit it, as you would.

However, as you learned earlier in this chapter, being a successful publisher requires a considerable amount of time, money, and effort. Time invested to research which artists are seeking songs; making CD copies or sending digital transmissions such as MP3s; typing cover letters; printing lyric sheets; and mailing or delivering your submission packages, as well as negotiating and issuing recording and synchronization licenses, is considerable time away from writing songs. But in the event that your efforts yield a hit, the financial and emotional payoffs are well worth the investment.

CHAPTER SIX

Copublishing Your Work

As you learned in Chapter 1, any income a song earns (with the exception of print licensing fees) is divided into approximately equal amounts between the writer's share and the publisher's share. In a standard publishing agreement, 100 percent of the writer's share of any income a published song generates belongs to the writer; 100 percent of the publisher's share belongs to the publisher.

Copublishing, also referred to as *copub* or *split publishing*, can be defined as a situation in which a writer is granted or retains a portion of his or her copyright ownership and a portion of the publisher's share of income when publishing one or more songs. When a song is copublished, the writer earns 100 percent of the writer's share of any income generated—and a specified percentage of the publisher's share. Similar to any publishing agreement, a copublishing deal may apply to a single song, to a specified group of songs, or to an exclusive (staff-writing) agreement.

In theory, any percentage of the publisher's share of income and copyright ownership may be allocated to the writer (as copublisher). However, in most copublishing agreements the publisher's share is split equally between the publisher and songwriter/copublisher, with each owning 50 percent of the publisher's share. Under this circumstance, for each dollar a song earns, 50 cents is the writer's share and 50 cents is the publisher's share. The songwriter (presuming he or she is the sole writer) receives 50 cents as the writer (100 percent of the writer's share) and an additional 25 cents as a copublisher (50 percent of the publisher's share) for a total of 75 cents.

Co-administering Your Material

Before continuing to discuss copublishing it will be helpful to understand that, depending on how a copublishing agreement is structured, in addition to owning a portion of the copyright, a writer might also negotiate the retention of specific rights typically granted to a publisher. These *administration rights* include permission to negotiate and issue recording, synchronization, and print licenses. When they are conveyed to, or retained by, a writer, he or she becomes an *administrating publisher*, also referred to as a *co-administrator* of his or her material. This affords the songwriter a degree of control over how his or her songs are used.

Co-administration can be set up in a variety of ways. In some instances, each administrating publisher controls its own share of the songs and both parties must agree to the issuance of any license. In other cases, all parties have the right to issue specified licenses, while other licenses are controlled solely by one of the administrators. For instance, some agreements allow each administrator to issue mechanical licenses without the other party's consent, provided the license specifies that all administrators will be paid the *statutory rate*, the mechanical royalty rate established by Congress (as explained in Chapter 9).

How to Get a Copublishing Deal

Publishers are, understandably, not eager to relinquish a significant portion of their income and ownership of their copyrights. They typically need a compelling reason to agree to copublishing. Writers may earn the status needed to copublish in any of several ways, but each scenario is predicated on the writer's level of clout—and how strongly a publisher wants to represent a particular song or writer.

Songwriters with a recent track record of hits are among those most likely to procure copublishing deals. Any time a publisher acquires an individual song or signs a writer to an exclusive songwriting agreement, the hope is that their efforts and expenditures will yield a profit. If a writer has demonstrated his or her ability to write songs that generate significant income, a publisher can assume there's a good chance that its investment of time and money will be recouped and earn revenue— even by acquiring only a portion of the writer's publishing rights and income.

A songwriter who brings something to the proverbial table, for example, a song that has already been recorded by an established artist, would be in a strong position to negotiate a copublishing deal, as would a writer who is collaborating with a successful recording artist or producer. Songwriter/artists who record their own material are also good candidates to secure copublishing deals if they have a record deal, or one that is pending. In these instances, publishers sometimes grant copublishing only for those songs that are recorded and released on the writer/artists' albums.

Some songwriters may be able to obtain a copublishing deal based on their history of procuring recordings of their songs. Writers who demonstrate that they have the connections and savvy to secure cuts share one of a publisher's primary responsibilities and, as such, are justified in requesting a copublishing agreement.

Publishers tend to have policies regarding copublishing, and some companies will be more likely than others to grant it. Smaller, independent publishers who may not have an established track record of placing songs may be more amenable to copublishing than larger companies. As with virtually every aspect of any song publishing agreement, whether the writer is permitted to share in the publishing and, if so, the percentage of the publisher's share to be conferred to the songwriter, are negotiable points. It doesn't hurt to ask; they can only say "no."

Analyzing Copublishing Provisions for Single Song and Exclusive Songwriting Agreements

Individual songs, as well as songs included as part of exclusive (staff-writing) agreements, may be copublished. When this occurs, the agreement signed by a songwriter and music publisher does not typically say "Copublishing Agreement" at the top of the page. Copublishing agreements are identical to other publishing agreements for songs, with the exception of additional provisions for the writer to share in copyright ownership and the publisher's share of income. It's likely that an agreement to copublish an individual song will be labeled "Single Song Agreement"; likewise, a contract for a staff-writing deal is typically labeled "Exclusive Songwriting Agreement."

In some single song and exclusive songwriting agreements it is specified that in the event certain conditions are met, copublishing will be invoked. For example, if a writer secures his or her own cut, he or she will receive copublishing (or "participation," explained later in this chapter) for that particular song. In other instances, an exclusive songwriting agreement might specify that songs delivered after a publisher has recouped its financial investment will be copublished by the writer. These are among the contractual points that should be addressed by the attorney negotiating on a writer's behalf.

The paragraphs that follow are intended to be inserted into the Exclusive Songwriting Agreement included in Chapter 4. By changing the introductory paragraph and Paragraph 9, as well as by adding Paragraphs 19, 20, and 21 (included and explained below) this agreement provides for the writer to copublish his or her work. (Please refer back to the Exclusive Songwriting Agreement on page 48.) Note that by replacing the references to multiple compositions with one specific song, these same provisions may be applied to Single Song Agreements in order to convert them to copublishing agreements.

COPUBLISHING PROVISIONS FOR AN
EXCLUSIVE SONGWRITING AGREEMENT

AGREEMENT made as of this _____ day of _____, 200_, by and between _____ ("Writer") individually and doing business as "_____" ("Co-Publisher") whose address is _____ and _____ ("Publisher") whose address is _____.

This paragraph establishes the date the agreement takes effect and states the names and addresses of the parties entering into it. The writer's name and address, as well as the name and address of the writer's publishing company, are also included.

9. Advances
Conditioned upon Writer's full and faithful performance of all of the material terms and provisions of this Agreement, Publisher shall pay to Writer or on Writer's behalf the following amounts, all of which shall be recoupable by Publisher from any and all royalties payable to Writer hereunder and any and all Net Receipts payable to Co-Publisher pursuant to Paragraph 19, below:

This paragraph states that provided the writer fulfills his or her contractual obligations (such as delivery of acceptable songs), the publisher must pay the specified amounts, which are recoupable from the writer's share of any mechanical (sales) royalties and licensing fees that his or her songs covered under this agreement might earn. The publisher also recoups from revenue due the writer as copublisher, including the copublisher's share of performance royalties.

19. Ownership and Administration

Notwithstanding any provision to the contrary herein contained, the Compositions shall be owned by Publisher and by Writer, in his/her capacity as Co-Publisher (the "Co-Publisher"), in the following shares:

> **Publisher: 50%**
> **Co-publisher: 50%**

and shall be exclusively administered by Publisher for the life of copyright protection, all in accordance with the following terms and conditions:

This paragraph establishes the division of ownership of the composition. Note that the percentages can be any number upon which the writer and publisher agree. However, a fifty-fifty split is typical. In this instance, the writer retains 100 percent of the writer's share—and 50 percent of the publishing portion.

The publisher retains the administration rights, as explained in the following provisions. Note that in some instances a copublisher may keep some or all of these rights. This is an important negotiation point.

(a) The Compositions shall be registered for copyright by Publisher in the names of Publisher and Co-Publisher in the office of the Register of Copyrights of the United States of America as and when Publisher deems necessary in its sole business judgment.

This subparagraph states that the decision as to when to copyright a song is up to the publisher. When a song covered by this agreement is registered with the Copyright Office, both the publisher and copublisher are to be listed on the form.

(b) Publisher shall have the sole and exclusive right to administer and exploit the Compositions, to print, publish, sell, dramatize, use and license any and all uses of the Compositions, to execute in its own name and Writer's publishing designee's name any and all licenses and agreements whatsoever affecting or respecting the Compositions, including, but not limited to, licenses for mechanical reproduction at customary industry rates, public performance, dramatic uses, synchronization uses and sub-publication, and to assign or license such rights to others throughout the world. Without limiting the foregoing, Publisher is entitled to receive and collect and shall receive and collect all Gross Receipts (as defined below) derived from the Compositions throughout the universe, and Publisher shall pay to Co-Publisher fifty percent (50%) of Net

Receipts (as defined below). All payments to Co-Publisher shall be made in accordance with the same accounting provisions of this agreement as with respect to payments to Writer and shall be subject to all of the same provisions concerning royalties payable to Writer, including, without limitation, those concerning recoupment, deductions, offsets and indemnifications. Without limiting the generality of the forgoing, it is specifically understood and agreed that Co-Publisher's share of Net Receipts shall be applied in reduction of any and all Advances and other recoupable costs attributable to Writer and/or Co-Publisher hereunder. For purposes of this paragraph 19(b) "Gross Receipts" is defined as the gross sums actually received by Publisher or its agent in the United States (or credited against an outstanding advance previously paid Publisher), reduced by collection fees actually charged by any collection agent or organization which is not owned or controlled by Publisher or legal fees, court costs, accounting fees or other direct costs incurred by Publisher in the collection of such sums. Gross Receipts shall not be deemed to include any portion of any advance payments, guarantee payments, or minimum royalty payments which Publisher may receive in connection with any sub-publishing agreement, collection agreement, licensing agreement or other agreement with respect to the Compositions unless such payments are made solely for the use of specific and separately identifiable Composition(s) and no other musical compositions or other works of authorship, in which event such sums shall be deemed Gross Receipts actually received by Publisher for such uses.

Noted here is that only the publisher has the right to enter into agreements for any and all uses of the compositions. The publisher shall collect all monies and pay copublisher 50 percent of the "net" amount, which is defined in subparagraph (c) below. Any money collected by the publisher on behalf of the copublisher is applicable toward recoupment before any money is paid to the writer/copublisher.

This paragraph defines "gross receipts" as any amounts collected by the publisher minus any fees paid to an individual or company that are not controlled or owned by the publisher and any costs incurred in order for the publisher to collect its money. It also states that gross receipts do not include any payments made to the publisher for subpublishing or other advances collected unless this money is paid specifically for the use of one or more of the writer's compositions.

(c) "Net Receipts" is defined as Gross Receipts less the following:
(i) Royalties which shall be paid by Publisher to Writer pursuant to this Agreement and royalties which shall be paid by Publisher to any other publishers or writers of the Compositions;

This subparagraph defines "net receipts" as gross receipts (the total amount received) minus any money due to this writer and/or other writers or publishers of a given composition.

(ii) Direct, reasonable, out-of-pocket, administrative and exploitation expenses of Publisher with respect to the Compositions, including, without limitation, registration fees, advertising and non-in-house promotion expenses directly related to the Compositions, Demo production costs related to the Compositions (to the extent not recouped from royalties otherwise payable to Writer), and the costs of transcribing for lead sheets.

Stated here is that all expenses incurred by the publisher regarding the compositions (for example, unrecouped demo costs, copyright registration fees, and fees paid for promotion by an outside agency) and money paid for the preparation of lead sheets are also deducted from gross receipts.

(iii) Attorneys' fees, if any, actually paid by Publisher for any agreements (other than the within Agreement) affecting solely the Compositions.

This subparagraph indicates that any attorneys' fees regarding compositions covered by this agreement (other than fees paid for the preparation of this agreement) will be deducted from gross receipts.

(d) To the extent permitted by law, small performing rights in the Compositions for the United States and Canada shall be assigned to and licensed by the performing rights society to which both parties belong. Said society shall be and is hereby authorized to collect and receive all monies earned from the public performance of the Compositions in the United States and Canada and shall be and is hereby directed to pay directly to Publisher the entire amount allocated by said society as the so-called "publisher's share" of public performance fees for the Compositions for the United States and Canada. Annexed to this Agreement as Exhibit "A" is the form of letter of direction from Co-Publisher to BMI, ASCAP, or SESAC (as the case may be) which shall effectuate the foregoing provisions. Co-Publisher shall sign and deliver to Publisher copies of said letter simultaneously herewith, and in default thereof Publisher is hereby authorized and empowered by Co-Publisher to sign copies of said letter for and on behalf of Co-Publisher and submit same to the appropriate society.

This subparagraph states that the "small performing rights" (the right to perform or broadcast music in a nondramatic setting) of compositions covered by this agreement are to be licensed by the performing rights organization to which the publisher and writer/copublisher belong. The PRO will be authorized to collect the total amount of the publisher's share of performance royalties and pay it to the publisher. The copublisher agrees to send a letter (or have the publisher do so) authorizing the PRO to pay the publisher on his or her behalf. A copy of this letter is to be given to the publisher. This applies only to compositions in the U.S. and Canada.

(e) Co-Publisher hereby ratifies and shall be subject to the same warranties, representations and covenants as set forth herein with respect to Writer.

Stated here is that everything in this agreement as it applies to the writer also applies to the writer as copublisher.

(f) Without limiting the generality of any of the foregoing, it is specifically understood and agreed that Publisher shall have the sole right to collect Co-Publisher's share of Net Receipts hereunder, including, without limitation, Co-Publisher's portion of the so-called "publisher's share" of performance income.

This subparagraph reiterates that the publisher will collect all money due to the copublisher. This includes performance royalties.

20. Administration; Reversion

Notwithstanding anything to the contrary contained in this Agreement, after the later of (i) the end of the second accounting period which occurs immediately following _____ (__) year(s) after expiration or termination of the Term hereof, or (ii) the end of the second accounting period, after expiration or termination of the Term, following the accounting period during which Writer and Co-Publisher are both fully-recouped hereunder, after thirty (30) days written notice from Co-Publisher to Publisher, Publisher shall promptly reassign to Co-Publisher the right to administer Co-Publisher's ownership interest in the Compositions. From and after the reassignment of Co-Publisher's administration rights, Publisher and Co-Publisher shall each have the separate right, throughout the universe, to administer and exploit their respective interests in the Compositions, all in accordance with the following:

This paragraph establishes conditions under which the copublisher acquires the administration rights to its percentage of ownership of songs covered by the agreement. These rights revert back to the writer/copublisher after the latter of the following occurs:

1. After the second accounting period following a specified number of years after this contract ends (typically 2 to 5 years)

2. At the end of the second accounting period during which the writer and copublisher are fully recouped, following the end of the term of this contract.

The copublisher must give written notice to the publisher in order to have these rights reinstated. When this has occurred, both the publisher and copublisher each have the right to administer and exploit the songs.

(a) The performing rights societies in the United States and Canada (e.g., ASCAP, BMI, SESAC and SOCAN) shall be notified to pay the publisher's share of performance income in respect of the Compositions as follows:
(i) 50% of such income shall be payable directly to Publisher; and
(ii) 50% of such income shall be payable directly to Co-Publisher.

This subparagraph states that after the administration rights revert to the writer/copublisher, the performing rights society to which the writer and publisher belong shall be notified to pay the copublisher's share of performance royalties directly to the copublisher.

(b) Co-Publisher shall have the sole right to collect the Writer's share of income and shall have the sole responsibility to pay Writer the royalties due as provided herein. Co-Publisher warrants and represents that Co-Publisher will at all times indemnify and hold harmless Publisher and any licensee of Publisher from and against any and all claims, liabilities, costs and expenses arising out of the breach by Co-Publisher of its obligation to pay such writer royalties.

Noted above is that following the reversion of administration rights, the copublisher will collect both the copublisher's and writer's share of any income and distribute the writer's share to the writer. The copublisher will have the sole responsibility to pay the writer that portion that is due the writer. The publisher will no longer have any obligation to pay the writer. Nor will it have any liability if the copublisher fails to pay the writer.

(c) Publisher and Co-Publisher each shall have the right to administer and retain third party administrators to administer their respective rights in the Compositions throughout the universe. Each such administrator shall be notified by the party retaining such administrator of the parties' respective rights in the Compositions;

This subparagraph maintains that after the administration rights revert to the copublisher, the publisher and copublisher each have the right to engage an outside administrator to handle their portions of the songs. However, they are required to notify their administrators of the other party's rights (their percentage of ownership).

(d) Publisher and Co-Publisher shall have the right to enter into non-exclusive licenses and agreements for the exploitation, performance, recording, synchronization, printing, publication or other use of the Compositions throughout the world and the universe. Publisher and Co-Publisher shall provide each other with copies of all such licenses and agreements, and all licensees and third parties to such agreements shall be notified of the parties' respective percentage interests in any royalties or fees payable thereunder. All licenses or agreements shall provide for direct payment to Publisher and Co-Publisher of their respective shares of any fees or royalties payable thereunder.

Affirmed here is that the publisher and copublisher each have the right to issue nonexclusive licenses and agreements (for example, recording licenses, synchronization licenses, and print licenses) throughout the world. They are required to notify the licensees of the percentage of royalties and fees due to each publisher. Each party is also required to provide a copy of any agreements or licenses to the other.

(e) Publisher and Co-Publisher shall each have the right to enter into exclusive licenses for the use of the Compositions and to enter into so-called "first use" licenses for the Compositions throughout the world and the Universe solely with respect to their own interest in the Compositions.

This subparagraph asserts that after the reversion of administration rights, the publisher and the copublisher (the writer) each have the right to issue licenses for their respective interests in the songs. These include exclusive licenses, as well as licenses to permit the first recording and release of a song.

(f) Each party shall have the right to inspect the other party's royalty books and records relating to the Compositions, such inspection to be made during regular business hours upon at least thirty (30) days prior written notice, and in no event more than once during any calendar year.

Indicated above is that the publisher and copublisher have the right to review each other's accounting records relating to the songs covered by this agreement. These audits are to be done during regular office hours. Thirty days written notice of intent to examine the records is required, and an audit may not be done more than once a year.

(g) Should Publisher or Co-Publisher commence any action or proceeding against an unrelated third party or parties for the infringement of copyright or other violation of the parties' respective rights in the Compositions, then the party commencing such action or proceeding shall promptly notify the other party in writing. In such event, the party so notified (the "Notified Party") shall have the right, but not the obligation, to participate in such action or proceeding. If the Notified Party elects to participate in such action or proceeding, then the Notified Party shall pay the costs thereof (including attorneys' fees) in proportion to the Notified Party's ownership interest in the Composition at issue, and receive that same proportion of any sums recovered in such action or proceeding. If the Notified Party elects not to participate in such action or proceeding, then the Notified Party shall have no right or interest whatsoever in any sums recovered therein.

This subparagraph declares that if the publisher or copublisher takes any legal action against another individual or company for copyright infringement or any other violation regarding the songs covered by this agreement, the other publisher must be notified in writing. The other publisher has the right to join in the legal action provided he or she pay the proportional share of any fees. If the notified party decides not to participate, then he or she will not share in any money that may be collected.

(h) If either party shall receive monies belonging to the other party, the receiving party shall account to the other party for its shares of all such sums at the times and in the manner provided for herein in respect of the rendition of royalties and royalty statements under Paragraph 10, above.

Stated here is that if the publisher or copublisher receives payment to which the other is entitled, they are required to provide accounting and payment to the other publisher as explained in Paragraph 10 of the Exclusive Songwriting Agreement. (See page 60.)

(i) In all other circumstances, Publisher and Co-Publisher will jointly administer the Compositions on such basis as is reasonably customary in the music publishing business.

This subparagraph declares that under any situation not specified in this contract, the publisher and copublisher will handle the registration of copyright, the issuing of licenses, and the collection and accounting of royalties based on commonly accepted music business practices.

(j) Both Publisher and Co-Publisher shall be responsible for affixing proper copyright notices on each copy of each of the Compositions that are printed under the authority of that party.

Noted above is that the publisher and copublisher are responsible for including the copyright notice on each printed copy they authorize.

21. First Right of Refusal: Matching Right
(a) If writer or Co-Publisher shall desire to sell, transfer, assign or dispose of Co-Publisher's interest in the Compositions (or any portion thereof), then before negotiating with any third party, Writer and/or Co-Publisher shall first give Publisher written notice of such fact and the parties shall engage in prompt continuous good faith negotiations concerning the terms of the proposal sale, transfer, assignment or disposition of such retained interests to Publisher. If the parties are unable to reach agreement on the material terms of such sale, transfer, assignment or dispositions within thirty (30) days after Writer and/or Co-Publisher's notice to Publisher, then Writer and/or Co-Publisher, as applicable, may elect to discontinue the negotiations with Publisher by written notice to Publisher. Thereafter, Writer and/or Co-Publisher, as applicable, may solicit offers to dispose of Co-Publisher's interest in the Compositions to third parties.

This subparagraph establishes that the writer/copublisher shall notify the publisher if he or she decides to sell all or any portion of his or her share of the publishing. This is to be done before the writer negotiates with any other company or individual. After receiving this notice, the publisher has thirty days to negotiate to buy the copublisher's share. At the end of the thirty-day period, if an agreement has not been reached, the copublisher must notify the publisher in writing that the negotiations are ending. The writer/copublisher may then offer his or her percentage of ownership in the songs to other companies and individuals.

(b) If Writer and/or Co-Publisher shall receive an acceptable bona fide offer from a financially responsible third party to acquire all or any portion of Co-Publisher's interest in the Compositions, before accepting any such offer, Writer and/or Co-Publisher, as applicable, shall first offer to Publisher the right to buy or acquire the such offered interests on the same terms and conditions as set forth in such third party offer. Writer and Co-Publisher agree to give Publisher a copy of any offer and the name of the proposed purchaser, and Publisher shall have fifteen (15) days after receipt of such third party offer in which to notify Writer and/or Co-Publisher, as applicable, whether or not Publisher desires to acquire that portion of Co-Publisher's interest offered for sale on the terms and conditions set forth in such third party's offer. In the event Publisher shall fail to give Writer and/or Co-Publisher, as applicable, written notice with said fifteen (15) day period that Publisher is exercising its option to buy or acquire the interest being offered for sale, Writer and/or Co-Publisher, as applicable, shall have the right to accept the offer of the proposed third party purchaser, but only on the terms and conditions as set forth in the third party offer delivered to Publisher, provided, however that: (i) if Writer and/or Co-Publisher, as applicable, do not accept any offer from a proposed purchaser which Publisher has reviewed and declined to accept as aforesaid within three (3) months after expiration of said fifteen (15) day period, or (ii) if after Writer and/or Co-Publisher's acceptance of any such third party offer previously reviewed by Publisher and rejected by it, Writer and/or Co-Publisher, as applicable, and the proposed purchaser agree to revise such offer so that it is less favorable to Writer and/or Co-Publisher, as applicable, than that set forth in the original offer, then, before Writer and/or Co-Publisher may dispose of all or any portion of its interest in the Compositions on such less favorable terms, Writer and/or Co-Publisher, as applicable, shall provide to Publisher the new terms, conditions and any other relevant information forming the basis of the revised offer including, without limitation, any so-called "due diligence" reports prepared by or on behalf of the proposed purchaser which are in Writer and/or Co-Publisher's possession or control and Publisher shall have the right to accept the revised offer on the new terms and conditions contained therein, provided that Publisher must exercise such right, if at all, within ten (10) business days after the date such offer shall have been resubmitted to Publisher. Publisher shall not have any obligation to meet any non-financial terms of any offer.

This subparagraph maintains that the publisher has the right to buy the writer's share of publishing before any other person or company. If the writer or copublisher receives a legitimate offer to buy his or her share of ownership of the publishing, he or she must give the publisher a copy of the offer and the name of the party making the offer. The publisher has fifteen days to decide whether to purchase the publishing for this same amount. If the publisher does not reply in writing within fifteen days of receipt of the notice, the writer/copublisher may accept the offer. However, if the copublisher/writer does not accept the offer within three months following publisher's fifteen day window to purchase has elapsed, or if the offer is reduced, then the writer must provide the publisher with the new offer. The publisher will then have ten days to accept the new offer. The publisher is not required to match any aspect of the offer other than the money being offered.

Exhibit "A"

An *exhibit* is the name given an attachment to a legal agreement. The first document attached is referred to as Exhibit "A." Subsequent attachments would be titled Exhibit "B," Exhibit "C," etc.

EXHIBIT "A"

This document is attached to the agreement to authorize a writer's performing rights organization to distribute the copublisher's share of the publisher's portion of performance royalties to the designated administrator.

Dated: As of _____

TO: ___name and address of the performing rights organization___
_____to which you are affiliated—BMI, ASCAP, or SESAC_____

Dear Sir or Madam:

You are hereby authorized and directed to pay to our administrator, _____ ("Administrator"), at _____, and we hereby assign to Administrator, all monies payable from and after the date hereof (regardless of when earned) as the publisher's share of performance royalties with respect to the compositions described as follows: All musical compositions which are or shall be co-owned by Administrator and the undersigned.

This paragraph instructs the writer's/copublisher's PRO to pay the total publisher's share of any performance royalties earned directly to their publisher. The publisher is listed as "Administrator" and it provides a space to include your publisher's address. It applies to all songs covered by your copublishing agreement.

Copies of all statements and all correspondence shall be sent to Administrator and to us.

This sentence requests the PRO to send copies of all royalty statements and any other communication to both the publisher and the copublisher/writer.

Until further notice, we understand and authorize that _____name of PRO_____ **'s records will reflect only** _____**'s address for our membership.**

In this paragraph, the writer states that unless he or she notifies the PRO of another arrangement, the only address listed for the copublisher and publisher shall be the publisher's address.

The foregoing authorization and direction shall remain in full force and effect until modified or terminated by both the undersigned and Administrator.

This sentence reiterates that the terms of this letter will remain in effect until the PRO is notified by the writer/copublisher and the publisher/administrator.

Very truly yours,

_____
      writer's name and address

_____,

d/b/a ____co-publishing company's name____

Understanding Participation Agreements

An agreement that grants a portion of the publisher's income to a writer, but does not confer copyright ownership or administration rights to the publisher, is referred to as a *participation agreement*. In theory, a participation agreement may grant a writer any specified percentage of the publisher's share of income. Presuming that a writer is granted 50 percent participation of the publisher's share of a song that has only one writer, for every dollar the song earns, the writer receives 50 cents (100 percent of the writer's share) as well as 25 cents (50 percent of the publisher's share)—a total of 75 percent of a song's income, as opposed to the 50 percent that would be earned if a participation agreement were not in place.

Participating in the publisher's share of income is certainly preferable to earning only the writer's portion, but it is not as beneficial to a writer as owning a portion of his or her own copyright. Copyright ownership (with administration rights) affords a writer a degree of control over the use of his or her material (for example, the right to issue licenses). But more importantly, a writer who owns a portion of his or her copyright (with or without administration rights) has the right to sell his or her catalog, which may become a very valuable asset.

By inserting the paragraphs that are analyzed below into the royalty section of the exclusive songwriting agreement on page 60, the agreement becomes a participation agreement, allowing the writer to share in the publisher's portion of income.

PARTICIPATION CLAUSE

(g) As additional royalties hereunder, Publisher shall credit Writer's royalty account (and make payment if applicable) with an amount equal to fifty percent (50%) of Publisher's "net publisher's share" of royalties derived and received by Publisher from the actual reproduction and other exploitation of Compositions. "Net publisher's share" for purposes of this subparagraph 10(g) shall mean the monies actually received by Publisher in the United States (or credited to Publisher's account in reduction of prior advances) for Publisher's own use and benefit and specifically allocated to the Compositions, less the following:

> This subparagraph provides for the publisher to pay the writer half of the publisher's share of any income credited to, or received by, the publisher for the writer's songs. This amount will be credited to the writer, and if all money advanced to the writer by the publisher has been recouped, payment will be made to the writer. The publisher will deduct the expenses that are detailed in the following two clauses.

(i). The amount of all monies paid and payable as "writer royalties" to Writer pursuant to the other provisions of this Paragraph 10, and to all other songwriters, publishers or parties entitled to payment by Publisher with respect to the Compositions; and

> This clause specifies that income collected by the publisher that belongs to the writer, any cowriters, or additional publishers will be deducted before calculating the writer's participation share of the publisher's income. In the example that follows, Publisher #1 is the sole administrator of a cowritten song which is copublished by another publisher.
>
> > $1,000.00 in mechanical royalties are collected
> > $ 250.00 is due the writer signed to Publisher #1
> > $ 500.00 is due Publisher #2 (who will pay its own writer)
>
> This leaves $250 for Publisher #1. Therefore, if the participation share is 50 percent, the writer receives $125 of the publisher's share for a total of $375 ($250 of the writer's share and $125 of the publisher's share).

(ii). The amount of all costs and charges incurred or paid with respect to the Compositions or which may properly be allocated (entirely or proportionately) thereto, including, without limitation and among other things, for musical arrangements, professional material, copyrighting fees and charges of licensing and collection representatives and agencies, and music publishers and administrators within or outside the United States, including Publisher's affiliates.

> This clause states that also deducted from royalties will be costs including

(but not limited to) producing musical arrangements, copyright registration fees, and fees charged by outside companies to collect royalties owed.

For the avoidance of doubt, it is specifically understood and agreed that any royalties payable to Writer pursuant to this Paragraph 10(g) (including, without limitation, the so-called "publisher's share" of performance royalties), shall be credited to Writer's account and applied to the recoupment of any advances paid to Writer pursuant to this Agreement or to any other recoupable charges to Writer's account hereunder.

Affirmed above is that any royalties earned under this clause will go toward repaying any money the writer owes the publisher, such as advances or other items in the contract that the publisher has paid for and the writer is contractually required to pay back out of royalties (for example, demos, office expenses, legal fees, etc.).

Publishers are understandably reluctant to share a portion of their income and copyright ownership. Only writers with proven track records, writers who are also recording artists or producers, and those who have demonstrated their ability to secure their own recordings will typically be granted copublishing or participation. In order to earn the right to copublish your material, you will need to write exceptional songs, hone your ability to network, and demonstrate that your work can generate significant income for your publisher. While it's unlikely that you'll be able to accomplish these goals during the initial phases of your career, hopefully they will be attained as your career develops—and you will be rewarded by being able to copublish your material.

Operating As a Performing Songwriter

As the name implies, a *performing songwriter* is a songwriter who performs and/or records his or her own compositions. Many people think of performing songwriters as primarily acoustic guitar- or piano-playing singer/songwriters, such as John Mayer, Norah Jones, Alicia Keys, James Taylor, Janis Ian, or Billy Joel. However, the majority of pop, Americana, rock, and hip-hop artists write or cowrite some or all of their own songs. As such, they can also be categorized as performing songwriters.

Many performing songwriters compose exclusively for themselves with no intention of pitching their songs for other performers to record. Artists in this category include Beyoncé, Green Day, Alan Jackson, Mariah Carey, Maroon5, Gwen Stefani, Jennifer Lopez, and Rob Thomas.

The Benefits of Publishing Deals for Performing Songwriters

Songwriters who are also recording artists composing primarily for themselves benefit by having an outlet for their material. They don't need a publisher to pitch their songs to other artists. However, many recording artists (and those aspiring to secure recording contracts) affiliate with publishers.

In many instances, publishers sign performing songwriters to publishing deals in the hopes that they will procure a recording contract. In these situations, publishers typically assist with song development, financing and production of demo recordings, and development of a press kit with photos and bio. Then, the publishers use their contacts and credibility to pitch the artist to record labels and producers; this is often referred to as *shopping* a deal.

There are a variety of benefits a performing songwriter can derive by affiliating with a music publisher. For instance, writer/artists who are already signed to a record label might enter into a publishing or copublishing deal in order to have songpluggers pitch their material for possible inclusion in television shows, films, and commercials. A publisher might also secure *cover recordings*, sometimes referred to as *covers*, of their writers' songs. These are recordings made subsequent to a song's first commercial release. An example of a cover recording is Ray Charles' version of Billy Joel's "New York State of Mind."

In some instances, artists sign with a publisher primarily to receive an advance against their future songwriting royalties. Recording artists who write their own songs may be able to command advances of $100,000 or more if they have secured a recording contract with a major label. In most instances, the publishing deals that successful performing songwriters enter into are either copublishing agreements or administration agreements (explained in Chapters 6 and 8).

Sources of Income for Performing Songwriters

Artists who write their own material earn royalties for the sale and performance of their songs, just as any nonperforming songwriter. In addition, performing songwriters generate earnings from a variety of sources, including *artist royalties*, payments made to the artist by the record label for CD and electronic sales (such as downloading) and licensing of their recordings for television, films, and commercials. They also earn money from concert performances, sales of merchandise such as T-shirts and souvenir booklets, and product endorsements.

Artists who are members of the American Federation of Television and Radio Artists (AFTRA), the vocalists' union, are paid for singing on their own albums. This money is paid from the artist's recording fund, as explained later in this chapter. Vocalists must join AFTRA prior to having their music released on a major label. (For more about AFTRA, read "Hiring Musicians and Vocalists" later in this chapter).

In the U.S. (unlike in Japan and most European countries), recording artists (singers and musicians) and record labels receive no payment when their recordings are played on the radio or broadcast on television. These uses are considered free advertising intended to encourage listeners to purchase an artist's music and attend performances. However, the *writers* of these songs are paid performance royalties by the PROs with which they are affiliated.

If a recording artist is also the writer (or a cowriter) of his or her own material and recordings are purchased, he or she is entitled to mechanical royalties; if works are broadcast on radio, television, or the Internet, that writer is entitled to receive performance royalties in his or her capacity as a songwriter.

Artists receive royalty payments from their record labels for the sale and use of their master recordings—and while a detailed discussion of this type of compensation is not within the scope of this book, it is important to understand that these payments are totally separate from any money paid for the use of songs an artist may have written.

The licenses issued by record companies for the use of their artists' recordings (for instance, in television, films, or commercials) are called *master use licenses* or *master licenses*. The right to reproduce or use an already existing sound recording (a *master*) is called a *master use right*. Master use licenses, agreements that grant the right to use master recordings, can be issued only by the owner of the master recording, typically a record label. Similarly, only the individual or company that owns a master recording may give permission to include a *sample*, an excerpt of prerecorded material used within another recording.

A song can be expressed as notes and words on a piece of paper. To authorize the use of a song, a mechanical license is required. A "master" refers an actual sound recording. To authorize its use or reproduction, the user must procure a master use license. Artists whose masters are licensed are entitled to a percentage of the licensing fees collected by their record labels.

Prior to 1995, sound recording copyright owners (SRCOs) in the U.S. were not entitled to compensation for the public performance of their works over the Internet. However, the Digital Performance Right in Sound Recordings Act of 1995 and the Digital Millennium Copyright Act of 1998 established that sound recording copyright owners be paid for the right to perform their music via satellite, cable, and Internet for specified digital transmissions.

In September 2002, Congress approved legislation under Section 17 of the Copyright Act, providing for statutory license fees for artists when their works are transmitted over the Internet as webcasts and other *ephemeral* recordings, such as streams. (See Chapter 9 for information about streams and digital licensing.) In addition to artists and record labels being paid for specified digital transmissions of their master recordings, payments are allocated for *nonfeatured vocalists* and *nonfeatured musicians* (background singers and musicians who are not otherwise entitled to artist royalties).

SoundExchange, a nonprofit performance rights organization that evolved out of the Recording Industry Association of America (RIAA), licenses, collects, and distributes public performance royalties for sound recording copyright owners—record labels and artists. Its membership includes more than eight hundred fifty major and independent record labels and thousands of recording artists.

SoundExchange's primary function is the collection and distribution of royalties for *noninteractive digital transmissions*, meaning those that do not allow users to choose specific songs or collections of songs. Examples of noninteractive digital transmissions include broadcasts on cable and satellite radio broadcasts, webcasts, and streaming (but not on-demand streaming). SoundExchange does not administer artists' or record label royalties for traditional radio or television broadcast, downloads, or services that allow listeners to select specific tracks that exceed one minute in length. For additional information, visit www.soundexchange.com.

In many instances, the mechanical and performance royalties paid to performing artists for their role as songwriters far exceeds the artist royalty paid by their record labels. One reason for this is that there are likely to be tremendous recording and promotion expenses that the record label is entitled to recoup before paying royalties to the artist. In some cases, artists have achieved what would be considered great chart success—before receiving a dime in artist royalties. But unless the writer/artist has received a recoupable advance from a music publisher, he or she is entitled to songwriting royalties regardless of whether the record label ever recoups its investment.

Another reason why songwriting income often surpasses artist royalties is that hit songs typically continue to receive radio airplay many years after their initial release (for example, on "oldies," "classic rock," or "classic country" stations). There are instances of classic albums by artists such as Pink Floyd, the Rolling Stones, and the Beatles that continue to generate sales as new generations of listeners are exposed to them. But in most cases, airplay of artists who may have achieved moderate chart success does not typically prompt many listeners to seek out and purchase albums that may have been released decades earlier and may no longer even be available.

Remember, recording artists are not entitled to royalties when their songs are played on the radio in the U.S., but the writers of these singers' songs continue to receive performance royalties for the airplay. This can be a significant source of income depending on the amount of airplay the song receives.

Recording Your Own CD

For many performing songwriters, recording their own independently released albums provides a way for them to share their music with listeners—and, hopefully, profit from it. By performing regularly at small venues such as coffeehouses, churches, nightclubs, and house concerts, and selling their albums and merchandise (such as T-shirts, hats, mugs, and souvenir booklets) after shows and on their Web sites, many artists are able to earn their living by doing what they love.

Ani DiFranco is a classic example of an artist who took the reins of her own career and achieved great success producing and marketing her albums on her own. However, this is a rare exception. The majority of self-produced albums sell less than a thousand copies—and the artist fails to recoup his or her investment. When deciding whether to release your own CD, if profit is one of your motives, it's a good idea to assess realistically how you will sell your product.

Making your album available on your Web site and at Internet music sales sites such as CD Baby (www.cdbaby.com) provides access to millions of listeners. But in actuality, very few potential buyers listen to artists with whom they are not familiar. With music by approximately one hundred thousand different artists available on CD Baby, it would be impossible for even the most ardent fans to listen to more than a fraction of them.

Artists who tour and play numerous live shows, generate a "buzz," garner media exposure, and have the financial backing to secure the professional promotion typically required in order to achieve widespread radio airplay, have the best access to potential buyers. Many artists who rely on music fans to somehow find their Web sites and other sites that sell their albums, wind up with closets filled with box loads of unsold CDs and disappointments.

Hiring a Producer

When a performing songwriter decides to record an album, one of the first and most important decisions to be made is whether to self-produce or to hire a producer. A producer's job includes both creative and administrative responsibilities. Analogous to a film's director, he or she is ultimately responsible for every aspect of the finished recorded product.

Before recording begins, a producer reviews the songs being considered and, along with the artist (and if applicable, the artist's manager), contributes to the decision of which ones are the strongest and should therefore be recorded. He or she might offer suggestions for rewriting, *instrumentation* (deciding which instruments will be used), and *arrangement* (how the song will be structured). The producer might also suggest recording one or more outside songs.

Sonic quality, the sound of the recording, also falls under the producer's domain. His or her choices of recording studio, recording engineer, microphones, use of effects to alter the sound of the recording (such as reverb and delay), and mixing and mastering engineers, will all contribute enormously to the overall sound of the recording. Of course, many of these decisions will be influenced by the recording budget.

If an artist is not *self-contained* (either playing all the instruments him- or herself, or part of a band) the producer hires musicians and background vocalists (if necessary) and is responsible for completing paperwork such as union contracts and issuing payments. During the recording process, one of the producer's most important jobs is to capture the best vocal and instrumental performances. It's crucial that producer and artist share a creative vision for the project and, ideally, the producer will create a finished product that reflects this.

For many artists it's difficult, if not impossible, to maintain objectivity regarding their songs and vocal performances. A producer provides a trusted set of ears to help the artist bring forth the music he or she hopes to create.

Typically, a producer is paid an advance as well as a percentage of the price of singles and albums after they've been sold. This percentage is typically referred to as *points*. These amounts are negotiable and vary greatly in different genres of music. For a major label recording deal, an artist can expect to pay a producer at least $4,000 per song, in addition to a percentage of royalties. For independent and self-produced recording deals, producers' advances are typically much lower. The producer's percentage, and what that amount is based upon (for instance, a percentage of retail selling price or wholesale selling price) is determined by the producer's level of clout. It typically ranges from 3 to 5 percent.

Top producers with track records of hits command payments of $50,000 or more per song, and considerably higher royalty percentages than those without a string of current hits. The producer's fee is paid out of the *recording fund*, the amount allocated by a record label for the costs of producing an album or single. The recording fund also includes the amount provided to cover all recording costs, as well as money for the artist to live off of during the production of the recording. This money, as well as most costs incurred by the record label to advertise and promote the product, is recoupable by the record label from the artist's royalties and licensing fees. Recording budgets range from $10,000 at small, independent labels to $1 million or more for an established superstar signed to a major label.

The ideal way to find a producer whom you feel would bring out the best of your artistry is to listen to a variety of albums in styles of music similar to your own.

Evaluate the sonic quality, the song selection, the emotion evoked by the vocals, the instrumentation, and other factors that are important to you.

It may not be as difficult to locate and contact producers as you might think. The monthly publication *New On The Charts* (www.notc.com) lists contact information for every producer whose work is represented on a given month's music industry chart (in addition to much more information). The *Producer & Engineer Directory* (www.musicregistry.com) provides contact information for more than sixteen hundred record producers and recording engineers, including their credits, phone and fax numbers, and e-mail addresses. It also includes listings of management firms that handle producers and recording engineers.

Many producers are also songwriters; if this is the case, you can contact them by sending a letter, fax, or e-mail to their publisher. It is easy to figure out to which publisher a writer (or writer/producer) is signed by studying the credits on an album that includes one of their songs.

While some producers with multiplatinum album credits may not be willing to work with unsigned or developing artists and may be out of your price range, others may be looking for the next big thing. Also bear in mind that many producers get their starts as recording engineers or songwriters. You may be able to find up-and-coming producers by listening to projects they have recorded.

Hiring Musicians and Vocalists

The top musicians and singers in any major music market are almost certain to be members of their respective unions, the American Federation of Musicians (AFM) for instrumentalists and AFTRA for vocalists. Union members join the *local*, the chapter that governs the area where they live.

When hiring union members for recordings and live performances, the minimum amounts they must be paid are mandated by their unions. These amounts are referred to as *union scale*. While union scale is the minimum that a union-affiliated musician or vocalist must be paid, the most successful musicians and singers command double or even triple union scale.

Individuals and companies who hire union members more than three times are required to become a *signatory* to the union. This means that a document has been signed agreeing to employ only union members, abide by the union's regulations, and pay the rates the union has established. All major record labels and music publishing companies are signatory to AFM and AFTRA. However, artists releasing product on their own or on small, independent labels have the option of hiring musicians and vocalists who are not union affiliated. In these instances, the amount each performer is paid is negotiated on a case-by-case basis.

As of this writing, AFTRA-affiliated vocalists are paid a minimum of $188.75 per song for sessions up to one hour. Additionally, a payment equal to 11 percent of their total compensation must be made to the Health and Retirement Fund (an account that provides for members' health insurance and pension), bringing the total for one song to $209.51. Different rates are established for artists who are entitled to partake in royalties, and for those singing as part of a group. For additional information contact AFTRA (www.aftra.org).

Again, as of this writing, union scale for musicians who are members of AFM (www.afm.org) is $345.98 per musician for each three-hour recording session, plus $19 for the Health and Welfare Fund. These rates remain the same regardless of how many songs are recorded in the three-hour period. For both demos and master recordings, one band member is designated the *leader*. This individual is paid twice as much as the other musicians on the session and is responsible for generating the chord charts as well as being certain that the session flows smoothly and efficiently. The AFM's rates typically increase 3 to 3.5 percent each year.

In Nashville, AFTRA and AFM have established a lower rate, referred to as *demo scale*, for recordings intended solely for demonstration purposes. For demo recordings, solo vocalists are paid $80 per song, with a minimum payment of $100 per session plus a mandatory contribution of 12.1 percent to the Health and Retirement Fund as of this writing. To hire AFTRA vocalists to record demos outside of Nashville, *master scale* (the full union rate) must be paid. Similarly, AFM-affiliated musicians recording demos in Nashville are paid demo scale, $150.72 per three-hour recording session, plus $19 that must be paid to their Health and Welfare Fund. However, outside of Nashville, master scale is applicable regardless of the intended purpose of the recording.

In the event that a demo recorded in Nashville (with the musicians and vocalists paid demo scale) is commercially released, AFTRA and AFM members who performed on the recording sessions must be upgraded to full master scale payment. Artists who manufacture a maximum of ten thousand copies are permitted to pay AFM members a reduced rate designated a *limited pressing* rate. The rate per musician for a three-hour recording session intended as a limited pressing is, as of this writing, $189.49 (plus $19.00 for the Health and Welfare fund), with the leader receiving $378.98 (plus $19.00 for the Health and Welfare fund). Members of AFTRA and AFM will provide the appropriate forms to be filled out. AFTRA does not have a reduced rate for limited pressings.

Paying Mechanical Royalties

When performing songwriters sell their own music, they serve the function of a record label and, as such, are required to issue accounting statements and pay mechanical royalties to all publishers whose music they sell. It is the publisher's responsibility to forward the appropriate payment to its writers. If an artist is the sole writer of all his or her songs, this is not an issue. However, if there are cowriters or outside songs involved, the artist (acting as a record label) has a legal obligation to obtain recording licenses from publishers and to issue royalty statements and payments. Unless otherwise agreed upon (for example, the *controlled composition clause*, which is explained in Chapter 9), the mechanical royalty is to be paid at the statutory rate. (See page 137 for statutory rates.)

When only modest sales are anticipated, the artist releasing his or her own album sometimes pays the publishers up front for the entire portion that would be due (based on the writer's percentage of ownership of the song) if all units were sold. This saves the artist the work of issuing royalty statements and payments; he or she knows that all writers and publishers have been paid everything they are due—until the artist has additional CDs manufactured.

Let's look at an example based on the statutory rate of $0.091 effective January 1, 2006. In this example, an artist produces a thousand of his or her ten-song, self-released CDs, and the CD includes one song that was written as a 50/50 split with one collaborator.

1,000 units x $0.091 = $91.00 (the total mechanical royalty to be paid per song)

$91.00 ÷ 2 = $45.50 (total per song for each writer and his or her publisher)

In the absence of a copublishing agreement or other arrangement, for each of the nine self-penned songs, the artist/writer is required to pay him- or herself $45.50 as the publisher and $45.50 as the songwriter. (Of course, in actuality it is unlikely that an artist would go through the effort of issuing a royalty statement and payment to him- or herself.)

For the one cowritten song, the writer/artist retains $45.50 as his or her own publisher. Half of this amount ($22.75) represents the writer's share of the mechanical royalty while the remaining $22.75 is the publisher's share. The writer/artist is required to pay his or her cowriter's publisher $45.50. That publisher in turn is responsible for paying his or her writer the writer's share ($22.75) of this income and retains the remaining $22.75 representing the publisher's share. Remember that this amount is for one song; if ten songs on the album were cowritten, the artist would be responsible for paying his or her collaborators' publishers $45.50 for each song—a total of $455.00 (half of the total mechanical royalties generated by ten songs) for each 1,000 units sold.

As you will learn in Chapter 9, the Harry Fox Agency (HFA) handles the issuing of mechanical licenses and royalty collection for more than twenty-seven thousand publishers.

When an artist requests a recording license from HFA for a pressing of five hundred to twenty-five hundred units, payment in full must be received before the license will be granted. Five hundred is the minimum number of units for which HFA will issue a license. (A detailed discussion of recording licenses and the Harry Fox Agency can be found in Chapter 9.)

CHAPTER EIGHT

Understanding Copyright Administration and Administration Agreements

Administration, as the term is used in music publishing, encompasses all actions necessary to protect musical works and ensure that the publishers of these works are paid the monies to which they are entitled. Administrative functions include copyright registration; issuing of mechanical and synchronization licenses; registration with performing rights organizations; preparation of lead sheets, sheet music and reprint licensing; and the collection and distribution of royalties.

Administration Deals

An *administration deal,* often referred to as an *admin deal,* is an arrangement in which a publisher, or a songwriter acting as his or her own publisher, engages a company to handle the administrative tasks required for one or more songs—without conveying ownership of the copyright. This can be an ideal situation for songwriters who do not need to rely on a publisher for creative input or for pitching and placing their songs.

Individuals in this category are typically either performing songwriters who record their own material; writers and/or publishers who secure their own recordings; or songwriters with tremendous clout, who prefer to have someone else handle the noncreative aspects of publishing. Having someone else deal with paperwork, licensing, and administrative responsibilities allows them to focus their energy on the creative aspects entailed in being a writer and/or publisher.

Administration deals are offered by most major publishing companies. However, Bug Music (www.bugmusic.com) is the primary company specializing in deals of this type, primarily representing songwriters and writer/artists who require only administrative functions from a publisher.

For songwriters in the enviable position of owning all, or a portion of, a song that has already been recorded, an administration deal covering this song allows them to retain a higher percentage of its income than would a standard publishing agreement. Some songwriters in this situation opt to use their recorded song as leverage to secure a staff-writing (exclusive songwriting) deal. Bringing a song that has already been recorded to the negotiations for a staff-writing deal (particularly if it has been recorded by a successful, established artist) typically results in the writer receiving a significantly higher advance than he or she might otherwise command.

Most administration deals last from three to five years. Unless a writer is already generating significant royalties, it's unlikely that any money will be advanced when signing a deal of this kind. Only writers who bring a guarantee of major recordings and income (such as successful writer/artists, writer/producers, and songwriters collaborating with hit artists) are typically able to command significant advances. Keep in mind, though, that as with any publishing advance, money advanced as part of an administration deal is essentially a loan, and as such, it will be recouped from future royalties.

Administrators typically charge a fee of 10 to 25 percent of the total revenue (both the writer's and publisher's portions) generated by a song. The administrator's payment comes solely from the publisher's share of income; the writer receives the full amount of the writer's royalties. Therefore, if an administrator charges 15 percent of the total dollars earned, it receives 30 percent of the publisher's share of income.

Any deductible expenses (as specified in the administration agreement) are paid by the publisher (or writer acting as his or her own publisher) and the administrator in a percentage equal to their respective shares of income. For example, if the administration fee is twenty percent of the total income, the administrator is responsible for 20 percent of deductible costs and the publisher pays 80 percent.

Although an administrator is engaged primarily to issue licenses and collect royalties, in some instances it also takes on the songplugging function of a publisher, pitching songs for inclusion in television and films, as well as to recording artists. Companies that serve this role typically include a provision in their agreements entitling them to a higher fee in the event that they secure a recording or placement in television, film, or other media. (See paragraph 4 (e) of the Administration Agreement on page 116 for an example of this provision.)

In some cases it is specified that the administrator receives a portion of the copyright (ownership of the song), or retains administration rights to a song for an additional period (for instance, extending the term of the contract by an additional year), in the event that it secures a recording or song placement. In these instances the following issues need to be addressed in the agreement:

- What criteria are necessary to invoke the administrator's receiving additional payment? (For example, does the administrator receive a higher percentage on all recordings and song placements it procures, or does this apply only to major-label recordings or licenses that generate payment above a specified amount?)

- If the administrator procures a recording or placement, does the higher percentage rate apply to *all* of the song's subsequent earnings, or simply to this one use?

It's crucial that an administrator be notified of all recordings and song placements a songwriter or anyone acting on his or her behalf procures. Failure to do so can result in potentially significant income slipping through the proverbial cracks.

Analyzing an Administration Agreement

The document that follows is a sample of the kind of agreement signed by a publisher and a copyright administrator to engage the administrator to assume specified functions. An explanation of each paragraph is included.

ADMINISTRATION AGREEMENT

THIS AGREEMENT is made as of the day of _____, 200_, by and between, on the first part, _____ (hereinafter referred to as "Administrator") c/o _____ (address) and, on the second part, _____ (hereinafter individually and collectively referred to as "Publisher") c/o _____ (address).

The date when the agreement is signed, as well as the names and addresses of the parties entering into the agreement, are inserted into the section above. Also established is that throughout this agreement, the individual or company who will be administering the copyright(s) is to be referred to as "Administrator" and that the copyright owner (the publisher, or the songwriter, if he or she owns the publishing) will be referred to as "Publisher."

1. Compositions

This Agreement is made with respect to Publisher's ownership and controlled share of compositions listed on Exhibit A (all of such musical compositions being hereinafter collectively referred to as the "Compositions" and individually referred to as the "Composition").

This paragraph notes that the contract covers specified songs, which are listed in an attached document referred to as Exhibit A. It further specifies that this agreement applies only to the portion of the songs owned and controlled by the publisher. In addition, it determines that throughout this agreement the covered songs will be designated as "Compositions." In the event that the administrator is being engaged to handle all songs written during a specified period, this paragraph would be changed to reflect this fact.

2. Rights

Subject to the terms hereof, Administrator shall, during the term hereof, have the exclusive right to administer and exploit Publisher's ownership and controlled share of the Compositions throughout the world; to print, publish, sell, use and license the performance and use of the Compositions throughout the world (subject to the rights customarily exercised by the performing rights societies with which Publisher is now or may hereafter affiliate); and to execute in Administrator's name on behalf of Publisher, or in Publisher's name, any licenses and agreements affecting the Compositions, including but not limited to, licenses for mechanical reproduction, public performance and synchro-

nization uses. During the term hereof, Publisher shall not sell, transfer, assign or convey Publisher's ownership or controlled share of any Composition.

This paragraph states that while this agreement is in force the administrator shall be the only one with the rights to:

• Represent and pitch the publisher's share of the songs and

• Issue all licenses on the publisher's behalf.

The rights listed above apply worldwide, subject to the rights of the performing rights societies to license and collect performance income related to the Compositions. This paragraph further states that while this agreement is in effect, the publisher may not sell its share of any composition covered by this agreement.

3. Collections
Administrator shall be entitled to collect all gross receipts earned by and derived from Publisher's ownership and controlled share of the Compositions during the term hereof. Administrator shall also be entitled to collect gross receipts generated by Publisher's ownership and controlled share of the Compositions during the term hereof for a period of two (2) years thereafter. "Gross receipts" is defined as any revenue derived from Publisher's ownership and controlled share of the Compositions less amounts paid to or deducted by collection agencies and performing and mechanical rights agencies. Gross receipts shall include, without limitation, mechanical royalties, synchronization fees, printing income, and the so-called "publisher share" of public performance income.

This paragraph affirms that the administrator has the right to collect all "gross receipts" generated by the publisher's portion of the songs during the term of the agreement and, with respect to gross receipts generated during the term for two years after it ends. "Gross receipts" are defined as all money collected minus fees paid to facilitate the collection of royalties. This includes revenue from sales, synchronization licenses, sheet music, reprint rights, and performance royalties due the publisher.

4. Royalties
Administrator shall pay to the Publisher the following royalties in respect of the Compositions; however Administrator shall be entitled to retain from gross receipts, prior to the following calculations, its reasonable expenses as set forth in 4(f):

This paragraph maintains that royalties shall be paid as described in the subparagraphs below.

(a) 12.5% of the retail selling price of each copy of each printed edition of the

Compositions (except inclusions in printed compilations and folios) sold in the Territory, paid for and not returned to Administrator;

> This subparagraph establishes that the administrator shall pay the publisher 12.5% of the retail price of each piece of sheet music sold (and not returned) in the countries covered by this agreement. This does not apply to books or compilations that include multiple songs.

(b) **That proportion of 12.5% of the retail selling price for each copy of each printed compilation or folio sold in the Territory, paid for and not returned to Administrator, as the Compositions bear to the total number of copyrighted musical compositions in such printed compilation or folio;**

> This subparagraph provides that the 12.5% of the retail price to be paid to the publisher for songs included in compilations is to be divided by the total number of songs included in the collection. For instance, if one song covered by this agreement is part of a ten-song compilation, the administrator would pay the publisher 10% of 12.5% of the retail price (1.25% of the retail price).

(c) **90% of all income royalties, fees and other monies arising in the Territory and received by the Administrator with respect to the exploitation, licensing or other uses of the Compositions throughout the Territory including without limitation, mechanical royalties, but excluding public performance fees, Synchronization, and Cover Recordings;**

> Subparagraph (c) states that the administrator shall pay the publisher 90% of all income received, with the exception of money earned for performance royalties, synchronization licensing fees, and recordings of "cover songs" as defined in subparagraph (e) and print uses as specified above.

(d) **90% of Publisher's share and 100% of composer's share of all public performance royalties received by Administrator with respect to the public performances of the Compositions in the Territory;**

> This subparagraph addresses performance royalties collected by the administrator. It states that the administrator shall pay the publisher 90% of the publisher's share and 100% of the songwriter's share of performance royalties.

(e) **60% of all royalties and other fees payable with respect to Synchronization and Cover Recordings procured by Administrator. The term "Synchronization and Cover Recordings" shall mean any commercial recording of the Compositions or synchronization license granted in respect of the Compositions, procured by the Administrator or Administrator's agent.**

> Subparagraph (e) establishes that in the event that the administrator, or someone acting on its behalf, secures commercial recordings or synchronization licenses for songs covered by this agreement, it is only required to

pay the publisher 60% of the income generated as a result of these uses.

(f) The term "reasonable expenses" shall mean for purposes of this Agreement, actual out-of-pocket administrative and exploitation expenses of Administrator directly related to the Compositions, including but not limited to, registration fees, the costs of transcribing lead sheets, and the cost of producing demonstration records; provided, however, Administrator's general office overhead will not be deducted as "reasonable expenses."

This subparagraph defines "reasonable expenses" as all actual costs the administrator incurs related to the compositions covered by this agreement. As provided in paragraph 4, this amount will be deducted from gross receipts before the publisher's share is calculated. Subparagraph (f) further clarifies that the administrator's office expenses are not to be considered as part of "reasonable expenses."

(g) All gross receipts not distributed pursuant to the above provisions of this paragraph 4 shall be retained by Administrator as its fee. All gross receipts paid to Publisher shall be inclusive of all royalties payable to the authors and composers and co-publishers of Publisher's ownership and controlled share of the Compositions. All royalties due authors and composers and co-publishers of Publisher's ownership and controlled share of the Compositions shall be paid by Publisher. All payments to Publisher hereunder shall be subject to all applicable taxation statutes, regulations and treaties. The foregoing royalties shall be calculated upon the earnings received in the Territory by the Administrator after deduction of any collective or society fees applicable within the Territory (e.g. Harry Fox, ASCAP, BMI, SESAC). No royalties or fees shall be paid to the Publisher for professional or complimentary copies of the Compositions.

This subparagraph states that all money collected by the administrator (minus deductible expenses) not specifically covered in the subparagraphs above will be retained by the Administrator. The administrator keeps the overage as its fee. Gross receipts paid to the Publisher include all money payable to songwriters, including any share the songwriters may be due as copublishers. The publisher is responsible for paying its writers and copublishers their appropriate shares. In addition, subparagraph (g) establishes that the publisher is required to pay applicable taxes and to abide by legal statutes, regulations, and treaties. This subparagraph also states that the royalties described above are based upon what the administrator actually receives from collection agencies. Finally, it asserts that there is no payment for free goods.

5. Warranties
(a) Publisher represents, warrants and agrees as follows:

In this subparagraph the publisher makes the following promises:

(i) the Publisher is not under any legal disability and has the full right and authority necessary to enter into this Agreement and to grant the rights herein granted;

This subparagraph states that the publisher has the legal right to enter into this agreement.

(ii) the Publisher has not heretofore made and shall not during the term hereof make any agreement granting rights in or to the Compositions to any other person, firm or corporation for the Territory or any part thereof;

In this subparagraph it is established that the publisher has not and will not enter into any other agreement(s) granting any rights regarding these compositions.

(iii) the Publisher has not heretofore entered into and shall not during the term hereof enter into any agreement which will detract or derogate from the acquisition or enjoyment by the Administrator of all of the rights to be administered hereunder with respect to the Compositions;

Subparagraph iii states that the publisher has not and will not enter into any agreement that would prohibit the administrator from exercising its full rights to the compositions.

(iv) the Publisher will pay any and all monies due to the writers/composers of the Compositions;

This subparagraph provides that the publisher is obligated to pay any money due to the writers.

(v) that the Compositions are original and to the best of the Publisher's knowledge, do not infringe upon the rights of any third party;

Subparagraph v establishes that the publisher believes the songs covered by this agreement are original and do not violate anyone else's rights.

(b) The Administrator warrants, represents and agrees that it has the power to enter into this Agreement and that it will use its best endeavors to administer the Compositions during the term hereof;

This subparagraph states that the administrator promises it has the right to enter into this agreement. In addition, the administrator promises to use its best efforts in its handling of the compositions.

6. Indemnification
The parties hereto shall indemnify each other, and their respective permitted assigns, licensees and their respective directors, officers, shareholders, agents and employees from any liability, including, without limitation, reasonable counsel fees and court costs, arising out of or connected with or resulting from

any claim inconsistent with any of the warranties, representations or agreements made by the other in this Agreement. Each party shall give the other prompt written notice of any claim or action covered by said indemnity, and in the event Publisher is the indemnitor, Administrator shall have the right to withhold payment of any and all monies hereunder in an amount reasonably related to such claim or action, provided (a) all of such withheld monies shall be deposited in an interest-bearing account in a federally insured bank or savings and loan association, and (b) shall be distributed (i) upon a settlement (with Publisher's consent) or final judgment of any such claim or action in accordance with the rights of the parties hereto, or (ii) if the claim is not pursued for a consecutive twelve (12) month period, or (iii) if Publisher posts a bond in an amount equal to such withheld amount.

This paragraph affirms that the publisher and administrator promise to be responsible for damages, losses, and legal fees incurred by the other party due to its own misrepresentation, false warranties, and agreements made in this contract. This includes claims against each party's employees and anyone to whom they assign rights related to this agreement.

The paragraph further states that notice of any claim against the other party must be issued in writing. In the event that the publisher has misrepresented itself, the administrator has the right to withhold enough money due the publisher to cover the claim. This money must be kept in an interest-bearing account in a federally insured bank or savings and loan company. The money that's been withheld is to be paid if any one of the following conditions are met:

- If the publisher agrees to a settlement or if there is a legal decision settling the case;

- If there is no action on the claim in twelve consecutive months; or

- If the publisher posts a bond.

7. Settlement of Claims

Administrator shall have the right, but not the obligation to prosecute, defend and settle all suits and actions with respect to Publisher's ownership and controlled share of the Compositions, and generally to do things necessary concerning the same and the copyrights and other rights with respect to Publisher's ownership and controlled share of the Compositions; provided, however, Administrator shall not settle any claim or action without the consent of Publisher. Publisher shall have the right to provide independent counsel for itself, to assist in or assume the prosecution or defense of any such matter, but at its own expense. If Administrator fails to prosecute or defend any such suit or action within a reasonable time after Publisher's request for Administrator to do so, Publisher shall have the right, but not the obligation, in Publisher's name and/or Administrator's name, to prosecute, defend and settle any such suit or action. In the event of recovery by Administrator or Publisher of any monies as a result of a judgment or settlement, such monies shall be divided between Administrator and Publisher in the same shares as provided in paragraph 4 above, after first deducting the expenses of obtaining said monies, including reasonable counsel fees. Without waiver of or prejudice to any other right or remedy hereunder or otherwise, any judgments or any settlements respecting any of the Compositions, together with costs and expenses, including reasonable counsel fees, shall be subject to the indemnity provisions of paragraph 7 hereof, and the indemnitor's payments thereunder shall be paid to the indemnitee from any sums that may become due or payable hereunder to the indemnitor hereunder, and/or promptly upon demand.

According to this paragraph, the administrator may take any action it deems necessary to protect the compositions. However, the publisher must agree to any settlement proposed by the administrator. The publisher may engage its own lawyer at its own expense. If the publisher asks the administrator to take action to protect its interests, and the administrator fails to do so within a reasonable amount of time, the publisher may proceed with legal action on its own. The paragraph also explains that any money recovered by either party will be divided as described in paragraph 4, after reasonable legal fees and expenses are deducted. The injured party is entitled to collect any fees to which it is due.

8. Royalty Accounting

Statements as to all monies payable hereunder shall be sent by Administrator to Publisher within sixty (60) days after the end of each calendar, semi-annual period, together with payment for any net sums shown due and owing for such period. Administrator shall not be obligated to account for any gross receipts not actually received by Administrator in the United States. Publisher shall be deemed to have consented to all statements and other accounts rendered by Administrator to it, and said statements and other accounts shall be binding upon Publisher and not subject to any obligation for any reason, unless specific objection, in writing, setting forth the basis thereof, is given by Publisher to Administrator within one (1) year from the date rendered. A Certified Public Accountant, on Publisher's behalf at reasonable intervals, may examine the books of Administrator pertaining to the Compositions, during Administrator's usual business hours and upon prior reasonable notice. Said books relating to activities and receipts may be examined during the one (1) year period following delivery by Administrator of the settlement statement for said accounting period.

This paragraph establishes that the administrator must send the publisher an accounting statement within sixty days after each six-month period. Payment for any money due must also be paid at this time. This only applies to payments that have actually been received by the administrator in the U.S. The publisher has one year in which to notify the administrator in writing of any objections. The publisher may hire a Certified Public Accountant to review the administrator's records. This must be done within one year of receipt of the royalty statement in question. Advance notice must be given and the audit must be conducted during the administrator's regular business hours.

9. Term of Agreement
The initial term of this Agreement shall be until the last day of the calendar quarter succeeding three (3) years after the date hereof. This Agreement shall thereafter continue until written notice of the termination of the term of this Agreement shall have been sent by either party hereto to the other. If such notice shall so be given, then any such termination shall be effective on the last day of the calendar quarter following at least thirty (30) days after the date of notice. Notwithstanding the foregoing, no such notice of termination shall be deemed effective unless prior to the date upon which the term of this Agreement is to terminate, Administrator shall have recouped or been paid by Publisher its reasonable expenses (as said term is defined herein) theretofore incurred. Notwithstanding the foregoing, the term of this Agreement with respect to any Composition commercially exploited as a result of Administrator's efforts in the form of a phonorecord or in a motion picture or television soundtrack or in a commercial during the term hereof shall extend for a period of at least five (5) years from the initial date of such exploitation to the general public.

This paragraph establishes the period the agreement will remain in effect. It states that this contract will run until the end of the calendar quarter following three years. Unless written notice is received the agreement will continue. If notice to end the agreement is received at least thirty days before the end of a calendar quarter, the agreement will terminate the last day of that quarter. However, all reasonable expenses owed to the administrator must have been recouped or paid in order for this agreement to end. Also stated here is that any recording or use in a television show, film, or commercial secured by the administrator remains covered by this agreement for five years from the date of the release of the recording, or use of the song.

10. Sub-publishing
Administrator may enter into sub-publishing or collection agreements with, and license or assign any of its rights hereunder to third parties throughout the world. In the event Administrator is or shall be a party of any sub-publishing, collection or administration agreement for any country of the world with a subsidiary or affiliate, such agreement shall be deemed to be an agreement with an unrelated third party.

This paragraph sets forth that the administrator has the right to sign sub-publishing or collection agreements and to assign its rights to other individuals and companies worldwide. If the administrator is affiliated with, or has an administration agreement with, a subpublishing company, that agreement will be treated as if it were with an unrelated company.

11. Entire Agreement

This Agreement sets forth the entire understanding between the parties, and cannot be modified, terminated or rescinded except by mutual written agreement of both parties hereto. This Agreement shall be governed and construed under the laws of the State of _____ applicable to agreements made and wholly performed therein.

This paragraph states that this document expresses the complete agreement between the administrator and publisher. It can only be changed by both parties signing an agreement. Additionally, it includes a space to insert the name of the state where the administrator's primary office is located, whose law the parties choose to apply to this Agreement. The laws of the specified state shall apply.

12. Power of Attorney

Publisher agrees to execute any document reasonably necessary to effectuate the intent of this Agreement, and irrevocably grants to Administrator a power-of-attorney, coupled with an interest, to execute any such documents in Publisher's name and on Publisher's behalf.

This paragraph establishes that the publisher agrees to sign any documents necessary to allow this agreement to be in force. It states as well that the publisher gives power of attorney and permission to the administrator to sign documents on the publisher's behalf.

IN WITNESS WHEREOF, the parties have executed this Agreement as of the day and year first above set forth.

BY: _____   BY: _____
Administrator   **Publisher**

The administrator and publisher sign in the spaces provided above. The agreement goes into effect on the date shown on its first page.

Administration deals are typically not appropriate for developing writers and those who need the creative input and songplugging expertise a full-service music publisher provides. But, for songwriters and writer/artists who have the ability to secure their own recordings, an administration deal can be the perfect way to retain full ownership and control of their copyrights, while having a professional handle the business of licensing, paperwork, and royalty collection for a relatively small fee.

PART II

HOW SONGS GENERATE INCOME

CHAPTER NINE

Understanding Mechanical Licenses and Mechanical Royalties

Among the rights granted copyright holders is the authority to determine (under specified circumstances) who may reproduce and sell their copyrighted works. Music publishers grant these rights by issuing recording licenses and are compensated by receiving mechanical royalties.

Mechanical Licenses

A *mechanical license* is the license granted by a copyright owner to a company such as a record label or digital download provider permitting it to record, manufacture, and distribute recordings of a song or musical composition. In exchange for these rights, referred to as *mechanical rights*, by signing a mechanical license the record label agrees to pay the publisher a specified price for each sale of tangible and electronically produced product, such as CDs and digital downloads.

Record labels, companies that sell karaoke recordings, and download providers are required by law to procure a mechanical license from a song's publisher prior to selling or distributing the song; failure to do so can result in fines of up to $150,000 levied by the U.S. Attorney General. In actuality, many recordings are released without the record label's completing the paperwork required to obtain the required license. But provided the publisher is willing to grant the license, no penalties are invoked.

As you will learn later in this chapter, the transition from music being sold as a tangible product (such as a CD) to distribution via digital transmission presents the music industry with enormous challenges. Among these challenges is defining those uses that require mechanical licensing as opposed to performance licensing. (Performance rights and licensing are discussed in Chapter 10.) This distinction is much less clear when no physical product is being sold.

Analyzing a Mechanical Licensing Agreement

The document that follows is a sample of the kind of agreement an administrating publisher signs, granting a record label the right to record, manufacture, and distribute audio recordings. It includes explanations of each paragraph.

MECHANICAL LICENSING AGREEMENT

DATE:

The date the agreement is signed is inserted in the space above.

TO: _____ **(Licensee)**
_____ **(Address)**
_____

The "Licensee" is the individual or company to whom the mechanical license is being granted. This would typically be a record label. The address of this company is inserted below the licensee's name.

TITLE: _____

The name (and any alternative name, if applicable) of the composition covered by this agreement goes into this space.

WRITER(S) and PERCENTAGES: _____
_____.

In the space provided above, each writer's name and percentage of ownership of the composition is listed.

PUBLISHER(S) and PERCENTAGES: _____

_____% **(percentage ownership)**

_____ **(PRO Affiliation)**

_____

_____ **(Address)**

_____% **(percentage ownership)**

_____ **(PRO Affiliation)**

_____

_____ **(Address)**

For each publisher of the composition covered by this agreement, the company name, its percentage of ownership of the song being licensed, the performing rights organization with which the publisher is affiliated (ASCAP, BMI, or SESAC), and the company's mailing address should be listed.

1. Right to Grant Mechanical License
To Whom It May Concern:
We own or control the mechanical recording rights in the copyrighted musical

work listed above. You have requested to use the listed musical work as related to the making and distribution of phonorecords. This license will be subject to all of the terms and provisions of Title 17 of the United States Code (Copyright Act).

This paragraph states that the publisher of the composition has the right to grant the license that has been requested. It also establishes that the work has been copyrighted. In the event that there are multiple publishers of the composition, each of the publishers has the right to issue this license. The *Compulsory License* provisions of the *U.S. Copyright Act (Title 17)* , as related to the making and distribution of phonorecords, refers to the rules set by Congress governing recordings such as those included on CDs.

2. Rights Granted

Contingent upon the conditions specified within this agreement, we grant to you, your successors and assigns, the non-exclusive and irrevocable right and license, during the term of the copyright and any extensions to use the work listed above, to use the title in the recording, manufacture, and sale of phonorecords in the United States only, unless we grant you additional written permission to the contrary, of the following recording:

TITLE: _____

ALBUM TITLE: _____

ARTIST: _____

RECORD #: _____

LABEL: _____

This paragraph asserts that the rights being granted by the signing of this agreement apply to the heirs and to any company or individual to whom the record company might transfer or sell its rights. The right to record this song is not being granted on an exclusive basis, meaning that the publisher(s) may allow others to record the song subsequently. The rights being granted may not be withdrawn during the period that the copyright and any extensions are in force. These rights apply only to recordings manufactured and sold in the U.S.

In the spaces above, the song's title, the title of the album (if applicable), the artist's name, the record number (which will be provided by the record label), and the name of the record label are to be filled in.

3. Musical Arrangements

We grant you the privilege of making a musical arrangement of the listed work, but your arrangement may not change the basic melody or character of the listed work and shall not be subject to protection under the Copyright Act as a derivative work by you.

In this paragraph the recording company is granted the right to create an arrangement of the work. However, no significant changes may be made to the song itself. The resulting arrangement of the song may not be construed as a copyrightable "derivative" work, separate from the original. (Note that this refers to the song itself. The resulting recording is copyrightable as a *sound recording.*)

4. Royalty Rate

You shall pay royalties at the statutory mechanical rate (as established by the Copyright Royalty Tribunal) in effect at the time of sale or download of the composition unless we grant a variance to such royalty rate in writing.

This paragraph states that the record company is required to pay the mechanical royalty rate established by Congress (the *statutory rate*). The applicable rate shall be the one in effect at the time the product is sold or downloaded. Note that in some agreements it is specified that the royalty to be paid will be the statutory rate in effect at the time the product is manufactured, or the one in effect the date this agreement is signed. Whenever possible, it is best to avoid agreeing to a specific amount, for example, 0.091 cents for each unit sold. One should participate in any increases mandated by Congress.

5. Royalty Accounting

You shall provide accounting statements quarterly, within forty-five (45) days after each calendar quarter-year conclusion (March 31, June 30, September 30, and December 31) for the calendar quarter year just concluded, whether or not royalties are due and payable for such period. The royalty basis is to be determined on the net records manufactured and sold, excluding works distributed for promotional usages or as "free goods." You shall have the right to retain as a reserve against charges, credits, or returns, such portion of payable royalties as should be reasonable.

According to this paragraph, the record label is required to provide royalty statements within forty-five days after the end of each quarter. Note that some agreements require this accounting to take place within thirty days of the end of the quarter, while others allow up to ninety days. Also established in this paragraph is that a statement, listing the number of recordings manufactured and sold, must be provided regardless of whether there is any money to be paid. The label is not required to pay royalties for promotional products and those given away for free. Finally, this paragraph affirms that the record label has the right to hold back a portion of the royalties to cover the possibility of recordings being returned.

6. Right to Audit

We retain the right to object to any royalty statement, provided we list in writing and mail by certified mail, any objections. You have forty-five (45) days to

respond by signed mail. We retain the right to audit your records pertaining to the royalty statement of the listed title for a period of one (1) year from receipt of a particular royalty statement.

This paragraph means that the publisher may dispute the information on any royalty statement by sending a list of their objections by certified mail. If this occurs, the record label is required to respond in writing within forty-five days and must obtain a signature as proof of delivery of its response. The publisher shall have the right to examine the record label's accounting records as they apply to any given royalty statement, provided that this occurs within one year of the receipt of the royalty statement in question.

7. License Termination
In the event that you fail to comply with the accounting or royalty payment provisions described above, and the default is not remedied within forty-five (45) days of our written (certified) notice, this compulsory license shall be automatically terminated. We retain all legal remedies provided by the Copyright Act.

This paragraph establishes that if the record label does not provide statements and/or royalty payments, and still does not do so within forty-five days of receiving a certified letter notifying them of their failure, then the agreement no longer remains in effect. The publisher is entitled to all rights established by law.

8. Definition of Phonorecords
The term "phonorecords" as used herein to describe the musical work listed above shall include any means of sound reproductions, whether currently known or unknown, including but not limited to records, cassettes, compact discs, pre-recorded tapes, and "sight and sound" devices.

This paragraph establishes that the term "phonograph record," as used in this agreement, refers to all current recording formats as well as any that might be developed in the future.

9. Copyright Acknowledgment
On the label affixed to each phonorecord (and/or permanent containers holding the phonorecord) you manufacture or sell containing above listed musical work, you will include the title, writer(s) name(s), publisher(s) name(s), and PRO(s).

This paragraph states that the record label will include the song title, writers' names, publishers' names, and performing rights organization affiliations on the label or in the insert of the product.

10. Limitation of Rights; Legal Disputes
All rights and uses not specifically granted within this license regarding the musical title listed above are reserved to the publisher(s). Any litigation concerning the interpretation and/or enforcement of this license shall be heard

only in the State or Federal Courts of _____. In any action, the prevailing party shall be entitled to recover its reasonable out-of-pocket attorneys' fees and court costs.

This paragraph asserts that the only rights and uses being granted are those specifically addressed in this agreement. In the second sentence, the name of the state in which the publisher has its main office should be inserted; this will be the state where any legal action (if applicable) will be decided. In the event that there is a legal proceeding, the losing party will be required to pay court costs as well as the other party's attorneys' fees.

Sincerely,
"Licensor"

_____

By:

The "licensor" is the publisher granting the license.

"Licensee"

_____

By:

The "licensee" is the record label to whom the license is being granted.

Compulsory Mechanical Licenses

In most instances, the owner of a copyright maintains the right to decide who may or may not use his or her work. However, copyright law mandates that in specified situations, a license must be issued regardless of whether a copyright owner chooses to do so. In these cases, the license issued is called a *compulsory license* or a *compulsory mechanical license*, which allows the recipient of the license to record, manufacture, and distribute a given song.

Copyright statute specifies six scenarios in which a copyright owner is obligated to issue a compulsory license. These are for:

• Cable television rebroadcast

• Public Broadcasting System shows

• Jukeboxes

• Performances on digital radio (such as webcasts)

• Digital distribution of recordings (such as downloading)

• Audio recordings of previously released songs.

As it applies to most songwriters, this final instance is the most significant. Section 17 U.S.C. 115 of the Copyright Act provides that a copyright owner is required to license a song to anyone who wants to record and distribute it providing that all of the following conditions are met:

- The song has been previously recorded and released in the U.S. with the copyright owner's permission;

- The song is a nondramatic musical work (it is not part of a larger work, such as a Broadway show or an opera);

- The recording will be used only as an audio recording; and

- The statutory rate will be paid.

In actuality, it is extremely rare that a compulsory license is issued. When the criteria for compulsory licensing are met, an administrating publisher typically issues its standard mechanical license with the mechanical royalty rate being the statutory rate.

First Use Licenses

A *first use license* is a mechanical license issued by a publisher authorizing the first recording and commercial release of a song. It is virtually identical to any other mechanical license and typically does not specify that it is licensing a first use.

The statutory rate does not apply to the first use of a song, and theoretically a publisher may demand any mechanical royalty rate it chooses. If a record label is not willing to pay the requested amount, the publisher has the right to deny the first license. In actuality, the statutory rate has become the standard mechanical royalty rate for the sale of virtually all recordings—including first uses of songs.

Holds

To understand the concept of holds it is beneficial to understand that when a publisher pitches a song to a recording artist, A&R representative, artist's manager, or record producer, he or she is likely to receive one of the following three responses:

1. "No."

2. "I'd like to hold onto a copy of this."

3. "I'd like to place this song on hold."

There is a world of difference between scenarios #2 and #3, but they are often confused and used interchangeably by songwriters who fail to understand what a hold entails. "I'd like to hold onto a copy" means "I like the song—and I want to listen to it again before making a determination or a commitment." In the vast majority of instances, this does not lead to the song being placed on hold—or being recorded.

Requesting a *hold* is tantamount to asking for the exclusive right to reserve a given song for possible inclusion in a specific artist's recording project. When an individual requests to place a song on hold, he or she believes the song is a strong contender and wants his or her artist to have the right to be the first one to release it. By granting a hold, a publisher agrees not to issue a mechanical license permitting any other artist to record the song until the artist for whom the hold has been requested has either recorded and released the song or has decided not to record it, thereby relinquishing the hold. This ensures that when it's time for an artist to commence recording his or her album, no competing artist will have already commercially released the song.

As addressed earlier in this chapter, once a song has been *commercially released* in the U.S. (meaning, the distribution of "phonorecords" has been made available to the public), any artist has the right to record ("cover") and release an audio recording of the song, provided that all of the following criteria are met:

- The song is a nondramatic musical work (meaning not part of an opera, ballet, or musical play);

- There has been a commercial release of recordings in the U.S.—and the initial recording was authorized by the copyright owner; and

- The record label agrees to pay the statutory royalty rate.

Therefore, it follows that once a song that meets these criteria has been commercially released, it cannot be placed on hold—even if the first release failed to garner any radio airplay or significant sales. In these instances, a publisher might agree to refrain from actively pitching a song until a given artist has an opportunity to record and release it, but the publisher has no legal right to stop any artist from recording it. Note that performance of a song on television or in a film does not meet the Copyright Act's definition of distribution of a "phonorecord." Therefore, having a song on a television show or in a film does not in and of itself trigger the compulsory licensing provision.

The right to choose to whom the first mechanical recording license will be granted allows publishers (and songwriters acting as their own publishers) to determine which artist may be the first to release a song. This right, to grant or withhold the first recording license, affords the copyright owner an important degree of control over the use of his or her work. For instance, it allows a publisher to deny a first recording license to an artist whom it believes does not have a high probability of success (for example, a fledgling artist on a new, independent record label or an artist whose style the publisher doesn't like).

A publisher might also refuse to issue a first recording license fearing that the cut might jeopardize the possibility of a more lucrative recording. For example, if an artist's release receives sufficient airplay or video broadcast to make the public and music industry professionals aware of the song, yet does not become a bona fide hit, it could effectively destroy the song's chances of being recorded by a more successful artist for several years or more. This is because many artists are hesitant to record songs that have been previously released; others may be concerned that the first release's failure to achieve chart success may be a reflection of the quality of the song.

When there are multiple publishers of a given song, copyright law allows each of the song's publishers (or writers acting as their own publisher) to act independently of each other. This allows each publisher of a jointly created work the right to grant a hold and issue a recording license—regardless of whether the song's other publishers choose to do so. A publisher cannot compel its copublishers to honor a hold, but ideally the publishers communicate with each other and agree upon a course of action they mutually believe will be best for the song.

Holds are typically granted to A&R executives, producers, artists' managers, and artists themselves for audio recordings, and in some instances, for inclusion in film or television projects. Publishers do not place songs on hold, although they may request to "hold onto" a copy of a song to listen again before deciding whether they choose to publish it.

Typically, a hold is expressed as a verbal agreement between a publisher and one of the individuals responsible for an artist's song selection. Only a handful of artists and their representatives have been known to request written acknowledgment of a hold.

Except for the rarest of instances (typically involving high-budget film projects), no money is paid when a song is placed on hold. If a major artist's representative expresses a desire to reserve a song, the incentive for a publisher is not any immediate financial reward, but the possibility of getting the song recorded.

The overwhelming majority of holds ultimately do not get recorded for the project for which they were placed on hold. There are numerous instances of songs that have been on hold ten or more times—without generating a released recording.

Some acts may have several hundred songs placed on hold by their managers, record label executives, and producers throughout the song-gathering process, and these songs may remain in limbo, essentially withdrawn from the marketplace, for long periods of time. For instance, a song placed on hold for an artist who has recently released an album might stay on hold for a year or more, until the artist records a subsequent album. After the year has elapsed, the artist may decide not to record the song, may attempt to record it and decide that he or she can't sing it well, or may conclude that it no longer fits the style of the album. (Typically artists record more songs than are actually included on their albums, allowing them to release only those that sound best.)

These situations are frustrating and disappointing, and there have been countless discussions regarding ways to compensate songwriters and publishers when their songs are placed on hold, as well as means to limit the time a song may remain on hold. But holds remain a necessary part of doing business with which songwriters and publishers must contend, as a hold typically represents the first hoop through which a song must jump en route to getting recorded—and few songwriters and publishers are willing to alienate the superstar artists and record label executives who have the power to record their songs.

Digital Licensing

The advent of technologies that made it possible for digital audio files to be compressed (such as in the MP3 format) and therefore easy to transmit via the Internet, and the resulting wave of unlicensed music file sharing, took the music industry by surprise. The decline in music sales was devastating, impacting songwriters' and publishers' incomes, as well as those of artists and record labels.

Digital licensing, the licensing of copyrighted musical works for transmission or sale in digital formats, is the solution, and it represents a potentially enormous revenue source for both songwriters and publishers. Digital licensing fees may be imposed for uses including, but not limited to, full permanent downloads, limited-use downloads, on-demand streaming, CD burning, and ringtones, which are explained later in this chapter.

In the past thirty years, vinyl records were replaced by cassettes and 8-track tapes, which were in turn supplanted by CDs. It has now become apparent that the latest mode of delivery and sale of albums and singles is going to be primarily via digital transmission, with consumers accessing and listening to music through computers and other electronic devices. The manufacture and sale of tangible products encompassing music (such as CDs) is about to go the way of the dinosaurs.

The Digital Performance Right in Sound Recordings Act (DPRSRA), enacted in 1995, and the Digital Millennium Copyright Act (DMCA), passed by Congress in 1998, contain provisions regarding licensing on the Internet and other digital media. These statutes laid the groundwork to ensure that songwriters, music publishers, recording artists, and record companies will be protected as new technologies are developed. However, the business is still facing the challenge of defining how copyright owners are to be compensated for digital transmission, reproduction, and distribution of their songs using the latest technologies and those that will develop in the future.

In many instances, licenses granting permission (as well as licensing fees) for sales and access to music by digital transmission are already in use. Payments for these uses and standardized agreements are still in the process of evolving.

Digital Permanent Downloads

A *digital permanent download* (*DPD*) refers to the digital transmission of a musical composition resulting in a permanent copy made by or for the recipient. DPDs remain in a recipient's computer indefinitely and may be transferred to portable devices such as an iPod or other MP3 player, or burned onto CDs. An example of a DPD is any song downloaded from a site such as Walmart.com or iTunes. These typically cost consumers in the range of 79 cents to $1.00 per song.

The licensing of digital permanent downloads was established in Section 115 of the U.S. Copyright Act, which provides for them to be licensed at the same statutory rate as tangible, physical recordings, such as CDs. Therefore, through December 31, 2007, a copyright owner is entitled to be paid $0.091 or 1.75 cents per minute (whichever is greater) each time one of its songs is downloaded as a DPD file. This fee is paid by the seller of the download and is split among the song's writers and publishers.

The licensing of songs for sale as digital permanent downloads is covered by agreements that are essentially identical to mechanical licenses. The only difference is the inclusion of references to sales via electronic and digital delivery.

At the close of 2004, the Recording Industry Association of America (RIAA) established standards for "gold," "platinum," and "multiplatinum" awards for digital permanent downloads. The sales required to attain these awards are lower than for physical products (such as CDs) because at the time these awards were instituted tangible product was outselling electronically transmitted music by a sizable margin:

Gold . . . . .100,000 digital permanent downloads

Platinum . . . . .200,000 digital permanent downloads

Double Platinum . . . . .400,000 digital permanent downloads

Additional multiplatinum certifications are awarded for each additional 200,000 downloads.

Limited or Tethered Downloads

Limited downloads, also sometimes referred to as *tethered downloads*, are digital files that are delivered electronically to a computer—but with specified restrictions. There are two categories of limited downloads:

- *Limited-time downloads* remain in a computer for a specified number of days—for instance, thirty, sixty, or ninety days, and

- *Limited-use downloads* permit a specified number of times that the song file may be accessed and played—for instance, ten, twenty, or thirty times.

While a permanent download is tantamount to purchasing a song, a limited download is analogous to renting it. At the time of this writing, no industry standard or legal statute was as yet in place governing payment for limited downloads.

Streaming and On-Demand Streaming

Streaming can be defined as the electronic delivery of an audio or video file to a computer, allowing it to be watched or listened to as the file is actually being transmitted. Analogous to a radio or television broadcast, it is intended for a one-time use. After a streamed song has been listened to, it does not remain in the listener's computer. When this book was written, more than five thousand Internet radio stations were streaming a total of more than four million titles each week and the number was rapidly growing.

On-demand streaming refers to accessing and playing a specific song from a catalog of works. Listeners typically access on-demand song files by joining an *online subscription music service*, a service that charges consumers a fee, allowing them to stream, download, or burn music from the company's catalog for a specified period of time.

Companies such as Napster, Rhapsody, and Liquid Audio provide their members with access to enormous catalogs of music—in some instances more than a million songs—via on-demand streaming over the Internet. These firms are required to obtain licenses from the copyright owners of the musical compositions, as well as master use licenses from the owners of the sound recordings they offer. Online subscription services charge their members a fee, typically in the range of $8.00 to $15.00 per month. A portion of this money funnels down to the songwriters, publishers, recording artists, and record labels of the works they offer. The National Music Publishers Association (NMPA) has reached agreements with several providers of streamed music that require a song's publisher be paid 10 cents when the song is added to the server's database and 25 cents each time the song is streamed. At the time of this writing, standardized agreements and fee schedules have not yet been established for streaming.

Burning

Burning refers to the process of transferring music from a computer to a CD, MP3 player, or another similar portable device, resulting in a permanent copy of the songs. This is analogous to purchasing the songs and, as such, the copyright owners are entitled to royalty payments covered by mechanical or digital licensing agreements.

Ringtones

A *ringtone* is a portion of a song or musical composition transmitted as a digital audio file, stored in a user's cell phone, and played each time the phone rings. The two types of ringtones are:

- *Phonic Ringtones*, which are sound files containing an original, recreated recording of a given song. These recordings, sometimes referred to as *Mega-Tones*, typically played on a synthesizer, are made specifically for the ringtone provider. Phonic ringtones may be either *monophonic* (using only one note at a time to play the melody line) or *polyphonic*, a musical arrangement created with multiple notes played simultaneously to create chords and harmonies; and

- *Prerecorded Ringtones*, sometimes called *real tones* or *HiFi Ringers*, which are excerpts of artists' actual master recordings.

With more than 250 million ringtone transmissions in the U.S. per year generating more than $500 million in revenue (and $3.1 billion earned each year internationally) and the market growing each year, this represents a significant source of income for songwriters and music publishers.

Billboard magazine compiles a *Hot Ringtones* chart based on sales information collected from leading ringtone providers. Songs that reach Number One on the *Hot Ringtones* chart have been known to generate more than one hundred thousand ringtone sales per week at the peak of their popularity.

Users purchase these audio files to load into their mobile phones from stores and Internet sites for prices that range from $1.00 to $3.00 per song, with an industry average of $1.25 per ringtone sold. Payments, shared by writers and publishers, average 5 cents per ringtone sold.

Ringtone licenses grant providers, sometimes referred to as *mobile entertainment providers*, the right to distribute a given song through their services for reproduction on mobile telephones, pagers, or other portable communications devices. When their songs are licensed for use as ringtones, songwriters and music publishers receive money from mechanical licensing fees (based on a percentage of the sale price) as well as performance royalties (collected and distributed by ASCAP, BMI, and SESAC). They also share in revenue known as a *fixing fee*, or *fixation fee*, which is paid by the provider when the song is initially recorded and added to a server's database for use as a ringtone.

When a prerecorded ringtone is used, the seller must also pay a master use fee to the owner of the master recording (typically a record label), which in turn compensates the artist.

In many instances, it is specified that the recipient of a digital license must provide copy-protection technology to prevent unauthorized reproduction and distribution of the licensed songs. Licensing fees differ widely, and the complex issues surrounding payment for digital transmissions of copyright-protected material such as ringtones, limited downloads, and streams are still in the process of being settled. At the time of this book's printing Congress was in the process of reevaluating and reforming Section 115 of the Copyright Act to better address the needs of music creators, sellers, and consumers in the digital era.

Mechanical Royalties

As explained in Chapter 1, mechanical royalties are payments a record label makes to copyright owners (publishers) for the sale of recordings made of their songs.

The term *mechanical royalties* was initially coined when Congress enacted the 1909 Copyright Law, mandating that music publishers be paid 2 cents each time their songs were reproduced "mechanically" onto a player piano roll. These payments were made by the manufacturers of the piano rolls.

Today, in the U.S., these royalties are paid by record labels and download providers to music publishers, who in turn pay their writers the "writer's share" of the mechanical royalty income. The percentage due the writer is determined by the agreement signed by the writer and his or her publisher. It is typically 50 percent of the mechanical royalties collected after deductions, as specified in the publishing agreement. In instances where songwriters and songwriter/artists act as their own publishers, they set up publishing companies (as explained in Chapter 5) to collect both their writer's and publisher's share of mechanical royalties.

Mechanical royalties should not be confused with money due artists and record labels for the use of specific recordings of songs. As explained in Chapter 7, this is referred to as a *master use right*, and is conveyed by the owner of a given sound recording. In most instances, "master" recordings are owned by a record label.

Mechanical royalties have gone up considerably since 1902, providing successful songwriters with a significant source of income. The current rates are listed below and are paid for the sale of tangible product such as CDs, as well as for product that is delivered electronically, such as by downloading and other means of sales by electronic or digital transmission.

Statutory Rate

The *statutory rate* is the mechanical royalty rate, established by the Copyright Arbitration Royalty Panel (overseen by the licensing division of the Library of Congress), to be paid for the sale of all audio recordings in the U.S. following the first authorized use. In simpler terms, it is the amount of money typically paid by a record label to a copyright holder for each copy of a song included on an album or single that is sold in the U.S. This amount is split between the song's writers and publishers.

This rate is set at $0.091 (a little more than 9 cents), or 1.75 cents per minute (whichever is greater) through December 31, 2007. Since 1976, Congress has been giving songwriters a raise by increasing the statutory mechanical royalty rate approximately every two years, so it's likely that a new rate will take effect January 1, 2008.

The statutory rate applies to each song included on an album or single. Using the rate in effect at the time this book was written, the sale of each song released as a single or included on an album in the U.S. generates a mechanical royalty of $0.091, presuming that it is less than five minutes long.

Using the statutory rate of $0.091, the chart below shows how much money a song earns from mechanical royalties. These amounts represent the total mechanical royalties earned for each sale or digital download and are divided among all of a song's writers and publishers.

1,000 units	$ 91.00
10,000 units	$ 910.00
100,000 units	$ 9,100.00
500,000 units (designated "Gold" in the U.S.)	$ 45,500.00
1,000,000 units (designated "Platinum" in the U.S.)	$ 91,000.00
10,000,000 units (designated "Diamond" in the U.S.)	$910,000.00

When negotiating any music publishing agreement, it is always advisable to include a provision stating that in the event the music publisher issues a recording license to any company it owns or with which it is affiliated, the license must be issued at the full statutory rate. This protects a songwriter from the potentiality of his or her publisher issuing recording licenses to its subsidiaries (and paying its songwriters) at 50 percent or three-quarters of the customary rate. While every publisher may not agree to this condition, it is wise to request it.

Note that the statutory rate is applicable only for sales within the U.S. Outside the U.S. the mechanical royalty rate varies from country to country and in most instances is based on a percentage of the selling price of the recording, as explained later in this chapter.

Controlled Compositions

Major record labels in the U.S. virtually always include a provision in their new artists' contracts specifying that songs written or cowritten by the artist (and in some instances, the producer) are subject to the terms of a *controlled composition clause*. These clauses typically define *controlled compositions* as songs written, owned, or controlled (meaning published) by the artist (or, in some instances, either the artist or the producer). The inclusion of this clause permits record labels to pay a reduced mechanical royalty rate, typically three-quarters of the statutory rate, to copyright owners (publishers) for the sale or download of these songs.

Record labels justify paying this lower rate, referred to as a *3/4 rate*, or a *controlled rate*, by citing the enormous expenditures required for the recording, promotion, and distribution of their artists' products. They assert that the 25 percent discount on the mechanical royalty rate reduces their costs and their risk, allowing them to operate successfully in a business where only a small percentage of new artists generate a profit.

In addition to affecting artists' incomes (if they write or cowrite their own material) this provision has a major financial impact on songwriters who collaborate with artists, as their mechanical royalty payments are reduced by 25 percent as well, in accordance with the controlled composition clause.

While writing songs with an artist increases a songwriter's chance of his or her compositions being recorded, in the event that this occurs under a controlled composition clause the songwriter earns only 75 percent of the money that would have been earned had the song not been the result of a collaboration with the artist or if the song had been recorded by an artist other than the one with which it was written.

In some instances, attorneys are able to modify a controlled composition clause to provide their writer/artists (and these writers' collaborators) higher mechanical royalty rates after an album has reached specified sales levels (for instance, stipulating that the full statutory rate must be paid after an album has exceeded one million sales). However, the inclusion of this clause requires a savvy attorney—and a record label that is very eager to sign the artist.

In most cases, the controlled composition clause includes a provision that permanently sets the mechanical royalty at the rate in effect at a specified time, such as the date the artist began recording the album, the release date of the album, or the date the recording was delivered to the record label. As years go by and Congress provides for increases in mechanical royalty rates, including this provision allows record labels to pay a considerably lower royalty than the statutory rate in place at the time of the sale. This is especially problematic for artists and songwriters whose works become classics, generating sales for many years after their initial release.

Record labels also typically stipulate a maximum number of songs for which they will pay the full statutory mechanical royalty rate; for example, an artist's contract might state that the record label will pay a full rate only for a maximum of eleven or twelve songs per album. In the event that the artist chooses to include additional songs, all songs on the album may be subject to a reduced mechanical royalty payment. In other cases—for instance, when an artist records ten songs by other writers, as well as four songs he or she has written—all of the money contractually allocated by the record label for mechanical royalties may be used to pay the full statutory rate for those songs written by those writers. The artist may receive no mechanical royalties for the songs he or she contributes.

Additional Reduced Mechanical Royalty Rates

Record labels typically have three price categories for their albums—top-line, mid-line, and budget. The newest releases are typically considered *top-line*, meaning they are sold at full price (for example, $18.98 retail for a CD). Unless there is a controlled composition clause in place, songs on top-line albums are licensed at the full statutory rate. In many instances record labels ask publishers to accept a lower mechanical royalty rate for songs included on mid-line and budget albums, which are marketed at reduced prices.

Mid-line recordings are defined in one of two ways, depending on the record label:

- Recordings sold at 65 percent to 80 percent of full price; or

- Recordings sold at least $2.00 below full price.

Recordings are typically relegated to lower priced categories when they are no longer current releases. For example, while an established artist's latest album is sold at full price, his or her early releases—those no longer in high demand—are likely to be discounted to mid- or budget-price categories.

Budget recordings are those sold at even lower prices—typically below 65 percent of full retail price. Note that mid-line and budget recordings are not temporarily discounted or "on sale"; these terms refer to products consistently marketed below full price. Albums in the budget category include those a record label believes can only be sold at a drastic price reduction.

Songs included on compilation albums, which bring together songs from other sources, are also typically subject to reduced mechanical royalty rates. Examples include movie soundtrack albums, collections of television theme songs, and albums such as *The Biggest Country Hits of the 1990s.*

While in theory a record label can request a mechanical license stipulating that it will pay any specified percent of the statutory rate (for instance, 64 percent or 92 percent), in actuality it almost always requests a 3/4 rate (meaning 75 percent of the statutory rate) for controlled compositions and mid-priced albums, or in the case of budget records and albums sold by discount record clubs, a 50-percent rate.

The Harry Fox Agency

The Harry Fox Agency (HFA) was established in 1927 by NMPA to issue mechanical licenses and to collect and distribute mechanical royalties on behalf of U.S. publishers. With more than twenty-seven thousand affiliated music publishers, it is the foremost organization of its kind in the U.S.

HFA issues mechanical and digital licenses on behalf of its publisher members for uses including the recording and reproduction of CDs, ringtones, and Internet downloads. In addition, the agency collects and distributes mechanical royalties, audits record labels, and investigates piracy claims on behalf of those who engage its services. HFA retains 6.75 percent of all money it collects as its fee.

The Harry Fox Agency issues licenses only to manufacturers within the U.S. and to importers who have U.S. addresses. At the same time, it provides mechanical royalty collection and mechanical royalty monitoring services to its publisher clients for music distributed and sold in more than seventy-five countries around the world through reciprocal agreements with mechanical rights organizations in those territories.

The Harry Fox Agency does not issue *synchronization licenses*, licenses used to grant permission for the use of music in television, films, and commercials. (For an in-depth discussion of synchronization licenses see Chapter 11.) Nor does HFA pitch or promote songs, provide clearance for the use of samples, grant performance rights (which are handled by the performing rights organizations, ASCAP, BMI, and SESAC in the U.S.), or provide *print rights* (the right to publish lyrics in sheet music, books, magazines, and other media, and to alter lyrics). All of these functions must be handled by publishers. HFA licenses songs, which are owned by music publishers (or songwriters acting as their own publishers), but does not license the use of master recordings.

To affiliate as a publisher with the Harry Fox Agency, a publisher must have at least one song available for licensing through HFA, and have had at least one song commercially released within the last twelve months. Additional information and application forms are available at www.harryfox.com.

Reserves and Returns

A discussion of how songs generate income would not be complete without addressing the fact that stores sell CDs essentially on consignment, meaning they have the right to return those they fail to sell. The term *returns* refers to those CDs that stores send back to the record label for credit.

Record labels reimburse stores for either 100 percent or a lesser percentage of the cost of returned CDs. Whether the retailer receives full credit or a partial credit is typically contingent on the percentage of product returned. For example, a store that returns less than 20 percent of a given CD may be credited with 100 percent of the amount it paid, while a store that returns 50 percent of a particular CD it has stocked may be reimbursed for only a portion of the amount it paid.

If a record label pays a mechanical royalty to a publisher and the product is later returned, the label deducts the money paid from the publisher's future royalty statements—but only for that same title. This debit is passed along from the publisher to the song's composers.

In some instances, as a result of product being returned, a writer's royalty statement might reflect a deduction instead of a payment due. In these instances, the songwriter is not required to write a check to reimburse his or her publisher; the money is recouped from future royalty statements. In the event that there is not sufficient income for the publisher to recoup its loss, the writer is not responsible for repayment.

Reserves is the term for royalties that record labels hold back in anticipation of product being returned. Record labels routinely withhold mechanical royalties for 50 percent to 75 percent of the product they ship. While this percentage may seem exorbitant, it is the record labels' only protection against overpayments to publishers.

Songwriters' royalties are based on the amount actually received by their publishers—not on the amount of units shipped. Therefore, although a record label might boast that a given CD has shipped five hundred thousand units, if three hundred thousand of these copies are returned, the songwriters and publishers are only paid for two hundred thousand copies. Even if all five hundred thousand copies shipped are sold, the record label will likely hold back payment for three hundred thousand copies until it is certain that its vendors will not be returning any unsold product. This explains why it sometimes takes a year or more after an album is sold before a songwriter receives his or her mechanical royalty payment. When music is sold exclusively as digital transmissions, as opposed to physical product, this issue will no longer apply.

Audits

An *audit* is an examination and assessment of a company's or individual's bookkeeping records to verify the accuracy of the reporting. Audits also investigate whether the companies whose records are being examined have fulfilled their obligations to compensate the other party, as established by their contractual agreement. In some cases, an audit may seek to establish whether the licensed material is being used as the agreement between the parties intended. Although on rare occasions songwriters have audited record labels and performing rights organizations, it is a much more common occurrence for them to audit their publishers.

Virtually all single song and exclusive songwriting agreements have provisions that specify the timeframe and conditions under which an audit may be conducted. The agreements typically stipulate that the writer may hire an attorney, accountant, or other qualified auditor, at his or her own expense, to review the publisher's records. It is usually stated that this review must be scheduled with reasonable advance notice and must take place during the publisher's normal business hours. Most songwriting agreements place a one- or two-year limit (after receipt of the royalty statement in question) on how much time the writer has to notify the publisher of his or her intention to initiate an audit.

Auditors are typically compensated in one of two ways:

- A flat fee payable by the writer—regardless of whether any missing royalties are found or recovered; or

- A percentage of any money recovered as a result of the audit.

The fees charged to audit a publisher vary widely, but typically range from $5,000 to $30,000 or more. Factors affecting the fee include the number of years or reporting periods being examined, as well as the extent of the documents to be reviewed. When an auditor is engaged on a contingency basis (receiving a percentage of the money regained), the percentage typically ranges from 15 percent to 25 percent. Most auditors review the writer's publishing agreement, as well as the royalty statements in question, in order to determine whether an audit is warranted. If their compensation is tied to the amount of money they retrieve, they will have to be relatively certain that there is a good likelihood of recovering enough money to make it worth their effort.

Some songwriting contracts contain provisions establishing that the cost of an audit is to be paid by the company being audited, in the event that the audit discloses that additional royalties, above a specified amount, are due. For instance, a contract may specify that the publisher is required to absorb the cost of the audit if it is determined that the royalty recipient was underpaid by 10 percent or more.

The Songwriters Guild of America (SGA) Collection Plan is a mandatory system of royalty collections and auditing for its members. SGA's accountants conduct periodic random audits of its members' publishers. SGA professional writer/artist members pay 5.75 percent of their writer royalties (up to a maximum of $1,750 a year) for this service.

Auditors look for discrepancies in the following areas:

- *Underreported Unit Sales* refers to discrepancies between the actual amount of product (for example, CDs or downloads) sold and the amount reported on the writer's royalty statements. For instance, an album may have been certified triple platinum for achieving sales of more than three million units in the U.S., while the publisher may have accounted for sales of only one and a half million copies.

- *Underreported Shares Rate* refers to whether the writer's percentage of owner-ship has been accurately reflected. For example, a writer who is the sole writer of a composition may have inadvertently been credited with only 50 percent of the writer's share of royalties.

- *Incorrect Royalty Rates* refers to whether the writer has been paid the royalty rates specified in the contractual agreement.

- *Excessive Affiliate Fees* examines whether deductions for subpublishing and ad-ministrative fees have been accounted for accurately.

- *Foreign Income Taxes*, taxes withheld by foreign affiliates and licensees, are also examined to be sure that the amounts are accurate.

- *Unreported Licensing Income* refers to money a publisher collected, such as print and synchronization licensing fees, that may not have been reflected on a songwriter's royalty statements.

- *Underreported Black Box Income* refers to *black box income*, that is, money paid a publisher from sources that have not specified the titles of the songs for which they are paying. In many instances this results from foreign royalty col-lection agencies collecting money that goes unclaimed because songs that are generating income were not registered with these agencies. In some cases the problem results from works being translated into a foreign language or as-signed a new title—and not properly registered.

The auditing process typically takes at least a year, and in some instances, much longer. Auditors submit their findings to publishers in the form of a report and, typically, a settlement resulting in additional payments to songwriters (including interest accrued on delinquent payments) is reached. In approximately 95 percent of cases, a compromise is reached and a financial settlement is agreed upon by the two parties. The remaining cases are settled through the courts or arbitration.

Foreign Mechanical Rights Organizations

In the U.S., record labels pay mechanical royalties directly to music publishers or to the Harry Fox Agency, if a publisher has designated HFA as its agent. Outside the U.S., mechanical royalties are collected by mechanical rights societies to which music publishers must belong in order to collect their money. In some instances, the same foreign society collects both mechanical and performance royalties and distributes them to publishers.

While in the U.S. and Canada the mechanical royalty rate is expressed as a spe-cific amount (for example, $0.091 per unit sold in the U.S. through December 31, 2007), the rate in other countries is a percentage of the selling price. Some coun-tries calculate the mechanical royalty based on retail price; others base the rate on a percentage of the *published price to dealers* (PPD), the price retailers pay for the product, which is essentially the wholesale price.

In continental Europe, forty-one mechanical royalties collection societies comprise the membership of Bureau International des Sociétiés Gérants les Droits d'Enregistrement et de Reproduction Mécanique (BIEM). BIEM, based in Paris, negotiates with the International Federation of the Phonographic Industry (IFPI), a recording industry trade association representing recording industry associations from forty-eight countries. Together, they establish standardized royalty agreements and mechanical royalty rates for their member organizations.

The mechanical royalty rate in countries that are members of BIEM is currently 11 percent of the PPD and is typically renegotiated every four or five years. Deductions for rebates, discounts, and packaging costs bring this figure to an effective rate of 9.001 percent of PPD, with reduced rates offered for budget products. Digital licensing rates, audiovisual use, and some other usages are negotiated on a territory-by-territory basis.

Throughout most of Europe, the mechanical royalty is collected for an entire album—regardless of the number of songs included; 9.001 percent of the price that retailers pay (the PPD) is divided among all of the album's songs and distributed to the publishers. Therefore, a song included on a European album of ten songs earns a higher royalty than a song included on an album of twelve songs—if both albums are sold to retailers for the same price.

BIEM societies collect more than $700 million annually from record labels in their respective territories on behalf of music publishers and composers. Examples of mechanical royalty rates currently paid in some other countries are listed below:

- The United Kingdom: 8.5 percent of PPD
- Australia: 5.98 percent of retail price or 8.7 percent of PPD
- Latin America: 6.75 percent of retail price
- Japan 5.6 percent of retail price.

When these percentages are converted to dollars and cents, most countries pay a higher mechanical royalty rate than the U.S.

CHAPTER TEN

Understanding Performance Royalties

Songs are considered *intellectual property*, assets that are nonphysical and cannot be perceived by the senses or possessed. While a particular performance or recording of a song, or its transcription onto paper, can be seen, heard, transferred, or purchased, the underlying song itself remains intangible—yet, it is a copyrightable creation.

Among the rights afforded copyright owners are the rights to perform their musical works publicly, prevent the unauthorized use of their works, and be paid when their works are used. *Performance royalties* refers to the money songwriters and music publishers earn as compensation when their *nondramatic musical works* (songs and compositions that are not part of an opera or musical theater piece) are "performed" publicly.

Most people think of a performance as a concert, a live show, but in this context, the term refers to much more. Public "performances" include, but are not limited to, broadcasting songs on radio and television; playing them in restaurants, shopping malls, roller rinks, nightclubs, elevators, hotel lobbies, theme parks, airplanes, and sports arenas; digital audio transmissions over the Internet; and ringtones on mobile phones. In order to comply with U.S. copyright law, any establishment that plays copyrighted music is required to secure permission to do so.

Performing Rights Organizations

With more than $4 billion collected and distributed annually by performing rights organizations (PROs) throughout the world, performance royalties represent an enormous revenue stream for songwriters and publishers. In many cases, the money earned as performance royalties by a particular composition far surpasses earnings from the sale of recordings.

In addition to the radio airplay they receive, popular songs are likely to be featured as live performances or in videos, broadcast on network and cable television, played over the Internet and in concert venues and cafés, as well as presented in a myriad of other uses that generate income. When these uses are totaled, the PROs log billions of performances each year. It would be impractical, if not impossible, for songwriters and publishers to monitor the individual performances of their songs and to collect the pennies generated.

For each dollar a song earns in performance royalties, approximately 50 cents is paid directly to the songwriter by the performing rights organization to which he or she is a member; the remaining 50 cents is paid by the PRO to the song's publisher. These payments are made in separate distributions. Songwriters acting as their own publishers must affiliate with a PRO, both as a writer and as a publisher, in order to collect the full amount (the writer's and publisher's portions of performance royalties) they are due.

In the U.S. there are three PROs, the American Society of Composers, Authors, and Publishers (ASCAP), Broadcast Music International (BMI), and SESAC (formerly known as the Society of European Stage Authors and Composers, now simply referred to as SESAC). By joining a PRO, songwriters and publishers essentially engage that organization to collect and distribute the performance royalties they are due. In addition, the PROs help developing songwriters by offering workshops, pitch opportunities, and career advice.

A songwriter is permitted to be a member of only one performing rights organization at any given time. However, publishers must join each society with which the writers of songs in their catalogs are affiliated. For instance, if a publishing company represents songs written solely by ASCAP-affiliated songwriters, it only needs to join ASCAP. If a publisher's catalog includes songs written by ASCAP-, BMI-, and SESAC-affiliated songwriters (as would typically be the case), in order to collect its performance royalties the publisher must establish three publishing companies—each with a different name, one affiliated with each of the PROs. When songwriters who are members of different PROs collaborate (as they often do), each PRO collects and distributes the performance royalties due its respective member and his or her publisher.

The licenses PROs issue to radio stations, television broadcasters, and establishments that wish to play music or have it performed on their premises are referred to as blanket licenses. A *blanket license* grants its recipient the public performance rights to all music owned by a given PRO's members. ASCAP, BMI, and SESAC determine what each establishment's licensing fees shall be, based on a variety of factors including its size and the amount of revenue it generates. For instance, major television networks and top radio stations pay far more to obtain blanket performance licenses than do retail stores, nightclubs, cable television networks, and tiny college radio stations.

In order to legally broadcast songs written by members of ASCAP, BMI, and SESAC, a radio station (or other user of music) must obtain a license from each of the PROs. While in theory, a radio or television station, nightclub, shopping mall, or other user of music has the right to negotiate a licensing fee directly with the songwriters and publishers of each song it broadcasts, it would be a logistical nightmare and is rarely attempted.

ASCAP

Created in 1914, ASCAP represents more than two hundred thousand songwriters, composers, and publishers. ASCAP's main offices are in Los Angeles, with additional offices New York, Nashville, Atlanta, Miami, Chicago, and London. Its Board of Directors is made up entirely of writers and publishers who must approve all changes in the calculation and/or method of royalty payments. Approximately 14 to 15 percent of the licensing fees it collects are retained to cover its operating expenses.

In 2004, ASCAP collected $698 million and distributed $610 million to its writer and publisher members. ASCAP distributes royalties eight times a year: four quarterly distributions cover performances in the U.S. and four cover foreign performances. Domestic royalty payments to writers and publishers are typically made six or seven months following the end of each performance quarter.

One distinguishing element of ASCAP's payment system is that licensing fees paid by radio stations are used solely to pay royalties for radio performances; likewise, fees collected from television stations are distributed only for television performances; licensing fees collected from Internet broadcasters are allocated only for payment for Internet performances, etc. This is referred to as a "follow-the-dollar" system of payment and ASCAP is the only U.S. performing rights organization that uses this method of distribution.

BMI

Headquartered in Nashville, with offices in New York, Los Angeles, Atlanta, Miami, Puerto Rico, and London, BMI represents more than three hundred thousand songwriters, composers, and publishers in the U.S., and licenses more than six and a half million compositions. Established in 1940, BMI is a non-profit-making company, retaining approximately 14.2 percent of the licensing fees it collects to pay for its administrative costs and distributing the remainder to its songwriter and publisher members.

BMI's revenue for fiscal year 2004–2005 was $728 million, with $623 million being distributed to its writers and publisher members. Domestic and international royalties are distributed four times a year, in January, April, July, and October, with the exception of payments for live concert performances. Royalties earned for concert performances are paid in April and October for pop concerts, and annually, in August, for classical concerts. Pay-per-view performances are paid once a year. Royalties are distributed approximately seven months following the calendar quarter during which the performance, broadcast, or airplay occurs.

SESAC

SESAC is the smallest of the three U.S. PROs. With a market share estimated at 3 percent to 8 percent, it collects an estimated $50 to $80 million dollars annually in licensing fees. A privately owned, for-profit company, its headquarters are in Nashville, with offices in New York, Los Angeles, and London.

Unlike the other performing rights organizations, SESAC has a selective process by which it affiliates songwriters and publishers; prospective writers and publishers must be approved for membership. When it was founded in 1930, most of SESAC's affiliated writers were European and/or writers of gospel music. Today, this organization represents between eight thousand and nine thousand songwriters, composers, and music publishers across virtually all genres of music.

SESAC royalties are distributed quarterly, with domestic payments made approximately three months after the quarter in which the music has been performed (at least three months faster than its competitors). Additionally, SESAC distributes foreign royalties four times a year.

How Radio Performance Royalties Are Monitored and Calculated

Each of the three U.S. PROs fulfills the same primary functions for its members—the collection and disbursement of performance royalties for nondramatic performances of music. But each of the societies identifies performances and assigns a monetary value to each performance in different ways.

At their peak, hit songs on the pop, adult contemporary, R&B, or country charts garner more than one hundred thousand radio airplays a week in the U.S. Depending on a song's genre and marketing, it may also accrue hundreds of thousands of international performances.

A variety of factors influence the amount of performance royalties a particular song earns. Songs that have a long, slow climb up the charts amass considerably more airplay along the way to the Number One position than do songs that zoom to the top of the charts quickly. The length of time a song spends at the top of the charts also affects the amount of airplay it receives, and, therefore, the amount of performance royalties it generates.

The ranges of performance royalties typically earned by pop, adult contemporary, R&B, and country songs during their first year of release are listed below according to peak chart position. Bear in mind that 50 percent of the amounts listed are paid by the PROs to the songs' writers, with the remaining 50 percent paid to their publishers (or to the writers, if they are serving as their own publishers).

Peak Chart Position	Range of Performance Royalties
#1	$600,000–$1,000,000
#5	$300,000–$ 600,000
#10	$200,000–$ 500,000
#20	$125,000–$ 400,000
#30	$100,000–$ 250,000
#50	$ 30,000–$ 150,000

The reason this range is so wide is that some songs that reach particular chart positions receive considerably more airplay than others. The figures listed above are intended as general guidelines, and any given song may earn more or less than these amounts. For example, there are instances of Number One country songs earning as little as $350,000, as well as exceptionally popular pop songs generating more than $2 million dollars in performance royalties during their first year of release—but these are not typical.

Songs that remain at Number One (or in the top 5) for multiple weeks receive significantly more airplay (and subsequently, royalties) than do songs that spend only one week at these chart positions. Several times throughout the year—including Thanksgiving, Christmas, and New Years—the chart positions remain *frozen*, meaning that radio stations' play lists are unchanged during these weeks. Songs on the charts during these periods garner an additional week of performances and a significant windfall for their writers and publishers. Additionally, songs that receive airplay in multiple formats (for instance, pop, adult contemporary, and R&B) garner many more performances than songs that are played on only one radio format. (A detailed explanation of the music charts is addressed in Chapter 15.)

Hit singles continue to generate performance royalty income for many years after their initial chart success. The amount a particular song earns in subsequent years is contingent on the amount of radio and television airplay it continues to receive. Some hit songs earn less than $1,000 a year after their initial success, while songs that remain popular on "oldies" stations may earn in the range of $10,000 to $50,000 a year—and this income may continue for decades. Songs that achieve worldwide popularity may earn double these amounts.

Songs in styles such as Christian, jazz, and rock earn considerably less performance royalties than their mainstream counterparts because there are fewer radio stations playing these formats, thus generating less radio airplay. For instance, during one particular week, according to *Billboard Radio Monitor*, the Number One pop song reached an estimated sixty-one million radio listeners while the Number One rock song reached roughly eleven million radio listeners; the song at the top of the jazz charts was heard by approximately eight million listeners; and the Number One Christian song was heard by an audience of approximately 4.7 million. Depending on the amount of airplay accrued, songs in these and other music genres outside the mainstream earn only a fraction of the performance royalties generated by their pop counterparts—in some cases, as little as 5 percent, 10 percent, or 20 percent.

The three U.S. PROs engage the services of companies that use technology known as *digital pattern recognition*, sometimes referred to as *fingerprinting*, to identify songs played on the radio and, in some instances, television. These research firms include Nielsen Broadcast Data Systems (BDS), MediaBase/Mediaguide, and BlueArrow. This process identifies songs within seconds by analyzing each composition's unique sound patterns and then runs it through a database of licensed compositions to credit the appropriate writers and publishers. Statistical projections are used by all the PROs to estimate actual airplay from the number of surveyed performances.

How ASCAP Monitors and Pays for Radio Performances

ASCAP licenses more than 11,500 local commercial radio stations and two thousand noncommercial radio broadcasters in more than twenty-five hundred markets. In addition to using the Nielsen BDS and Mediaguide monitoring systems, as well as log sheets submitted by radio stations, ASCAP monitors radio airplay by recording and reviewing more than sixty thousand hours of radio station broadcasts each year. This provides a system of checks and balances, circumventing the potential of airplay logs being inadvertently or intentionally altered by reporting radio stations.

In keeping with ASCAP's "follow-the-dollar" system of payment, licensing fees collected from radio stations are disbursed as royalties only for the type of music these stations play. For example, a Latin song's royalty is based upon licensing fees collected from radio stations that broadcast Latin music, not from those with a pop, rock, or R&B format.

Credit Weights

Every performance identified by ASCAP is assigned a number of credits, determined by factors including how the music is used, the licensing fee paid by the radio station, and the time of broadcast. These variables combine to comprise what ASCAP refers to as the "weight" of the performance. For instance, a song played in full on a major radio station carries more weight, and therefore earns more credits, than a twenty-second excerpt of a song used as a jingle and broadcast on a smaller station. Each quarter, the dollar value of an individual credit varies, determined by the total amount of licensing fees collected and the number of credits earned by all writer and publisher members.

Radio Feature Premium Payments

Songs in ASCAP's catalog that attain specified threshold numbers of *feature performances* (a performance that lasts a specified period of time, which varies by PRO standards, during which the song is the sole sound broadcast) on radio in any one quarter receive additional credits in that quarter. These bonuses, known as *radio feature premium payments*, allow for hit songs to be paid at higher rates. These additional payments vary based on each quarter's revenue and the number of times a song is performed.

How BMI Monitors and Pays for Radio Performances

BMI assesses data from digital airplay-measurement technology providers, such as BDS and BlueArrow, to calculate the number of radio performances received by songs in its repertory. Additionally, it factors in information derived from log sheets provided by radio stations, which list all songs the station has played during a three-day period each year. Various stations are surveyed different days throughout the year, amassing a sample of almost four million hours annually. This sample is factored to project a statistically reliable survey of all feature performances on all commercial radio stations throughout the U.S. (A feature performance in this case is defined by BMI as ninety seconds or more of a song being the sole sound broadcast.)

BMI's radio performance royalty payments are based upon the licensing fees collected from each individual station on which a particular song is broadcast. Major stations that reach millions of listeners pay higher licensing fees than their counterparts that reach smaller audiences. Therefore, a performance of a song played on a station that reaches millions of listeners earns more money than the same performance on a smaller station.

The amount BMI pays each time a particular song airs on the radio varies each quarterly accounting period. The royalty payment rate is based on the licensing fees BMI collects from stations that play the song during a given quarter. In addition, the rate varies depending upon the total amount available for each quarter's commercial radio distribution.

BMI's radio performance payment system is quite complex, and songs may be categorized and paid in three ways: the "Current Activity Payment," the "Hit Song Bonus," and the "Standards Bonus." Payments for songs in each of these categories are calculated differently, as explained below.

Current Activity Payments

BMI's *Current Activity Payment* is essentially its base royalty rate; all songs performed on the radio are included in this category, unless they are upgraded to a higher payment level as a result of attaining specified levels of airplay. BMI calculates the royalty rate for each particular work by using a formula that takes into account the licensing fees collected from stations that performed the song and the number of times it aired on those stations. For instance, when a song is performed on five hundred radio stations during a given quarter, its per-airplay royalty rate is determined by the licensing fees collected by BMI from those particular five hundred stations. Another song receiving airplay on five hundred stations in this same quarter will be paid at a different rate because it's likely that the stations on which it was aired paid different licensing fees than those referenced in the first part of this example. The majority of BMI's radio performance royalties available for distribution each quarter are allocated to Current Activity Payments.

Hit Song Bonus

Any work performed more than ninety-five thousand times during a given quarter is eligible for BMI's *Hit Song Bonus*. Therefore, the writers and publishers of "hit" songs played on the same (or equivalent radio stations) receive a higher royalty per airplay (approximately one and a half times the base rate) than songs with lower current quarter performance counts.

Standards Bonus

BMI defines a song as a *Standard* if it has been performed on commercial radio stations in the U.S. at least two and a half million times since its release and is performed at least fifteen thousand times in a quarter. These songs are eligible for the *Standards Bonus* and receive BMI's highest per-performance royalty rate.

Commercial Radio Performance Payments

Commercial radio encompasses all stations other than classical, college, and National Public Radio stations. The BMI performance royalty rate paid for a local commercial radio performance is determined by the amount of the licensing fee paid to BMI by the station broadcasting the performance.

For airplay on stations that paid among the top 25 percent of the highest licensing fees in the previous year, each full performance of a song earns a minimum of 12 cents, which is divided among the song's writers and publishers. Stations in this category are referred to as *Radio 1*. Each full performance of a song on the remaining 75 percent of radio stations, known as *Radio 2*, earns a minimum of 6 cents, which is split among all participants.

These rates are minimum payments and may be increased contingent on the amount of radio income available in any particular quarter. Since BMI operates on a nonprofit basis, they periodically increase their royalty rates by instituting what they call *Voluntary Quarterly Payments*, additional payments to distribute the licensing fees that have been collected.

Additional Radio Performance Payments

A *classical work* is defined by BMI as a symphonic, chamber music, solo, or other work originally written for classical concert or opera performance. Each feature performance of a classical work on local commercial radio is paid a minimum of 32 cents per minute, which is divided among the works' writers and publishers. Feature performances of songs played on college radio stations (stations affiliated with colleges and universities) are paid at a minimum rate of 6 cents, divided among all of the songs' writers and publishers.

The royalty rate paid for performances on National Public Radio (NPR) is based upon the amount of license fees received by BMI from the Corporation for Public Broadcasting (CPB), as compared with the total number of monitored performances of BMI works on NPR stations. As a result, the royalty rate changes each quarter as a different number of performances is paid from the amount of fees received.

Radio Feature Performance Bonus Payment Rates

BMI pays higher "per-performance" royalty rates for songs that have received more than twenty-five thousand radio or television broadcast performances. These higher rates do not apply to performances on college radio stations. There are four bonus levels; the one applicable in any given quarter to a particular song is determined by the total (cumulative) number of performances of the work, and the number of performances the work receives in that quarter.

Super Bonus Payment Rates

BMI's *Super Bonus Payment Rate* is its highest "per-performance" rate for radio airplay in a given quarter. This rate is four times the amount paid for songs in BMI's

Current Activity Payment category (base rate). A song's eligibility to receive payment at the Super Bonus level is based on the total number of performances it has accrued since its inception, as well as the number of airplays received in a particular quarter.

Of the total number of performances in any given quarter, 10 percent receive this highest royalty rate. The BMI song that has accumulated the highest total number of performances since 1960 is entitled to this bonus level of payment for any airplay received during the accounting quarter. In descending order, each of BMI's most popular songs (as defined as amassing the most airplay since 1960) are paid at this bonus rate for all current quarter performances until the top 10 percent of all performances in this quarter have been accounted for. Songs in this category include "You've Lost That Lovin' Feelin'" (Barry Mann, Phil Spector, and Cynthia Weil), which has received more than eight million performances, and "Never My Love" (Donald and Richard Addrisi) and "Yesterday" (John Lennon and Sir Paul McCartney), which have each accumulated more than seven million performances.

Upper-Level Bonus Payment Rate

Continuing down the descending list of songs that have accumulated the most airplay, BMI identifies those works whose current quarter's performances collectively constitute approximately 15 percent of the current quarter's radio feature performances of all BMI works. These songs are eligible for the *Upper-Level Bonus* and are paid at two and a half times the base rate.

Mid-Level Bonus Payment Rate

Those songs with the next lower cumulative history, whose current quarter's performances together constitute approximately 25 percent of the current quarter's radio feature performances of all BMI works, are paid the *Mid-Level Bonus Rate*. Songs in this category earn double the BMI base rate.

Entry-Level Bonus Payment Rate

All other works with a cumulative history of twenty-five thousand or more performances are paid at the Entry-Level Bonus Rate of one and a half times BMI's base rate.

Additional Bonuses

Any song that receives one hundred thousand performances in a given quarter is paid at the next higher level bonus rate than it would otherwise be entitled to. While the bonus systems previously explained are partly based on past airplay, the Hit Song Bonus is determined solely by airplay received in the current quarter.

Hit songs routinely receive one hundred thousand or more performances in the quarters during which they are at the peak of their popularity. Since these songs have not received prior airplay, without this bonus they would be paid at the Entry-Level Bonus Payment rate. This bonus rewards BMI writers and publishers of a new hit by bumping their payment levels to Mid-Level Bonus Payment during those quarters in which the song receives a minimum of one hundred thousand performances.

Songs written specifically for and performed in full-length motion pictures or made-for-television movies are paid at no less than the Upper-Level Bonus Payment rate, provided that a minimum of forty-five seconds of the work is used or it is played during the film's opening (a "main title theme") or during the closing credits. Additionally, BMI pays the Super Bonus Payment rate to compositions from original musical theater works, musical revues, and operettas when they are played on the radio.

How SESAC Monitors and Pays for Radio Performances

There is a widely held misconception that SESAC's radio performance royalty payments are based on songs' rankings on music charts, such as those compiled by *Billboard* magazine. In actuality, SESAC was the first of the domestic PROs to use digital pattern recognition technology for tracking and determining payments for radio airplay performances. It is the only U.S. PRO to use this technology as the sole basis for estimating airplay.

More than ten million hours of radio broadcasts are monitored annually by SESAC. This data, collected by Nielsen BDS, is used to identify the performances of SESAC's songwriters' songs for royalty distribution purposes, and is extrapolated to estimate each song's total radio performance activity.

Radio performances are weighted according to the licensing fees paid by the stations. After operating expenses are deducted from the radio station licensing fees collected in a particular quarter, each song is paid according to its share of the total credits. Performances broadcast via commercial radio services (such as satellite radio) and paid music services such as Muzak are assessed by electronic performance logs, listing all performances from these sources. Payments are based on the license fees collected and the number of payable performances occurring in each quarter.

Songs achieving specified levels of airplay are paid at one of three incremental bonus levels, with songs receiving the most airplay being paid at the highest "per-performance" rate. The number of BDS detections a song receives in a performance period and the radio format on which it airs determines its bonus level.

How Television Performance Royalties Are Monitored and Calculated

In the U.S., more money is collected and distributed by the PROs for television performances than for any other type of performance. The PROs each assign a dollar value to music performed on television by factoring in the type of performance (for instance, visual vocal, background music, theme song, jingle, etc., as explained opposite), the length of the performance, the number of stations airing the performance, and the licensing fees paid by the stations airing the work.

Categories of Television Music and the Royalties They Generate

Television music is categorized according to the way it is used in the context of a program. The various uses (as well as their abbreviations) are listed below:

- *Main Title* (*MT*) or *Theme*. A song or instrumental piece that is played during the opening credits and is regularly associated with a television show, such as the theme song (TS) from *Bewitched* or *I Love Lucy*

- *End Title* (*ET*). A song or instrumental piece played while the credits roll at the end of the show

- *Visual Vocal* (*VV*). A song performed by one or more vocalists on camera; the viewer can actually see the song being sung (for example, a scene in a television show that features a singer performing in a nightclub or a choir singing in a church)

- *Visual Instrumental* (*VI*). A performance that features one or more musicians playing their instruments on camera, such as a strolling violinist or an instrumental jazz trio

- *Background Instrumental* (*BI*). Underscore; instrumental music played in the background that is not the focus of the audience

- *Background Vocal* (*BV*). One or more vocalists singing off camera

- *Logo Performance* (*LP*). A performance of music regularly accompanying the visual identification of a production company or program distributor

- *Infomercial Performance* (*IP*). Music performed in a short-form or long-form advertisement, the content of which typically includes a product demonstration and invites direct consumer response

- *Promotional Announcement* (*Promo*). An announcement that advertises an upcoming program

- *Commercial Jingle* (*J*). Music (either preexisting or written specifically for an advertiser) used to advertise a specific product or service.

The abbreviations listed above are not universally recognized. Many cue sheets (as per the sample included in the next section) include a key, defining the abbreviations used.

The amount of royalty paid by the PROs when songs and musical compositions are broadcast varies widely, contingent on factors such as the way in which the music is used, the time of day of the broadcast, the length of the musical composition, and the licensing fees paid by the broadcaster. The figures that follow provide a general idea of the range of the amount of performance royalties that may be generated for various usages of music on television. These amounts are for one usage unless otherwise specified. They include the writers' and publishers' shares and do not include synchronization licensing fees:

Network television prime time series theme song . . . . $800–$1,500

Visual vocal (on camera) performance on
prime time network television . . . . $3,000–$4,500

Hit song used in a nationally-aired
commercial for one year . . . . $125,000–$200,000

Jingle aired once on a major network . . . . $75–$200

Ten minutes of background/underscore
on a prime time network series . . . . $5,000–$10,000

Theme song on local or cable television (depending
on number of stations airing the work and their size) . . . . $30–$600

Thirty seconds of background on cable television (depending
on number of stations airing the work and their size) . . . . $0.25–$200

Cue Sheets

Each piece of music included in a television show or film is referred to as a cue. In addition to other tracking methods, a *music cue sheet*, a log of all the music used in a production, enables the performing rights organizations to credit the composers and publishers of these works properly.

It's the responsibility of a TV show or film's production company to provide a cue sheet to the PROs. But it is always a good idea for a publisher (or songwriter serving as his or her own publisher) with songs included in a television show or film to request a copy of the cue sheet in order to verify its accuracy—and that it has indeed been submitted.

For each segment of music included in a television show or film, a cue sheet must provide the name of the film or television show, the air date, the episode name and number (for television series), the names and PRO affiliations of the composers and publishers, the percentages of ownership (if there are more than one writer of a given cue), the title and length of each cue, and an abbreviated description of the way the piece of music is used. A sample cue sheet is shown on the opposite page.

How ASCAP Monitors and Pays for Television Performances

In order to identify musical works performed on both broadcast and cable television, ASCAP surveys approximately thirty thousand hours of local television programming annually. It uses local TV guides, log sheets supplied by local television stations, cue sheets provided by television producers or broadcasters, and tapes of actual broadcasts.

MUSIC CUE SHEET

Episode 12: "Opie Learns to Fly"

Original Air Date: February 22, 2006

Cue #	CueTitle	Use*	†Timing	Composer/Affiliation	Publisher/Affiliation
1	Harpeth Hills Drive	MT	1:12	Jason Blume/BMI	Dreamer's Moon Music/BMI
2	I'm Just Big-Boned	BI	:23	Duncan Rice/ASCAP	British Blue Songs/ASCAP
3	Watch Out for Coin	BI	:17	Duncan Rice/ASCAP	British Blue Songs/ASCAP
4	Bite Me	VV	:49	Claire Ulanoff/ASCAP	After the Flood Music/ASCAP
5	Digging Iris	VI	:51	Neil Thurston/SESAC (50%) Virginia Cliff/BMI (50%)	Garden Boy Music/SESAC (50%) Green Run Songs/BMI (50%)
6	Getting Younger Every Day	BI	1:04	Janice Cook (BMI)	Empress Songs (BMI)
7	I Can Fly	ET	1:22	Jason Blume (BMI)	Dreamer's Moon Music (BMI)

*BI = Background Instrumental; VI = Visual Instrumental; VV = Visual Vocal; MT = Main Title; ET = End Title.
†In minutes and seconds.

ASCAP pays performance royalties for all music included in programs and promotional announcements on the major networks (ABC, CBS, and NBC), as well as on Fox and the WC. It also pays royalties for all music used in commercials that air on the major networks; for Fox, UPN, and the WC, royalties are paid for music included in commercials only if these are identified in a survey.

For local TV broadcasts, ASCAP pays royalties for all music included in syndicated programs and movies, while works included in commercials and other uses are paid based on whether they appear in surveys. (*Syndication* refers to the distribution or leasing of television programs by production companies to multiple stations and networks.)

Royalties are paid for all music used on public television (PBS) station programs, syndicated shows, and films airing on stations that pay ASCAP an annual licensing fee of $20,000 or more. Music from ASCAP's catalog that is performed in highly rated network and local TV series earn additional credits as *TV Premium* payments.

Weighting for Various Television Music Uses

Similar to its method of payment for radio performance, ASCAP payments to composers and publishers of television music are based on the number of credits their music amasses. The number of credits assigned to a given television performance is determined by factors including how the music is used (for instance, as a feature performance, theme song, background, or part of an advertisement); the length of the performance; whether the performance is on network, local, or cable television; and the time of day the music is broadcast.

Feature Performances

A feature performance, defined by ASCAP as music that is the principal focus of audience attention that lasts forty-five seconds or more, receives 100 percent credit from ASCAP's weighting program. This is the highest weighted television music performance; all other uses are assigned weights relative to this. For uses that are less than forty-five seconds in length, songs that have received at least twenty thousand television and/or radio performances may qualify for 100 percent crediting if they meet several additional criteria. Television feature performances of fifteen to forty-four seconds are credited at 50 percent, while those shorter than fifteen seconds are credited at a 25-percent rate.

Theme Songs

Television theme songs, compositions used to identify a television program or series or a television personality (such as the music played each time Jay Leno takes the stage), are credited at various rates:

- 35 percent for a local television series theme

- 50 percent for a prime time network series theme

- 50 percent for a theme song from a prime time network series subsequently syndicated to local or cable television stations

- 50 percent for a previously released hit song (defined as a song that has received a specified number of performances under particular circumstances) used as a TV series theme

- 35 percent for a network series theme aired other than during prime time

- 35 percent for a theme for a series made for local television syndication or cable TV

- 16 percent for each minute of a theme for a feature film, TV movie of the week, or miniseries.

If the same song is used as the opening and closing theme, it receives one full payment. If different songs serve this function, they are each credited as one full performance.

Background Music

Background music, sometimes referred to as *underscore*, is music intended to evoke a mood and emotion; it is not intended to be the audience's focus. With some exceptions, background music is credited by ASCAP as follows:

- 16 percent per minute for television series, movies of the week, TV specials, and feature films airing on television

- 50 percent for songs that have previously been hits or 16 percent per minute (whichever is greater).

Music in Television Commercials

Advertising jingles and preexisting songs used in television commercials are credited as follows:

- 3 percent for any composition written specifically for inclusion in a commercial

- 3 percent for any work written for purposes other than advertising, provided the work has received less than one hundred fifty feature radio and/or television performances in the previous five years

- 3 percent for any hit song with lyrics rewritten specifically for advertising purposes

- 5 percent for songs originally written for purposes other than advertising that received more than one hundred fifty feature radio and/or television performances in the previous five years

- 12 percent for a song that has previously been a hit (as defined by its previous performances) and used with its lyric unchanged.

How BMI Monitors and Pays for Television Performances

BMI identifies music used on television through information derived from music cue sheets and logs provided by licensees, as well as from outside research firms including the TV Data Corporation. For the ABC, CBS, and NBC television networks, BMI pays royalties for all performances aired during prime time, as well as for the vast majority of morning, afternoon, and weekend programming. Music included in *network originating programming* (local, network-affiliated stations broadcasting shows created by the networks) is paid for by the network instead of by the local TV station carrying the program. Performances of music on these networks are listed separately on writers' and publishers' royalty statements.

Performance royalties for music broadcast on smaller television networks, such as Fox, the WC, and PAX, are calculated from licensing fees paid by the individual local stations broadcasting the programs. The royalties BMI pays for music used in promotional announcements aired on the ABC, CBS, Fox, and NBC television networks is determined by the time of day of the performance and varies from quarter to quarter, depending upon the number of promotional announcements aired in a given quarter. At the time of this book's publication there were no payments for promotional announcements on any other medium.

Payment is made for feature performances of commercial jingles (works used to advertise products and/or services for sale on television and radio) on broadcast and cable networks, local television, and radio. Royalties are paid for background performances only in commercials airing on the ABC, CBS, Fox, and NBC television networks. In both cases, rates vary from quarter to quarter depending on the number of commercials aired in a given quarter.

Explanations of the various factors that contribute to determine the amount of royalty paid for a particular television performance follow:

Time of Day
The categories that follow are listed in descending order, according to the amount of royalty they generate for an equivalent performance. For network television: Prime time (6:00 P.M.–10:59 P.M.); late night (11:00 P.M.–1:59 A.M.); morning/daytime (6:00 A.M.–5:59 P.M.); overnight (2:00 A.M.–5:59 A.M.).

Length of Performance
A *feature performance*, defined by BMI as a performance with a duration of forty-five seconds or longer, receives the highest royalty rate. Shorter uses are prorated.

Number of Network Stations
The number of network stations that carry a particular program affects the royalty rate paid for every song performance in that program. Music included in shows that air on the most stations are paid at the highest rate.

BMI Royalty Payments for Music on ABC, CBS, and NBC
Royalties for music performed on ABC, CBS, and NBC are paid at the following rates, which are split between all of a composition's writers and publishers. These rates are multiplied by the number of local stations airing the show. As is the case with radio, the television performance royalty rates listed reflect minimum payments and may be considerably higher, depending on the amount of licensing revenue generated in any given quarter.

Prime time	Late Night	Overnight	Morning/Daytime
Full Feature Performances (forty-five seconds or more):			
$11.50	$9.00	$5.00	$6.00
Theme Song:			
$5.00	$3.32	$0.58	$1.00
Background:			
$1.10	$0.72	$0.52	$0.60
Logo:			
$0.30	$0.24	$0.22	$0.28

BMI Royalty Payments for Music on Local Television

BMI licenses more than eleven hundred local stations. These stations have the option of obtaining a blanket license (which most choose), covering all the works in BMI's catalog, or licensing music on a "per program" basis. Fees collected from stations that negotiate licenses "per program" are distributed only to those songwriters, composers, and publishers whose music is used on the programs.

For performances broadcast on local stations that opt for a blanket license, royalty rates (to be divided among a work's writers and publishers) are listed below and may be considerably higher, depending on the television licensing revenues received in a particular quarter. Note that for local television, while the rate is contingent on the time of day of airing, these rates are separated into only two categories (as opposed to the four categories previously listed for network broadcasts).

Daypart A (4:00 P.M.–12:59 A.M.)	Daypart B (all other times)
Full feature performances (forty-five seconds or more):	
$5.00	$1.50
Theme Song:	
$2.00	$1.00
Background:	
$0.76	$0.42
Logo:	
$0.18	$0.16

BMI Royalty Payments for PBS and Cable Television

BMI collects licensing fees from PBS stations and distributes these fees to songwriters, composers, and music publishers whose works are broadcast on PBS stations. The rates vary in different quarters, depending on factors such as the amount of the licensing fees collected, the way the music is used, the length of the musical cue, and the time of day during which it is aired.

Licensing fees are collected by BMI from pay cable networks, such as HBO, Cinemax, and Showtime, as well as from basic cable networks such as Lifetime, MTV, and the History Channel. Royalty rates vary each quarter and are determined by dividing the amount of license fees collected from each cable network (less an administrative fee) by the performances aired on that network.

How SESAC Monitors and Pays for Television Performances

To identify the majority of music contained in television performances, SESAC reviews listings of television shows, compiled by Tribune Media Services (TMS), coupled with music cue sheets provided by television production companies. SESAC tracks, and pays royalties for, 100 percent of its repertory's television broadcasts.

For performances in television commercials, SESAC conducts a complete survey of all networks and approximately thirty cable channels. For the purposes of royalty payment, SESAC defines a network as: ABC, CBS, NBC, Fox, and the WC. A sample survey is used for jingles in syndicated programs airing on local television. To track television performances of music videos on outlets such as MTV and VH-1, SESAC uses the same "fingerprint" technology it uses for monitoring radio performances.

Payments for television performances are based upon several factors:

- The number of stations broadcasting the program in which the performance occurs

- The way the music is used (for instance, as a feature performance, background music, program theme, commercial, jingle, etc.)

- The time of day when the performance occurs (for example, during prime time, overnight, early morning, etc.)

- The duration of the performance

- Where the performance occurs (network, local station, cable TV, etc.).

Feature Performances

SESAC defines a feature performance as "a visual vocal or instrumental work that is the principal focus of audience attention, or a background vocal work that is prominent, but not necessarily the sole focus of audience attention":

- Feature performances of thirty-one seconds or longer receive 100 percent credit

- Feature performances of sixteen to thirty seconds receive 50 percent credit

- Feature performances of one to fifteen seconds receive 25 percent credit.

Full payment is made for up to a maximum of twelve feature performances per one-hour program. Payments for feature performances exceeding twelve per one-hour program are prorated among participating affiliates.

Theme Performances

A theme performance is defined by SESAC as "a vocal or instrumental work used as the identifying song at the opening and/or closing of a program." Television themes are credited with 60 percent of the value of a full feature performance. Theme songs used within a program additionally, as anything other than opening or closing themes (for instance, a theme song used to segue to a commercial, or as a transition between scenes), are paid at the background rate.

Background Performances

Background performances are credited with 16.67 percent of the value of a full feature performance per minute of usage. If a song in a single program (or episode) is used as background music repeatedly, the duration of those uses are combined for that single program (or episode).

Jingle, Promo, and Logo Performances

For the purposes of royalty payment, SESAC defines a jingle as "an existing or original work performed on television as part of an advertisement for a product or service." A promo is "a work used to advertise or promote the airing of an upcoming television program." A logo is "a work used to identify a program's creator, producer, or distributor."

Jingle, promo, and logo performances receive credit equal to 3.5 percent of the applicable full feature performance value:

- Jingle and promo performances thirty seconds or longer receive 100 percent credit (3.5 percent of the credits allotted to a full-feature performance)

- Jingle and promo performances one to twenty-nine seconds receive 50 percent credit (1.75 percent of the credits allotted to a full-feature performance).

Time of Day

Television performance credits are determined by the time of day during which performances air. SESAC refers to this as the *day part factor*:

- Prime (Weekdays, 7:00 P.M.–10:59 P.M.;
  Weekends, 12:00 P.M.–10:59 P.M.) 100%

- Late Fringe (11:00 P.M.–1:59 A.M.) 75%

- Early Fringe (Weekdays, 4:00 P.M.–6:59 P.M.) 60%

- Day (Weekdays, 6:00 A.M.- 3:59 P.M.;
  Weekends, 6:00 A.M.–11:59 A.M.) 50%

- Overnight (2:00 A.M.–5:59 A.M.) 25%

Value Factor

All performances of SESAC's repertory are assigned a *value factor*, determined by the ratio of the total number of performance credits of SESAC works in a given quarter to the revenue available for distribution after operating costs are deducted. This is essentially its base rate. Since revenues and performances vary from quarter to quarter, the value factor varies depending on the source of the performance and the performance period in which it occurs.

Royalties for Live Performances

Performing rights organizations license thousands of restaurants, nightclubs, lounges, coffeehouses, cabarets, concert halls, and other venues where live music is performed. ASCAP and BMI estimate the number of performances hit songs are likely to receive in such venues, and royalty payments are made based on these estimates. However, this does not provide for payments to writers of songs that have not received significant performances in other mediums, such as radio and television.

ASCAP and BMI pay royalties for songs performed as part of the top two hundred grossing tours each year. The songs that generate these payments are determined by listings provided by tour promoters and artists' managers. Songwriters and publishers with songs being performed in major artists' tours would be wise to confirm that their PRO has been apprised of this fact. Failure to do so can result in loss of income.

SESAC is the only domestic PRO that pays royalties for all reported live performances. SESAC affiliates can claim payments for performances occurring in all licensed live music venues by completing the Live Performance Notification Form. Payments for live performances vary according to the licensing fee collected from the venue, the number of tickets sold, and whether a song is performed by an opening act or headlining act.

The ASCAPLUS Awards

The ASCAPLUS Awards Program (formerly known as "Special Awards") provides payments for songwriters of works that are performed outside of broadcast media, meaning songs that are not included in ASCAP's surveys of television, radio, and the Internet. Examples of songs that are not typically credited, despite receiving performances in licensed venues, include songs performed in cabarets, coffeehouses, and nightclubs.

Writers earning less than $25,000 annually in domestic performance royalties are eligible to apply for these awards. Those who tour extensively, performing their original compositions in cafés, hotel lounges, or supper clubs, as well as writers whose songs are performed by other artists in these types of venues, may be awarded several hundred dollars or more each year. The amount of each award is based on factors including the number of performances and the licensing fees received from the venues in which the performances occur.

To be considered for an ASCAPLUS Award, ASCAP members complete an application by June 1st each year, including a listing of the venues in which their material has been performed during the previous year, as well as a list of the titles performed. For additional guidelines, and to request an ASCAPLUS Award application, visit ASCAP's Web site.

Internet Royalties

When this book was written, transmissions over the Internet accounted for a mind-boggling five billion or more performances annually—and this number was growing exponentially. Using digital audio recognition technologies, such as BDS, Mediaguide, and BlueArrow, as well as information obtained directly from licensees, the PROs analyze millions of hours of Internet airplay data. Webcasts (concerts and performances broadcast over the Internet), music embedded in Web sites (such as "Flash" introductions), performances of videos broadcast over the Internet, and songs broadcast by streaming services are among the performances for which licenses are issued and performance royalties are paid.

Royalty payments for Internet performances vary widely and may be less than one cent for each performance. But songs that are major hits can receive hundreds of thousands of Internet performances, adding up to substantial income. Each of the U.S. performing rights organizations license satellite radio, ringtone providers, and additional technologies that allow for the public performance of music in new media. As these technologies continue to evolve they will likely lead to additional sources of revenue for songwriters and music publishers.

Why, How, and When to Join a Performing Rights Organization

The primary reason to join a performing rights society is to facilitate the collection of performance royalties. In the absence of PROs, countless performances would have to be identified and monitored, not only throughout the U.S., but in every country that provides for payment of performance royalties throughout the world. In addition, a licensing fee would have to be negotiated and agreed upon by each user of music and the music's copyright owner. A performing rights license would have to be drafted and signed, and the money would have to be collected. Affiliating with a PRO takes care of all of these functions for songwriters and music publishers whose compositions are being publicly performed.

In addition to collecting and distributing performance royalties, ASCAP, BMI, and SESAC offer excellent workshops to help songwriters, television and film composers, and writers for musical theater hone their craft, network with other writers and music industry professionals, and advance their careers. In some instances, these classes are available only to members of the respective societies. An additional benefit of joining a PRO is access to representatives who meet with members and prospective members to offer career guidance.

To be eligible for ASCAP or BMI membership, a songwriter must meet one or more of the criteria listed below. They must have written or cowritten one or more songs or instrumental musical works that have been, or are about to be:

- Commercially recorded and released (for example, included on an artist's CD)

- Performed publicly in any licensable venue (for example, a nightclub or concert hall)

- Included in a film, television show, or radio broadcast

- Available to be heard on the Internet (for example, posted on a Web site)

- Published and available for sale or rental.

The U.S. performing rights societies collect and distribute royalties only on behalf of songwriters, composers, and publishers. They do not collect royalties for record labels or recording artists. If artists are writer/artists, performing their own compositions, the PROs collect and distribute their songwriting performance royalties as they do for any songwriter.

When a songwriter or a music publisher joins a PRO, they sign a binding legal contract. ASCAP's contracts are not negotiated; each member signs the same agreement, agreeing to the same terms. Therefore, there is no need to have an attorney review this document. This is also typically the case with BMI and SESAC; however, in some exceptional instances the provisions of their agreements are negotiated.

There is no fee for writers to join any of the U.S. PROs and no annual dues. ASCAP publishers pay annual dues of $50. BMI-affiliated corporate publishers pay a onetime fee of $250, while individuals applying for membership as publishers are subject to a onetime fee of $150. There are no fees for publishers to affiliate with SESAC.

Membership applications can be downloaded from the ASCAP and BMI Web sites, www.ASCAP.com and www.BMI.com. SESAC determines membership eligibility on a case-by-case basis. Those interested in affiliating with SESAC are advised to contact a membership representative.

Resigning from a PRO

The PROs' writer membership agreements are renewed automatically at the end of each term, meaning that members join for perpetuity, but with specified windows during which they have the opportunity to resign. ASCAP's membership agreements last for a period of one year; six to nine months prior to the agreement's expiration, members who wish to resign are required to complete a Writer Resignation Notification Form. BMI's writers may resign by notifying the organization in writing, three months prior to the end of their two-year term; the same applies for SESAC; however, SESAC's affiliation agreement extends for three years.

When a member resigns from one of the performing rights organizations, he or she has the right to remove his or her songs from its catalog. All of the PROs have clauses within their agreements that specify circumstances and criteria that must be met prior to songs being taken back; SESAC imposes the least of these constraints.

Registering Works

ASCAP, BMI, and SESAC require the registration of all their members' songs that are receiving public performances. A song may be registered by its writer or publisher by completing a simple form, either online or by mailing it to the PRO. There is no fee for members to register their songs, and failure to do so results in lost royalties, so it's a good idea to register all songs that have any possibility of receiving airplay or public performance.

As previously stated, for songs included on television shows, in films, or in other audiovisual media, production companies or broadcasters are required to submit a cue sheet. It is not necessary for songwriters and music publishers to register short musical cues contained in television shows and films, provided these cues are listed on a cue sheet. It is advisable to register any actual songs and musical compositions that might possibly be broadcast on television or radio, or performed in any other licensed medium.

How to Decide Which PRO Is Right for You

Without the assistance of a crystal ball it is impossible to predict which of the three U.S. performing rights organizations will pay the most royalties over the course of a given writer's career. Each PRO can point to instances in which songs cowritten by a member of their organization and a writer affiliated with one of the other PROs earned more money for their own affiliated writer.

Indeed, in some instances, a PRO will outpay its competitors for a particular song. But on average, despite the disparate ways in which they monitor performances and calculate royalties, ASCAP, BMI, and SESAC tend to pay about equally in order to remain competitive. Since songwriters have the option of resigning from one PRO and joining a different one, if one society were clearly the best for everyone, all songwriters and publishers would join that organization and the others would cease to operate.

Songwriters who meet membership eligibility requirements should meet with a representative from each PRO prior to deciding which one to join. Since in most situations, it is impossible to predict accurately which PRO will pay the most over the long term, the decision of where to affiliate might best be made by assessing factors such as which PRO's systems of monitoring and calculating royalties you prefer; which membership representative is the most enthusiastic about your work—and is willing to set up meetings with publishers and others who might further your career; and which organization offers beneficial workshops.

Foreign Performing Rights Organizations

More than sixty countries throughout the world have performing rights organizations that serve the same functions as ASCAP, BMI, and SESAC. In many of these countries, the PRO serves a dual purpose, also collecting mechanical royalties. The U.S. is one of only a few countries with more than one PRO.

International foreign performing rights societies include:

Australia—APRA (Australian Performing Rights Association Ltd.)

Canada—CAPAC (Composers, Authors, and Publishers Association of Canada Ltd.)

Germany—GEMA (Gesellschaft fur musikalische Auffuhrungs und mechanische Vervielfaltigungsrechte)

England—PRS (Performing Rights Society Ltd.)

Japan—JASRAC (Japanese Society of Rights of Authors and Composers).

When music from ASCAP, BMI, and SESAC's catalogs is performed outside the U.S., performance royalties are collected by the PRO located in the country where the performance takes place. The three U.S. performing rights societies have reciprocal agreements with their international counterparts. As a result of these agreements, income from performances outside the U.S. is forwarded to ASCAP, BMI, and SESAC, which distribute it to their writer and publisher members. Foreign performance royalties account for a significant amount of the money distributed by the U.S. PROs.

CHAPTER ELEVEN

Writing and Marketing Music for Film and Television

In recent years, the music industry has seen decreased sales of singles and albums as a result of illegal downloading and other factors, but there are more films being produced and, with the advent of cable and satellite television, more television stations broadcasting more hours of programming than ever. Music makes a vital contribution to films and television shows, evoking emotions as well as a sense of time and place to scenes. Virtually every film and television show includes music, providing an exceptional outlet and source of revenue for songwriters and composers.

By marketing their existing songs and creating new ones specifically targeted to film and television projects, songwriters can expose their works to enormous audiences. Additionally, compositions that are not geared to mainstream radio (such as instrumental works, electronica, world, and ethnic music, and songs that seem to be from another era) may be perfectly suited for a particular scene in a film or television show. In addition to the satisfaction derived from hearing their works on television or in films, by placing songs and instrumental compositions in these media, writers and publishers earn substantial licensing fees and royalties (explained later in this chapter).

Pitching Music for Film and Television

Submitting songs and music for television and film productions is similar to pitching songs to publishers and record label executives—but there are some differences. For one thing, as noted in Chapter 5, it is never appropriate to describe your songs when pitching to publishers and A&R executives, for instance, stating in a cover letter, "I've enclosed two positive, mid-tempo rock songs" or "a female hip-hop song." But when sending songs to a *music supervisor*, the individual in charge of selecting music for possible inclusion in a film or television production, it is not only appropriate, but advisable to categorize your songs according to style and tempo. For instance, you might send several CDs, one labeled "Up-Tempo Pop with Male Vocals," another containing "Latin Instrumentals," a third, "Country Ballads," and another "Alternative Rock." A succinct description of the musical style helps music supervisors categorize and locate the kinds of songs they're seeking for a given project.

When submitting instrumental compositions it's a good idea to submit several versions of the same piece, each edited to a different length (15 seconds, 30 seconds, and 60 seconds). This allows music supervisors to consider the same composition for various placements.

When pitching songs for possible inclusion in films and television it's crucial that the rights to these songs be readily available. This means that if you have collaborators, it's important to know their publishing information—and who controls the rights to grant synchronization licenses on their behalf. Some major publishers are notorious for taking weeks (or longer) to respond to licensing requests, unless these are for top-paying, high-prestige projects. If a music supervisor needs material that can be cleared quickly and with minimal hassles (as is typically the case for television licensing), there's no point in interesting him or her in your work if an honest assurance of an expedited clearance cannot be provided.

Just as when pitching material to publishers and A&R representatives, it's important to include all pertinent information, such as the writer's name, music publisher(s), contact information, and PRO affiliation. It is not appropriate to include extraneous details such as the name of the studio, engineer, and musicians, or biographical information about yourself, unless you have major credits in the music industry.

Unlike publishers, who look for potential hits to be pitched for various projects, at any given moment it's likely that a music supervisor is looking for music to fit one particular film or television show. Therefore, when pitching songs it's important to do your homework. In some instances you may read a description of a film in a trade newspaper or magazine (such as *The Hollywood Reporter* or *Variety*) and be able to deduce the kinds of music that would likely be appropriate for the film. A film set in Harlem in the 1940s may need sultry jazz songs to evoke the era; sending rock or country songs for this project is a waste of your time—and the music supervisor's.

Music for film and television is rarely re-recorded to transform a demo to a master quality recording. If your music is selected, in most instances the recording you send is exactly what will be used in the film or television show. Therefore, pitching for film and television shows almost always requires finished master recordings. While these recordings may have been produced in a home studio, the vocals, instrumental performances, and overall sonic quality must meet high industry standards in order to be competitive. The only exception to this is song demos submitted for consideration as an opening credit or end title. In these instances, when the right song is found, a master recording may be produced.

Lists of music supervisors and their contact information can be found in *The Music Business Registry: Film & Television Music Guide* (www.musicregistry.com) and *The Hollywood Reporter's Blu-Book Production Directory* (www.hollywoodreporter.com). *The Hollywood Reporter* also includes beneficial information regarding film and television music in its *Film & TV Music Special Issue*, published four times a year (January, April, August, and November). Additionally, by regularly reading the television and film industry's trade publications you can glean valuable information such as descriptions of films that are entering production.

When submitting songs to music supervisors, remember that in addition to placing music in a particular film or on a particular television show, a primarily goal is the establishment of long-term business relationships. In order to become someone music supervisors go to when they need music, present yourself professionally, follow up once (several weeks after submitting your material) but don't be a pest, and present quality material that matches the descriptions of the songs they seek.

Indienotes.com (www.indienotes.com) is a company that researches and compiles up-to-date listings of films and television shows that are seeking music. It provides subscribers with online pitch sheets, leads sent via e-mail describing the type of music being sought, and contact information for the music supervisors seeking it.

Indienotes.com sells three separate pitch sheets, each covering different styles of music. The subscription price at the time of this writing is $45.00 per quarter for listings of films and television shows seeking music in each of the following three categories:

- Country / folk / inspirational / gospel / holiday / big band / jazz / blues / classical / underscore

- Hip-hop / R&B / reggae / urban / dance / electronica / Latin / techno

- Pop / rock / adult contemporary / alternative / horror / metal-rock / rave / surf.

CueSheet (www.cuesheet.net) is a tip sheet that focuses exclusively on television, film, and other media projects requiring soundtrack music, composers, and songs. The publication, available only to professional subscribers, is delivered by e-mail twice a month. Its listings describe the music requirements of upcoming productions seeking songs and/or instrumental compositions, as well as information about the cast, director, producer, and, in some instances, a plot synopsis. Contact information and addresses are provided.

The majority of *CueSheet*'s listings are for film or television productions based in the U.S., Canada, and the United Kingdom. Companies having sought music through listings in *CueSheet* include the BBC, Granada TV, Imagine Entertainment, Fox 2000, Fox Searchlight, Nickelodeon, Paramount, TouchStone, and Universal Pictures, as well as numerous independent music supervisors. A three-month subscription (six issues) costs $234.00; one year (twenty-two issues) costs $773.00. A free sample issue can be ordered at *CueSheet*'s Web site.

Taxi (www.taxi.com), as discussed in Chapter 5, provides its members with listings of outlets for music for television and film projects. This organization has had great success, connecting countless songwriters with music supervisors and music libraries, resulting in Taxi members placing their music on networks including ABC, NBC, CBS, Fox, MTV, HBO, CNN, PBS, ESPN, Showtime, Nickelodeon, Discovery, and more.

In addition to its biweekly listings, Taxi offers *Taxi Dispatch*, an additional service geared exclusively for songwriters and composers who hope to have their songs included in television and film projects. For an additional fee of $149.00 a year, members who upgrade their membership are e-mailed requests from television and film supervisors who are urgently seeking material. Listings are e-mailed to members within an hour of receipt and those wishing to submit music must do so within twenty-four to forty-eight hours, either online or by overnight mail or courier. As with regular Taxi submissions, there is a $5.00 fee for each song or piece of music sent for consideration. *Dispatch* submissions do not receive critiques.

BMI, in conjunction with the Sundance Institute, presents the Annual Sundance Institute Composers Lab, held in Sundance, Utah. Composers chosen to participate in the two-week event attend workshops under the guidance of leading film composers and film music professionals. BMI also awards the BMI/Jerry Goldsmith Film Scoring Scholarship to partially underwrite a recipient's participation in the University of California, Los Angeles Extension Film and Television Scoring program. For additional information and submission guidelines, visit www.bmi.com. The U.C.L.A. program, designed to help composers develop the skills and contacts needed to pursue a successful career in film and/or television scoring, is among the top programs of its kind.

ASCAP presents a workshop at New York University for composers and songwriters who wish to enter the field of film and TV. High-profile film composers teach participants the mechanics of timing, and the art of composing music intended to accompany visual images. Students have the opportunity to compose, orchestrate, conduct, and record a musical work with a group of New York's top musicians. Those applying should have music composition and orchestration experience at the undergraduate level. Additional registration information can be found at www.ascap.com.

Production Music Libraries

Production music libraries, also referred to as *music libraries*, are companies that acquire songs and musical compositions from composers and, for a fee, issue synchronization licenses for these works, primarily to film and television production companies. Production music libraries also provide songs and music for inclusion in video games, advertising, audiovisual presentations, and virtually any other source that uses music.

These companies maintain enormous catalogs of music, which their clients may review either online or by previewing CDs. By providing preexisting music for their customers' use, they offer a low-budget alternative to hiring a composer. Library tracks are licensed in a variety of different ways. Library music customers may purchase the rights to use one particular track, all of the music included on one or more of a library's CDs, or a blanket license, the right to unlimited use of some or all of the music in a company's catalog, for a specified period of time.

With the top music libraries such as FirstCom and KPM offering tens of thousands of musical compositions to their customers, there is an enormous ongoing need to acquire new music. A few music production services hire *in-house composers*, individuals who compose music and produce recordings on a full-time basis, usually on a work-for-hire basis. But most music libraries rely on submissions from independent songwriters, composers, and recording artists.

Music represented by production music libraries is referred to as *library music* or *library tracks,* and may include vocal and instrumental music in virtually every imaginable musical style. While music publishers typically seek only the kinds of songs they can place with current recording artists, production music libraries supply film and television clients, as well as others whose musical needs may run the gamut from African tribal rhythms to Gregorian chants, punk rock, new age instrumentals, old-time country, rap, Delta blues, arrangements of classical works, surf music, a variety of ethnic music, polka songs, and every style in-between.

The majority of library music is recorded by instrumentalists who play most of the instruments themselves (in many cases programming all or most of the sounds using synthesizers) in home recording studios. From a financial standpoint, it's rarely feasible for songwriters and composers to pay to rent recording studios and hire musicians to record library tracks.

Analogous to when a song is signed to a music publisher, composers typically earn nothing when they place music with production libraries—unless their works are selected for use. Licensing fees tend to be low, most often $25 to $1,000 per track, with the majority of uses earning fees on the low side of the range. However, when library music is broadcast on television or radio, it earns the same performance royalties as would any other composition.

As an inducement to use their music, some music libraries offer *royalty-free music,* the use of their music for free—provided it is used in televised network broadcasts, and cue sheets are filed with the applicable PROs. Although companies offering royalty-free compositions forego up-front licensing fees, they (and the composers whose material they represent) may earn significant performance royalties on the back end after their works air. As explained later in this chapter, musical compositions included in films do not earn performance royalties when they are screened in the U.S. Therefore, production libraries do not offer music for inclusion in films on a royalty-free basis.

Composers who earn significant income from library music placements are typically those who are the most prolific, submitting hundreds of compositions for consideration—and those who are lucky enough to have their works air on television. In some instances, music production libraries provide a financial advance to a composer, but this is usually only the case with composers who have already attained a level of credibility and success. Many artists who record and distribute their own CDs find additional outlets for their work in television shows and films by placing it with music libraries.

Typically, production libraries acquire the publishing rights to the works they represent, leaving the writer with the writer's share—50 percent of any income generated. Some music libraries do not request the publishing rights when they acquire a song or musical composition, simply retaining 50 percent of any income the works might earn—but leaving ownership with the composer. Works that are already published are not appropriate for placement with music production libraries.

An agreement, expressing the terms agreed upon, is signed by a composer when assigning one or more musical compositions to a music production company. When entering into a library music agreement, a composer is typically required to affirm that he or she is the copyright owner of both the musical composition and the master recording. In the event that a musical work is the result of collaboration, and a cowriter has a contractual right to approve synchronization or other types of licensing, this composition is not appropriate for library music licensing. In addition, library music must be available for licensing throughout the world without restrictions.

Music production libraries have varying submission policies. Some prefer to receive music on CDs, others may request a link to a writer's Web site so that they can audition his or her work, while still others may ask for MP3s. Prior to sending material, always contact the company you're targeting to learn the name of the individual to whose attention your music should be addressed, as well as any specific requirements it may have. Many companies outline their submission procedures on their Web sites.

Similar to submissions to music supervisors, when sending instrumental compositions for consideration by music libraries it's advisable to send several versions of the same composition, edited to various lengths. Composers can increase their chances for success by including alternate mixes of the same composition; for instance, a version with the lead instrument featured lower in the mix might be better suited for a scene for which a director does not want the music to distract the viewers from focusing on the dialogue.

The Music Business Registry: Film & Television Music Guide is an excellent resource, providing contact information for more than one hundred fifty production music libraries, as well as movie studios; network and independent television production companies' music departments; music supervisors, managers, and agents who represent film and television composers; companies specializing in the placement of music in film and television; and much more.

Legal Considerations When Placing Demos in Film and on TV

A sticky issue arises when songwriters place their demos in films or television shows. Many songwriters assume that because they pay to produce their demos, they own the master rights to these recordings. But this is not necessarily the case.

As you've previously learned, when music is selected for inclusion in a television or film project, the recording submitted is almost always the version used (as opposed to a new, re-recorded version). Technology has made it possible for many songwriters to produce relatively inexpensive recordings that rival high-priced, professional studio productions. The difference between a demo and a master recording can sometimes be defined only by usage—not by sonic quality. Therefore, songwriters may be able to place recordings that were initially intended as demos into television shows and films. But do they have the legal and ethical right to do so?

Kelly Clarkson, Sheryl Crow, Faith Hill, Gretchen Wilson, Pink, and Garth Brooks are among the many successful recording artists who supplemented their income by singing demos for songwriters while awaiting their big break. But does a songwriter, who may have paid one of these artists $75 to sing a demo, have the right to manufacture and sell the demo as a commercial recording when the artist becomes famous? Of course not. An individual who added his own voice to a Trisha Yearwood demo and attempted to market it as a duet was quickly slapped with a lawsuit.

When a singer or musician is hired to perform on a demo, unless otherwise stated the implied understanding is that the resulting recording is to be used for demonstration purposes only. Therefore, in the absence of an agreement such as the one that follows, it is neither legal nor ethical to market recordings containing these performances as "masters" for inclusion in film or television projects.

Songwriters and music publishers who anticipate pitching their demos for possible use in television and film productions can circumvent this problem by requesting the demo musicians and vocalists they hire to sign an agreement waiving their rights to ownership and/or any additional income generated by licensing the demo. This document, essentially a work for hire agreement, when signed by a musician or vocalist, grants the songwriter and/or publisher the right to license demo recordings featuring their performances for inclusion in television, films, and for placement by a production library.

Some publishers who pitch material for television and film projects refuse to represent songs unless all musicians and vocalists performing on the demos have signed waivers establishing their performance as a work for hire. It's advisable to present musicians and vocalists with an agreement (such as the one that's shown on the next page) prior to the date of the recording session so they have an opportunity to read it carefully and decide whether it is something they are willing to sign. If a musician or singer is unwilling to enter into such an agreement, the songwriter has the option of not employing this musician—or agreeing to not pitch demos that feature this performer for inclusion in films, television shows, and other projects that require a master use license.

While a signed waiver, such as the one that follows, affords songwriters and music publishers the legal right to exploit their demo recordings for use in television and film, it fails to address an ethical issue. In the event that a short excerpt of a musical composition contained in a demo is included in a film or television show, the master use licensing fee and performance royalties generated may amount to a few hundred dollars or less. This may not even cover the cost of producing the demo recording. In this instance, it would not be financially feasible for a songwriter or publisher to compensate the musicians and vocalists who contributed their performances to the recording.

If a recording initially intended as a demo generates significant income (for example, $5,000 or more from master use licensing fees and performance royalties), a case can be made that the musicians and vocalists deserve to be compensated

DREAMER'S MOON MUSIC

9 Music Square South, PMB 352, Nashville, TN 37203 • (615) 665-2381
JBSongdoc1@aol.com

Musician/Vocalist Waiver

This letter is to confirm that your work on any demonstration recordings for ___Jason Blume or Dreamer's Moon Music___ ("Employer") is deemed as a work for hire as defined in Section 101 of the U.S. Copyright Act. Accordingly, you hereby irrevocably grant to Employer, its successors, and assigns, all rights and proceeds of services and performances for any and all copyright terms throughout the world. Employer shall have the sole and exclusive right to copyright the sound recording under Employer's name as the sole artist and author thereof. These recordings will be manufactured, advertised, sold, or distributed only as demonstration recordings and not for sale to the public as commercial records.

Notwithstanding the above, it is agreed that we and our affiliates may license these recordings for television, films, and production music library purposes. The payment you receive for each of these recordings is the full and complete payment. No additional sums will be due to you as a result of the exploitation of these recordings.

Accepted and Agreed: Date:

_____   _____

Sample musician/vocalist waiver.

for their contribution—despite having signed a waiver. Some songwriters and publishers choose not to do so, arguing that the money they earn by placing their demos in films and television shows helps balance their operating costs, because the majority of their recordings never generate income.

For other songwriters and publishers, sending musicians and vocalists an unexpected bonus payment, acknowledging that their creative contributions are valued and rewarded, feels like the right thing to do. Performers who feel appreciated and well-compensated may add that extra spark that leads to even greater successes when they are hired in the future.

Note that while an argument can be made for musicians and vocalists being entitled to share in a portion of master use licensing fees generated by recordings that embody their work, synchronization licensing fees (as discussed later in this chapter) are paid for the use of the underlying composition—not for the use of any specific recording, and as such belong solely to the copyright owners of the song or musical work.

Most song publishing agreements grant ownership of demo recordings to the publisher. Writers may be able to have their attorneys negotiate co-ownership of these recordings, thereby generating additional income in the event their demos are placed in television shows or films, generating master use licensing fees.

As explained in Chapter 7, if demo musicians and singers are members of the Nashville chapters of their respective unions (AFM and AFTRA), demo producers are required to upgrade payments to master scale in the event that recordings initially produced as demos are used as master recordings. This is applicable only for demos produced in Nashville, as there is no differentiation between demo and master scale payments for union members affiliated outside of Nashville.

In actuality, many songwriters and publishers place their demos in film and television projects without securing permission from those who perform on the recordings. The musicians and vocalists whose performances are embodied on these recordings rarely become aware that their performances are being licensed. But this doesn't make it legal—or the right thing to do.

Synchronization Licenses

The document a music publisher (or a songwriter acting as his or her own publisher) signs, granting permission for a song or musical composition to be "synchronized" to accompany visual images, is a *synchronization license* (typically referred to as a *sync license*). This is used to authorize the inclusion of a song or instrumental music as part of the soundtrack of a film, television show, video, or television commercial.

The right to use music in a film, television show, or other visual media is referred to as *broad rights*, and is protected by U.S. Copyright law. As you learned in Chapter 9, anyone has the right to record and release a song after its first commercial audio release, provided the user obtains a mechanical license and pays the statutory rate. There is no analogous statute regarding the inclusion of music in motion pictures and television. To include songs or music in a film or television show legally, a production company must negotiate and reach an agreement with the copyright owner (the song's publisher).

As discussed in Chapter 1, a synchronization license covers the use of a song—but not the right to use any preexisting recording of the song, such as a particular artist's version. In the event that a film or television production company, or an advertising firm, wants to include an existing recording of a song in its production, a master use license must be negotiated with the owner of the sound recording. For instance, in order to include Coldplay's "Speed of Light" in a television show, the show's producer must obtain a license from the song's copyright owner (the publisher) authorizing the use of the song itself, as well as a master use license from the copyright owner of Coldplay's recording of the song (the record label) for the use of the band's recording.

Each aspect of copyright ownership (ownership of a song itself and ownership of a particular sound recording) is sometimes referred to as a *side*. If the same individual or company owns both sides, the synchronization and master use licenses are typically combined in what is called an *all-in license*.

In the event that a music publisher grants permission for the use of a song, but no agreement is reached with the record label to authorize the use of a specific master recording of the song, in some instances, a new recording, known as a *sound-alike*, is produced. But if the publisher refuses to grant permission, no version of the song may be used.

Music Supervisors and Music Clearance

A music supervisor's job is to compile songs he or she believes would best contribute to a production and then submit them to the director and/or producer for final approval. But finding the perfect song is of no benefit if an agreement to license the song for inclusion in the project cannot be reached.

The process of negotiating and securing synchronization licenses for music to be used in film and television productions is typically referred to as *music clearance*. Television networks, film studios, and TV production companies typically hire individuals or companies who specialize in this. In many instances, the ease with which a piece of music can be cleared is a deciding factor for which songs are included in a film or show.

When a song being considered for inclusion in a film or television show has multiple songwriters and publishers, it's important for the person in charge of music clearance to ascertain which publisher has the right to grant a synchronization license. Depending on what has been agreed upon, one publisher may have the right to issue a synchronization license on behalf of all of a given song's publishers, making the clearance process relatively simple. But this is not typically the case.

When multiple publishers each control a share of the copyright, and must all agree upon the terms and fees of a sync license, the negotiation process may become too complicated and lengthy to accommodate a production's needs. A solution is to designate one as the administrating publisher with regard to licensing for film and television.

Major publishing companies will rarely agree to give up control over such important and potentially lucrative uses of their copyrights. But songwriters interested in placing songs in television shows and films, and who act as their own publishers, might establish written agreements with collaborators, designating one of them as the company in charge of issuing sync licenses.

Synchronization Fees

The fee paid by a film or television production company for the right to include a song or an instrumental composition in its production is known as a *synchronization fee* or *sync fee*. Sync fees vary tremendously and are negotiated on a case-by-case basis. A copyright owner has the right to demand any price it chooses for the use of its works in advertising, television, or film; a film, television show, or commercial's producer can either pay the price—or choose another piece of music.

Sync licensing fees are based on a production's music budget and a variety of additional factors. Among the most important of these is the manner in which the music is to be used. Songs used as *theme songs* (music that is identified with a show or film and played at its beginning or during its opening credits, such as "Thank You for Being a Friend" on *The Golden Girls*) tend to command the highest fees. Short snippets of instrumental background music generally earn the lowest sync fees.

The synchronization fee a song earns is also determined by the *duration* (the length of the song used), with a minute-long excerpt obviously being worth more than a ten-second snippet. The *term* of the agreement (as mentioned earlier, the length of time it will be in force) also affects the price of the sync license. A license granting rights for the life of the copyright (as is requested in most cases) garners a higher sync fee than one that expires after five or ten years.

The right to distribute a film or television show in various media is sometimes referred to as the *scope* of the agreement and is an additional factor to be considered when negotiating a sync fee. A publisher will likely be able to collect higher fees by granting rights for a wide variety of distribution methods, such as video, DVD, Internet broadcast, iPod, cell phone, pay-per-view, and laser disc, than if it licenses only the rights to screen a film in theaters.

Most synchronization licenses include a clause that allows for distribution and sale in any and all forms of media now known, as well as those that may be invented in the future. This protects the production company from having to secure an additional license each time a new technology is developed.

The *territory* covered by the license—the countries in which it is applicable—is another factor assessed when determining a synchronization licensing fee. Most licensees require worldwide rights, and a considerably higher price is typically paid for this than when a license covers only one specified territory, such as North America.

Whether a song is slated to be included in a soundtrack album is also a factor in determining a sync licensing fee. Some publishers may grant a synchronization license at a reduced fee if the license stipulates that a song will be included on a motion picture or television show's soundtrack album, such as *Music from and Inspired by Desperate Housewives*. The potential to earn mechanical royalties and additional performance royalties (in the event the song is released as a single) are a huge incentive for a publisher to strike a deal. Songs that have attained great success after their initial inclusion in a film include *Titanic*'s "My Heart Will Go On," *Armageddon*'s "I Don't Want to Miss a Thing," *8 Mile*'s "Lose Yourself," and the theme from *The Godfather*.

In the case of films produced specifically for release on DVD (as opposed to those for theatrical distribution), sync fees are typically lower and are influenced by the amount of product manufactured. Whether a specific song is deemed vital to a scene is a major factor in determining its value when a sync license is negotiated.

Let's look at a situation where a song is sought to help evoke the sense of a scene in a film being set in 1965. If a music clearance specialist is unable to persuade a publisher to agree on a price and other terms to procure the rights to a song by the Beach Boys, he or she might be able instead to substitute a song recorded by Jan and Dean, The Supremes, Leslie Gore, or The Temptations, if these are available for a lower price. These alternatives may work equally as well in a particular scene without sacrificing the director's intent. But if a character in the film specifically refers to a particular song, for example, The Beach Boys' "Help Me, Rhonda," the director may be adamant about procuring the rights for this specific song. In this instance, the song's publisher will be in a strong negotiating position to demand a price at the highest end of the range.

A final factor in determining the price of a synchronization fee is the *stature* of the copyright; songs that have been hits command significantly higher licensing fees than unknown compositions—and songs such as "Proud Mary," "Satisfaction," and "Let it Be," which have reached legendary status, earn even higher amounts.

Most favored nations (*MFN*), sometimes referred to as *favored nations*, refers to situations in which a licensee (for instance, the producer of a television show, simulcast concert performance, or DVD) specifies that all licensors are to be subject to the same terms. As it applies to synchronization licensing, this means that the licensing of all music included in a particular project (such as a pay-per-view concert performance) will be the same; all publishers are required to agree to the same sync licensing fee and agreement terms, such as the territory covered, the duration of the agreement, and formats for distribution (for instance, pay-per-view, Internet download, or DVD).

In instances in which different music publishers negotiate varying fees and/or contractual terms for inclusion of their music in a particular project, those publishers who include a most favored nations clause in their licensing agreement are assured that no other publisher will be paid more or receive more beneficial terms. When a most favored nations clause is in effect, each songwriter and music publisher is compensated equally—whether the song covered by the agreement was written by Madonna, Bono, or a songwriter who has never before had a song recorded.

Synchronization Fees for Major Studio Films

As in any negotiation, the price agreed upon will be a function of how strongly the product (in this case, a particular piece of music) is desired—and the user's ability to pay for it. A Hollywood blockbuster with a $100 million dollar budget will likely have a much higher budget for music than will a film produced for a fraction of this amount. The licensing fee ranges presented below are extremely wide; the amount paid to use a particular piece of music will be based on the factors discussed in Chapter 10:

- *Main Title.* Fees range from $25,000 to $500,000. In exceptional instances, current hit songs and songs written and/or performed by superstar artists have generated more than $1 million.

- *Background Instrumental.* This typically is written by an individual hired as a film's composer and is licensed as part of an overall music agreement. In the event that an outside piece of music is used for this purpose, the fees vary too widely to estimate accurately, and may be as low as $300. (Composers who write the entire score for a major studio film can earn from $50,000 to more than $1 million, depending on their stature and the film's budget.)

- *Background Vocal.* Fees depend largely on the stature and usage of the song, as well as the film's budget. Well-known songs can command $15,000 to $60,000.

- *Visual Vocal.* Fees fall in the $20,000 to $60,000 range.

- *End Credit.* These fees range from $25,000 to $100,000. Again, current hit songs and songs written and/or performed by top artists can earn substantially higher amounts.

Music used in independent films is licensed at considerably lower rates contingent on the budgetary limitations of the production. Some independent films are produced on a shoestring and have no money budgeted for music while others, with budgets of several million dollars or more, may offer significant payments to license music.

Songwriters and publishers sometimes license their works to low-budget, independent films for as little as $50 or $100. Others allow their music to be used in exchange for a film credit and wide audience exposure—and in the hopes that the film will generate performance royalties in the event that it airs on television.

In addition to the money earned from synchronization licensing, songs in films earn performance royalties when the films are shown in most countries outside the U.S. These royalties vary widely, depending on the music's usage and the amount of revenue the film garners outside the U.S. Some songs included in major films have earned as little as $300 in performance royalties for foreign screenings, while songs used as opening or closing themes in Hollywood blockbusters have generated more than $500,000 in these payments.

Writers' royalties for performances in films screened outside the U.S. are collected by performing rights societies in foreign territories and forwarded to the U.S. PROs, which distribute them to their writers. In most cases, publishers' shares of these royalties are collected by the publisher's agent or subpublisher in each territory. Performance royalties are not earned when films play in movie theaters in the U.S.

When licensing music for minimal fees, it's advisable to request a clause be included in the synchronization license specifying that the music publisher is to be paid additional money in the event the film is acquired and released by a major distributor, or distributed via DVD, laser disc, or some other future technology.

Synchronization Fees for Television Shows

Synchronization licensing fees paid for the inclusion of music in television shows can provide a significant source of income for songwriters and publishers, as there are hundreds of channels broadcasting thousands of hours of programming—and they virtually all include music. But the sync licensing fees paid for television tend to be considerably lower than the amounts paid for feature films. This is primarily because television shows typically have much lower budgets than do major motion pictures. While the music budget for a major Hollywood film may range from $200,000 to more than $1 million, network television shows are more likely to allot $10,000 to $15,000 for each thirty minutes of programming.

Television themes (songs played at the beginning of each episode) and well-known songs included in network television shows usually earn licensing fees in the range of $5,000 to $15,000 per episode. This covers worldwide synchronization rights for the life of the copyright. In some cases, the term of the license is limited (in most cases to five years) and must be renegotiated, with additional fees being paid, in the event that the show is broadcast in reruns or syndication. Songs and musical compositions that have not previously been hits garner lower sync fees, typically in the range of $500 to $2,500. Depending on the way a song is used, its duration, and the show's budget, fees may go considerably higher.

When a synchronization license confers the right for a song to be included on home videos or DVDs, as well as additional methods of distribution (referred to as *home video option rights*), the licensing fees listed above may increase by as much as two-fold.

Synchronization licensing fees are almost always collected by a song's publisher and split 50/50 between the publisher and songwriter(s). These fees are paid up front, when the licenses are signed.

In addition to the sync licensing fee, songs earn performance royalties when they air on television. A portion of a song played on a prime time, major network show can earn its writers and publishers a total of $1,000 to $2,000 in performance royalties (depending on the length of the excerpt and how it is used)—and this does not include reruns or syndication, which generate additional payments. In many cases, performance royalties earned for television broadcasts far exceed the synchronization fees.

A sync license is not required for a live television performance, such as a singer performing his or her latest hit on *Saturday Night Live*, because sound is not being "synchronized" to an existing visual image. But if the show is later rebroadcast, the producer is required to obtain a synchronization license.

Composers hired to write and produce the instrumental background score for a major network (ABC, NBC, CBS) television series typically earn in the range of $5,000 to $15,000 per thirty-minute episode and $10,000 to $25,000 per one-hour episode. Fees are usually lower for non-network and some cable series.

In most cases, music composed as television or motion picture background score is created as a work for hire, with the show's (or film's) producer owning all rights to the work, as well as any income it generates. Only composers with significant clout may be able to retain a portion of the publishing rights to their background scores.

Analyzing a Synchronization Licensing Agreement

The document that follows is a sample of the kind of agreement signed by a music publisher and a film producer to license the use of a musical composition in a film.

FILM SYNCHRONIZATION LICENSING AGREEMENT

FOR AND IN CONSIDERATION OF THE SUM OF _____
Dollars, for the synchronization rights hereinafter set forth and for the performing rights and other rights set forth in Paragraphs 4 and 5 below, said sums payable upon the execution and delivery hereof, and in consideration of all the other promises and agreements contained herein, Publisher listed below, hereby grants to _____ and its successors and assigns, hereinafter referred to as "Producer" the non-exclusive irrevocable right, license, privilege and authority to record in any manner, medium or form, whether now known or hereafter devised, the music and the words of the musical composition set forth below only in connection with the motion picture entitled below in any language, to make copies of the recording in any and all gauges of film and to import the recording and/or copies of the recording into any country within the territory covered by this license and to perform, as set forth below, the musical composition in the territory, subject to the terms, conditions and limitations set forth below:

This paragraph establishes the fee to be paid for the nonexclusive right to use the musical composition named below in a motion picture. It also states that a performance license is being granted, according to the provisions of paragraphs 4 and 5. Further stated is that the specified fee must be paid when this contract is signed and delivered. The paragraph provides a space in which to insert the producer's name. Additionally, it affirms that the producer has the nonexclusive right to record the musical composition in any media, but only as related to the motion picture. It also states that this agreement is binding to all parties, even if the producer's or publisher's company is bought or assigned to someone else. Finally, it states that the rights granted by this agreement, including the right to make copies of the recording in any medium of film, and in any language, extend to any country covered by this contract, as specified by the provisions contained in the agreement.

1. Musical Composition

The musical composition (hereinafter the "Composition"), and the sole use of the musical composition, covered by this license is:

TITLE: "_____"
WRITER(S): _____
PUBLISHER: _____
USE: Motion Picture Synchronization, including, worldwide theatrical distribution, video release rights, broadcast television rights, cable television rights, public institutions and airline screening rights.

This paragraph provides spaces to insert the title of the musical composition being licensed, as well as the names of the writers and publisher. It also defines the uses for which permission is being granted as inclusion in films, videos, broadcast and cable television, and performances in public institutions, as well as on airlines throughout the world.

2. Motion Picture Title

The title of the only motion picture with which the recording is to be used is:
"_____" (hereinafter the "Motion Picture").

In this paragraph, the title of the film for which the musical composition is being licensed is listed. It further specifies that this is the only film for which the composition is being licensed.

3. Territory

The territory covered by this license is: the World.

This paragraph establishes that the license covers all countries throughout the world.

4. Performance License—United States

Publisher grants to Producer the non-exclusive right and license in the United States and its possessions to perform publicly, either for profit or non-profit, and to authorize others so to perform the Composition only in synchronization or timed relationship to the Motion Picture and trailers thereof as follows:

This paragraph describes the performance rights granted by the music publisher, and to the film producer within the U.S. and its possessions (for instance, Puerto Rico and the Virgin Islands). It states that the right to perform the composition within the film and its advertising trailer is granted on a nonexclusive basis, regardless of whether the performance is for profit.

(a) Theatrical Performance
In the exhibition of the Motion Picture to audiences in theatres and other public places where motion pictures are customarily exhibited, and where admission fees are charged, including but not limited to, the right to perform the Composition by transmission of the Motion Picture to audiences in theatres and such other public places for the duration of United States copyright of the Composition.

This subparagraph grants the right to show the motion picture in all venues where films are typically screened.

(b) Public Television Performance
In the exhibition of the Motion Picture by free television, pay television, networks, local stations, pay cable, closed circuit, satellite transmission, and all other types or methods of television or electronic reproduction and transmissions ("Television Performance") to audiences not included in Subparagraph (a) of this Paragraph 4 only by entities having performance licenses therefor from the appropriate performing rights societies. Television Performance of the Motion Picture by anyone not licensed for such performing rights by ASCAP, BMI or SESAC is subject to clearance of the performing right either from Publisher or ASCAP, BMI, SESAC or from any other licensor acting for or on behalf of Publisher and to payment of an additional license fee therefor.

Subparagraph (b) states that the film embodying the musical composition may be shown on any television station, providing the broadcaster is licensed by the performing rights organization with which the work is registered. It further establishes that for any television broadcaster not licensed by the PROs, the producer, broadcaster, or someone acting on their behalf must obtain a performance license from the publisher, the PROs, or an agent acting on the publisher's behalf, which may require payment of an additional licensing fee.

5. Foreign Performing License
It is understood that the performance of the Composition in connection with the exhibition of the Motion Picture in countries or territories outside of the

United States and its possessions shall be subject to clearance by performing rights societies in accordance with their customary practice and the payment of their customary fees. Publisher agrees that to the extent it controls the performing rights, it will license an appropriate performing rights society in the respective countries to grant such performing right.

This paragraph states that when the film is shown outside the U.S., it is subject to the customary practices and payments of the PROs in various countries. It further establishes that it is the publisher's responsibility to license the applicable PROs in the foreign countries where the film is shown, to the extent that the publisher has the right to do so.

6. Videogram License

Publisher hereby further grants to Producer, in each country of the territory, the non-exclusive right to cause or authorize the fixing of the Composition in and as part of the Motion Picture on audiovisual contrivances such as video cassettes, video tapes, video discs, DVD and similar compact audiovisual devices reproducing the entire motion picture in substantially its original form ("Videogram"), and:

This paragraph provides the nonexclusive right to include the musical composition in "videogram" versions of the film. Videograms include DVDs, video tapes, and other similar film reproduction technologies. The paragraph further specifies that this right applies only when the complete film is reproduced in what is essentially the version in which it was initially released.

(a) To utilize such Videogram for any of the purposes, uses and performances hereinabove set forth; and

This subparagraph establishes that all rights conveyed in this contract apply to videograms.

(b) To reproduce, and to sell, lease, license, or otherwise distribute and make such Videogram available to the public as a device intended primarily for "home use" (as such term is commonly understood in the phonograph record industry) in the United States.

Subparagraph (b) states that videograms may be sold and distributed to the public as long as they are intended primarily for private, noncommercial uses.

7. "Most Favored Nations"

Notwithstanding anything herein to the contrary, Producer hereby warrants and represents that no other musical composition will be licensed for a substantially similar use to the Composition licensed hereunder in connection with the Motion Picture by or on behalf of a publisher on a more favorable basis to such publisher than is provided to publisher hereunder. If a musical composition is so licensed in connection with the Motion Picture on a more favorable basis in any of the areas hereunder, Producer hereby agrees that such more favorable basis shall also be extended to the licensing of the Composition hereunder. By way of clarification of the foregoing and not in limitation thereof, if another musical composition is licensed in connection with the Motion Picture, and the publisher thereof is paid amounts for such composition exceeding the sums paid to Publisher hereunder, Producer shall immediately pay to Publisher an amount equal to the difference between the amount paid for such other musical composition and the sums and/or royalties theretofore paid Publisher hereunder.

In this paragraph, the producer promises that no other musical composition will be licensed for inclusion in the film at a higher rate, or with better terms, if it is used in a manner similar to the composition covered by this agreement. It further states that, in the event another composition used similarly is granted a higher licensing fee or better terms, the producer will give these more favorable terms to the publisher of the composition covered by this agreement.

8. Restrictions
This license does not include any right or authority:

Paragraph 8 lists rights that are not granted by this license.

(a) to make any change in the original lyrics or in the fundamental character of the music of the Composition;

Subparagraph (a) states that the music may not be significantly changed and there may not be any alterations to the lyrics.

(b) to use the title, the subtitle or any portion of the lyrics of the Composition as the title or subtitle of the Motion Picture;

According to subparagraph (b) neither the title of the musical composition nor any lines of the lyric may be used as the title or subtitle of the movie.

(c) to dramatize or to use the plot or any dramatic content of the lyrics of the Composition; or

Subparagraph (c) establishes that the ideas, story, or scenario expressed in the lyrics may not be portrayed in the film.

(d) to make any other use of the Composition not expressly authorized herein.

In this subparagraph, it is affirmed that the musical composition may only be used in the ways described in this agreement.

9. Warranty
Publisher represents and warrants that it owns or controls the aforesaid extent of interest of the composition licensed in the aforesaid Territory hereunder and that it has the legal right to grant this license and that Producer shall not be

required to pay any additional monies, except as provided in this license, with respect to the rights granted herein. Publisher shall indemnify, defend and hold harmless Producer, its successors, assigns and licenses from and against any and all loss, damages, liabilities, actions, suits or other claims arising out of any breach, in whole or in part, of the foregoing representations and warranties, and for reasonable attorneys' fees and costs incurred in connection therewith; provided, however, that such Publisher's total liability shall not exceed the consideration paid hereunder.

In this paragraph, the publisher asserts that it owns or controls the composition, and has the right to enter into this agreement. It further states that the producer shall not have to pay any money to secure the rights to the composition, other than the fee specified in this agreement. The publisher is responsible to defend any claims or legal actions that result from its statement that it owns or controls the composition. The paragraph also states that the producer is not liable for any costs or damages resulting from the publisher's misrepresenting itself. Finally, it states that the maximum amount the publisher may be responsible for paying to the producer is the amount of the fee it received by entering into this agreement. It is likely that a producer would negotiate to try to have this stipulation removed, so that the publisher would be liable for any costs that result from its misrepresentations.

10. Publisher's Reservation of Rights
Subject only to the non-exclusive rights hereinabove granted to Producer, all rights of every kind and nature in the Composition are reserved to the Publisher together with all rights of use thereof.

According to this paragraph, although the publisher grants nonexclusive rights specified in this agreement, it retains all rights to the composition.

11. Advertising
The recording and performing rights hereinabove granted include such rights for air, screen and television trailers solely for the advertising and exploitation of the Motion Picture.

This paragraph affirms that, in addition to the rights specified previously within this agreement, permission is granted to broadcast the musical composition for advertising and promoting the movie.

12. Cue Sheet
Producer agrees to furnish Publisher a cue sheet of the Motion Picture within thirty (30) days after the first public exhibition of the Motion Picture at which admission is charged (except so-called "sneak previews").

This paragraph states that the producer shall provide the publisher with a cue sheet within 30 days of the first paid public screening.

13. Remedies

If Producer, or its assigns, licensees, or sub-licensees, breaches this Agreement by, among other things, failing to pay timely any license fees required hereunder, and fails to cure such breach within thirty (30) days after notice of such breach given by Publisher to Producer, then this license will automatically terminate. Such termination shall render the distribution, licensing, or use of the Composition as unauthorized uses, subject to the rights and remedies provided by the laws, including copyright, and equity of the various countries within the Territory.

This paragraph addresses what happens in the event that the producer (or any individual or company to which it assigns its rights) fails to live up to its contractual obligations, such as neglecting to pay the licensing fee. It states that this agreement becomes void if payment has not been received within 30 days after the producer has been notified it is in violation of the terms of this agreement. It further states that if the agreement is terminated, any use of the composition shall be deemed unauthorized, and as such, the publisher will be entitled to compensation provided by the copyright laws of the countries in which the uses take place.

14. Notices

All notices, demands or requests provided for or desired to be given pursuant to this Agreement must be in writing. All such documents shall be deemed to have been given when served by personal delivery or three days following their deposit in the United States mail, postage prepaid, certified or registered, addressed as follows:

This paragraph establishes that all correspondence regarding this agreement must be in writing. It further states that notices and other correspondence will be deemed to have been delivered at the time when the correspondence is personally delivered, or three days after being mailed within the U.S., by certified or registered mail.

(a) To Publisher:

In subparagraph (a), the name and address of the publisher is provided.

(b) To Producer:

In subparagraph (b), the name and address of the producer is given.

or to such other address in the United States as either party may later designate in writing delivered in the manner aforesaid.

According to the continuation of this paragraph, if the publisher or producer wants correspondence to be sent to an address different from the one listed above, they must notify the other party as previously specified.

15. Entire Agreement

This license is binding upon and shall inure to the benefit of the respective successors and/or assigns of the parties hereto, but in no event shall Producer be relieved of its obligations hereunder without the express written consent of Publisher. This Agreement shall be construed in all respects in accordance with the laws of the State of Tennessee applicable to agreements entered into and to be wholly performed therein. The recording and performing and other rights hereinabove granted shall endure for the periods of all copyrights in and to the Composition, and any and all renewals or extensions thereof that Publisher may now own or control or hereafter own or control without Producer having to pay any additional consideration therefor except as otherwise might be specifically set forth herein, including, without limitation, pursuant to the provisions of Paragraph 7, above.

> This paragraph affirms that this Agreement is legally binding and that (as required by law) there is benefit to both parties (or individuals or companies to whom they may assign their rights). It further states that the producer may only be released from its obligations by the publisher's written consent. Also stated is that this Agreement is subject to the laws of Tennessee (in this instance, the state where the music publisher is located). Additionally, this paragraph declares that the recording and performing rights being granted shall continue as long as the composition's copyright and renewals remain in force, and that the producer shall not be required to pay any fees, other than those specified in this Agreement, including in Paragraph 7 of this Agreement.

IN WITNESS WHEREOF, the parties have caused the foregoing to be executed as of the _____ day of _____, 2_____.

"Publisher":

By: _____

_____

(print name and title)

"Producer":

By: _____

_____

(print name and title)

> In the spaces above, the date, printed names, and signatures of the publisher and producer are inserted.

To license music for use in a television show, a license similar to the one explained above is issued, addressing the length of the term and the various uses being granted, such as pay television, free television, basic cable, and subscription television.

CHAPTER TWELVE

Targeting Special Markets

The musical interests of many songwriters lie outside the mainstream pop, country, adult contemporary, and R&B markets. For these writers, who channel their creativity into songs that can be both emotionally and financially rewarding, there are unique considerations when writing and marketing work.

Marketing Songs for the Christian Music Market

With more than forty-five million albums sold annually, and sales exceeding $700 million, the Christian music market represents an important outlet for songwriters who choose to express their faith and religious beliefs through their music.

The terms *Christian* and *gospel* are used interchangeably to designate any music that incorporates the Gospel or Christian themes into its lyrics. Many people use *gospel* to describe the Southern gospel style of music popularized by artists such as the Oak Ridge Boys and the Gaither Vocal Band, and *black gospel* to describe the style of music identified with artists such as Cissy Houston and André Crouch. There's also a genre called *contemporary Christian music* (*CCM*), which refers to any musical style with Christian lyrics, other than traditional gospel. This includes adult contemporary, rock, pop, and hip-hop.

Christian music is comprised of a wide variety of musical styles, sharing one common denominator—their lyrics deal with Christian themes. Business is conducted in the Christian music market in virtually the same fashion as in the secular music market.

As in nonreligious genres, publishers who focus primarily on Christian music sign single song and exclusive songwriting agreements; songwriters and music publishers earn the statutory mechanical royalty rate when their music is sold or downloaded; and ASCAP, BMI, and SESAC pay performance royalties for Christian music played on radio, television, and the Internet, and at other venues where music is licensed. When their songs are sold as sheet music, writers and publishers of Christian music are paid in the same manner as are secular songwriters.

As is the case with secular music, a large percentage of the songs placed with successful recording artists are pitched by established music publishers and/or songwriters aligned with them. Songwriters hoping to break into the Christian music market need to produce professional-sounding demo recordings of their songs before approaching music publishers. When pitching songs for the Christian market, with its added emphasis on lyric content, a well-produced guitar/vocal or keyboard/vocal demo may be sufficient, depending on the style of music.

As in any genre of music, it's always advisable to seek reliable professional feedback before investing significant sums in demo recordings. The Gospel Music Association (www.gospelmusic.org) offers a song-critiquing service for songwriters focusing on the Christian music market. At the time of this printing, their fee was $30 per song.

Despite the fact that more than fourteen hundred radio stations program gospel music exclusively, this still represents only a small percentage (approximately 6 percent) of overall music sales and radio airplay. Therefore, songwriters in this market tend to earn only a fraction of the money earned by their counterparts writing nonreligious music.

In 2004, fourteen Christian music albums were awarded gold certification by the RIAA for sales exceeding five hundred thousand. Eight Christian music albums were certified platinum, for sales exceeding one million, and five reached multi-platinum status, but these are exceptions. Many successful Christian albums sell fewer than one hundred thousand copies, with the majority being sold by artists following performances at churches and small venues, such as coffeehouses, garnering sales of ten thousand copies or less.

Radio performance income for Christian songs tends to be only about 10 percent of what mainstream songs generate. This is because there are so many fewer stations playing exclusively Christian music formats than those playing secular music. An additional factor contributing to the lower performance royalties is that the stations featuring this programming tend to be smaller, reaching fewer listeners than their mainstream equivalents.

Listed below are some of the most popular genres of Christian music and some of their representative artists:

- Pop/adult contemporary: MercyMe, Jaci Velasquez, Matthew West, Steven Curtis Chapman, Michael W. Smith

- Rock: Jars of Clay, Casting Crowns, P.O.D., Tobymac, Thousand Foot Crutch

- Praise and worship: Brooklyn Tabernacle Choir, Matt Redman, Chris Tomlin

- Country/bluegrass: the Oak Ridge Boys, Ricky Skaggs, Randy Travis, Charlie Daniels

- Black gospel: Yolanda Adams, Kirk Franklin, BeBe and CeCe Winans

- Southern gospel: the Crabb Family, the Gaither Vocal Band, the Martins

- Inspirational/easy listening: Sandi Patty, Kathie Lee Gifford, Selah, Steve Green, Darlene Zschech

- R&B/hip-hop: GRITS, Mary Mary, Tonéx

- Latin: Samuel Hernandez, Julissa, Rojo, Marcos Witt

- Instrumental: Jim Brickman, John Tesh, Phil Keaggy, Kirk Whalum

- Children's: Cedarmont Kids, Songtime Kids, Veggie Tales, Wonder Kids.

Pop/adult contemporary and black gospel, each having a 20-percent market share, are the best-selling styles of Christian music. They are closely followed by rock (the fastest growing style), with a 19-percent market share. Praise and worship music accounts for approximately 10 percent of Christian music sales. Children's Christian music and country/bluegrass formats each capture a 5-percent market share, with instrumental Christian music accounting for 4 percent of gospel music sales. Southern gospel and inspirational music each represent approximately 3 percent of Christian music sold, with the remaining gospel music sales being split among R&B/hip-hop and Latin music.

A majority of the Christian music publishing companies and record labels are based in Nashville and Franklin, Tennessee. While any music publisher can pitch songs to Christian recording artists, music publishers who focus primarily on the gospel industry typically have the best contacts and credibility, and may be best able to discern a "hit" for this market.

The most successful publishers of Christian music include the following: Brentwood-Benson Music (www.brentwood-bensonmusic.com), Provident Music (www.providentdistribution.com), Word Music (www.wordmusic.com), Daywind Music (www.daywind.com), Sony BMG (www.sonybmg.com), Warner/Chappell (www.warnerchappell.com), EMI Christian Music Publishing (www.emigospel.com), Gaither Music Company (www.gaithernet.com), Marantha! Music (www.maranthamusic.com), Integrity Music (www.integritymusic.com), and Universal Christian Music Publishing (www.umpgnashville.com).

Christian music sales are monitored by *Christian SoundScan*, operated by the Christian Music Trade Association (www.cmta.com), which provides weekly sales information. More than thirteen hundred stores nationwide currently report to *Christian SoundScan*, including national chains such as Family Christian Stores and Lifeway Christian Stores, regional chains including Berean and Mardel, hundreds of independent stores, and Internet retail sites such as www.musichristian.com and www.cbd.com.

As is the case with virtually all styles of music, networking is crucial for writers hoping to break into the Christian music market. The Gospel Music Association (GMA) presents its annual Gospel Music Week each April in Nashville, Tennessee. The conference includes exhibitions, concerts, and panel discussions. Participants include music publishers, record labels, recording artists, and retailers. GMA also presents Music in the Rockies, an annual week-long Christian music seminar and talent competition, each August in Estes Park, Colorado. Both of these events offer invaluable networking opportunities.

The Nashville Songwriters Association (NSAI) sponsors a monthly Christian songwriting workshop in Nashville, as well as an annual Christian Music Songwriters Retreat featuring Christian music industry panels, lectures, and feedback from industry professionals, including GMA award–winning songwriters and music publishers.

The *Annual Gospel Music Association's Music Industry Networking Guide* is the Christian music industry's most comprehensive listing of recording artists, artist's managers, booking agents, record labels, and music publishers. Free to GMA members and $19.95 for nonmembers, this excellent resource is available only through GMA.

Songwriters composing material that is performed in churches should be aware of Christian Copyright Licensing International (CCLI). One of the rights afforded copyright owners is the right to authorize the reproduction of their songs and lyrics. It is illegal to copy lyrics without first obtaining a license from the copyright owner, and infringements can result in fines up to $30,000 for each infraction. Thousands of churches photocopy and distribute lyrics or sheet music to their congregants to aid in sing-alongs. But to be in compliance with copyright law, churches should secure permission from the publishers of each song reproduced every time it is copied. This would be a laborious, if not impossible task. The *Church Copyright License* is a convenient and cost-effective way for churches to legally copy song lyrics and music used in congregational singing.

Church Copyright Licenses, provided by CCLI, are blanket licenses that grant churches the right to copy songs and lyrics for their congregations. Reproductions may be in the form of bulletins, song sheets, transparencies, computer projections, custom arrangements, or live recordings of services.

For an annual fee, based primarily on the size of the congregation, a church receives the right to copy for congregational singing more than one hundred fifty thousand songs represented by more than twenty-five hundred music publishers and songwriters functioning as their own publishers. This includes songs published by top companies including Brentwood-Benson, EMI, Hillsong, Integrity, Marantha!, Mercy/Vineyard, and Word. Publishers and songwriters pay a onetime fee of $50 to have their songs listed among those licensed by CCLI.

CCLI provides licensing to more than one hundred seventy thousand churches worldwide, including more than one hundred forty thousand congregations in North America. Churches that obtain licenses from CCLI maintain a record of the authorized songs they copy and provide this listing once every two and a half years. A royalty is calculated, based on the number of times each song has been copied, the type of reproductions made, and the amount of licensing fees collected. Royalties are distributed to copyright owners twice annually, on February 15 and August 15.

Royalties distributed by CCLI can be substantial for the most popular songs sung in churches. Songwriters hoping to encourage the use of their songs in churches are advised to perform them for multiple congregations. The Church Copyright License provides payment for the use of songs that touch thousands of hearts but may not receive sales or airplay.

Marketing Children's Songs

While many children listen to pop, rap, rock, and hip-hop music, *children's music* refers to songs written specifically for very young listeners—typically preschoolers. The vast majority of children's songs are written by entertainers who write, perform, and produce recordings of their own material exclusively, leaving limited opportunities for songwriters to place these songs. Those songwriters who do secure recordings of this music are typically those who write exceptional songs—and are skilled at networking with performers of children's music.

Children's music encompasses a wide variety of styles, including pop, rock, rap, hip-hop, country, jazz, folk, and blues; the common thread is that the lyrics are applicable to and appropriate for young audiences. Some writers mistakenly assume that songs composed for children need to be lyrically and melodically simplistic. While this may be the case when writing songs intended for toddlers, a significant segment of the children's music market is comprised of songs that can be listened to by the entire family.

Songs targeted for audiences that include various age groups need to be sophisticated enough to capture an adult's interest while being lyrically appropriate and relevant to children. Examples of this kind of material can be found by listening to songs featured in soundtracks of films such as *Beauty and the Beast*, *The Lion King*, and *The Little Mermaid*.

Celine Dion ("Miracle") and Collin Raye ("Counting Sheep") are among the mainstream recording artists who have recorded albums of children's music and music intended for families to enjoy together. Writers who subscribe to tip sheets and who excel at networking are likely to learn about opportunities to pitch for similar projects.

Children's music superstar Raffi has recorded thirteen albums, selling more than twelve million albums, but the majority of children's entertainers earn a modest living, performing and selling their product from the stage at venues such as shopping malls, private parties, libraries, fairs, and theme parks.

More than sixty *terrestrial radio stations* (non-Internet), a growing number of Internet radio stations such as www.kidmixradio.com, and satellite radio's *XM Kids* program children's music, providing exposure to a wide audience as well as performance royalties for songwriters and music publishers of children's songs. A listing of radio stations that play children's music, as well as their music submission policies, can be found at www.kidsmusicplanet.com.

Record labels that distribute children's music include Music for Little People (www.musicforlittlepeople.com), Rounder Kids (www.rounderkids.com), Putumayo (Putumayo Kids division, focusing on world and ethnic music for children) (www.putumayo.com), Casablanca Kids (www.casablancakids.com), Sony Wonder Records (www.sonywonder.com), Walt Disney Records (www.disney.go.com/disneyrecords), Sugar Beats (www.sugar-beats.com), and Twin Sisters Productions (www.twinsisters.com). It is always advisable to contact record labels prior to submitting songs or artist's demos for consideration.

Television shows and DVDs are among the most lucrative outlets for writers of children's songs. Programs and videos/DVDs such as *Sesame Street*, *Barney*, *Dora the Explorer*, *Care Bears*, *Scooby Doo*, *The Rugrats*, the *Barbie* movies, and *Teletubbies* present hundreds of opportunities for writers of children's music to market their work. In addition, the Cartoon Network, Nickelodeon, Toon Disney, and many other cable channels specifically offer children's programming—and virtually all of it includes songs and/or music geared to children.

The soundtracks of animated children's feature films also typically feature songs. Phil Collins (*Tarzan*), Elton John (*The Lion King*), and Melissa Manchester (*102 Dalmations*) are among the songwriters who have composed music for successful children's films. In many instances, the songs for these shows and films are written by staff-writers and may be treated as works for hire. Securing one of these positions typically requires previous success composing for children and, as in most areas of the music business, excellent networking skills. But there are still opportunities for songwriters to place material on a freelance basis in venues such as television shows, videos, computer games, and audio recordings.

Songwriters who have success placing their material in the children's music market are typically entrepreneurs who think outside the box and work hard to create avenues to sell their products.

Blue Vision Music is one of the few companies representing both performing and nonperforming songwriters of children's music. They work to license children's songs and music throughout the U.S. and internationally for use in CDs, videos/DVDs, musical toys, computer games, and other formats. Visit www.bluevisionmusic.com for additional information and submission guidelines.

The Children's Music Network (CMN) (www.cmnonline.org) is a nonprofit association whose membership is comprised of performers, songwriters, music educators, record producers, music distributors, broadcasters, and others involved in the children's music industry. With chapters throughout the U.S., CMN hosts regional gatherings, which are open to members and nonmembers alike. CMN also presents an annual conference including workshops, community dialogue, performances, and excellent networking opportunities.

The Children's Entertainment Association (CEA) (www.kidsentertainment.com) is the country's leading trade association for those involved in children's entertainment. CEA members come from all areas of the children's entertainment industry, including songwriters, performers, music publishers, film/television/video/radio professionals, attorneys, agents, and managers.

The "tween" market targets preteens, typically eight to twelve years of age. Music written and marketed for this age group represents an enormous source of income for songwriters. *Radio Disney*, a radio station exclusively targeting the tween and younger audience, is at the center of this extremely lucrative market. Available on cable and satellite radio, on the Internet at www.radiodisney.com, and on terrestrial radio in more than fifty-five major U.S. cities, Radio Disney airplay guarantees exposure to millions of preteen music buyers.

Songs popular among this age group are primarily the same pop, R&B, rap, and hip-hop hits heard on Top 40 radio. Kelly Clarkson, Jesse McCartney, Avril Lavigne, Hilary Duff, and Bowling for Soup are among the mainstream artists who have topped the Radio Disney charts. Quite a few very young artists, such as Aly & AJ, LMNT, Cheetah Girls, Aaron Carter, Raven, and JoJo found tremendous success (and in some cases gold or platinum sales) as a result of their Radio Disney airplay—without the benefit of significant airplay on mainstream radio stations. Compilations of Radio Disney hits, marketed by Walt Disney Records, have sold millions of copies.

Pitching songs to artists who target tweens requires the same process as pitching for mainstream acts described in Chapter 5. The only difference is that when pitching for the tween market, the lyrics need to be appropriate for young artists and their audiences.

Licensing Songs for Video Games

More than twice as many video games are sold in the U.S. than movie tickets, generating sales exceeding $14 billion annually—and virtually all of these games include music. Original music in video games, sometimes referred to as *interactive games*, is a key element to enriching a player's experience and contributes to game sales. The increasing popularity of music culled from the soundtrack of electronic games is evident in the proliferation of soundtrack albums, radio stations, and Web sites devoted exclusively to these compositions.

Further indication of the burgeoning popularity of music from video games can be found in the fact that symphonic concerts at the Hollywood Bowl and throughout Europe have featured works from video game soundtracks, and the National Academy of Recording Arts and Sciences (NARAS) has established a Grammy Award category for best music composed for a video game. Music licensing for inclusion in video games represents one more potentially lucrative outlet for songwriters and composers.

Music composed for this market is analogous to soundtracks for television shows and films in that its primary function is to enhance the emotional impact of the visual imagery. A significant amount of video game music underscores high-energy chase and battle scenes; approximately 40 percent of it is orchestral, performed either on synthesizers or by live orchestras. Roughly another 40 percent of the music included in interactive games tends to be instrumental techno, trance, or electronica, with the remaining music most often being rap, hip-hop, and rock. While these styles predominate, songs in virtually all popular styles have been used in interactive games.

Peter Gabriel, Sisqo, Marilyn Manson, Snoop Dogg, the Beastie Boys' Mixmaster Mike, and Bow Wow are among the artists who have had their music licensed for inclusion in video games. Well-known artists have commanded licensing fees of $100,000 or more. In addition to licensing fees, songwriters, composers, and recording artists gain additional exposure to an audience that is among the prime music-buying demographic.

If an existing recording is being used (such as an artist's hit song), a video game's manufacturer (typically referred to as the game's "publisher") must obtain a master use license from the owner of the sound recording (in most cases, a record label), as well as a synchronization license from the composition's copyright owner (a publisher, or a songwriter functioning as his or her own publisher).

Unlike the sale and download of audio recordings, Congress has not mandated a statutory mechanical royalty rate for CD-ROMs (the format in which many video games are sold) and no standard for payment has been established. Video game music licensing deals are negotiated on a case-by-case basis.

In the overwhelming majority of instances, music written for this market is treated as a work for hire, and composers are paid a onetime fee, referred to as a *buyout*. This amount typically ranges from $500 to $750 for each minute of music used in the soundtrack, typically totaling $10,000 to $35,000 or more for an entire score. Top composers, creating music for the highest budget video game projects, can earn twice this amount.

Some video game publishers hire in-house composers who may earn salaries of $75,000 a year or more. Other companies hire freelance composers. In some cases, music is licensed by composers to game companies. In these instances, composers are paid a flat fee, but retain ownership of the music. In other cases, a publisher of a video game may control all rights to the music included in its games, but pays the composer the writer's share of any income earned subsequent to his or her initial composing fee. It is always preferable for a composer to retain ownership of the writer's share—if a game's publisher is willing to grant this.

Composers with a track record of composing for successful video games may have the bargaining power to demand bonus payments, for instance, an additional $5,000 to $10,000 for each two hundred fifty thousand units sold, as well as a supplementary payment in the event a game is made available in additional formats or systems (referred to as *platforms*) such as GameCube, Game Boy Advanced, Playstation 3, and Xbox.

A *composer's fee*, money paid for the writing of music, is separate from the *recording budget*, an amount allocated for the payment of musicians, vocalists, and recording studios. A recording budget is typically determined by the sales predicted for a particular game based on its publisher's market research. For low-budget projects, many composers use synthesizers and perform the entire score themselves. In these instances, the composer's fee may include the recording budget.

Music budgets of $100,000 to $200,000 (including composing, recording fees, and the design of sound effects) are not uncommon, with the top echelon of interactive games having a $1 million audio budget. Games with high-end budgets have been known to allocate $200,000 or more for symphonic scores recorded by live orchestras. In many instances, composers record orchestral scores outside the U.S., typically in Prague (in the Czech Republic) or Budapest, Hungary, where the fees for musicians are considerably lower than domestically.

In exceptional cases, instead of a buyout, composers are paid a royalty for each game sold. This royalty typically ranges between 8 cents and 15 cents for each copy sold. With many games selling more than five hundred thousand copies, and top video games such as *Tony Hawk Pro Skater* and *Grand Theft Auto* selling more than ten million copies worldwide, it's easy to see that these royalties can be substantial.

The payment a particular musical composition can command is determined by factors including the composer's bargaining power, whether it has previously been a hit, the anticipated sales, the term of the agreement (for instance, five years, ten years, or life of the copyright), whether the license grants the right to include the musical composition in advertising and ancillary products (such as audio CDs, DVDs, and other formats), and whether the game will be sold solely as a physical product, or available to play for a fee on the Internet.

Songs are not often used within the games themselves because lyrics can distract players from the dialog and action, which are intended as the primary focus. Most games include only one song, typically played during opening credits or closing credits. These songs are typically written or cowritten by the composer of the game's background score or by a well-known recording artist.

Although songs are not typically pitched for inclusion in interactive games, songwriters, and more often, successful recording artists, are sometimes commissioned to create songs specifically for a game. In these instances, video game producers and audio directors work closely with songwriters to craft songs that are tailormade for the project. Unknown songwriters have their best shot at getting songs included in low-budget games produced by the smaller companies.

When songs are used in video games, they are almost always presented as finished master recordings. While a band might place master recordings of their songs in interactive game soundtracks, it is not appropriate for a songwriter to pitch a demo with the expectation that a video game producer will say, "I like that song. Let's get Jack Johnson to record it." But by pitching demos and master recordings of their songs, songwriters have a chance of capturing the attention of video game music supervisors, composers, or producers who may commission future songs.

Composers pursuing work in the video game industry need a *demo reel*, a recorded compilation showcasing some of their strongest work. While there is no consensus regarding the number of compositions that are typically included, three to five musical works, each between two and three minutes in length, should be sufficient to demonstrate your capabilities.

Companies such as Bob Rice's FBI/Four Bars Intertainment (www.fourbarsintertainment.com) and Position Soundtrack Services (www.positionmusic.com) are among the firms that represent composers, songwriters, and independent artists for the placement of their music in video games. They also work to place their clients' music in film, television, soundtrack albums, and commercials. Production houses such as Tommy Tallarico Studios (www.tallarico.com) and Convergent Entertainment (www.convergententertainment.com) also periodically contract freelance composers.

As is the case in virtually every area of the music business, networking and establishing professional relationships is a crucial component of achieving success composing for, and placing songs in, video games. The E³ Expo (www.e3expo.com), held each May in Los Angeles, is the video game industry's foremost trade show and conference. In addition, game developers' conferences such as those offered by Game Connection (www.game-connection.com) and the Game Developers Conference (www.gdconf.com) present outstanding networking opportunities. The International Game Developers Association's Web site (www.igda.org) and Gamasutra (www.gamasutra.com) are also excellent resources.

Composers seeking to work in the video games industry can interact and network with other professionals by joining the Game Audio Network Guild (G.A.N.G.) (www.audiogang.org), an organization of composers, sound designers, voiceover directors, video game designers, producers, and other associates and executives within the interactive entertainment industry. G.A.N.G. hosts educational opportunities, such as panels, and its members can access online articles regarding video game music contracts, negotiations, and creative and technical issues.

Licensing Songs for Musical Theater

Songs included in theatrical productions are typically intended to advance the show's story line and provide insight into the characters' feelings and motivations. Therefore, it is extremely rare for unknown existing songs to be pitched to, or placed in, musical shows, or for musicals to include songs written by various songwriters. (One notable exception is the short-lived *Urban Cowboy*, which included country songs by a variety of Nashville songwriters.)

With few exceptions, the songs included in *book musicals*, shows that use songs to help tell a story (such as *The Sound of Music, The Producers,* and *Hairspray*), are written by lyricists and composers writing specifically for the show. For instance, Elton John and Tim Rice composed the songs for *The Lion King* in conjunction with the writer of the show's story and dialog (the *libretto,* or *book*), allowing them to create songs integral to the plot of the show.

In many instances, a show's producer acquires the rights to a book or story and then commissions a composer and lyricist to write the musical score. In other cases, composers and lyricists work with a writer to create a show that is subsequently pitched to producers. Exceptions are primarily situations in which a show is written to showcase existing songs, such as *Ain't Misbehavin'* (the songs of Fats Waller), *Movin' Out* (the songs of Billy Joel), and *Mamma Mia!* (the songs of Abba).

The rights to perform *dramatic musical works* (those included in musical and dramatic plays, operas, and ballets) are called *grand rights.* The rights to license *nondramatic musical works* (songs or musical compositions that are not part of a larger theatrical production) are called *small rights.* Small rights include the right to perform music on television and radio and in concert halls—provided that it is not presented as part of a dramatic musical work. These rights are typically retained by songwriters.

Performing rights organizations license only nondramatic musical works. The rights to include and perform songs and other music in theatrical productions are licensed directly by a composer or, if applicable, the composer's music publisher. Composers and lyricists of music for musical theater are typically paid a percentage of gross weekly box office receipts, with a weekly minimum guaranteed, regardless of whether any profits are generated. Producers of musicals do not typically acquire any portion of the publishing rights to the songs in the shows they produce.

The Dramatists Guild of America (www.dramatistsguild.com) is an invaluable resource for musical theater composers and lyricists. Its *approved production contract (APC)* is the template for virtually all agreements used to license music for Broadway theatrical productions. In most instances, this contract, which is available to all members of the Dramatists Guild, is modified during a process of negotiation, but members agree to have the Guild approve all changes to it.

Under the terms of the Dramatists Guild's approved production contract, writers and composers of music for theatrical productions retain ownership of their work, including all publishing rights to their compositions, granting only specified rights to a show's producers. These rights include stage production rights in the U.S. and other English-language territories, the right to create and sell merchandise (referred to as *commercial use products*), and the right to create a cast album.

By maintaining ownership of their publishing rights, composers and lyricists are entitled to mechanical royalties for the sale and download of cast albums, print and other licensing fees, as well as performance royalties, when their compositions are performed on television, radio, and in venues licensed by ASCAP, BMI, and SESAC. The Dramatists Guild's approved production contract provides that a show's producer is entitled to a percentage of the revenue paid to composers and lyricists from subsidiary uses of their music licensed in the context of the show, such as licensing revenue from audiovisual works (including television and motion pictures), stock and amateur production rights, and stage rights in foreign territories. The producer's percentage of the writers' *subsidiary rights* income typically ranges from 10 percent to 40 percent, with shares of audiovisual uses at a maximum of 50 percent.

The rights conveyed to a show's producer typically include specified option periods during which he or she may present "first class" stage productions (such as Broadway and its equivalent), second class productions (off-Broadway and its equivalent), and touring productions in the U.S. and Canada, as well as in the United Kingdom, Australia, and New Zealand.

Since the Dramatists Guild's contract provides that writers own and control their work, lyricists and composers retain the right to approve any changes to their material, including any additions and deletions of songs, as well as the right to approve the artistic personnel working on the show, such as the director, designers, cast, orchestrators, and musical director.

In the past, composers, lyricists, and the writers of a Broadway show's book shared a royalty of 4.5 percent of box office receipts, which increased to at least 6 percent, subsequent to a show's investors recouping their outlay. Currently, most musical productions calculate the payment due composers and lyricists by using a system referred to as a *profit pool*, a means of allocating the weekly net operating profits earned by a production, in lieu of paying a percentage of gross box office receipts.

Composers and lyricists are typically guaranteed a minimum weekly payment (for instance, $2,000 per week) during the run of their show. This payment is an advance against a percentage of the show's profits. A production's operating expenses, such as salaries for the cast and stage crew, rental of the theater, advertising, insurance, legal fees, management fees, office expenses, and overhead, are deducted from gross box office receipts to determine profits.

Using the Broadway profit pool model, 35 percent of a production's weekly net operating profits are allocated to the show's composer, lyricist, book writer, director, choreographer, costumers, lighting designers, scenic designers, sound designers, orchestrators, and designated others (including the producers themselves) who comprise the *creators' royalty pool*. The composer, lyricist, and *librettist* (the show's book writer) share a minimum of 15.56 percent of the weekly net operating profits, increasing to at least 17.78 percent after the show has recouped its production expenses. The remaining 65 percent is paid to the production's investors.

After the investors have recouped their outlay, the share allocated to the composer, lyricist, book writer, director, and other members of the creative team (aforementioned) increases from 35 percent to 40 percent and the producer's 60 percent share of the profits is split equally between the producers and investors. Royalty pools are sometimes used off-Broadway as well, with slightly different parameters.

When music is used in dramatic shows either as background score or as *source music* (music that emanates from a specific source, for instance, a song playing on a jukebox, radio, or television within a scene), it is licensed on a case-by-case basis. The writers of material used in this fashion are typically compensated with an up-front fee, as well as a weekly payment. Depending on how important the use of a specific song is to a production, and the songwriter's clout, a royalty payment may be negotiated, but this is not typically the case.

Original cast albums are recordings that combine performances of a show's songs (by the members of the original cast), portions of its musical underscore, and excerpts of dialog. Typically, after recording costs have been recouped by the record label, 40 percent of royalties (analogous to an artist's royalty, as explained in Chapter 7) are paid to the show's producer, with the remaining 60 percent being divided among the composer, lyricist, and book writer.

In addition to the royalty described above, the statutory mechanical royalty rate is paid by a record label to the lyricist and composer's music publishers when copies of their songs are sold or downloaded. Album expenses are rarely recouped on a cast album, so in actuality, shows' composers and lyricists typically make their money only from mechanical royalties. A show's cast and orchestra are paid a fee out of the album's production budget and do not share in cast album royalties.

Songwriters and their music publishers also earn performance royalties when their songs are performed or broadcast beyond the context of the musical for which they were written, on radio or television or in venues licensed by PROs, such as nightclubs, concert halls, and restaurants. Neither a show's producer nor its librettist is typically entitled to any portion of a composer's or lyricist's mechanical or performance royalties.

While the recording of *Highlights from Phantom of the Opera: The Original Cast Recording* has sold more than 4.8 million copies in the U.S., and *Les Misérables*, *Rent*, and *Mamma Mia!* have each sold more than one million copies, few original cast albums come close to these sales figures—and many sell less than fifty thousand copies. Still, composers and lyricists of long-running shows such as those previously mentioned, as well as *Cats*, *Miss Saigon*, and *Evita*, earn millions of dollars in production royalties and licensing fees.

Companies such as Tams-Witmark (www.tams-witmark.com), Samuel French (www.samuelfrench.com), Music Theater International (MTI) (www.mtimusical-worlds.com), Dramatic Publishing (www.dramaticpublishing.com), and Dramatists Play Service (DPS) (www.dramatists.com) license the right to perform dramatic and musical theatrical productions throughout the U.S. and internationally. In addition, they rent scripts, piano accompaniments, and full orchestral musical arrangements.

Broadway musical extravaganzas such as *Spamalot*, *Les Misérables*, and *Wicked* typically cost more than $10 million to mount, and with the majority of Broadway musicals failing to earn a profit, only a handful of new musicals reach Broadway each year. But there are more than forty-five thousand amateur and professional theatrical organizations in the U.S. and Canada presenting more than fifteen thousand musical theater productions, totaling more than sixty thousand performances by professional and amateur troupes regionally—and each of these performances generates a royalty for composers and lyricists. In addition, innumerable schools, youth groups, churches, and senior citizen organizations license the right to perform musical theater works.

While Tams-Witmark, Samuel French, and Dramatists Play Service typically represent only shows that have previously been produced on Broadway, off-Broadway, or in London's West End, Music Theater International (MTI) and Dramatic Publishing also represent new musical theater works and accept unsolicited submissions.

TheatreworksUSA (www.theatreworksusa.org) is the premier provider of musicals created specifically for schools and youth organizations. They represent works by both new and established musical theater writers. The vast majority of the works TheatreworksUSA produces are commissioned. They go through an intensive development process during which the writers, composers, and lyricists work closely with their staff. For this reason, almost all of the individuals they commission live in the New York City area.

TheatreworksUSA typically finds the writers whom they commission by reviewing works from students of Juilliard, New York University (NYU), and the BMI Lehman Engel Workshops (described below), and by attending theater festivals. Writers, lyricists, and composers are welcome to submit works for consideration. Submission guidelines can be found at the agency's Web site.

Composers and lyricists of regional and other non-Broadway musical productions are compensated with a percentage of gross box office receipts. Theatrical licensing agencies typically charge organizations that present shows (for instance, high schools, community theater groups, and professional theatrical producers) a licensing fee of 8 percent to 15 percent of gross box office receipts. An average fee is 10 percent, with shows in high demand commanding higher percentages.

Depending on the contract negotiated when a show was first produced, the show's initial producer is typically entitled to a percentage (for example, 40 percent) of licensing fees earned for a specified period of time. The licensing agency retains 10 percent of the gross box receipts as its fee, with the remaining revenue typically being divided among the show's writer, composer, and lyricist.

Each agency has its own submission procedures, but in most cases it is necessary to submit a bound script and a recording (a CD) of all songs included in the production. A professionally produced piano/vocal demo is typically sufficient. Including a videotape recording of the production is helpful, but not mandatory. A synopsis of the play, its production history, cast, set, and technical requirements should be submitted, in addition to the author's bio or resume. For shows that have previously been produced, it can be helpful to include any positive reviews. Visit the Web sites listed throughout this section for additional guidelines and addresses.

For writers hoping to have their musical shows professionally produced, a production at a musical theater festival can sometimes provide a first crucial step toward that goal. The New York Musical Theater Festival (www.nymf.org) and the National Alliance for Musical Theatre (www.namt.net) have been important sources of new material, showcasing musical theater works by both upcoming and established writers. Both of these festivals have spawned numerous successful productions.

BMI sponsors the Lehman Engel Musical Theatre Workshop, an exceptional educational and networking opportunity, held every year in New York City. Workshop alumni include writers and composers of successful Broadway musicals such as *A Chorus Line*, *Avenue Q*, *Titanic*, *Little Shop of Horrors*, and *Beauty and the Beast*. Applicants for the BMI Lehman Engel Musical Theatre Workshop are required to submit three samples of their work along with a completed application form. August 1st is typically the deadline for submissions and there is no cost to writers who are accepted. Applications may be requested by sending an e-mail to musicaltheatre@bmi.com. For additional information visit www.bmi.com.

Similarly, ASCAP offers musical theater workshops in New York City, Chicago, and Los Angeles. The New York workshop, directed by Academy Award-winner Stephen Schwartz (*Godspell, Wicked, Pippin, Pocahontas,* and *The Hunchback of Notre Dame*), offers opportunities for musical theater writers to receive constructive feedback from top industry professionals.

ASCAP's Los Angeles and Chicago Musical Theater Workshops are offered in conjunction with Disney. They are also directed by Stephen Schwartz, with the Chicago workshop co-anchored by theater composer Craig Carnelia (*The Sweet Smell of Success, Is There Life After High School?,* and *Working*). For additional information and submission guidelines visit www.ascap.com.

CHAPTER THIRTEEN

Tapping Additional Sources of Income

For many songwriters, success is defined as switching on the radio and hearing one of their songs; others hope to have their work included on albums appearing on *Billboard*'s charts; while for some songwriters, hearing their music in a feature film or television show is their ultimate ambition. But most aspiring songwriters share one element in their definition of success: they hope to earn a living from the music they write.

Many successful songwriters derive the majority of their income from mechanical and performance royalties, earned primarily for the sale, downloading, radio airplay, and television broadcast of their songs. But there's considerable additional money to be made by savvy songwriters and publishers who tailor and market their work for a variety of other uses.

Writing and Marketing Jingles and Music for Commercials

Music, typically in the form of a commercial jingle, is an integral component of television and radio advertising, contributing tremendously to an ad's impact. Incorporating melody with an advertiser's message enhances listeners' abilities to remember the products or services being promoted. For instance, while listeners may find themselves humming "You Deserve a Break Today," few would think of, or recite, a spoken advertising slogan.

It's often a song that is the most memorable aspect of a commercial. For instance, it's impossible for many listeners to hear "I'd Like to Teach the World to Sing" without an instant association with Coca-Cola, yet it's unlikely that many viewers would be able to recall the dialogue or visual components of these ad campaigns.

A *commercial jingle* is a musical composition with or without a lyric, written specifically for use in a television or radio advertisement, promotion, or public service announcement, or a song originally written for other purposes, sometimes with a new or altered lyric intended for advertising a product or service. Many people think of a jingle as a catchy "mini-song" created to advertise a product. But this represents only one of the categories into which jingles can be classified.

Radio and Television Station IDs

Radio and television station IDs are brief musical works (typically six seconds in length) including lyrics. These *spots*, as they are sometimes called, are specifically created to identify the call letters of the radio or television station, the name of an on-air personality, specific programs, or features. Examples include musical and vocal arrangements of names and phrases, such as "KISS-FM," "Magic Country 103," or "John Johnson in the Morning." This type of jingle receives the most airplay, perhaps ten times each hour.

The majority of radio station IDs heard in the U.S. are produced by a few firms specializing in this service and located in Dallas, Texas and Seattle, Washington. The same instrumental tracks are typically used dozens of times for station IDs in different cities, with the only changes being in the vocal track, which includes the name of the DJ, station, or feature.

Generic Jingles

Generic Jingles are short pieces of preexisting or *stock* music, with or without lyrics, typically sold by production music libraries and used by radio stations as part of advertising and featured programming. Examples include snippets of music, accompanied by lyrics such as "Oldies All the Time," "Weekly Top 40," or "Hot Country."

Product Advertising Jingles

Product advertising jingles are essentially short songs (under twenty seconds in duration), including lyrics, created specifically for use in television or radio advertisements. They typically have exceptionally catchy melodies and include the name of the product or service being promoted. Examples of this type of jingle include the Oscar Mayer Wiener Song, Campbell Soup's "Mm, mm, Good," and Chia Pets' "Ch-Ch-Ch-Chia." Typically, jingles such as these are commissioned as works for hire by an advertising agency.

Preexisting Songs in Jingles

Sometimes songs that have previously been hits are used in commercials. When compositions are used in commercials in their original version, with no changes to the music or lyric, this is referred to as an *integral use*. A *derivative use* refers to instances in which a new version of a song is created, typically to include lyrics altered to fit the advertiser's needs.

Songwriter/artists whose songs have been featured in commercials include Missy Elliot; Mary J. Blige; Bob Dylan; Sting; Alan Jackson; Crosby, Stills, and Nash; Collective Soul; Moby; and Barenaked Ladies.

Nationally broadcast commercials featuring well-known celebrities' songs and performances benefit from the audience associating the product or service with the artist whose music is used. Tens of millions of viewers (or listeners, in the case of radio) are repeatedly exposed to this association (and in the case of the Super Bowl, more than one hundred thirty million viewers), and this connection pays off for advertisers.

Licensing Songs for Commercials

While synchronization licenses are used to license songs for television commercials, the license issued to grant permission to incorporate a song in a radio commercial is called a *transcription license*. The sky's the limit for sync and transcription licensing fees of well-known songs written and performed by superstar artists, with the top echelon of stars, such as the Rolling Stones and Madonna, reported to have earned up to $12 million for the use of their songs and master recordings.

Songwriters who have not reached superstar status can expect to earn fees of $75,000 to $150,000 for a license granting use for a one-year advertising campaign broadcast nationwide in the U.S., incorporating a song that has not previously been a hit. Well-known songs are likely to garner fees in the range of $150,000 to $500,000, with some fees topping $1 million. Songs included in ads that air only locally or regionally earn a fraction of these amounts.

In addition to licensing fees, which are paid by advertisers to music publishers (who distribute the writer's portion), performance royalties are earned when commercials are broadcast on television and radio. The three U.S. performing rights societies each calculate performance royalty payments differently. But each of them pays considerably less (for instance, 3 percent to 12 percent) for a performance embodied in a commercial than for a full television or radio feature performance.

Most of the largest advertising agencies responsible for national campaigns are located in New York, Los Angeles, and Chicago. In most cases, these companies have their own staff of jingle writers and rarely accept material from outside writers. Smaller advertising agencies, and those producing commercials for local and regional broadcast, are located in every major city and typically hire freelance writers and producers.

Writers hoping to break into this market need a *sample reel*, a collection of their demo recordings to play for prospective clients and employers. If a writer has already amassed credits as a jingle writer, the demo should feature a collection of jingles he or she has written previously. Ideally, this demo will include at least five commercials, written and produced to demonstrate the writer's ability to craft imaginative, effective jingles.

For writers who have not yet written jingles that have been broadcast on television or radio, demos are typically comprised of one of two types of compositions:

- Original jingles created by the writer for actual products. These are intended to demonstrate what the writer would be capable of creating if he or she were given an opportunity to compose a jingle to promote an existing product or service. Examples include a new jingle for BMW or for Allstate Insurance.

- Jingles produced to promote imaginary products. In these instances, the writer creates jingles for products or services that do not yet exist. Examples include jingles to promote Rover's Dog Grooming or Mitzi's Tennessee Corn Bread.

In addition to composing jingles, many successful jingle writers produce their own recordings, hiring musicians and vocalists, overseeing musical and vocal arrangements, and being responsible for the overall sonic quality of the music. Jingle writers who also hope to produce their own recordings need demos to illustrate their ability to create recordings that sound competitive with the commercials airing on television and radio.

The Standard Directory of Advertising Agencies (National Register Publishing), also known as *The Agency Red Book*, is the most comprehensive directory of advertising agencies in the U.S. and Canada. With a price of $799, many readers may want to access this book from the reference section of their local libraries. Offering an interactive online course for songwriters and composers interested in pursuing this potentially lucrative field, Jingle University (www.jingleuniversity.com) is another excellent resource.

Print Licensing

Among the rights conveyed to copyright holders is the right to authorize the printing of a transcription of a musical work. Permission to reprint copies of the musical notes and lyrics that comprise a song or other musical work is granted by *print licensing*—and the fees this generates for songwriters, composers, and music publishers can be substantial.

Three companies manufacture and sell the vast majority of printed music in the U.S. and Europe. These firms are the Hal Leonard Corporation (headquartered in Milwaukee, Wisconsin), Warner Brothers Publications U.S., Inc. (a division of Warner/Chappell Music, located in Miami, Florida), and the Music Sales Group (based in London, England).

Through exclusive licensing agreements, these three companies produce musical arrangements, design artwork, market, and distribute printed copies of songs and musical compositions for virtually every major U.S. music publisher. They also negotiate and grant permission and licenses for music and lyrics to be printed in books and magazines on behalf of the publishers who engage their services.

Print Music Licensing Fees

Printed music encompasses sheet music, folios, mixed folios, and matching folios—and songwriters (and their publishers) earn royalties for all of these configurations. In addition, licensing fees are generated when lyrics are printed in books and magazines.

As you learned in previous chapters, royalties derived from the sale, downloading, and performance of songs and musical compositions is typically divided equally between a work's composer and publisher. But this is not the case for royalties generated for the sale of printed music.

The sections that follow describe the various kinds of printed music and explain how songwriters are compensated when these items are sold.

Sheet Music

Sheet Music can be defined as a printed copy of the words, notes, and harmonic accompaniment (chords) that comprise a single song or musical work. Sheet music for a given song typically includes a piano arrangement, guitar chords, the melody notes, and lyrics. This configuration is sometimes referred to as *PGV, Piano/Guitar/Vocal*. Some sheet music is also sold with *guitar tablature*, meaning that in addition to the names of the chords, diagrams are shown illustrating where fingers are placed on the guitar frets to voice the chords properly.

Musicians and singers buy sheet music so they can learn and perform their favorite songs. Therefore, recent popular songs and standards account for the majority of individual sheet music sold. Few customers would buy sheet music for a song with which they and their listeners are unfamiliar, so producers typically generate sheet music only for well-known songs. While sheet music royalties can contribute significantly to a hit songwriter's income, they typically represent only a small percentage of the revenue generated by a hit song.

Music publishers are typically paid a royalty equal to 20 percent of the marked retail price of sheet music. This payment is made by the company that manufactures and distributes the sheet music, in most cases, Hal Leonard, Warner Brothers, or the Music Sales Group. At the time this book was written, sheet music for an individual song retailed for $3.95, generating 79 cents for the song's publisher.

In many music publishing agreements, the royalty rate paid to songwriters for the sale of sheet music is expressed in pennies—as opposed to a percentage of the money collected by the publisher for these sales (as is the case for mechanical royalties and other licensing income). Depending on the rate negotiated and agreed upon in their publishing agreement, songwriters typically earn in the range of 7 cents to 10 cents for each unit of sheet music sold. Superstar writer/artists and songwriters with maximum clout may be able to negotiate a royalty rate as high as 12 cents for each copy of sheet music sold.

It's preferable for a songwriter's royalty to be expressed as a percentage of the amount collected by their publisher (such as 50 percent of the money earned for sheet music royalties), or a percentage of the wholesale price. This allows songwriters to share in increased earnings as the price of sheet music goes up. In many cases, publishing companies insist on paying the considerably lower "penny" rates previously listed.

Some attorneys negotiate a sheet music royalty rate that increases at various sales thresholds. For example, an agreement might specify that the writer will be paid 10 percent of the wholesale selling price of the first one hundred thousand copies or less, 12 percent of the wholesale selling price for copies in excess of one hundred thousand, and 15 percent for copies in excess of two hundred fifty thousand.

Folios

A *folio* is a collection of sheet music for songs that share a common bond. Folios are categorized according to their contents. A *matching folio* is a compilation of all the songs included in a particular album. It typically has the album's artwork on its cover and, in addition to sheet music, it includes photos of the artist. An example of a matching folio is Jesse McCartney's *Beautiful Soul*, which includes sheet music for the twelve songs included on this album.

Mixed folios are collections of sheet music for songs that share a common bond, but were written by a variety of artists and writers. Examples of mixed folios include *The World's Greatest Love Songs* or *Favorite Wedding Songs of 2006*.

A *personality folio* features songs recorded by a particular artist. It may include songs culled from various albums and written by a variety of songwriters, for instance, *Cher Classics*. Similar to matching folios, personality folios typically include photos of the featured artist.

Sheet music of songs from popular Broadway musicals and television and film soundtrack albums are also compiled into folios along with photos from the productions. Examples of these folios include *Wicked, Music from the O.C.*, and *Rent*.

Publishers are typically paid a prorated amount of 10 percent to 12.5 percent of the suggested retail selling price of a folio. At the time of this writing, the majority of folios ranged from $16.95 to $19.95 retail. The amount paid by a publisher to a songwriter whose song is included in a folio is contingent on the royalty agreed upon in their publishing agreement. This most often ranges from 10 percent to 12 percent of the wholesale price, which typically is approximately half of the amount collected by the publisher.

In addition to payments to music publishers, companies that license, produce, and distribute personality folios typically pay 5 percent of the wholesale selling price to the artist whose songs are featured. Artists with maximum clout may be able to command up to 5 percent of the retail selling price (approximately double the wholesale price).

Instructional, Classical, and Additional Kinds of Sheet Music

There are thousands of school jazz bands, concert bands, marching bands, orchestras, chamber orchestras, and choruses, as well as innumerable churches and local community groups with choirs, organists, pianists, and other instrumentalists. In addition, countless students take lessons to learn how to play piano, guitar, and every imaginable musical instrument—and all of these individuals and organizations use printed music. Writing choral and instrumental music, and orchestrations for these markets, can generate substantial revenue for composers and songwriters who target them.

Writers whose songs and music are sold as band arrangements, recital pieces for soloists, orchestrations, arrangements for voices, and as instructional folios receive the royalty specified in their publishing agreements. This amount is typically 50 percent of the royalties collected by their publishers for these uses.

Music publishers interested in tapping into the instructional and/or classical music market should contact one of the three major licensors and distributors of this material to obtain submission guidelines. Contact information for these companies can be found at www.halleonard.com, www.warnerchappell.com, and www.musicsales.com.

Unpublished writers, composers, and music arrangers who hope to have their works marketed may need to target smaller companies initially, as the companies previously listed have a policy of not accepting unsolicited material. RYCUN Music, a small company that sells instructional music on the Internet, accepts submissions of original compositions for publishing consideration in the following genres: brass/wind ensemble, Christian, concert band, educational, instrumental solo/duet (brass/wind, guitar, percussion, piano, strings, vocal), jazz ensemble (big band), orchestra, saxophone quartet, string quartet, and various mixed ensembles. For submission guidelines contact www.rycunmusic.com.

Electronic Sheet Music

Electronic sheet music is sheet music that can be downloaded digitally from an Internet site. At sites, such as www.sheetmusicplus.com, www.jwpepper.com, and www.sheetmusicdirect.com, hundreds of thousands of titles are available.

The cost of electronic sheet music and folios is approximately the same as if they were purchased at stores, but online distributors offer a far greater selection than companies that stock physical product as well as the convenience of instant delivery. In addition, in many instances, customers may have their sheet music printed in any key they choose. Royalties for electronically delivered sheet music and folios are typically the same as for physical copies of sheet music sold in stores.

Reprinting Lyrics in Books and Magazines

Copyright law provides that lyrics (and excerpts of lyrics) may not be printed in books or magazines without the consent of the copyright owner. Licenses that grant this permission are commonly referred to as *lyric reprint licenses*. In most instances, the fees earned when lyrics are reprinted range from $100 to $1,500, depending on the number of copies being printed, the retail price, the number of lines being reprinted, the number of lyrics being printed, whether the book or magazine will be available in multiple languages, the territory in which the books or magazines will be sold, and the reprint licensing budget.

A sample reprint licensing agreement with explanations of each paragraph follows.

Analyzing a Lyric Reprint Licensing Agreement

The document that follows is typical of the kind of agreement a music publisher (or songwriter acting as his or her own publisher) signs in order to grant permission for a lyric to be printed in a book or magazine.

LYRIC REPRINT LICENSING AGREEMENT

July 1, 2006

Cookda Books
(insert book publisher's address)

To Whom It May Concern:
This agreement, when signed by you and us, constitutes our permission to you as stated below ("Agreement"). If not signed by both parties within sixty (60) days this offer is automatically withdrawn.

1. Grant of Rights
We grant you the non-exclusive right to print, publish, distribute and sell at your sole cost and expense, the following copyrighted musical composition ("Composition"), in the following format, with the following notice:

MY FOREVER FRIEND
By Jason Blume
© 2006 Dreamer's Moon Music (BMI)
Administered by Moondream Music Group
All Rights Reserved Used by Permission

Format: Inclusion of Lyrics; Hard cover book; 322 pages; retail selling price: $22.95
Title: What Unicorns Dream
Author: Maureen Custer
Publisher: Cookda Books
Number of copies: Permission to print maximum of 50,000 copies
Use: ONE-TIME USE ONLY
Language: English language only
Territory: Such rights shall be exercised in World (the "Territory")

This paragraph establishes that the music publisher grants permission to include the specified lyric in the book referenced above. It also states that the book's publisher may print, market, and sell copies of the book at its own expense. This right is granted on a nonexclusive basis, meaning that the music publisher may allow this lyric to be printed in other books as well.

The "notice" refers to the copyright symbol (©), the year of the first publication of the work, and the name of the copyright owner, the work's title, the author, the PRO affiliation, and the notifications "All Rights Reserved" and "Used by Permission."

In addition, this paragraph specifies the book's title, author, publisher, number of pages, retail price, conditions of usage, language, maximum number of copies that may be printed under this license, and countries for which these rights are granted.

2. Remuneration

In respect of such right, you shall pay the sum of Two Hundred-Fifty ($250.00) dollars, payable in US funds, within sixty (60) days, as full payment for your use of the Composition as granted herein. If a higher fee is paid to any other publisher for a similar or like usage, such higher fee shall automatically be paid to us hereunder, and this paragraph shall be deemed amended accordingly.

Affirmed here is that the book publisher is required to pay $250 (U.S.) to the song's publisher within sixty days of the signing of this agreement. This is the full payment for the right to reprint the lyric. It further includes a most favored nations clause, stating that if any other publisher is paid more for a comparable use in this book, the music publisher is to receive an equal amount.

3. File Copy

You shall supply us with one (1) gratis copy of any publication in which the composition is utilized.

This paragraph asserts that the music publisher is to receive one free copy of the book in which its lyric is printed.

4. Publication Expenses

The entire cost of printing and offering for sale (including all preparation and production expenses for artwork, engraving and printing costs) shall be your expense.

In this paragraph it is clarified that all expenses incurred in the publication of the book are to be paid by the book's publisher.

5. Term of Agreement

This Agreement and all of the rights granted to you by us hereunder shall be in full force and effect for a period of three (3) years from the date first written hereinabove (the "Term"). Following the expiration of the Term, you shall have the non exclusive right to sell and distribute copies of the Folio on hand as of the expiration of the Term for a period of one (1) year (the "Sell-Off Right").

This paragraph notes that the book publisher has the right to sell the book (referred to as the "Folio") for three years from the date of this contract. After the term has expired, the book publisher has the right to sell remaining copies for one additional year.

6. Status of Parties

Nothing contained herein is intended to constitute a partnership or joint venture between the parties hereto, it being understood that the relationship between us shall be that of independent contractors, and you shall have no authority to bind us in any way to any third party.

This paragraph maintains that the two parties entering into this agreement are independent of each other. It further specifies that the book publisher may not enter into any legal agreement that affects the music publisher or the song being published.

7. Right to Audit

You shall keep and maintain full and complete books and records concerning the Composition. We shall have the right, at our expense, to examine and audit, at your offices and upon prior reasonable notice, that portion of your books which relates to the Composition.

This paragraph states that the book publisher is required to maintain bookkeeping records regarding the song. It further affirms that the music publisher may audit the book publisher's records regarding the licensed composition. If the song's publisher chooses to do so, it must provide reasonable notice and conduct the audit at its own expense.

8. Right to Enter into Agreement

We grant and represent that we have the right to enter into this Agreement, and to grant all of the rights herein granted to you, and that exercise of such rights by you in accordance with the terms and provisions of the Agreement shall not infringe upon the copyright, property, private, contractual or other rights of, or constitute unfair competition with, any third party.

In this paragraph, the music publisher affirms that it has the right to enter into this agreement and grant the stated rights. It also states that by including this work in the book, the book publisher is not violating any other individual's or company's rights.

9. Assignment

This Agreement shall be binding upon and shall insure to the benefit of the parties hereto and their respective successors and shall not be assignable (except by us to any party acquiring all or substantially all of the business assets of Moondream Music Group).

This paragraph states that the parties shall be legally bound by this Agreement and that there is a benefit to both parties. It further states that the Agreement shall not be transferred by the book publisher to anyone else.

10. Controlling Law

This Agreement represents the entire agreement between you and us and may only be modified or terminated by an agreement in writing signed by you and us. The Agreement shall be governed and construed under the laws of the State of Tennessee applicable to agreements executed and to be wholly performed within the State of Tennessee, the County of Davidson.

In this paragraph it is affirmed that the terms specified in this Agreement represent the entire understanding between the two parties. In addition, it states that this Agreement may only be changed by or ended by another agreement signed by both parties. Finally, it states that this Agreement is subject to the laws of Tennessee, the state where the music publisher is located.

Sincerely,   ACCEPTED AND AGREED TO:

MOONDREAM MUSIC GROUP
9 Music Square South
Nashville, TN 37203

By: _____   By: _____
Jason Blume   Duncan Rice
President, Moondream Music   Director, Business Affairs
                                                       Cookda Books

Pitching Songs to Foreign Markets

Reaching the Number One spot on a U.S. airplay or sales chart earns a writer more money than attaining this distinction in any other country throughout the world. For instance, a Number One pop, country, R&B, or adult contemporary album released in the U.S. is virtually guaranteed being certified gold for sales of at least five hundred thousand copies. It's very likely that these albums will also earn platinum status for sales of at least one million copies.

A "gold" designation in Canada is awarded for sales of only fifty thousand units, with "platinum" being presented for one hundred thousand sales, while in countries such as Greece and Norway, a "gold" award is earned for sales of twenty thousand units and sales of forty thousand units earn "platinum" status. These lower award thresholds reflect these countries' smaller populations—and, therefore, reduced sales.

Likewise, hit singles outside the U.S. receive considerably less airplay (and, subsequently, less revenue from performance royalties) than their American counterparts. But there is still the potential of substantial earnings for U.S. songwriters who have hits in foreign territories.

Songwriters and music publishers who expand their pitching beyond the U.S. borders may not only find opportunities to pitch to hundreds of additional recording artists, but may also find outlets for styles of music that might not currently be in vogue in the U.S. For instance, there may be more opportunities to pitch pop and dance music in Europe than in the U.S.

The largest music publishing companies maintain offices throughout the world. Companies such as Sony BMG, Warner/Chappell, Universal Music Group, and EMI have offices in New York, Los Angeles, and Nashville, as well as throughout Europe and Asia. Smaller publisher Peer Music also has offices worldwide and has had considerable success in international markets.

The guidelines for pitching to music publishers outside the U.S. are the same as those discussed regarding submissions to domestic publishers (as explained in Chapter 2). It is always best to secure a referral when approaching a music publisher. A U.S. music publisher whose company has international offices will be likely to forward material deemed appropriate for the international market to their counterparts in other countries.

International music events such as Popkomm and Midem are attended by music publishers and record label representatives, as well as by songwriters, composers, and recording artists from around the world. Countless music publishing and licensing deals have been struck at these events, which offer unsurpassed networking opportunities.

Midem (originally abbreviated from "Marché Internationale de l'Édition Musicale," but now simply referred to as Midem) (www.midem.com) is a five-day event that takes place each January in Cannes, France. More than nine thousand participants from over ninety countries attend each year. Popkomm (www.popkomm.de) is a three-day conference held each September in Berlin, Germany. More than fifteen thousand visitors from more than forty countries typically participate.

Both of these events attract independent and major record companies, music publishers, online and traditional music distributors, recording artists, songwriters, composers, A&R executives, booking agents, music producers, concert promoters, import/exporters, retailers, music business attorneys, and mechanical and performing rights organizations.

Participants also include music buyers from ancillary fields and industries, including advertising, video games, and film and television. These conferences offer trade show exhibitions, panel discussions, and performance opportunities at concerts, showcases, and recitals, but much of the business is done as a result of networking in the nightclubs and lounges and at the parties and receptions that last until dawn.

SongLink International and *SongQuarters* are tip sheets whose listings include a high percentage of recording artists in countries other than the U.S. who are seeking songs. (See Chapter 5 for information about these tip sheets.) These can be invaluable resources for songwriters and music publishers seeking to place their material with artists throughout the world.

In some instances, when recordings are secured in foreign countries, songs' lyrics are translated to another language. In many cases, translations retain the essential meaning of the original lyric, although, in order to accommodate the melody and rhymes, some changes are typically made. In other instances, a completely new foreign language lyric is created. When this occurs, the lyricist who created the original English-language version retains his or her percentage of ownership of the song—despite the fact that his or her contribution to the composition is no longer relevant.

Translators are typically paid and credited as cowriters only for the foreign-language version to which they contribute; they retain no ownership of subsequent English language versions and/or additional translations.

In rare instances, translations are considered as works for hire, with the translator being paid a flat fee and entitled to neither royalties nor songwriting credit. But in most cases, a translator becomes a cowriter of the new-language version. The percentage of ownership conveyed to a translator typically ranges from 12.5 percent to 40 percent, depending on the country—and the translator's level of clout. As in any cowriting situation, if the translator earns 30 percent as a cowriter, he or she is also typically entitled to 30 percent of the publishing income for any revenue generated by the foreign language version.

New versions must be registered with their alternate (foreign-language) title with the writers' U.S. PROs. Failure to do so can result in lost performance royalty revenue.

Entering Songwriting Competitions

Entering songwriting competitions is a step hundreds of thousands of songwriters take in their quest for recognition. Contests are offered by local songwriting organizations as well as on an international level.

One of the primary incentives for songwriters to enter the largest competitions is the opportunity to have their work listened to by top industry professionals, including music publishers, A&R executives, and successful recording artists named in the contests' advertisements. In actuality, it is only the top tier of finalists (in some cases, less than 1 percent of the entrants) whose songs are ever listened to by these advertised professionals. This is because the most successful international competitions receive as many as one hundred thousand entries. Only the top ten to twenty songs in each category are forwarded to the celebrity judges, who make the final determination.

Entry categories typically include pop, rock, folk/Americana, country, R&B, hip-hop, Christian, holiday, comedy/novelty, children's, Latin, world, lyrics only, and instrumental songs. Fees to enter these competitions range from $10 to $35 per song, with additional fees imposed to have the same song considered in multiple categories.

When entering songs that are the result of collaborations, it's advisable to discuss how entry fees and prizes are to be divided among cowriters. Prizes, listed at each competition's Web site, most often include cash, musical instruments, recording equipment, guitar strings, CD duplication, subscriptions to publications and tip sheets, inclusion in a compilation CD (for distribution to music publishers and record labels), and in some instances, a single song publishing agreement.

Virtually all of the contests stress that it is the quality of the song itself, not the demo production, that is judged. However, it's very difficult for even the most skilled industry professionals to remain unaffected by the instrumentation and performances used to demonstrate a song's potential—especially when faced with the daunting task of quickly sorting through box loads of hundreds, if not thousands, of songs for review.

By listening to winning entries, it quickly becomes clear that songs that secure top prizes are almost always represented by professional-quality demos. Of course, it's possible that a reason for this is that those songwriters who have honed their craft to a level where they can beat tens of thousands of other entrants are likely to have grasped the importance of a demo that can demonstrate a song's highest potential.

Entering competitions can be an expensive proposition, especially for songwriters who enter multiple songs in various categories. Possible benefits, in addition to any prizes, include the validation, recognition, and credibility earned by the winners. Songwriters hoping their contest entry will serve as a springboard to success should be aware that this has rarely been the case. If previous years' winning entries had gone on to achieve significant commercial success, this fact would surely be advertised on the contests' Web sites and entry forms.

Competitions for performing songwriters (in which both the song and performance are judged) have led to artists receiving recording contracts and, in some instances, great success. Abba was catapulted to fame when their song "Waterloo" won the top prize at the Eurovision Song Festival (www.eurovision.tv/english) in 1974. The phenomenally successful Eurovision festival is televised throughout Europe but is open only to songwriters residing in Europe. The Kerrville Folk Festival's New Folk Competition (www.kerrville-music.com), held each Spring in Kerrville, Texas, is the most prestigious competition of its kind. Past winners include Lyle Lovett, Steve Earle, Robert Earl Keen, Jr., John Gorka, David Wilcox, and Nanci Griffith.

Some contests are open only to writers who have earned less than a specified amount of royalties from their songs (for instance, only songwriters who have earned less than $1,000 in royalties may enter the North Carolina Songwriters Co-op Song Contest). But many of the major contests are open to all songwriters, regardless of professional stature.

In many cases, top prizes have been won by writers whose credits include chart-topping singles—a fact not widely publicized by these contests that earn the majority of their revenue from hopeful amateurs. Those considering entering songs in competitions should check the eligibility requirements to determine whether amateurs compete against professionals.

National and international songwriting competitions include:

- *American Songwriter Magazine*'s Lyric Writing Competition (www.americansongwriter.com)

- Belfast Nashville Songwriters' Contest (www.belfastnashville.com)

- CMT/NSAI Song Contest (www.nashvillesongwriters.com)

- Great American Song Contest (www.greatamericansong.com)

- I Write the Songs Love Song Competition (www.iwritethesongs.com)

- International Narrative Song Competition (www.narrativemusic.ca/insc.html)

- International Original Christmas Song Contest (www.themusiclibrary.org)

- International Songwriting Competition (www.songwritingcompetition.com)

- John Lennon Songwriting Contest (www.jlsc.com)

- Just Plain Folks (www.jpfolks.com)

- LadySixString Annual Lyric Contest (for females only) (www.ladysixstring.com/lyricwritingcontest)

- Songs Inspired by Literature Contest (www.artistsforliteracy.org)

- Pacific Songwriting Competition (www.pacificsongwritingcompetition.com)

- Song of the Year (benefiting VH-1's *Save the Music*) (www.songoftheyear.com)

- Songprize.com International Songwriting Competition (www.songprize.com)

- Songwriters Guild of America Song Contest (www.songwriters.org)

- U.S.A. Songwriting Competition (www.songwriting.net)

- Univision (www.unisong.com)

Local and regional songwriting competitions include:

- Austin Songwriters Group Annual Song Contest (www.austinsongwritersgroup.com)

- Cooch Music's Amateur Songwriting Competition (www.coochmusic.com)

- Dallas Songwriters Association (www.dallassongwriters.org)

- FlightSafe Music QuickLaunch Song Contest (www.flightsafemusic.com)

- Metro Detroit Songwriting Contest (www.detroitsongs.com)

- Mid-Atlantic Song Contest
  (www.saw.org or www.sonicbids.com/midatlanticsong)

- North Carolina Songwriters Co-op Song Contest (www.ncsongwriters.org)

- Texas Songwriters' Cruise Contest (www.texassongwriterscruise.com)

Christian songwriting contests include:

- Christian Songwriting Competition
  (www.christiansongwritingcompetition.com)

- Contemporary Christian Songwriting Contest
  (www.christiansongwriting.com)

- Positive Pop Song Contest (www.positivepopsongcontest.com)

CHAPTER FOURTEEN

Understanding Subpublishing

The largest music publishing companies, such as EMI, Sony BMG, Universal Music Group, and Warner/Chappell, have offices located throughout the world. However, the majority of music publishers rely on third-party, local publishers in various countries to act as their agents, handling administrative functions in their respective countries.

Subpublishing refers to an arrangement in which a music publisher (referred to as an *original publisher*) engages another music publisher (referred to as a *subpublisher*), located in a foreign country, to represent one or more songs on the original publisher's behalf. The contract signed by both music publishers when entering into an arrangement of this kind is called a *subpublishing agreement*.

The Role of a Subpublisher

In some instances, publishers sign a deal to subpublish with a large company, such as Sony BMG, for worldwide representation. Other publishers find it advantageous to sign individual deals in various territories. For instance, a publisher may sign a subpublishing deal with EMI for Scandinavia, a separate deal with Universal to cover the rest of Europe, and another deal with Warner/Chappell to cover Australia and Asia.

Typically, a subpublisher issues recording licenses and collects the writer's and publisher's share of mechanical royalties and the publisher's share of performance royalties. The subpublisher distributes them to the original publisher, after deducting a specified percentage as its fee. The subpublisher is also responsible for issuing additional licenses, such as synchronization and print licenses, in its territory.

As stated in Chapter 10, the writer's share of foreign performance royalties is sent to the writer's U.S. performing rights organization, which distributes it appropriately. In some instances, subpublishers ask to retain a higher percentage of the performance royalties they collect, as they only collect half of the total performance royalties (only the publisher's share). Whether this is granted is determined by the bargaining power and negotiating skills of the parties.

In many instances, in addition to their administrative functions, subpublishers also work to secure recordings and other placements in their respective countries for the songs they subpublish. Subpublishing agreements may encompass one song, multiple songs, or entire catalogs of songs.

The term of a subpublishing deal is specified within the agreement and in most cases ranges from three to five years. As compensation, subpublishers generally retain between 15 percent and 25 percent of all money they collect on an original publisher's behalf. If a catalog includes established hits with guaranteed earnings, a subpublisher may be willing to accept as little as 10 percent—but this is not typical. Subpublishers are entitled to percentages of income generated only in their own territories; for instance, a Japanese subpublisher earns no portion of the income earned by a song for sales or performances in the U.S. or other countries.

Most subpublishing agreements include a provision specifying that in the event the subpublisher secures a recording in its territory of a song covered by the agreement, it is entitled to a higher percentage of income. In these instances, the subpublisher's fee is typically 40 percent to 50 percent of the revenue this particular recording generates.

In the event that a subpublisher manufactures and sells printed music, it usually pays the original publisher 10 percent to 15 percent of the retail selling price. If the subpublisher secures a local print licensing deal (but does not actually manufacture the materials itself), its compensation is generally the same percentage negotiated for all other royalties generated in its territory.

It is always advisable to include a provision in a songwriting agreement stating that money due a publisher from its subpublishing agreements is to be computed *at source*. This means that the amount the songwriter is paid is calculated based on the amount collected in the country in which it was earned. Without this clause, writers may wind up paying double commissions—paying a subpublisher, as well as the subpublisher's foreign divisions in different countries where the song is released. Only writers with considerable bargaining power are usually granted this provision.

Subpublishers normally pay original publishers an advance against future earnings. The amount a publisher can command is contingent on factors including whether the subpublished material has previously achieved significant success in the U.S. or other markets, the number of songs included, the size of the territory covered by the subpublishing agreement, and the currency exchange rate.

In some instances, referred to as *collection deals*, no money is advanced. When negotiating these deals, a publisher may be able to persuade a subpublisher to accept a lower percentage as its fee. Because the subpublisher assumes no financial risk in a collection deal, its fee is typically 10 percent to 15 percent of the money collected in its territory.

How to Get a Subpublisher

When a songwriter signs a single song or an exclusive songwriting publishing agreement, the writer foregoes the right to enter into subpublishing agreements covering the published composition(s). Only a song's publisher (or a writer acting as his or her own publisher) may enter into subpublishing agreements.

In most instances, publishers in foreign territories subpublish only songs and catalogs from established writers and publishers. Writers operating as their own publishers, who have not established a track record of hits, tend to enter into subpublishing agreements when they require representation in other countries for one or more songs that have already been recorded and are generating income.

Writers without income-generating catalogs who seek foreign subpublishers are in actuality looking for a publisher (as opposed to a subpublisher) to pitch and represent their songs outside the U.S. Subpublishers' primary functions are usually administrative, and if there is no income being produced, their services are not required.

As mentioned earlier in this chapter, EMI, Sony BMG, Universal Music Group, and Warner/Chappell all maintain offices throughout the world. By contacting these publishing companies' U.S. offices, writers may be able to gain referrals to the individuals who might offer subpublishing deals in these firms' foreign offices. As in the U.S., there are innumerable smaller publishing companies located on every continent. The Midem and Popkomm conferences, discussed in Chapter 13, provide unparalleled networking opportunities for songwriters and publishers to meet publishers from throughout the world.

In some instances, songwriters who live in the U.S. enter into publishing agreements with companies based outside the U.S. These deals as a rule cover only the country in which the music publisher is based and any specified additional countries. For example, a songwriter might sign a publishing deal in Sweden to cover all of Scandinavia. In these instances, the foreign publishers provide full publishing services, pitching the writer's catalog, setting up collaborations, and providing creative input, as well as handling administrative duties.

Analyzing a Subpublishing Agreement

The agreement that follows is an example of the contract a song publisher, or a songwriter acting as his or her own publisher, enters into with a music publisher outside the U.S., to have that publisher act on his or her behalf.

SUBPUBLISHING AGREEMENT

AGREEMENT made, entered into and effective as of the _____ day of _____, 2006, between _____, whose principal place of business is at _____, USA ("Owner") and _____, whose principal place of business is at _____, ("Sub-publisher").

This paragraph establishes the date the agreement goes into effect, the names of the publisher ("Owner") and the foreign publisher ("Subpublisher"), and their business addresses.

WHEREAS, Owner does now and will own and/or control the copyrights of certain musical compositions during the Term hereof; and

With this statement, the publisher affirms that it owns or controls the compositions listed in this contract and will continue to maintain ownership or control throughout the period of this agreement.

WHEREAS, Sub-publisher is engaged in the business of music publishing within the territory of _____ (hereinafter referred to as the "Licensed Territory").

In this paragraph, the subpublisher affirms that it operates as a professional music publisher in the country or countries covered by this agreement. These countries are referred to as the "Licensed Territory."

NOW, THEREFORE, in consideration of the covenants, promises, representations and warranties, hereinafter made by the parties hereto, Owner and Sub-publisher hereby agree as follows:

This statement means that in recognition of the statements and promises made within this agreement, the parties entering it agree to abide by the terms listed within the agreement.

1. Compositions

For purposes of this Agreement the term "Compositions" shall mean Owner's interest in all musical compositions now owned and/or controlled by Owner, or which may become owned and/or controlled by Owner during the Term hereof, in whole or in part (the "Compositions").

This paragraph defines "Compositions" as the owner's share of all songs he or she owns or controls, as well as those acquired during the term of this agreement. If the agreement were applicable to a writer who publishes only his or her own songs, it would likely refer to songs "written" or acquired during the term of the agreement.

In this instance, the agreement covers all songs in an existing catalog, as well as songs that are acquired by the publisher during the term of the agreement. Depending on how a specific subpublishing agreement is structured, it may cover only pre-existing songs. Other agreements may exclude pre-existing songs, covering only songs acquired during the term of the agreement.

2. Sub-Publisher's Rights

In consideration of the agreement for payment by Sub-publisher to Owner of the royalties fees and other sums hereinafter set forth, Owner hereby grants to Sub-publisher the following rights during the Term hereof:

This paragraph establishes that specific rights are being granted to the subpublisher in exchange for royalties and fees to be paid to the owner. The rights being conveyed are listed below.

(a) The exclusive right to print, publish, vend and cause to be printed, published and vended, printed copies of the Compositions in the Licensed Territory;

This subparagraph states that only the subpublisher shall have the right to authorize the printing, publishing, and sale of printed copies (such as sheet music and reprints of lyrics in books or magazines) of the covered works in the countries to which this agreement applies.

(b) The exclusive Rights of public performance, including broadcasting and television rights, and of licensing such rights in and for the Licensed Territory;

This subparagraph grants the subpublisher the right to be the only one in the covered territory permitted to authorize licenses for public performances, such as radio and television broadcasts.

(c) The exclusive right to grant non-exclusive licenses to manufacture parts serving to produce and reproduce, and make mechanical and electrical reproductions for phonograph records, CDs, pre-recorded tapes and transcriptions, to license the rental of such reproductions, to license such rights in and for the Licensed Territory, and to collect all royalties and fees payable therefor on sales and rental within the Licensed Territory;

This subparagraph establishes that the subpublisher shall be the only one in the covered territory with the right to issue nonexclusive mechanical licenses and collect royalties.

(d) The non-exclusive right, with prior written approval of Owner in each instance, to grant non-exclusive licenses for the synchronization, recording and use in and with motion pictures, television productions, commercials, videograms and all similar audio visual devices, produced in the Licensed Territory, and to make copies of the recordings thereof, and export such copies to all countries of the world;

This subparagraph states that the subpublisher has the right to grant synchronization licenses for the use of the covered compositions in television, films, and other media produced in the Licensed Territory—but only with the copyright owner's written approval. This right is not granted on an exclusive basis.

(e) The right to make new adaptations and arrangements of the Compositions, to procure any new or translated lyrics or titles thereof and to publish, sell or use such new matter and to authorize others to do so in the Licensed Territory; provided, however, that, Sub-publisher shall not make any such adaptations, arrangements, changes or translations without the prior written consent of Owner and all copyrights in such adaptations, arrangements, changes or translations shall be the exclusive property of Owner.

This subparagraph provides that the subpublisher may create or authorize and license new versions (including translations) and musical arrangements of the covered compositions. It further specifies that any such alterations must be authorized in writing by the copyright owner and that the resulting, altered works are owned by the copyright owner.

3. Retention of Rights
Sub-publisher shall retain the rights herein granted with respect to each of the Compositions until the expiration of the Term of this Agreement, at which time such rights shall terminate, absolutely, and revert to Owner free of any claim thereto by Sub-publisher, or any person, firm or corporation claiming rights from or through Sub-publisher.

This paragraph states that the subpublisher's rights remain in effect only until the end of the term of this agreement, at which time all rights revert to the copyright owner. Finally, it states that when the rights revert back to the copyright owner, he or she will not be held liable for any claims of ownership by or through the subpublisher.

4. Term of Agreement
The Term of this Agreement shall be three (3) years commencing with the date hereof, provided that in the event that Sub-publisher has not recouped any and all advances paid to Owner hereunder, then the Term shall be automatically extended until the end of the accounting period during which such aforementioned advances have been fully recouped, provided that no such extension shall last longer than one (1) year. Notwithstanding the foregoing, the rights granted to Sub-publisher herein shall remain with Sub-publisher for an additional period of one (1) year after expiration of the Term hereof solely with respect to any Composition for which Sub-publisher has procured a local commercially released recording of that Composition during the Term of this agreement (a "Cover Recording"), it being agreed, however, that a local commercially released recording shall not be deemed to be a Cover Recording unless and until such recording has sold at least fifty thousand (50,000) copies in total across all formats during the Term of this Agreement. During the Term of this Agreement, Sub-publisher shall collect on behalf of Owner, all income heretofore unpaid and now payable and all income earned during the Term of this Agreement which shall become payable during the Term and within one (1) year thereafter in connection with all sales and uses of the Compositions in the Licensed Territory.

This paragraph establishes that the agreement shall last for three years following the date it is signed. If the subpublisher has not recouped all money it advanced to the owner, the contract shall automatically continue until the end of the accounting period during which the advance is recouped. Regardless of whether the advance is recouped, the contract shall not extend more than one year.

It further states that the terms of the agreement shall apply for one year after the agreement expires for any locally released recording of a covered song for which the subpublisher secures a recording that sells more than fifty thousand copies during the time the agreement is in effect. Note that the extension period is typically one to three years.

This paragraph also establishes that the subpublisher will continue to collect any money earned in the covered territory during the term of the agreement that is paid within one year of the agreement's expiration.

5. Territory
The Licensed Territory shall be _____.

This paragraph provides a space to enter the name of the country (or countries) covered by the agreement.

6. Royalty Payments
Sub-publisher agrees to pay to Owner the following royalties.

This paragraph establishes the royalties the subpublisher will pay the copyright owner for various uses of the covered songs.

(a) Twelve and one-half percent (12$\frac{1}{2}$%) of the marked retail selling price of each copy of the Composition in any and every printed edition (except folio, book, album or similar edition) sold, paid for and not returned to the Sub-publisher;

This subparagraph establishes that the subpublisher will pay the copyright owner 12.5 percent of the retail selling price of every copy of sheet music of the covered compositions sold. This does not include printed copies of songs sold as part of a collection of sheet music. It further states that royalties are not due for items unsold and returned to the subpublisher.

(b) An amount equal to that proportion of twelve and one-half percent (12$\frac{1}{2}$%) of the marked retail selling price of each copy of folio, book, album or similar edition sold, paid for and not returned to Sub-publisher, which the number of Composition(s) contained therein bears to the total number of copyrighted musical compositions contained therein;

This subparagraph states that the royalty rate for copies of sheet music sold as part of a folio, book, album, or other similar collection will be based on the covered work's percentage of the total songs included in the collection. For example, if there are ten songs in a book and only one is covered by this agreement, the subpublisher must pay the owner 1.25 percent of the marked retail selling price (one-tenth of 12.5 percent).

(c) Eighty percent (80%) of any earnings received for each licensed use of the Composition in any and every printed edition, folio, book, album, magazine or newspaper;

This subparagraph establishes that the subpublisher will pay the copyright owner 80 percent of all money it receives as licensing fees for granting the right to include a covered composition in a printed edition, folio, book, album, magazine, or newspaper.

(d) Eighty percent (80%) of the publisher's share of all gross broadcasting, television and other performing fees with respect to the Composition, it being understood and agreed that Sub-publisher shall cause the performing and broadcasting rights of the Composition to be registered with the performing rights society in the Licensed Territory and shall authorize and direct the performing rights society to pay to it one hundred percent (100%) of said publisher's share and that Sub-publisher shall remit to Owner the above percentages thereof;

This subparagraph states that the owner will be paid 80 percent of all fees received by the subpublisher for the broadcast of the owner's works in the covered territory. It also establishes that it is the subpublisher's responsibility to register the compositions with the appropriate performing rights organization and to instruct the PRO to pay the full publisher's share to the subpublisher. It further states that the subpublisher will then pay the appropriate percentage (80 percent) of this amount to the owner.

(e) Eighty-seven and one-half percent (87½%) of all gross monies received by Sub-publisher or credited to Sub-publisher's account as royalties for all mechanical reproductions of the Compositions embodied in records or other devices sold in the Licensed Territory; provided, however, that, if Sub-publisher procures a Cover Recording of a Composition in the Licensed Territory, then Sub-publisher shall pay to Owner seventy percent (70%) of all gross monies received as royalties for all mechanical reproductions of said Cover Recording;

This subparagraph establishes that the subpublisher will pay the owner 87.5 percent of all mechanical royalties the subpublisher receives or is credited with in the covered territory. However, if the subpublisher is responsible for securing an additional recording in the territory covered by this agreement, it retains a higher percentage, paying the copyright owner 70 percent of all mechanical royalties generated by the cover recording.

(f) Eighty-five percent (85%) of any and all other sums received by Sub-publisher from any and all other sources, including synchronization rights, with respect to the exploitation of Compositions within the Licensed Territory;

This subparagraph states that the subpublisher will pay the copyright owner 85 percent of all other money it receives, generated by covered compositions in the territory. It further states that this includes fees for synchronization rights.

(g) No royalties shall be paid by the Sub-publisher upon professional copies distributed for professional exploitation or advertising purposes.

This subparagraph declares that the subpublisher is not required to pay the owner royalties for promotional copies.

(h) All monies that shall become payable by Sub-publisher under this Agreement in respect to the Compositions shall be the gross monies accruing at the source first payable, without any deduction whatsoever for fees, charges, commissions, or otherwise, either by Sub-publisher or by any other party or parties, except the amount thereof to be deducted and retained by Sub-publisher as herein in each instance specifically provided. Any fees which Sub-publisher shall pay in order to secure the collection of royalties earned by the Compositions (other than fees paid to any appropriate mechanical rights or performing rights societies in any portion of the Territory) shall be borne by Sub-publisher out of its retained share of earnings hereunder.

The provision expressed in this subparagraph is typically referred to as "at source." It states that the money due the publisher from the subpublisher is to be calculated based on the total income earned in the country or territory where the revenue is generated. Subparagraph (h) further states that the only amounts which may be deducted from the "at source" collections are the subpublisher's fees specified in this contract. Any other costs or fees are paid by the subpublisher, other than fees due to PROs or mechanical rights societies.

7. Advances
Sub-publisher shall pay to Owner as a non-returnable but fully-recoupable advance against royalties hereunder the sum of _____ US Dollars (US $_____) within fourteen (14) days following the date of this Agreement.

This paragraph establishes that the subpublisher will pay the copyright owner a specified advance within fourteen days of the date of this agreement. It further states that this advance, to be paid in U.S. currency, is fully recoupable from the owner's future earnings. But in the event that the covered songs do not generate sufficient income for the subpublisher to recoup the total amount of the advance, the copyright owner is not required to repay the money it was advanced.

8. Accounting
Payment of royalties by Sub-publisher to Owner shall be made semiannually within (60) sixty days following June 30th and December 31st of each year

covering income received by Sub-publisher in the preceding six month period and said payment shall be accompanied by a statement containing no less than the following information:

1. Title of Composition(s)
2. Number of printed copies and recorded versions of compositions sold
3. The performance credits for the Composition(s)
4. The source and gross amount of income
5. Sub-publisher's percentage and share of income
6. Owner's percentage and share of income
7. The period during which the income was earned

This paragraph states that the subpublisher is required to pay royalties to the copyright owner twice a year, within sixty days following June 30th and December 31st. These payments will cover money received by the subpublisher within the preceding six months. It also states that the subpublisher is required to provide an accounting statement that includes the seven items listed in this paragraph.

All statements to be rendered hereunder shall be certified by a certified public accountant or the local equivalent thereof, and certified as accurate by an officer of Sub-publisher. Statements shall be accompanied by the relevant portions of statements received by Sub-publisher from its licensees and sub-publishers in the Licensed Territory.

This paragraph further states that the royalty accounting statements are to be certified as accurate by a certified public accountant, as well as by an executive of the subpublisher's firm. In addition, it requires the subpublisher to attach copies of pertinent portions of the statements it has received detailing payments for the covered compositions.

9. Method of Payment

All payments to be made hereunder shall be made by wire transfer or check to the bank of Owner. In the event that a payment is to be made in foreign currency, the rate of exchange shall be the same as the rate prevailing at the time the royalties which are the subject of such payments were received by Sub-publisher. The parties hereby agree that taxes required to be withheld or to be paid upon earned income in accordance with local law shall be deducted from the amounts payable to Owner unless or until Owner shall deliver to Subpublisher a certificate of exemption, or some like certificate. In the event that a local government shall not permit a payment to be made to Owner, Sub-publisher shall so notify Owner immediately and Sub-publisher shall, when so instructed by Owner, deposit such payment to the account of Owner in a local bank.

This paragraph states that payments by the subpublisher to the copyright owner shall be made by either a wire transfer or a check sent to the owner's bank. It further establishes that if payment is made in foreign currency, the exchange rate must be the same as the rate in effect when the subpublisher was paid. In addition, this paragraph declares that any taxes due in the covered territory will be withheld from the owner's royalties unless the copyright owner provides the subpublisher with a certificate exempting it from taxation. Finally, the paragraph maintains that if the government in the subpublisher's territory will not allow payment to be made to the owner, the subpublisher is required to immediately contact the copyright owner and, if requested, deposit the money in the owner's account in a local bank.

10. Audits

Sub-publisher shall permit Owner or its representatives to inspect and audit at the place of business of Sub-publisher, during usual business hours, and upon reasonable notice, all books, records and other documents and to make copies or excerpts therefrom, to the extent that they relate to the Compositions, during the Term of this Agreement and for one (1) year after the expiration thereof, or, in the case of Cover Recordings, for so long as Subpublisher shall be collecting income with respect thereto.

This paragraph establishes that the copyright owner has the right to inspect and make copies of the subpublisher's bookkeeping records. In the event the owner chooses to audit, the inspection must be carried out at the subpublisher's office during its regular business hours. It also affirms that any such audit must take place either during the term of the agreement or within one year after its expiration. In addition, it asserts that in the case of cover recordings, the owner may audit as long as the subpublisher is continuing to collect income from the cover recordings.

11. Copyright Notice

Sub-publisher agrees that it will cause to be printed on the title page of each and every copy of each Composition published and distributed in the Licensed Territory pursuant to this Agreement, proper notice of copyright together with the name(s) of the composer(s), the author(s) and the copyright owner of the Compositions.

In this paragraph, the subpublisher agrees to be sure the proper notice of copyright is included on each copy. This typically includes the copyright symbol (©), the year the composition was copyrighted, and the name of the copyright owner. In addition, the names of the songwriters and publisher are to be included on the title page of every copy of any of the covered compositions sold in the subpublisher's territory.

12. Copies
Sub-publisher agrees to forward to Owner two (2) copies of each printed edition and local release containing the Compositions or any adaptations thereof immediately upon publication.

This paragraph states that the subpublisher will, upon publication, immediately provide the copyright owner with two copies of each printed version of a covered composition (such as sheet music) or recording released within the subpublisher's territory.

13. Sub-Publisher's Representations and Warranties
Sub-publisher hereby represents and warrants to Owner that it knows of no actions, suits, proceedings, agreements or other impediments, actual or threatened, which could prevent or impair it from performing its duties hereunder.

In this paragraph, the subpublisher asserts that it is not aware of any lawsuits or other actions that would cause it to be unable to legally fulfill its obligations.

14. Owner's Representations and Warranties
Owner represents and warrants that it has full right, power and authority to enter into this Agreement and grant to Subpublisher the rights hereinabove set forth, upon the terms and conditions herein contained.

In this paragraph, the owner affirms that it has the right to enter into this agreement and grant the rights contained within the agreement.

15. Reservation of Rights
Owner hereby reserves all rights of every kind and nature not specifically granted to Sub-publisher herein, and the right to all fees, monies or other considerations derived from such reserved rights. Without limiting the generality of the foregoing, the following rights and any fees, monies or other considerations derived therefrom, except as herein provided, shall be reserved to Owner:

This paragraph states that the copyright owner retains all rights and any income that is not specifically conveyed to the subpublisher by the terms of this agreement. It clarifies the owner's reserved rights further in the subparagraphs below.

(a) All copyrights in the Compositions and in any adaptations, arrangements and new lyric versions thereof throughout the universe and all rights existing under such copyrights in the Licensed Territory.

This subparagraph states that the copyright holder retains ownership of the copyrights to all the covered compositions, including any new versions, in the subpublisher's territory and throughout the world.

(b) The exclusive right throughout the universe to dramatize the Compositions and to license the use and performance of such dramatic versions.

This subparagraph affirms that the owner shall be the only one with the right to have dramatic works based on the musical compositions created and licensed.

(c) The exclusive right throughout the universe to make cartoon, literary and other subsidiary versions of the Compositions and to publish and sell such versions.

This subparagraph establishes that the copyright owner retains the exclusive right to authorize, publish, and sell cartoons and books based upon the songs covered by the agreement.

(d) The exclusive right to grant licenses for the entire world and universe for the synchronization of the Compositions with sound motion pictures and television films, together with the right to grant permission for the public performance for profit of the Compositions as contained in such sound motion pictures and television films, if same are produced and originated outside the Licensed Territory, and Sub-publisher shall not share in any fees received by Owner or any local publisher in respect thereto.

This subparagraph states that the copyright owner maintains the exclusive right to issue synchronization licenses (as explained in Chapter 11) to include covered compositions in films and television shows produced outside the subpublisher's territory. It further establishes that the subpublisher is not entitled to any income earned from synchronization licenses generated outside of the territory covered by this agreement.

16. Failure to Comply

In the event that Sub-publisher fails to account and make payments hereunder when due and such failure is not cured within ten (10) days after written notice thereof has been served on Sub-publisher, or fails to perform any obligations required of it hereunder and such failure is not cured within thirty (30) days after written notice has been served on Sub-publisher, or becomes inactive, ceases doing business, or shall go into compulsory liquidation, or shall go into bankruptcy or make an arrangement for the benefit of or with creditors, or any insolvency or composition proceedings are commenced by or against Sub-publisher, then and in any of such events, in addition to such other rights or remedies which it may have at law or otherwise under this Agreement, Owner may elect to cancel or terminate this Agreement without prejudice to any rights or claims it may have, and then all rights in the Compositions hereunder automatically and immediately shall revert to Owner and

Subpublisher may not thereafter exercise any rights hereunder. Owner's failure to terminate this Agreement upon any default or defaults shall not be deemed to constitute a waiver of Owner's rights to terminate the same upon any subsequent default.

This paragraph addresses the consequences of the subpublisher's failure to live up to its contractual obligations. It establishes that the copyright owner may terminate the agreement under the following circumstances:

- If the subpublisher does not provide accounting and payments due and still does not do so within ten days of receiving written notice

- If the subpublisher fails to live up to its obligations and fails to remedy the problem within thirty days of receiving written notice

- If the subpublisher goes out of business

- If the subpublisher enters bankruptcy or a similar arrangement.

All rights revert to the copyright owner if it chooses to cancel the agreement because of the circumstances listed.

17. Assignment of Agreement

This Agreement shall be binding upon and inure to the benefit of the parties hereto and their respective successors and assigns, provided that Subpublisher shall not assign this Agreement or any of its rights herein to any person, firm, LLC or corporation without the prior written consent of Owner.

This paragraph declares that the agreement shall remain in force provided the subpublisher does not assign any of its rights to an individual or company without obtaining written permission from the copyright owner.

18. Addresses

Any notice, accounting or payment which either party hereto is required or desires to give to the other party shall be addressed to such other party's address first set forth above, or to the most recent of such other addresses as such party shall have designated in writing to the other party.

This paragraph states that accounting statements, payments, and correspondence are to be sent to the addresses entered on the first page of this agreement. It further states that notification of change of address by either the copyright owner or subpublisher must be done in writing.

19. Disclaimer

This Agreement shall not be construed to constitute a partnership or joint venture between the parties hereto and neither party shall become bound by any representation, act or omission of the other.

This paragraph declares that the copyright owner and subpublisher are neither in partnership, nor in a joint business venture together. Therefore, neither party is liable for the other's actions.

20. Jurisdiction

This Agreement shall be governed by and construed under the laws of the State of New York applicable to contracts executed and wholly to be performed therein. The venue for any action, suit or proceeding brought by either party against the other, respecting this Agreement shall be in a court of competent jurisdiction.

This paragraph establishes that the agreement shall be enforced according to the laws of the state which the parties choose (in this instance, New York). Any legal action regarding this agreement must be heard by a court authorized to render an enforceable decision.

21. The Entire Agreement

This Agreement constitutes the entire agreement between the parties with respect to the subject matter hereof, and cannot be altered, amended or modified, in part or in full, in any way except by an instrument in writing signed by the parties hereto, unless otherwise expressly provided herein.

This final paragraph states that the agreement contains the complete understanding between the copyright owner and subpublisher. It further states that the terms of the agreement may only be changed if both parties agree to the revisions in writing.

IN WITNESS WHEREOF, the parties hereto have caused this Agreement to be duly executed upon the day and year first above written.

_____   _____

OWNER   **SUBPUBLISHER**

Both parties sign in the spaces included above.

A major component of being a successful music publisher is establishing close business relationships. By engaging the services of subpublishers, music publishers based in the U.S. gain the benefit of having their songs represented by publishers with connections throughout the world. Additionally, they gain the advantage of having their material represented by individuals who are fluent in each respective country's language, and knowledgeable about the customs and manner in which business is successfully conducted in various cultures. This can expedite royalty payments, facilitate licensing, and possibly lead to recordings and other uses that generate income a publisher and its writers might otherwise never earn.

CHAPTER FIFTEEN

Learning How the Music Charts Work

Almost every songwriter dreams of having a song reach Number One on the charts—but many writers don't understand how chart positions are determined. *The charts* refers to the rankings of popular songs and albums in a variety of categories by the two main music industry resources—*Billboard* and *Radio & Records* (typically referred to as *R&R*). These companies publish the information they compile in their magazines and on their Web sites.

Singles Sales Charts

Before proceeding further it will help to understand the meaning of singles. When an album is completed, the record label chooses a song to be released as a *single*, a song targeted by the label to be publicized and promoted to radio stations. Typically, only one song from a particular album is designated as a single at any given time. Songs that are not selected as singles are referred to as *album cuts*.

If a song is available for purchase in a separate configuration from the album (such as a CD single) it is referred to as a *commercial single*. Commercial singles typically include several songs from the artist's album in addition to the one being promoted as the "hit" single, or may include alternate mixes of the same song. Most albums yield three or four singles. Only singles garner significant radio and video airplay—and performance royalties that can exceed a million dollars for songwriters and music publishers. Hit singles are a primary means of maximizing product exposure and album sales.

Although the artist and producer are consulted about which song they think should be a single, the decision is ultimately made by their record label's A&R and promotion staff. The single selection process typically relies on input from a record label's radio promotion staff, the artist, the artist's manager, the producer, and the A&R staff. To a large extent, the final decision rests in the hands of whoever has the most clout. Record labels are likely to defer to an artist with superstar stature, granting the artist the final say regarding the choice of singles. The singles selected to promote a new or developing artist are typically chosen by the record label with the justification that, in the case of a mainstream artist, it will have invested more than a million dollars in the recording and promotion of the artist's album.

A single is chosen based on the belief that it will have the best chance of garnering radio and video airplay, thereby compelling listeners to buy the album on which it is included. Although there are artists who have sustained successful careers without the benefit of hit singles, this scenario is not typical.

In some instances, a single is released without being part of an album. This most often happens in the dance music genre. An extended version of the song, as well as several alternate mixes, are typically included on dance singles. In some cases, a record label may sign a new artist to a *singles deal*, meaning that the label is obligated only to release one or two singles. This gives the record label an opportunity to "test the waters" without investing the money to record an entire album. An album will be completed and released only if the single receives significant airplay and sales.

Some superstars' singles may race to the top of the charts in eight or ten weeks. Other songs, especially those by new artists, may take twenty-five weeks or more to reach the top of the charts. But it typically takes a pop, country, adult contemporary, Christian, Latin, or R&B/hip-hop single between sixteen and twenty-two weeks to reach the Number One position in the *Billboard* and *R&R* charts. Most songs maintain their peak position one or two weeks, but depending on their popularity (and the clout of the record label's promotion staff), many songs have remained at Number One for several additional weeks. In the rarest instances, recordings by Mariah Carey, the Beatles, Usher, and the Bee Gees have remained at Number One for fourteen weeks or more.

After peaking, songs often have a slow descent back down the charts, remaining on the chart ten or more additional weeks. After this has occurred, a subsequent single is chosen and the process begins again.

Billboard singles charts rank individual songs in categories including Hot 100, Hot Digital, the Billboard Pop 100, Hot Rap Tracks, Hot R&B/Hip-Hop Songs, Adult R&B, Rhythmic, Hot Latin, Hot Country, Modern Rock, Mainstream Rock Tracks, Adult Top 40, Adult Contemporary, Blues, Reggae, World Music, New Age, Hot Dance Music/Club Play, Dance Radio Airplay, Hot Christian Singles and Tracks, Hot Christian Adult Contemporary, and Hot Gospel Tracks. The magazine also includes selected international singles charts.

R&R features music charts including Adult Contemporary, Hot Adult Contemporary, Rock, Active Rock, Alternative, Americana, CHR (Contemporary Hit Radio) Pop, CHR Rhythmic, Smooth Jazz, Triple A, Christian Adult Contemporary, Christian Rock, Christian Inspirational, Christian CHR, Country, Gospel, Latin Contemporary, Regional Mexican, Tropical, Urban, and Urban Adult Contemporary.

Understanding Radio Formats and Singles Charts

In order to understand how chart positions are calculated, one must be aware of how a station chooses which songs it plays and how often these songs are played; this is known as a station's *play list*. To the casual listener, it may seem as if disc jockeys play whatever their favorite tunes might be, but in actuality, this is rarely the case.

With the exception of the small percentage of airtime allotted for approved requests and "oldies," DJs play only songs chosen by a station's *music director* or *program director*, the individual in charge of selecting the songs that comprise a station's play list. The station's music director decides not only which songs are played during each one-week period, but also how many times a day each of these songs is broadcast. The play list is revised each week.

In many instances, the decision of which songs to play is determined by a consultant. Radio consultants conduct research, and analyze data, to assess which songs are preferred by various age groups and genders in a variety of geographic locations. They test listeners' responses to new music and older songs to determine which songs the station's targeted demographic wants to hear more of—and which ones the audience is tired of hearing. This information, as well as an assessment of the songs being played at the most successful competing stations, is used to develop stations' play lists.

Many radio stations are owned by media conglomerates that own hundreds of stations. In many of these instances, the parent companies dictate their stations' play lists. Clear Channel Communications, the most successful company of its kind, owns approximately 9 percent of the thirteen thousand radio stations in the U.S., accounting for 18 percent of the industry's revenue. Clear Channel also owns concert promotion companies, concert venues, magazines, research and consulting services, news networks, advertising services, Web sites, high-speed Internet service providers, a company that sells products related to Broadway shows, digital audio software manufacturers, and more. Cumulus Media is the second largest company of its kind, owning more than three hundred radio stations in the U.S.

There have been allegations that Clear Channel and Cumulus restrict airplay of specific artists and songs while promoting other artists and songs as well as specific political agendas. The companies deny these charges, citing various facts to refute the charges. Although Clear Channel reports that it employs nine hundred program directors, each in charge of their respective stations, there are ongoing concerns that a relatively small number of individuals and companies wield an inordinate amount of influence over the songs and recording artists played on radio stations throughout the U.S.

Record labels' promotion staffs supply copies of their artists' singles to radio stations' music directors and do their best to persuade them to add the songs to the stations' play lists. Broadcasters are prohibited from accepting cash or gifts of any value in exchange for playing specific songs—unless the transaction is disclosed to listeners. Such payments, known as *payola*, whether as outright bribes, paid vacations, gifts (such as high-end electronics), drugs, or other inducements violate a federal statute.

In 2005, when Sony BMG admitted to payola (in some cases, with independent promoters acting as middlemen), the company was fined $10 million by the Attorney General's office, and the money was donated to charity.

During any particular week, a station's play list typically includes twenty-five to thirty songs. A slot opens up only when a song is removed from the list, either because it is not performing well with audiences, or because it has run its course, having peaked and then retreated. The competition for one of these coveted slots is intense.

The frequency with which a song is played on a particular station is referred to as its *rotation*, and it is determined by a station's music director. Songs in *heavy rotation* receive the most airplay—six or seven spins a day. Songs placed in *medium rotation* are played four or five times a day, while those in *light rotation* are typically played two or three times daily. Most play lists allot a small percentage of overall airtime for "recurrent" songs, recent hits that have peaked and are no longer being promoted. Music directors typically also include slots for "oldies."

Reporting Radio Stations

Billboard and *R&R* designate specific radio stations in each music format as *reporting stations*. In each genre, leading stations are selected to be reporting stations based on their Arbitron ratings—provided that they broadcast a specified minimum percentage of current music. Arbitron is the leading marketing research firm that ranks radio stations according to their audience share.

Radio stations that play various music formats allocate different percentages of airtime for current songs versus older material. For instance, to be considered by *Billboard* as a reporting country music station, 60 percent of the music a station plays must be current country music. Rock stations play a much higher percentage of older songs and might only be required to play 30 percent current songs to be considered as a reporting station.

Every *Billboard* reporting station is monitored electronically twenty-four hours a day, seven days a week by Nielsen's Broadcast Data Systems' (BDS') Radio Track Service, which provides *Billboard* with the number of detections for each song played during a given week. With a few exceptions (explained below), songs are assigned their chart positions based on the amount of airplay they receive on reporting stations; so a Number One song on a particular chart is one that received the most performances in the previous week, at stations that report to this publication.

R&R has two levels of reporting stations—"Monitored" and "Indicator" reporting stations. The songs played on *monitored stations* are reported to *R&R* by Mediabase, a company that uses technology designed to electronically detect and identify songs played on the radio. *Indicator stations* are those that reach smaller audiences; they provide *R&R* with their weekly play lists. A song is assigned a *bullet*, an indicator of upward movement on the chart, when its number of detections increases from the previous week.

Many stations report to both *Billboard* and *R&R*; some report only to one or the other of these publications. The groups of stations designated as reporters in any particular musical format are sometimes referred to as *panels* by the publications that compile charts. A station's reporting status may change based on a shift in their format or their ratings. Therefore, the number of reporting stations in any particular format is not a fixed number; for instance, some months there may be 115 country reporters, while other months, the number may be 122.

At the time of this writing, *Billboard* had the following numbers of reporting stations in these popular formats: 117 country stations, thirty-five Latin pop stations, 137 R&B/hip-hop stations, and 115 mainstream Top 40 stations. *R&R*'s panels ranged in size from sixteen stations reporting Tropical music (a category of Latin music), to 117 stations for CHR/Pop (Contemporary Hit Radio, a term for Top 40), and 121 stations reporting country music airplay.

These numbers represent only a small percentage of the stations playing these musical formats—for instance, there are more than two thousand stations playing a country music format in the U.S. The reporting stations typically lead the way, with nonreporters playing many of the same songs as the stations that are monitored.

In most cases, for a song to attain the Number One position, it must be in heavy rotation on almost every reporting station—at the same time. In some instances, a song may reach this slot although it is not being played on one or two reporting stations, or despite being in light or medium rotation at some of the stations.

In each weekly edition, *R & RP* magazine publishes a list of the singles each reporting station has added to its play list. Online subscribers can view the play lists and the actual number of spins received by each song played on every one of *R&R*'s reporting stations. An additional publication, *Billboard Radio Monitor*, provides analogous information regarding the play lists at stations that report to *Billboard*.

How Singles Chart Positions Are Determined

While *R&R*'s charts are based solely on radio airplay, *Billboard* uses a complex formula that, in addition to radio airplay, factors in the number of sales and permanent digital downloads of singles to compile their Hot 100, Pop 100, and Hot R&B/Hip-Hop charts. The Hot 100 chart positions are based on a ratio of two thirds airplay to one third sales.

This ratio is applicable only to the entire Hot 100 songs averaged together; it's a misconception that every song's ranking is based 33.3 percent on its sales and 66.6 percent on the airplay it receives. For instance, the chart position for a song receiving a great deal of radio airplay, but few sales may be determined by a formula that weighs 90 percent on airplay and only 10 percent for sales—or vice versa. Similarly, rankings on the Pop 100 chart are based on an approximately 50/50 ratio of sales (including digital sales) and airplay.

The R&B/Hip-Hop songs chart positions are determined by a ratio of approximately 95 percent airplay and 5 percent sales. This is because at the time of this book's printing, digital sales were not being incorporated into the equation and there were relatively few sales of physical singles in this genre. All other *Billboard* singles charts (other than those that specifically tally only sales, such as the Hot 100 Singles Sales chart) determine rankings solely by the amount of airplay songs receive on reporting stations.

Country charts are *weighted* by *R&R*. This means that a formula is used to assign a greater number of points for airplay on stations that reach the widest audiences. So, being played on one of the nation's biggest country radio stations contributes more to a song's position on the *R&R* Country chart than would a spin on a station that reaches a smaller audience. Country music is the only format for which stations are weighted and points are factored by *R&R*. Similarly, *Billboard* uses a formula that assigns a higher value to songs being played at peak hours, and to airplay on the largest radio stations.

Defining the Music Ranked on Various Charts

Billboard and *R&R* compile charts monitoring airplay in a wide variety of radio music formats. While some of the formats (such as reggae, blues, country, and new age) are self-explanatory, the section that follows explains those that can be a bit confusing.

Pop music encompasses an exceptionally wide range, including hip-hop by artists such as Ciara and the Black Eyed Peas, rap by artists such as Ludacris and 50 Cent, rock by acts in the category of 3 Doors Down and Green Day, the R&B stylings of Mario and Usher, the jazz/pop of Nora Jones and Michael Bublé, and songs that are sometimes referred to as "pure pop," by artists such as Kelly Clarkson and Maroon5. *Billboard* ranks pop singles on its Pop 100 chart; *R&R*'s CHR Pop chart serves this same function. These charts monitor radio formats that play mainstream music, songs that are typically thought of as Top 40.

Billboard's Hot 100 chart differs from its Pop 100 chart in that it tallies airplay from reporting stations in all musical formats that Nielsen BDS monitors, whereas the Pop 100 chart monitors only *mainstream Top 40* stations (those that play songs by pop artists such as Madonna, Nickelback, the Black Eyed Peas, Shakira, and Lifehouse). Songs appearing on the Hot 100 chart also appear on the chart that applies to their specific formats. For instance, songs that are in the Top Ten on the Pop 100, Hot Country, and Hot R&B/Hip-Hop are almost certain to also be listed on the Hot 100 chart.

Songs that reach the Top Ten on charts such as the Christian, dance, and Latin charts typically do not garner sufficient airplay to be included in the Hot 100. This is because relatively few radio stations feature these formats, and, therefore, these songs do not amass nearly the amount of airplay as do songs in more mainstream genres.

Billboard's Adult Top 40 and *R&R*'s counterpart, Hot Adult Contemporary, monitor stations that play Top 40/pop music, but without aggressive rock or rap titles. Rob Thomas, 3 Doors Down, and Gavin DeGraw are among the artists who might be played on these stations; Missy Elliot and Queens of the Stone Age would not.

Adult Contemporary is a lighter version of Adult Top 40, playing fewer up-tempo titles and featuring artists such as Kimberley Locke, Jim Brickman, Celine Dion, Michael Bublé, and Phil Collins. Older songs from artists such as Journey, Paul McCartney, and the Manhattans are featured on these formats.

Billboard's Modern Rock Tracks and *R&R*'s Active Rock charts reflect airplay reported by stations that play an aggressive, hard rock format, featuring artists such as Nine Inch Nails, Foo Fighters, Weezer, and Gorillaz. *Billboard*'s Mainstream Rock Tracks and *R&R*'s Rock charts rank airplay garnered by rock songs and artists with a bit more mainstream appeal. Artists played on these stations include 3 Doors Down, Green Day, Papa Roach, and Trapt.

R&R's Alternative chart features artists such as Beck, Jimmy Eat World, Crossfade, and System of a Down, as well as many of the same artists whose songs are on the Rock charts. While some *alternative* stations target a male eighteen- to thirty-year-old demographic, featuring primarily guitar-driven, hard rock songs, others in this format are more inclusive of the softer songs within the genre that tend to be more popular with female listeners. But in all instances, stations playing an alternative format play primarily current music, while the other rock formats tend to include high percentages of older songs.

The Americana charts track songs played on radio stations whose formats are a hybrid of alternative country, folk, and music by singer/songwriters who don't quite fit in any other category. Artists such as Dwight Yoakum, John Hiatt, Mary Gauthier, Robert Earl Keen, Lucinda Williams, Willie Nelson, Michelle Shocked, and John Prine are included in this format.

Christian music encompasses various styles of music, their common bond being the lyric content. To reflect these different musical approaches, *Billboard* and *R&R* have several Christian music charts. *Billboard*'s Hot Christian Singles and Tracks and *R&R*'s Christian CHR charts rank the songs played on radio formats that feature artists such as Tobymac, Casting Crowns, Matthew West, and Jars of Clay, artists whose contemporary sounds are similar to those heard on the pop charts.

Billboard's Hot Christian Adult Contemporary chart and *R&R*'s analogous Christian Adult Contemporary chart monitor stations whose formats target a more mature demographic, playing artists including MercyMe, Michael W. Smith, Point of Grace, and Steven Curtis Chapman. The Hot Gospel chart featured in *Billboard* and *R&R*'s Gospel chart track airplay of songs recorded by artists such as Yolanda Adams, CeCe Winans, Mighty Clouds of Joy, and Anointed.

R&R also has a Christian Inspo (Inspirational) chart that reports airplay of worship-oriented songs recorded by artists such as Nicol Sponberg, Selah, Andy Chrisman, and Jadon Lavik. In addition, *R&R* charts Christian Rock, ranking the airplay of songs by artists such as Plumb, Wedding, Pillar, and Jeremy Camp.

Latin music covers a wide spectrum of styles, the common denominator being that it is geared to Spanish-speaking listeners and is typically recorded in Spanish. Various charts monitor airplay in several Latin formats. *Billboard*'s Latin Pop and

R&R's Spanish Contemporary charts rank airplay for mainstream songs by artists such as Shakira, Juanes, and Paulina Rubio.

Both *Billboard* and *R&R* compile charts that report airplay in the *Regional Mexican* format that features artists such as Patrulla 81, Los Tigres Del Norte, and Intocable. *Tropical Latin* music, with songs by artists such as Marc Anthony, Frankie Negrón, and Daddy Yankee are reported by both of the trade publications as well.

Billboard's Rhythmic Top 40 and *R&R*'s CHR/Rhythmic charts include songs that are also on the R&B/Hip-Hop and Rap charts. But the songs on the Rhythmic charts tend to be a bit more mainstream pop, featuring artists such as Nelly, Missy Elliot, and 50 Cent.

A *crossover hit* is a song that is successful in more than one radio format and, therefore, appears on multiple charts. For example, songs by artists such as Mariah Carey, Mario, and R. Kelly have been on the Pop, R&B/Hip-Hop, Rhythmic, and Adult Contemporary charts. Shania Twain, Faith Hill, Lonestar, Martina McBride, Tim McGraw, Rascal Flatts, and Keith Urban have all crossed over from the Country charts to success on the Pop and Adult Contemporary charts; MercyMe's songs have been hits of the Christian, Pop, and Adult Contemporary charts.

Pop and Adult Contemporary charts have featured Dido, Kelly Clarkson, Five for Fighting, Celine Dion, Sheryl Crow, and Maroon5. Likewise, 3 Doors Down, Hoobastank, and Coldplay have had songs on the Rock and Pop charts, and in some instances, the Adult Contemporary charts as well.

As you learned in Chapter 10, performance royalties are based on the amount of airplay a song receives. Therefore, it follows that songs that become hits in multiple formats garner considerably more airplay than songs played in only one. A song that reaches Number One on the Pop, R&B, and Adult Contemporary charts may earn in excess of $2 million in performance royalties. In addition, crossover songs are exposed to a wider audience of potential buyers.

Limited access to the *Billboard* and *R&R* charts is available at no charge at www.billboard.com and www.radioandrecords.com. Full access to all charts is available to paid Internet subscribers and to those who purchase the magazine.

Album Sales Charts

While *R&R* focuses exclusively on reporting radio airplay, *Billboard* magazine also charts the sales of singles and albums. Entire albums do not receive radio airplay—only selected cuts. Therefore, *Billboard*'s album charts are based exclusively on sales; airplay is not a factor in determining an album's chart position.

Billboard's album charts include the Top 200 (which ranks the top two hundred selling albums regardless of musical style), Top R&B/Hip-Hop Albums, Top Country Albums, Top Bluegrass, Top Rap Albums, Top Comedy Albums, Top Latin Albums, Jazz, Contemporary Jazz, Classical, Classical Crossover, and Soundtracks, as well as international charts.

Billboard's Pop Catalog chart ranks sales of albums that have been released for at least two years and have fallen below 100 on the *Billboard* Top 200 chart. This chart also includes reissues of older albums, such as a CD version of an album that had previously been available only as a cassette. The Pop Catalog chart is where one would likely find albums by artists such as the Beatles, the Beach Boys, Pink Floyd, Led Zeppelin, Elvis Presley, and Jimi Hendrix.

Sales figures are compiled and delivered to *Billboard* on a weekly basis by Nielsen SoundScan (typically referred to simply as SoundScan). *SoundScan* is an electronic information collection system that tracks the sale of music and music videos from more than seventeen thousand merchants throughout the U.S. and Canada, including stores such as Target, Tower, and Wherehouse; online stores such as Amazon.com and Walmart.com; mail-order music providers; and in some instances, concert venues where music is sold. The figures compiled by SoundScan reflect more than ten million sales transactions per week, representing more than 85 percent of retail music sales in the U.S.

SoundScan uses barcodes and information obtained from Internet download providers to track sales figures. Therefore, it is critical for artists selling independently produced CDs to include barcodes if they want the sales of their products included in *Billboard*'s music sales charts. A *barcode* is a Universal Product Code identification number that allows a product to be scanned and tracked. Most professional CD duplication services provide bar codes for their customers, included in the price of a duplication package.

Digital Sales Charts

Prior to the advent of the digital age and the development of MP3s, in many instances, record labels released a commercial single. Instead of buying an entire album, this allowed fans to acquire their favorite song, typically packaged along with one or two additional songs, which were referred to as *"B" sides.*

Now, only a small percentage of radio singles are commercially released and distributed by record labels as CD singles. However, at Web sites such as Music-Match, Apple's iTunes, and Napster, customers can choose from more than 1.5 million tracks to download for a fee, essentially making every song on most commercially released and distributed albums available as a single.

Sales figures for digitally delivered music are increasing exponentially. Nielsen SoundScan reported in 2004 that download sales were up 733 percent over the previous year, with more than 140 million downloads sold in the U.S. More than twice as many singles are sold in digital form over the Internet than as CDs sold in stores.

Although sales of permanent digital downloads are factored into all of *Billboard*'s sales charts (with the exception of the Top Internet Albums chart, which ranks sales of physical albums ordered by mail order through the Internet), the magazine also compiles charts that rank only digital sales. Sales by all major sellers of digital tracks, such as Liquid Media, Apple's iTunes, Download Punk, Mix & Burn, MusicMatch, MusicNow, Sony, and Napster are monitored. The tracks on the Hot Digital Songs chart may come from an album, a single, or an *EP* (the abbreviation for an *extended play* recording, containing more songs than a single, but less than an album; EPs typically include three or four songs).

Billboard's Hot Digital Songs chart reports sales of permanent digital downloads in all music formats. A song's ranking on this chart reflects all available versions of the song. *Billboard*'s Hot Digital Tracks chart differs from the Hot Digital Songs chart in that the download of each version of a particular song is treated as a unique entity.

Various mixes of the same song may appear simultaneously on the Hot Digital Tracks chart. For example, different recordings of the same song might include an explicit language version, an extended dance mix, an R&B mix, and the album version.

For most songwriters, there are few thrills that can equal seeing their song reach Number One on a music chart. While there is typically little that songwriters can do to influence the chart positions of their songs, by understanding how these rankings are determined, they can assess both sales and airplay of their own and other writers' works.

PART III

HOW TO PROTECT YOUR SONGS

CHAPTER SIXTEEN

Copyrighting Your Songs and Working with Attorneys

Most songwriters have heard that they should copyright their work—but few understand what this really means. *Copyright* can be defined as a collection of exclusive rights and protections afforded by law to the authors of original literary, dramatic, musical, and other works. As discussed in Chapter 10, songs are intellectual property, and analogous to tangible property, copyright law provides that they cannot be sold, altered, performed in public, or distributed without their owners' consent.

To copyright a song means to register it with the U.S. Copyright Office. The term copyright is also frequently used in the music business to describe a copyrighted composition itself. For instance, *exploiting the copyright* typically refers to placing a song with a recording artist, in a film, or on a television show, or licensing it for any other use that generates income.

Many developing songwriters fear their songs will be stolen. As a result, they may avoid playing their works in public, sharing them at critique sessions, or pitching them to publishers. In some instances, these writers "protect" their songs so well that no one who might record them ever gets to hear them. In actuality, songs are rarely stolen, although writers are routinely taken advantage of. Writers are best protected by copyrighting their material, and having all contracts reviewed by a music business attorney.

The Rights and Protections Afforded by Copyright

While ideas, concepts, and, in most instances, titles, are not protected by copyright law, the particular musical notes and words a songwriter uses to express his or her ideas are. A melody, a lyric, or a combination of these may be copyrighted; a unique concept or a great story line (for example, an opera about a deaf, mute, and blind kid) may not. However, the expression of a concept or story line is eligible for copyright protection.

Regardless of whether a copyright form has been registered with the U.S. Copyright Office in Washington, D.C., the rights conferred by copyright law automatically belong to the author of a work as soon as both of the following two conditions are satisfied:

1. The creation of an original work

2. Fixation of that work in any tangible medium of expression.

Fixation of a work means establishing a physical record of it. For instance, a melody hummed by a songwriter does not meet the criteria for copyright. But recording that melody onto a cassette, or writing the notes onto a sheet of paper, fulfill the requirements of copyright law for "fixing" the work. Similarly, reciting a lyric aloud does not satisfy the copyright requirement, but scribbling it onto a napkin does.

Section 106 of the U.S. Copyright Act grants the following exclusive rights to authors of a copyrighted work:

1. To reproduce the work (for example, to make printed copies or recordings)

2. To prepare derivative works (meaning works based upon the original work, such as translations, abridgments, parodies, or other adaptations)

3. To distribute copies to the public (for instance, to sell, rent, or lend recorded or printed copies)

4. To perform the work publicly (referring not only to live performances, such as concerts, but also to broadcasts of recorded performances via digital transmission; on radio and television and in films; and in venues such as roller rinks, shopping malls, elevators, and restaurants)

5. To display the work publicly (applicable only to tangible objects such as sculpture or paintings—not songs or musical compositions).

These rights and protections are conveyed regardless of whether a work is published or unpublished, and regardless of whether a work's author is a citizen or resident of the U.S. For works created on or after January 1, 1978, in the U.S., the copyright lasts for the author's lifetime plus seventy years after his or her death. For compositions deemed works for hire, the copyright remains in force for one hundred twenty years from the time the work was created, or ninety-five years after its first publication, whichever is shorter.

Although registration with the Copyright Office is not a requirement for basic protection, the law confers several significant benefits available only to works that have been registered. Among these advantages is the fact that copyright registration establishes a public record of the claim of ownership. Additionally, only songs that are registered with the Copyright Office may be the subject of an infringement suit; a work must be registered prior to its author or publisher instituting legal action to defend it from unauthorized use.

Another benefit of registering a copyright is that copyright registration made before or within five years of a work's publication may be used as *prima facie* (meaning without investigation) evidence in a court of law to establish the validity of a copyright, as well as the statements affirmed on the application (such as authorship).

One of the most important benefits of copyright registration is that under specified circumstances, the owner of a registered copyright may be entitled to additional money in the event that copyright infringement is proven. As explained on page 266 of this chapter, this money may be provided as statutory damages and attorneys fees.

While no worldwide or international copyright exists, more than one hundred countries provide some form of copyright protection, under specified conditions, to works created in the U.S. and other countries. The rights and protections granted vary, depending on the laws of each particular country and the international copyright treaties to which it subscribes. For additional information about copyright protection afforded in foreign countries and a list of countries that offer protection to works copyrighted in the U.S., view "International Copyright Relations of the United States," a brochure accessible by visiting www.copyright.gov/circs/circ38a.pdf.

A copyrighted work, such as a lyric, a song, or another musical composition, is an owner's property and, as such, may be sold, transferred, or inherited, subject to applicable state laws. To convey any or all of the exclusive rights afforded by copyright legally, an agreement must be signed by the copyright owner. This is essentially what occurs when a songwriter signs a publishing contract, transferring ownership of one or more of his or her songs to a music publishing company.

In some circumstances, copyright law provides that individuals other than a work's copyright owners are permitted to use and reproduce copyrighted material. These usages, collectively known as *fair use*, are outlined in Section 107 of the Copyright Act, sometimes referred to as the *Fair Use Statute*. They include the use of a work for purposes of criticism, comment, news reporting, education, and research. The determination as to whether an unauthorized use falls into one of these categories is subjective and determined on a case-by-case basis by the courts. There is no way to ascertain in advance whether a particular use will be ruled "fair use" or not.

How to Copyright Songs and Sound Recordings

The first step in copyrighting material is determining the proper form to use, keeping in mind the distinction between the copyright of a song versus the sound recording of a particular performance and production of a work. *Form PA* (Performing Arts) is used to register songs, lyrics, and musical compositions.

Form SR (Sound Recordings) is the form required to register ownership of the performance and production of a particular recording. Copyright law defines sound recordings as "works resulting from the fixation of a series of musical, spoken, or other sounds, but not including the sounds accompanying a motion picture or other audiovisual work."

Artists and record labels use Form SR to register the ownership of their master recordings. Songwriters and music publishers use Form PA to register ownership of songs, lyrics, and instrumental compositions. If the same individual is the owner of the sound recording and the underlying song or composition, both copyrights may be registered by using Form SR.

When registering a song, lyric, or musical composition, if all the following conditions are met, *Short Form PA* may be used:

- The author is alive at the time of registration

- The individual registering the copyright is the only author and the sole copyright owner of the work

- The copyright claimant is not a business organization

- The work must be completely new, not containing any material that has previously been published or registered, or that is in the public domain

- The work must not be a work made for hire. The Copyright Office defines a "work made for hire" as "a work prepared by an employee within the scope of his or her employment; or a work specially ordered or commissioned for certain uses, if the parties expressly state in a written agreement signed by them that the work shall be considered a work made for hire"

- The copyright registrant is not an anonymous author (one whose name does not appear on the copy of the work) who does not want to reveal his or her identity.

If all the above conditions are not met, the *Standard Form PA* application must be used.

A copyright registration may be made at any time after a work's creation. It is not necessary to reregister a song in the event that it becomes published, although the publisher has the option of doing so.

Copyright forms are downloadable free of charge at the U.S. Library of Congress Web site (www.copyright.gov). The fee to register a copyright is $30, payable by check or money order to "Register of Copyrights." Copyright fees are subject to change, so it is best to confirm the cost by visiting the Web site, writing the copyright office, or calling (202) 707-3000 prior to submitting an application. A copy of the standard version of Copyright Form PA follows on pages 252–253.

Analyzing Copyright Form PA

Form PA is the application used by a songwriter or music publisher to register a work of performing arts, including a song, lyric, or musical composition, with the Copyright Office. This form may also be used to register a "collective work," a collection of unpublished songs, lyrics, or instrumental compositions as described later in this chapter.

Copyright Office fees are subject to change. For current fees, check the Copyright Office website at *www.copyright.gov*, write the Copyright Office, or call (202) 707-3000.

Form PA
For a Work of Performing Arts
UNITED STATES COPYRIGHT OFFICE

REGISTRATION NUMBER

PA   PAU

EFFECTIVE DATE OF REGISTRATION

Month   Day   Year

DO NOT WRITE ABOVE THIS LINE. IF YOU NEED MORE SPACE, USE A SEPARATE CONTINUATION SHEET.

1

TITLE OF THIS WORK ▼

PREVIOUS OR ALTERNATIVE TITLES ▼

NATURE OF THIS WORK ▼ See instructions

2 a

NAME OF AUTHOR ▼

DATES OF BIRTH AND DEATH
Year Born ▼   Year Died ▼

Was this contribution to the work a "work made for hire"?
☐ Yes
☐ No

AUTHOR'S NATIONALITY OR DOMICILE
Name of Country
OR { Citizen of _____
Domiciled in _____

WAS THIS AUTHOR'S CONTRIBUTION TO THE WORK
Anonymous?   ☐ Yes ☐ No
Pseudonymous?   ☐ Yes ☐ No

If the answer to either of these questions is "Yes," see detailed instructions.

NATURE OF AUTHORSHIP Briefly describe nature of material created by this author in which copyright is claimed. ▼

NOTE

Under the law, the "author" of a "work made for hire" is generally the employer, not the employee (see instructions). For any part of this work that was "made for hire" check "Yes" in the space provided, give the employer (or other person for whom the work was prepared) as "Author" of that part, and leave the space for dates of birth and death blank.

b

NAME OF AUTHOR ▼

DATES OF BIRTH AND DEATH
Year Born ▼   Year Died ▼

Was this contribution to the work a "work made for hire"?
☐ Yes
☐ No

AUTHOR'S NATIONALITY OR DOMICILE
Name of Country
OR { Citizen of _____
Domiciled in _____

WAS THIS AUTHOR'S CONTRIBUTION TO THE WORK
Anonymous?   ☐ Yes ☐ No
Pseudonymous?   ☐ Yes ☐ No

If the answer to either of these questions is "Yes," see detailed instructions.

NATURE OF AUTHORSHIP Briefly describe nature of material created by this author in which copyright is claimed. ▼

c

NAME OF AUTHOR ▼

DATES OF BIRTH AND DEATH
Year Born ▼   Year Died ▼

Was this contribution to the work a "work made for hire"?
☐ Yes
☐ No

AUTHOR'S NATIONALITY OR DOMICILE
Name of Country
OR { Citizen of _____
Domiciled in _____

WAS THIS AUTHOR'S CONTRIBUTION TO THE WORK
Anonymous?   ☐ Yes ☐ No
Pseudonymous?   ☐ Yes ☐ No

If the answer to either of these questions is "Yes," see detailed instructions.

NATURE OF AUTHORSHIP Briefly describe nature of material created by this author in which copyright is claimed. ▼

3 a

YEAR IN WHICH CREATION OF THIS WORK WAS COMPLETED   This information must be given   Year in all cases.

b DATE AND NATION OF FIRST PUBLICATION OF THIS PARTICULAR WORK
Complete this information ONLY if this work has been published.   Month _____ Day _____ Year _____
Nation

4

See instructions before completing this space.

COPYRIGHT CLAIMANT(S) Name and address must be given even if the claimant is the same as the author given in space 2. ▼

TRANSFER If the claimant(s) named here in space 4 is (are) different from the author(s) named in space 2, give a brief statement of how the claimant(s) obtained ownership of the copyright. ▼

APPLICATION RECEIVED

ONE DEPOSIT RECEIVED

TWO DEPOSITS RECEIVED

FUNDS RECEIVED

DO NOT WRITE HERE
OFFICE USE ONLY

MORE ON BACK ▶ • Complete all applicable spaces (numbers 5-9) on the reverse side of this page.
• See detailed instructions.   • Sign the form at line 8.

DO NOT WRITE HERE
Page 1 of _____ pages

DO NOT WRITE ABOVE THIS LINE. IF YOU NEED MORE SPACE, USE A SEPARATE CONTINUATION SHEET.

PREVIOUS REGISTRATION Has registration for this work, or for an earlier version of this work, already been made in the Copyright Office?

☐ Yes ☐ No If your answer is "Yes," why is another registration being sought? (Check appropriate box.) ▼ If your answer is No, do **not** check box A, B, or C.

a. ☐ This is the first published edition of a work previously registered in unpublished form.

b. ☐ This is the first application submitted by this author as copyright claimant.

c. ☐ This is a changed version of the work, as shown by space 6 on this application.

If your answer is "Yes," give: **Previous Registration Number** ▼   **Year of Registration** ▼

5

DERIVATIVE WORK OR COMPILATION Complete both space 6a and 6b for a derivative work; complete only 6b for a compilation.

Preexisting Material Identify any preexisting work or works that this work is based on or incorporates. ▼

a

6

Material Added to This Work Give a brief, general statement of the material that has been added to this work and in which copyright is claimed. ▼

b

See instructions before completing this space.

DEPOSIT ACCOUNT If the registration fee is to be charged to a Deposit Account established in the Copyright Office, give name and number of Account.

Name ▼   **Account Number** ▼

a

7

CORRESPONDENCE Give name and address to which correspondence about this application should be sent. Name/Address/Apt/City/State/ZIP ▼

b

Area code and daytime telephone number   (   )   Fax number   (   )

Email

CERTIFICATION* I, the undersigned, hereby certify that I am the

Check only one ▶

☐ author
☐ other copyright claimant
☐ owner of exclusive right(s)
☐ authorized agent of

Name of author or other copyright claimant, or owner of exclusive right(s) ▲

of the work identified in this application and that the statements made by me in this application are correct to the best of my knowledge.

8

Typed or printed name and date ▼ If this application gives a date of publication in space 3, do not sign and submit it before that date.

Date

Handwritten signature (X) ▼

𝑥 _____

Certificate will be mailed in window envelope to this address:

Name ▼

Number/Street/Apt ▼

City/State/ZIP ▼

9

*17 U.S.C. § 506(e): Any person who knowingly makes a false representation of a material fact in the application for copyright registration provided for by section 409, or in any written statement filed in connection with the application, shall be fined not more than $2,500.

Rev: June 2002—20,000 Web Rev: June 2002 ♲ Printed on recycled paper

U.S. Government Printing Office: 2000-461-113/20,021

ⓒ Form PA
For a Work of Performing Arts
UNITED STATES COPYRIGHT OFFICE

REGISTRATION NUMBER

PA   PAU

EFFECTIVE DATE OF REGISTRATION

Month   Day   Year

DO NOT WRITE ABOVE THIS LINE. IF YOU NEED MORE SPACE, USE A SEPARATE CONTINUATION SHEET.

1

TITLE OF THIS WORK ▼

PREVIOUS OR ALTERNATIVE TITLES ▼

NATURE OF THIS WORK ▼ See instructions

1. Title of this Work

Every work registered must be given a title by which it will be indexed. The complete and exact title of the composition must be written in this space. In the event that the work is a collective work, the overall title of the collection should be given. If registering one or more songs that are part of a collection, the title of each song, followed by the title of the collection must be listed. For instance: "To Be Loved by You" (part of "The Greatest Unknown Hits of Jason Blume 2006").

Some songwriters circumvent the cost of registering each song they write by grouping their unpublished songs into a collection. For instance, they might copyright ten songs under the shared title, "The Future Hits of Anita Cutt." The Copyright Office's term for this is a *collective work*. Unpublished songs may be included on one copyright registration application Form PA and paid for as one submission if the following conditions are met:

• The elements of the collection are assembled in an orderly form

• The combined elements bear a single title identifying the collection as a whole

• The copyright claimant in all the elements and in the collection as a whole is the same

• All the elements are by the same author, or, if they are by different authors, at least one of the authors has contributed copyrightable authorship to each element.

Unpublished collections of songs and other musical compositions are not indexed under the individual titles of the contents but under the title of the collection; the individual songs will not show up in a search of copyright records. In the event that a song included in a copyrighted collection is commercially released, it needs to be registered individually for its author to derive all the protections and benefits copyright registration affords.

After a collection has been registered (and a certificate of registration has been received), *Form CA* may be filed for an additional fee of $100. Doing so causes each song in the collection to be indexed individually. There is a financial benefit in filing this form (as opposed to registering each song individually) only if five or more songs are included in a collection.

If the work is an unpublished collection, after listing the collection's title, the titles of the individual songs that comprise it may be listed. For instance: "The Greatest Unknown Hits of Jason Blume 2006": "To Be Loved by You," "I Think It's Gonna Rain," "Any Minute Now," and "One More Dream."

Previous or Alternative Titles

This space should be completed only if the work has previously been known or is currently known by different names. If this is the case, the Copyright Office suggests including all names by which someone might refer to the song in the event he or she is conducting a search for it. For instance, "To Be Loved by You," "2 B Loved by U," and "Be Loved by You."

Nature of this Work

A description of the registered work should be inserted in this space. For example: "Song lyrics," "Instrumental musical composition," or "Song." It is neither necessary nor appropriate to provide a more detailed description, such as "Up-tempo love song" or "Sad country song lyric."

2 **a**

NAME OF AUTHOR ▼		DATES OF BIRTH AND DEATH
		Year Born ▼ Year Died ▼

Was this contribution to the work a "work made for hire"?	AUTHOR'S NATIONALITY OR DOMICILE Name of Country	WAS THIS AUTHOR'S CONTRIBUTION TO THE WORK
☐ Yes	OR { Citizen of _____	Anonymous? ☐ Yes ☐ No	If the answer to either of these questions is
☐ No	Domiciled in _____	Pseudonymous? ☐ Yes ☐ No	"Yes," see detailed instructions.

NATURE OF AUTHORSHIP Briefly describe nature of material created by this author in which copyright is claimed. ▼

NOTE

Under the law, the "author" of a "work made for hire" is generally the employer, not the employee (see instructions). For any part of this work that was "made for hire" check "Yes" in the space provided, give the employer (or other person for whom the work was prepared) as "Author" of that part, and leave the space for dates of birth and death blank.

b

NAME OF AUTHOR ▼		DATES OF BIRTH AND DEATH
		Year Born ▼ Year Died ▼

Was this contribution to the work a "work made for hire"?	AUTHOR'S NATIONALITY OR DOMICILE Name of Country	WAS THIS AUTHOR'S CONTRIBUTION TO THE WORK
☐ Yes	OR { Citizen of _____	Anonymous? ☐ Yes ☐ No	If the answer to either of these questions is
☐ No	Domiciled in _____	Pseudonymous? ☐ Yes ☐ No	"Yes," see detailed instructions.

NATURE OF AUTHORSHIP Briefly describe nature of material created by this author in which copyright is claimed. ▼

c

NAME OF AUTHOR ▼		DATES OF BIRTH AND DEATH
		Year Born ▼ Year Died ▼

Was this contribution to the work a "work made for hire"?	AUTHOR'S NATIONALITY OR DOMICILE Name of Country	WAS THIS AUTHOR'S CONTRIBUTION TO THE WORK
☐ Yes	OR { Citizen of _____	Anonymous? ☐ Yes ☐ No	If the answer to either of these questions is
☐ No	Domiciled in _____	Pseudonymous? ☐ Yes ☐ No	"Yes," see detailed instructions.

NATURE OF AUTHORSHIP Briefly describe nature of material created by this author in which copyright is claimed. ▼

2(a–c). Name of Author

This section of the application provides spaces to include information for up to three authors. In the event that there are more than three authors, *Continuation*

Sheets, additions to Form PA that provide additional space, may be requested or downloaded. For copyright purposes, the term "author" is used to denote any contributor to a song, lyric, or musical composition; lyricists and composers are considered authors. If a collective work is being registered, the name of the author of the collection is listed.

The full legal name of each author should be listed, unless the work was created as a work made for hire, as explained in Chapter 1. In the event that the work being registered was made for hire, the person or company for whom the work was created is considered the author, and as such, their name (and not the name of the actual creator) is listed in this space. It is also acceptable to give the name of the person or company for whom the work was created, followed by the employee/creator's name. For example: Moondream Music Group, employer of Jason Blume.

Dates of Birth and Death
Also included in Section 2, for each author, are spaces to include the year of birth and, if applicable, death. Including the author's birth date is optional, but it is recommended as it serves as a useful form of identification. Copyright statute requires including the year of death if an author is deceased, unless his or her contribution is anonymous, pseudonymous, or was done as a work made for hire.

Was this Contribution to the Work a "Work Made for Hire"?
This section of the form includes a box to denote whether each author's work was made for hire as previously defined.

Author's Nationality or Domicile
Section 2 additionally requires a statement of each author's citizenship or the name of the country in which the author lives. For citizens and/or residents of the U.S., "U.S.A." should be listed in one or both of these spaces.

Was this Author's Contribution to the Work Anonymous? Pseudonymous?
An author's contribution is considered "anonymous" by the Copyright Office if he or she chooses not to include his or her name on copies or phonorecords of the work. An author's contribution is considered "pseudonymous" if he or she chooses to use a fictitious name instead of his or her legal name on copies and phonorecords.

If an author's work is anonymous, he or she may leave the space blank, write "anonymous," or list his or her name.

If an author's work is pseudonymous, the author may leave the space blank, write the fictitious name he or she chooses to use followed by the word "pseudonym" (for example, "Ima Riter, pseudonym"), or list his or her real name and pseudonym (for example: "Jason Blume, whose pseudonym is Juan A. Grammy").

Nature of Authorship

A description of each author's contribution to the work is required in this section. Examples include: "Words," "Music," "Words and music," "Coauthor of words," "Coauthor of music," and "Coauthor of words and music."

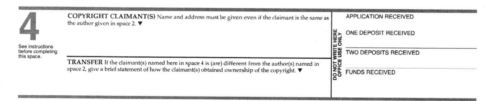

3a. Year in Which Creation of the Work Was Completed

According to copyright law, a work is "created" the first time it is fixed in a copy or phonorecord. The date listed in this space should be the year in which the author completed the version currently being registered.

3b. Date and Nation of First Publication of this Particular Work

This section should be completed only if a work has been published. Copyright law defines "publication" as "the distribution of copies or phonorecords of a work to the public by sale or other transfer of ownership, or by rental, lease, or lending"; a work is also "published" if there has been an "offering to distribute copies or phonorecords to a group of persons for purposes of further distribution, public performance, or public display."

For works that meet the above criteria, the month, day, and year of the first publication must be provided. In the space marked "Nation," the country in which the work was first published should be listed. In the event that the work was published in multiple countries including the U.S., it is only necessary to state "U.S.A."

4. Copyright Claimant(s)

The copyright claimant(s) is either the author(s) of the work, or an individual or company (such as a music publisher) to whom ownership of the work has been transferred. If no publishing agreement has been signed, the copyright claimant(s) is (are) the author(s) of the work. Even if the copyright claimant is the same individual listed as "author" in Section 2 of this form (and in many instances, this will be the case), the name and address of the person or company that owns the copyright must be listed in this space.

Transfer

If any copyright claimant named in space 4 is not an author named in space 2, a brief statement must be included explaining how the claimant came to own the copyright. Examples of explanations include "By written contract" (which would be appropriate for a song that has been published) and "By will" (meaning inheritance). Contracts or any other documents to substantiate this should not be attached. If ownership has not been transferred, this space can be left blank or the applicant may write "Not Applicable."

DO NOT WRITE ABOVE THIS LINE. IF YOU NEED MORE SPACE, USE A SEPARATE CONTINUATION SHEET.

PREVIOUS REGISTRATION Has registration for this work, or for an earlier version of this work, already been made in the Copyright Office?

☐ **Yes** ☐ **No** If your answer is "Yes," why is another registration being sought? (Check appropriate box.) ▼ If your answer is No, do **not** check box A, B, or C.

a. ☐ This is the first published edition of a work previously registered in unpublished form.

b. ☐ This is the first application submitted by this author as copyright claimant.

c. ☐ This is a changed version of the work, as shown by space 6 on this application.

If your answer is "Yes," give: **Previous Registration Number** ▼   **Year of Registration** ▼

5

---

5. Previous Registration

In this section, the applicant is asked whether this work, or a previous version of it, has previously been registered with the Copyright Office. Only one registration for the same version of a particular song, lyric, or musical composition is permitted, unless it meets the following criteria:

1. The work has been published since its previous registration

2. Someone other than the author was named as "claimant" in the previous registration, and the author is now seeking registration in his or her own name.

If one checks "Yes"(stating that the work has previously been registered), box "a," "b," or "c" must be checked, providing the reason why a new registration of the same work is being sought. The applicant must also provide the previous copyright registration number, which can be found on the upper right side of the certificate of registration.

If the answer is "No" (the work has not previously been registered), there is no need to complete the remainder of Section 5. If the composition, or any previous version of it, has been registered, there are three additional questions to be answered. The applicant checks the box that applies.

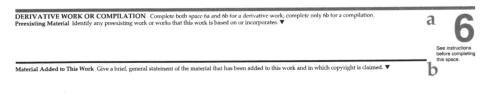

DERIVATIVE WORK OR COMPILATION Complete both space 6a and 6b for a derivative work; complete only 6b for a compilation.
Preexisting Material Identify any preexisting work or works that this work is based on or incorporates. ▼

a **6**

See instructions before completing this space.

Material Added to This Work Give a brief, general statement of the material that has been added to this work and in which copyright is claimed. ▼

b

6a. Derivative Work or Compilation

This section is completed only if one of the following criteria is met:

• The composition being registered is a "changed work," "compilation," or "derivative work," and it includes one or more works that have previously been published or registered with the Office of Copyright, or one or more works that are in the public domain.

- The Copyright Office does not specifically define what constitutes a "changed work." But it is not necessary to reregister a song unless the changes are substantial; altering a few words or notes does not require a new registration; completely rewriting a chorus melody or adding a bridge does. This section should be completed for the registration of substantially rewritten versions of existing songs, including those with significant additional or revised lyrics added to a previously registered melody, and/or substantially different, new melody to a previously registered lyric.

- The Copyright Office defines a *compilation* as "a work formed by the collection and assembling of preexisting materials or of data that are collected, coordinated, or arranged in such a way that the resulting work as a whole constitutes an original work of authorship." Examples of compilations include medleys of preexisting songs and musical reviews or productions comprised of preexisting songs.

- A *derivative work* is defined by the Copyright Office as "a work based on one or more preexisting works." Examples of derivative works include musical arrangements, dramatizations, translations, abridgments, condensations, motion picture versions, or "any other form in which a work may be recast, transformed, or adapted." Derivative works also include works "consisting of editorial revisions, annotations, or other modifications" if these changes, as a whole, represent an original work of authorship. Examples of derivative works include translations and musical arrangements.

In 6a if the current work is based on a preexisting work, the title of the previous work must be listed.

6b. Material Added to this Work

If the work being registered is a changed work or a derivative work, both 6a and 6b must be completed. Only 6b should be completed if the work being registered is a compilation. Section 6b requires a brief description of the additional, new material that has been added since the work's previous registration. Examples include: "New chorus melody and lyric," "Added a bridge," and "Added a third verse."

In the event that the work being registered is a compilation, a brief, general statement describing the material that has been compiled and the compilation itself must be provided. An example of this is "Compilation of Jason Blume Love Songs."

7a. Deposit Account

The Copyright Office allows individuals and companies that copyright materials frequently to maintain an account so that they do not have to send payment each time they register a work. A deposit account may be opened with a minimum of $250 dollars, and each time a work is registered the appropriate fee is withdrawn by the copyright office from the account. If the applicant maintains a deposit account, the name on the account and the account number are entered in this space.

This typically applies only to large publishing companies that register hundreds of works. For additional information about this, see *Copyright Circular 5: How to Open and Maintain a Deposit Account in the Copyright Office*. The circular is accessible online at the Copyright Office's Web site.

7b. Correspondence

The name, complete address, daytime telephone number (including area code), fax number (if applicable), and e-mail address (if applicable) of the person to be contacted if the Copyright Office has any questions about the application should appear in this space.

8. Certification

The copyright registrant defines and certifies his or her involvement with the song in this section. The appropriate box should be checked, designating whether the applicant is the author, another copyright claimant, the owner of exclusive rights (typically, a music publisher), or an authorized agent (acting on behalf of the author, claimant, or owner of the copyright). If the person completing the registration application checks the bottom box ("authorized agent of"), the name of the author, claimant, or copyright owner on whose behalf he or she is working must be stated.

As explained in Chapter 1, when a song is "published" the writer conveys all, or a portion of, the copyright ownership to a publisher. A song may be published regardless of whether it has been registered with the Copyright Office. When an individual or company publishes a song that has previously been registered with the Copyright Office, the publisher does not reregister the song. However, as provided by Section 205 of the Copyright Act, the publisher may (on a voluntary basis) record the transfer of copyright (or any other legal document pertaining to the copyrighted work) with the Copyright Office. While in most cases this is not mandatory, officially recording the transfer of ownership confers special legal advantages.

A publisher may document its ownership of a copyrighted song by "recording" the publishing agreement with the Copyright Office. This is accomplished by mailing a copy of the publishing agreement to the Copyright Office along with a fee determined by the number of titles to which the document pertains. The cost to register a publishing contract for one title is $80.00; there is an additional $20.00 fee per title for documents pertaining to a maximum of ten titles. Additional details can be found in *Copyright Circular 12*, available at the Copyright Office's Web site.

Typed or Printed Name and Date

The name of the applicant is typed or printed, along with the date of the application, in this space. In the event that a date of publication was included in Section 3, this application should not be signed and submitted prior to the date listed.

Handwritten Signature

The handwritten signature of the individual registering the copyright is required in this space.

Certificate will be mailed in window envelope to this address:	Name ▼	YOU MUST: • Complete all necessary spaces • Sign your application in space 8	**9**
		SEND ALL 3 ELEMENTS IN THE SAME PACKAGE	
	Number/Street/Apt ▼	1. Application form 2. Nonrefundable filing fee in check or money order payable to *Register of Copyrights* 3. Deposit material	Fees are subject to change. For current fees, check the Copyright Office website at www.copyright.gov, write the Copyright Office, or call (202) 707-3000.
	City/State/ZIP ▼	**MAIL TO:** Library of Congress Copyright Office 101 Independence Avenue, S.E. Washington, D.C. 20559-6000	

*17 U.S.C. § 506(e): Any person who knowingly makes a false representation of a material fact in the application for copyright registration provided for by section 409, or in any written statement filed in connection with the application, shall be fined not more than $2,500.

9. Address for Return of Certificate

The applicant's name and address must be entered legibly in the allotted space.

In addition to the application and payment, applicants must include one nonreturnable copy of the work, recorded clearly and audibly onto a CD or cassette tape, or accurately transcribed onto a lead sheet. (Note that it is not necessary to submit both a recording and a lead sheet—just one or the other.) For lyrics, one legible copy of the printed lyric is required. It is advisable to register works prior to their publication. However, if the work being registered is sheet music that has already been published, two copies are required. All items should bear the title of the work.

For musical works published in forms other than sound recordings, subsequent to January 1, 1978, two nonreturnable copies are required to be sent to the Copyright Office. This typically applies to printed music such as sheet music and musical arrangements. Works that have been published solely as sound recordings require only one deposit copy.

The application, payment, and copy(ies) should be sent to:

Library of Congress
U.S. Copyright Office
101 Independence Avenue, S.E.
Washington, D.C. 20559-6000

It typically takes the Copyright Office four to five months to issue a certificate of copyright registration, provided that the forms are completed correctly. Depending on the volume of applications being processed this process sometimes takes up to eight months, as well as an additional two months for the information to be added to the Copyright Office's online database. But registration takes effect on the day the Copyright Office receives an application, payment, and copy(ies) in acceptable form.

Copyright Registration Agencies

There are companies (accessible on the Internet) that will file copyright registration on an applicant's behalf for a fee. These companies provide applicants with a questionnaire that requires the identical information one provides when completing a copyright registration form. After the songwriter returns the questionnaire along with the required recording(s) or sheet music, the agency completes the copyright form and mails it to the Library of Congress. In some instances, the entire process can be completed online by attaching an MP3 recording, which the company transfers onto a CD and forwards to the Copyright Office. As mentioned above, the Copyright Office requires a tangible copy of works being registered, such as sheet music or a CD.

These companies generally charge $75 to $150 for their services. But the copyright application is a relatively simple one and anyone who can provide basic facts and write a check should be able to complete the copyright registration process without paying for legal assistance.

Copyright Infringement

Infringement refers to a violation or breach of the protections and exclusive rights afforded by copyright law. There are two primary categories of copyright infringement:

- Unauthorized use of a copyrighted work (for example, the reproduction, sale, performance, or distribution of a song without obtaining a license)

- Claiming another author's work as one's own (for instance, using a significant portion of another composer's melody or lyric).

There have also been instances in which, although a license has been obtained, courts have ruled that a copyright was infringed because licensees failed to live up to the terms of the agreement (such as not paying royalties as specified).

Conditions of Copyright Infringement

Three conditions must be fulfilled in order to prove that a copyright has been violated. In the event that copyright ownership, access, and substantial similarity are proven to the satisfaction of a judge and/or jury, infringement has occurred.

Proving Ownership

In order for an individual to establish that his or her copyright has been infringed, ownership of the copyright must first be proved. The best way to demonstrate a claim of ownership is to produce a certificate of copyright registration. In the absence of this registration or, if copyright ownership is disputed, there are other ways to affirm ownership, such as the "poor man's copyright."

The *poor man's copyright* refers to mailing a copy of a song and/or lyric to oneself via registered mail. In the event that ownership is contested, producing the unopened envelope serves as evidence that ownership of the work was claimed on the date of the postmark by the individual in possession of the sealed envelope.

As previously stated, copyright protection exists the moment a work is created and fixed in a tangible form; registration is a formality that provides a public record of an author's claim of ownership—and affords the additional rights previously addressed. These added benefits are not derived from mailing a copy of a song to oneself, and many attorneys consider the poor man's copyright worthless.

Nonetheless, producing a poor man's copyright as evidence in a court of law may conceivably help persuade a judge or jury that an author created a work on a given date. Witnesses, such as audience members, members of songwriting organizations, music publishers, and songwriting instructors who attest to the fact that they heard a song on a given date, or that they heard a song in progress, can have the same effect.

The majority of professional music publishers do not typically copyright the songs they represent until those songs are scheduled for commercial distribution or public performance. For companies with tens of thousands of copyrights, the cost of registration would be prohibitive.

Establishing Access

It does not matter whether a copyright was violated intentionally to constitute infringement. In many instances, the melodies and lyrics of songs have been copied unconsciously. In other cases, authors have created original works that, by complete coincidence, have been identical or very similar to ones previously created by other authors. In the eyes of the law, it is not infringement merely because a significant portion of a song is the same as, or similar to, another composition. A ruling of infringement requires proof that a writer accused of copying another author's work indeed had access to the work.

As the term is used in copyright law, *access* means that the defendant (the individual accused of copying a second author's work) had an opportunity to hear the other composer's work. If a song has been recorded and received widespread radio airplay, it is assumed that access was available. Likewise, if an accuser can prove that a copy of his or her song was sent to the defending author or to someone with a direct link to the defending author, a judge or jury would likely presume the author had access to the material. For this reason it is a good idea to maintain a log of all song pitches and submissions, including to whom your songs were sent (or, in the case of a face-to-face meeting, to whom they were played) and the date of the submission.

The issue of providing access is a major reason why many music publishers and record labels refuse to accept material that comes from nonprofessional and unsolicited sources. By returning an author's work in its original unopened envelope, these companies avoid the possibility of a songwriter claiming that a songwriter or artist affiliated with the company had direct access to the writer's work.

There have been instances when courts ruled that similarities between unique musical passages of two compositions were so striking, that although access could not be proven, it could be assumed. But as a rule, for infringement to be demonstrated there must be at least circumstantial evidence provided that the defendant had access to the material allegedly infringed upon.

Demonstrating Substantial Similarity

The final element that must be proven to lead to a finding of infringement is that the infringer's work is "substantially similar" to the original composition. Contrary to popular belief, copyright law specifies no particular number of notes or musical bars that may be copied legally. Conversely, there is no stated number of notes or bars that, if copied from another composition, constitutes copyright infringement.

Substantial similarity is determined, not by the quantity of notes shared by two compositions, but by the quality and significance of the similarity. Whether two musical compositions are substantially similar is determined on a case-by-case basis by the courts. *Musicologists*, expert music scholars, are often hired by defendants and plaintiffs to testify in infringement cases. These authorities compare the works in question in extreme detail, analyzing the ways in which the compositions are the same as well as how they differ. They assess elements including the songs' melodies, harmonies, rhythms, tempos, phrasing, structures, and chord progressions, and share their conclusions with the judge and jury.

The estimated contribution of specific musical phrases or combinations of notes and lyrics to the public's recognition of a particular song is a critical factor in courts' decisions. While in many songs, the melody expressed in one particular musical bar may not be identifiable to the majority of listeners, the seven notes that comprise the opening measure of "Over the Rainbow" are instantly recognizable as the Harold Arlen/Edgar Yip Harburg classic immortalized by Judy Garland.

Titles cannot be copyrighted, as evidenced by a search of BMI's catalog that yielded 628 songs titled "You and I." However, writing new songs with titles such as "White Christmas" and "Over the Rainbow," while not a breach of copyright law, could cause you to be sued under the laws of *Unfair Competition*. A jury would likely decide that the public would probably be misled and expect the original compositions when purchasing recordings with these unique titles that are so closely associated with classic songs.

In many instances, song titles and lines from songs have been lifted verbatim from movies and books. Notable examples include George Strait's "Blue Clear Sky" (written by Mark D. Sanders, John Jarrard, and Bob Piero, based on a line from the film *Forrest Gump*), Jamie O'Neal's "There Is No Arizona" (written by Lisa Drew, Shaye Smith, and Jamie O'Neal, using a line from Steven King's *Delores Claiborne*), and Chely Wright's "Single White Female" (written by Carolyn Dawn Johnson and Shaye Smith, and sharing its title with a film of the same name). These instances do not constitute copyright infringement, because while the words are the same, they have been used in a new way and in a different artistic medium, and do not lead to consumer confusion regarding the source of the work.

The Legality of Incorporating Celebrity, Company, and Product Names

Janis Joplin asked the Lord to buy her a Mercedes-Benz; Prince had a Number One hit with "Little Red Corvette"; Bruce Springsteen sang about "Cadillac Ranch"; Alan Jackson was "Crazy 'bout a Mercury"; and in one of the most famous uses of a product name, Paul Simon wrote and sang "Kodachrome." Mary Chapin Carpenter's "I Feel Lucky" mentions Dwight Yoakum and Lyle Lovett, as well as Barq's root beer and Camel cigarettes; Bowling for Soup's "Ohio" includes references to Troy Aikman, Willie Nelson, the Bush twins, Pantera, and Blue Belle ice cream; and countless country songs have referenced Patsy Cline ("Bottle of Wine and Patsy Cline"), George Jones, Hank Williams, Waylon Jennings, Willie Nelson, and Merle Haggard.

Are these uses permitted? The issue of whether it is legal to include the names of products, celebrities, and companies falls within the realm of trademark and other areas of civil law, as opposed to copyright law. The best protection against any potential legal action is to secure prior permission from the trademark owner. This hardly ever happens, though, and individuals and companies rarely object unless a song presents them in a negative light.

Remedies for Infringement

Copyright law falls primarily under the category of *civil law*, meaning that an individual who violates it is typically sued, but not charged with a crime. In the event a court rules that the conditions of ownership, access, and substantial similarity have been established, and infringement has occurred, it may issue an *injunction*, a court order forbidding continued distribution of the infringed work. In addition, the court has the right to order the destruction or seizure of all remaining infringing copies, as well as plates, computer discs, molds, and other items used specifically in the reproduction of the infringing composition. In actuality, this rarely occurs.

Copyright law also provides for financial restitution, determined on a case-by-case basis. One option is for the injured party to receive *fair market value*, the estimated amount the owner of the violated composition would likely have earned if the work had been properly licensed. In other instances, a court may award compensation equal to the amount of profit the infringer earned as a result of illegal use of the infringed composition.

Copyright may be deemed to have been violated regardless of whether there has been any financial loss. Copyright law prescribes *statutory damages*, financial remuneration intended to compensate the victims of infringement in circumstances when actual financial damages cannot be calculated. At the court's discretion, statutory damages in the range of $750 to $30,000 may be ordered, as well as attorneys' fees, for songs that were registered with the Copyright Office. In the event that an infringed work has not been registered with the Copyright Office, the author can only receive *actual damages*, meaning the amount of money potentially lost by the author, plus any money gained by the defendant.

The Copyright Act states that legal action must begin within three years of the time a copyright infringement claim is made. If a court rules that infringement was intentional (for instance, if a defendant continues infringing subsequent to receiving written notice), higher penalties (up to a maximum of $150,000) may be imposed. If an act of infringement is determined to have been unintentional, the court may reduce penalties to as little as $200.

If a judge determines that a criminal act has been committed in conjunction with the infringement, he or she may refer the case to the Office of the U.S. Attorney General for possible criminal prosecution. The Copyright Act states that intentional infringement by an individual for commercial advantage or financial gain is punishable by the imposition of a fine not to exceed $250,000, five years imprisonment, or both. In the event the infringement was perpetrated by an organization or a business (as opposed to an individual), the maximum fine is $500,000.

In one of the most famous copyright infringement cases, when George Harrison was found guilty of the "subconscious imitation" of the melody of The Chiffons' "He's So Fine" (written by Ronnie Mack) in Harrison's "My Sweet Lord," he was ordered to pay nearly $600,000.

In other cases, the Rolling Stones and Led Zeppelin settled accusations of infringement by blues legend Willie Dixon by paying undisclosed amounts rumored to exceed a million dollars. Similarly, the Beach Boys' Brian Wilson reputedly paid a substantial amount and added Chuck Berry's name to the credits when Wilson's "Surfin' U.S.A." was found to have infringed upon Berry's "Sweet Little Sixteen."

Once infringement of a song has been proved, all parties who subsequently exploit the song (such as a record label, retail store, or online seller of downloads) are also held liable—regardless of whether they knew they were infringing a copyright.

Many successful songwriters and artists have incurred considerable expense defending unfounded accusations of infringement, with attorneys' and musicologists' fees typically exceeding $30,000. In one notable case, despite having successfully defended against an accusation of copyright infringement, Creedence Clearwater Revival's John Fogerty was not permitted to recover the $1.35 million he'd spent to defend himself. The courts have been most likely to award attorneys' fees to the prevailing party in instances when they have ruled that the case was frivolous or brought in bad faith. In these instances, the courts' awards have rarely exceeded $10,000, which is typically only a fraction of the amounts incurred.

The instances previously discussed represent cases of copyrights being violated as a result of *plagiarism*; claiming another writer's work as one's own. Illegal downloading and selling songs without obtaining a license also constitute forms of copyright infringement, as these actions violate "mechanical rights," a copyright owner's right to control the reproduction and distribution of his or her material.

Grammy-nominated artist Sophie B. Hawkins was awarded $346 when it was determined that a small number of unauthorized promotional copies of her CD were being sold on e-Bay. More commonly, financial settlements, ranging from $3,000 to $12,000, have been imposed upon individuals found guilty of illegal downloading.

Including Proper Copyright Notice

In the U.S., songs (other than works for hire) created after April 1, 1989 are copyrighted and protected whether they have a notice or not. Although it is not mandatory to include a notice of copyright, in some cases doing so may help establish that a defendant knew that the material in question was copyrighted, and chose to infringe upon it intentionally. This often leads to higher financial awards in the event that infringement is found to have occurred.

The letter c enclosed in a circle (©) is used to denote copyright registration on "visually perceptible" copies, meaning printed materials, such as lyric sheets. It is also acceptable to spell out the word "copyright." The correct form for a notice includes:

- The copyright symbol, the word "copyright," or the abbreviation "copr"

- The year of the first publication

- The name of the copyright owner (or an abbreviation of the copyright owner's name, by which it can be recognized), as in the following sample:

© 2006 Dreamer's Moon Music

The phrases "All Rights Reserved" and "Used by Permission" are not legal requirements but are usually added.

Copyright notices for sound recordings do not include the copyright symbol ©, but the letter P in a circle (℗) , the year of first publication of the recording, and the name of the copyright owner, as in the example below:

℗ 2006 OneWorld Records, Inc.

Using Samples

The unauthorized use of samples constitutes a form of copyright infringement. A *sample* can be defined as a segment of a sound recording extracted with the use of digital technology. *Sampling* refers to using digital recording devices, often referred to as *samplers* or *digital samplers*, to copy excerpts of existing recordings and then incorporate them into new compositions. This practice has become a mainstay in genres such as rap, hip-hop, and techno.

One of the first and most famous examples of sampling was MC Hammer's use of Rick James' "Super Freak" in his song "Can't Touch This." Since then, artists including Eminem, Snoop Dogg, Moby, Will Smith, Janet Jackson, Beck, Mariah Carey, Alicia Keys, Nelly, and countless others have incorporated samples into their work. Recordings that have been sampled come from a diverse group of artists such as Queen, Martika, the Steve Miller Band, Dido, Ohio Players, and Kool & the Gang, with James Brown reportedly being the most widely sampled artist.

As explained in Chapter 9, anyone has the right to record and release a song or musical composition subsequent to its first commercial release regardless of whether the copyright owner grants permission—provided that a license is obtained and the statutory rate is paid. There is no analogous compulsory licensing for actual recordings, however. Therefore, permission must be obtained from the owner of a sound recording prior to the release of a musical work that incorporates any portion of their work.

As discussed earlier in this chapter, for a court to rule that copyright infringement of a song has occurred, "substantial" similarity must be proved. Depending on a variety of factors, small portions of a composition, such as multiple notes, words, and/or musical bars of a song or lyric may be copied without the song's copyright necessarily being deemed infringed. But this concept does not apply to sound recordings.

No portion of a sound recording may be used without obtaining permission from its owner—not even one note. Federal courts have ruled that the use of every musical sample—including brief, unrecognizable excerpts—must be licensed. Failure to do so constitutes copyright infringement.

Unauthorized sampling violates two copyrights—those of the sound recording and the underlying composition. To legally include samples from an existing recording, one must obtain licenses from both of these copyright owners, typically a record label and a music publisher.

In most instances, the writers of a sampled composition are credited as cowriters of the new composition encompassing their work. As such, they and their publishers are entitled to a portion of mechanical and performance royalties, as well as any licensing fees earned by the new composition. The percentage of ownership conveyed is determined by a number of factors, including the length and significance of the sampled excerpt—and the bargaining power of the respective parties.

In cases where a sample is significant and readily identifiable, the writers of the sampled composition may be assigned 50 percent (or more) of the resulting new song. Incorporating several lines from the chorus of a superstar's prior hit generally costs considerably more than licensing a bass line or drum beats from an obscure independent artist's album cut. Less substantial uses may earn the writers of the sampled composition as little as 10 percent or 20 percent ownership of the new composition.

In many cases, when an exceptionally high number of writers are listed in a song's credits, it is because a song has incorporated one or more samples, and the writers of the sampled composition(s) are entitled to share in the ownership of the new work. Mariah Carey's chart-topping "We Belong Together" included two samples, and credits ten writers and thirteen music publishers.

An advance is typically paid by the publisher of the new song to the publishers and composers of the sampled work. This advance is based on the amount earned by the anticipated sale of a specified number of units (for instance, one hundred thousand copies) of the new composition.

In some cases, when record labels license the rights to include samples of their copyrights, they are paid a royalty based on the new composition's sales. This royalty varies widely, but usually ranges from 8 cents to 10 cents for each sale of the recording embodying the licensed sample. In addition, an advance for a specified number of units (for example, payment for fifty thousand copies) is typically paid. In some instances, record labels accept a onetime, flat fee, known as a *buyout*, but this is not typically the case.

If a music publisher and record label determine that use of their sampled composition is relatively insignificant, they may accept a buyout. When this occurs, licensing fees vary greatly, but may range from $200 to $15,000, although there have been instances of much higher fees being imposed. In most cases, when a buyout is negotiated the fees range from $1,000 to $2,000 for the record label, with an equal amount paid to the music publisher.

According to copyright law, infringement of a master recording occurs only when the recording itself is actually copied—not imitated. By recording a new version (referred to as a *sound-alike* or a *replay*) of the original recording, one can eliminate the necessity of obtaining a license and paying a fee to the owner of the master. But it is still necessary to secure a license from the publisher and pay a royalty for the use of the underlying song.

Writer/artists seeking to incorporate samples into their work can seek the assistance of a music business attorney or a company specializing in music clearance, such as The Music Bridge LLC (www.themusicbridge.com) and EMG (www.clearance.com). It would usually not be financially feasible for a nonperforming songwriter to incorporate samples into his or her demo recordings.

Public Domain

In the U.S., music and lyrics written and published in 1922 or earlier are considered to be in the *Public Domain*, sometimes referred to as PD. This means that their copyright protection has expired; no one legally owns the songs. Therefore, these compositions may be used by anyone who desires to do so—without paying any royalties. Note that this refers only to the song itself—not to any specific sound recording of a song. (The law provides that copyright protection for existing sound recordings will remain in effect, and these recordings will not enter the public domain, until 2067.)

New versions of songs in the public domain may be copyrighted, and these new versions (and recordings of them) may not be used without the owners' permission. The song itself remains in the public domain, and anyone else has the legal right to make and copyright his or her own original version of the same PD song. Web sites such as www.pdinfo.com include lists of thousands of songs that are in the public domain.

Termination of Copyright

The *Copyright Term Extension Act of 1998* (CTEA) provides that copyrights for works written in the U.S. on or after January 1, 1978, may revert back to the author (or owner, in the case of works for hire) during two specified periods of time. This means that there are two periods during which an author or his or her designated heirs are able to terminate a transfer of rights. A *transfer of rights* typically occurs by entering into a song publishing agreement; this law allows songwriters to reclaim all rights to their songs from their publishers.

One of the windows during which a songwriter may regain his or her works is during the five-year period following the end of thirty-five years after the work's publication date. The other period of time during which a songwriter may reclaim his or her copyright is during the five-year period beginning forty years and one day after the signing of the transfer agreement.

Prior to the passage of CTEA, copyright lasted a term of twenty-eight years. At the end of the twenty-eight-year term, the copyright was automatically renewed for an additional twenty-eight years. For pre-1978 copyrights still in effect, the author, or his or her heirs, is able to terminate the renewal rights extension during the five-year period beginning after fifty-six years after the original copyright date.

An author, or his or her designated heirs, must notify the existing copyright holder in writing of his or her intention to reclaim the copyright. This must be done between two and ten years before the actual date the original copyright terminates. If the author is not living at the date of termination, changes in CTEA now permit not only specified heirs listed in the Copyright Act of 1976 to initiate termination, but also the author's estate, if no direct heir survives. If there is more than one writer of a work, then a majority of the cowriters, or their designated heirs, must agree on the termination of transfer.

When and Why You Need an Attorney

Few songwriters are knowledgeable enough in the practice of music business law to understand and negotiate the agreements successful songwriters likely will encounter throughout their career. Music business attorneys are expensive—sometimes as much as $350 an hour. But failure to use an attorney can ultimately be even costlier.

The simple answer to "When do you need an attorney?" is, "Before signing any song publishing agreement." Many aspiring songwriters become thrilled at the prospect of signing a publishing agreement, and indeed, this can represent a major milestone along the journey to songwriting success. Some of these writers are so eager to publish their songs that they fail to seek the expert advice of an attorney, and this can lead to unscrupulous deals that may remain in force for thirty-five years or more.

As stated in Chapter 4, there are no "standard" song publishing agreements—despite the fact that many small publishing companies may present writers with contracts that have "Standard Song Publishing Agreement" printed across the top of the first page. Virtually every clause in a song publishing agreement may be negotiable—and it's easier to be certain an agreement is in order before signing it than it is to extricate yourself from a horrendous contract after it has been signed.

An attorney skilled in the art of negotiation may be able to secure higher monetary advances, increased payments for print and other licensing fees, and additional rights for you than you might be able to obtain on your own. Percentage points and contractual clauses that may seem insignificant when entering into an agreement become critical in the event that a song becomes a hit. For instance, the difference between participating in a share of the publisher's income (or not doing so) can total hundreds of thousands of dollars for songs that reach the Top Ten on mainstream charts.

Additionally, music business attorneys have established relationships with music publishers and others "in the loop." This may allow access to important information regarding the contractual points and financial parameters a particular publishing company has agreed to in the past, under similar circumstances. For all of the reasons discussed above, never sign a song publishing agreement without having a music business attorney review it.

> Having contracts reviewed by an attorney who does not specialize in the field of music is analogous to consulting an eye doctor to treat a heart problem; the eye doctor may know more than a layman, but is unlikely to possess the experience and expertise of a top cardiologist. Attorneys who regularly negotiate song publishing contracts know what can be reasonably expected, both financially and in terms of the rights they may be able to secure for their clients.

Working with an Attorney to Shop a Deal

Some music business attorneys represent clients seeking publishing and recording contracts. If an attorney believes strongly in an artist's or songwriter's potential, the attorney may use his or her industry contacts to secure meetings with music publishers and/or record label executives. This process, typically referred to as *shopping a deal*, happens more often for songwriters who are also aspiring recording artists, but can also occur for non-artists seeking a staff-writing deal (an exclusive songwriting publishing agreement).

Attorneys are compensated in one of two ways for their work when they shop publishing and recording deals. Some are paid their hourly rate (typically $250 to $350 per hour), while others may be willing to work on a commission basis, earning a percentage (typically 15 percent to 25 percent) of specified income in the event that their efforts secure a deal. Attorneys place their credibility on the line when recommending a songwriter or recording artist to music publishers and record label executives, and therefore represent only those artists and writers they feel are truly exceptional.

How to Find an Entertainment Attorney

Information about lawyer referral programs in each state is available at The American Bar Association's Web site, www.abanet.org/legalservices/lris/directory.html. The bar associations in major music centers can be excellent resources for songwriters and recording artists seeking legal representation. The Beverly Hills Bar Association operates a nonprofit lawyer referral and information service (www.bhba.org/lawyerref.htm), which, for a $25 fee, recommends two attorneys. This fee entitles an individual to one consultation (a maximum of thirty minutes) with each referred attorney. In the event one chooses to continue working with a recommended attorney, fees are negotiated between the lawyer and client.

The Nashville Bar Association (www.nashbar.org) offers a lawyer referral service, which makes more than five thousand referrals each year. There is no fee for this service. Additionally, between 6 P.M. and 8 P.M. on the first Tuesday of each month, volunteer attorneys from the Nashville Bar Association answer questions from members of the public who call (615) 242-9272.

The Association of the Bar of the City of New York (www.abcny.org) provides lawyer referrals within the New York metropolitan area. Lawyers taking part in the referral program agree to accept a reduced fee of $35 for the first thirty-minute consultation. Beyond that, fees are negotiated between the lawyer and client.

Representatives of the PROs may be willing to share recommendations for music business attorneys, and the Nashville Songwriters Association (NSAI) provides its members with attorney referrals as well. The *Martindale-Hubbel Directory*, available in local libraries, includes a comprehensive listing of lawyers categorized by specialties and location.

CHAPTER SEVENTEEN

Hiring Independent Songpluggers and Avoiding Scams

Attaining success as a songwriter is not impossible, despite the fact that it may sometimes feel that way—but it is almost always challenging. The prospects of having to network, meet with music publishers, and pitch songs can be daunting, and even more so for songwriters who lack access to a major music center, like New York, Los Angeles, or Nashville. Faced with the frustrations that are so often part of the songwriting business, it's only natural that many writers grasp at what appear to be easy ways to achieve their goals, by working with independent songpluggers, and by falling victim to a variety of scams.

Working with Independent Songpluggers

An *independent songplugger* is an individual hired by a songwriter to pitch his or her songs to A&R executives, record producers, recording artists, and, in some instances, television and film music supervisors. The hope is that the "plugger" will secure recordings that generate sales, airplay, and/or licensing fees. Independent pluggers do not handle administrative tasks, such as copyright registration, synchronization license negotiations, and the collection and distribution of royalties, which are among the services music publishers provide; their sole function is to pitch songs.

Some unpublished songwriters hire independent pluggers in order to circumvent the networking, the visits to music centers, and the rejection typically included in the process of seeking a legitimate publisher. For many writers, mailing a monthly check is far less painful than putting forth the effort of trying to find a publisher to represent their songs.

A considerable number of published songwriters, including successful staff-writers and writers who have written chart-topping songs, engage independent pluggers to augment their publishers' efforts. This is because the competition to get songs recorded is intense—and these writers want every advantage. The illustration that follows may make this even clearer.

A major music publishing company may have twenty-five or more staff-writers. When a music publisher attends a meeting to pitch songs to a top recording artist, he or she may only be granted enough time to play eight to ten songs. Looking at the numbers, this would mean that more than half of the company's staff-writers will not get even one song pitched—and some of these writers may feel they have several potential hits for the artist with whom their publisher is meeting.

Getting a song pitched may be even tougher than the numbers imply, because the publisher, wanting to maximize his or her chance at getting a song cut, may play three or four songs written by the company's "star" writer, who may have had a recent Number One hit. By hiring an independent plugger, staff-writers supplement the number of pitches their songs get, thereby increasing their chances for success.

> In the event that a staff-writer secures a cut as a result of an independent plugger's efforts or by any other means, his or her publisher still earns the contractually agreed-upon publisher's share of any income the song generates.

The most effective songpluggers have credibility that affords them face-to-face meetings with the top decision makers—record producers, high-level A&R executives, and artists themselves. Their reputations are earned as a result of playing exceptional songs and representing the hit writers who create them. In contrast, songpluggers who pitch songs that are "good," but not "great," and represent writers who have not yet had hits, quickly find that the doors they need to walk through are locked.

Most of the independent songpluggers who represent unpublished writers lack the connections and clout to secure meetings, and instead, drop off songs that may or may not ever be listened to. While many of these individuals are honest and have the best intentions, this is not the case for others. Songpluggers only remain effective by representing the top echelon of songs, but some unscrupulous pluggers will represent any songwriter who can write a check.

In assessing which category a songplugger falls into, it can be helpful to ask the plugger the following questions:

- How many other songwriters are you representing?

- What are some of your other writers' credits?

- What recordings have you secured?

- What percentage of your pitches are made at face-to-face meetings, and how many are dropped off?

- Who are some of the music business professionals with whom you meet?

How Independent Songpluggers Are Compensated

Music publishers earn money only when the songs they represent generate income. As explained in Chapter 1, their compensation is typically 50 percent of a song's revenue, referred to as the publisher's share of the income. Publishers represent songs because they believe they will be able to get some of them recorded—and will share in the considerable income that may result. In contrast, songpluggers are typically paid a monthly *retainer*, a specified fee paid by a songwriter, in exchange for the songplugger's efforts in pitching his or her songs. Songpluggers get paid regardless of whether they ever get a song recorded.

Monthly retainer fees typically range from $200 to $1,000 per month. In many instances, this covers a specified number of songs—which could be anywhere from five to ten, twenty, or more. In other cases, the plugger may represent a songwriter's entire catalog. The use of songpluggers is more prevalent in Nashville than in New York or Los Angeles, and the fees paid in Nashville tend to be on the lower to mid portion of the range. Some pluggers charge a fee for each song they represent for a specified period of time. For instance, they may charge $200 to $500 per song, for a one-year period.

In addition to fees paid as a monthly retainer, most songpluggers earn either a percentage of any income generated as a result of their efforts, or a bonus payment. Percentages most often range from 15 percent to 25 percent of any income the writer receives. In the event that a writer is acting as his or her own publisher, it's crucial to specify whether this percentage is limited to the writer's portion, or includes the publisher's share (which effectively doubles the payment due).

In rare instances, in lieu of a percentage of the writer's income or a bonus payment, a songplugger representing an unpublished writer may request a share of ownership of the copyright of any song for which he or she generates income.

Some songpluggers (generally, those who believe strongly that they will be able to generate income) may be willing to forego a monthly payment, providing their services, essentially, on a commission basis. They earn money only if they generate income for the songwriters they represent. The bonuses or percentages received in the event their efforts generate income tend to be higher than those paid to pluggers who are paid monthly retainers. In these cases, songwriters have nothing to lose, as they pay nothing unless a recording is secured.

Independent Songplugger Agreement

The document that follows is a sample of the type of agreement songwriters enter into to engage the services of independent songpluggers.

INDEPENDENT SONGPLUGGING AGREEMENT

July 1, 2006

Following are the complete terms of the understanding between _____ writer's name _____ **(hereinafter referred to as "Writer") and** _____ songplugger's name _____ **(hereinafter referred to as "Songplugger").**

In exchange for using (his/her) best efforts to secure major label recordings and licensing fees (including, but not limited to synchronization licenses), Songplugger will be paid $500 per month (to be paid quarterly, on January 1st, April 1st, July 1st, and October 1st).

In addition to the $500 monthly retainer, Writer agrees to pay Songplugger fifteen percent (15%) of any royalties or licensing fees that (he/she) receives as a direct result of Songplugger's efforts. Such payments will be made within thirty (30) days of when monies are received by Writer.

It is understood that this is a nonexclusive relationship, allowing both parties to work with additional writers and songpluggers. This agreement will remain in effect for a one-year period.

AGREED AND ACCEPTED:

_____   _____
(insert writer's name)   (insert date)

_____   _____
(insert songplugger's name)   (insert date)

Bonus Schedules

In addition to monthly fees, most songpluggers' agreements provide for them to receive a bonus payment when they secure a recording. While some pluggers earn a percentage of the income they generate (as in the preceding agreement), others earn specified amounts listed on a document known as a *bonus schedule*. Bonus schedules establish the payments to be made by a songwriter to an independent plugger, in the event that specified criteria are met. They also specify the time period during which these payments are to be made.

Bonus payments are determined by a number of factors, including whether the recording is an album cut or a single, the number of copies sold or downloaded, and chart position (for singles). When reviewing the sample bonus schedule that follows, be aware that the amounts are negotiable and vary widely.

BONUS SCHEDULE

In addition to the monthly retainer agreed upon in the Independent Songpluggers' Agreement, the following bonuses are to be paid for recordings secured as a direct result of songplugger's efforts. All payments must be made within thirty days of the attainment of each threshold:

Initial Recording Bonus
For album release in the United States by a new artist on a "Major" label
(or on a label distributed by a major label) .... $ 500
For album release by "Major" artist
(whose previous album release sold at least 500,000 copies) .... $ 1,000
Mechanical Bonus (certified by RIAA)
For 500,000 units sold ("Gold" in the U.S.) .... $ 2,500
For 1,000,000 units sold ("Platinum" in the U.S.) .... $ 3,500
(Total paid for one platinum cut) .... $ 6,000
For each additional 1,000,000 units sold .... $ 2,500

<u>Performance Bonus (for Singles)</u>
(Based on Billboard's U.S. Pop, R&B, Country, and Adult Contemporary Charts)
Performance bonuses are in addition to fees paid for album release and mechanical bonuses. The amounts listed are not cumulative.
Total performance bonus paid if single peaks between #31–40 . . . . . . $ 2,500
Total performance bonus paid if single peaks between #21–30 . . . . . . $ 3,500
Total performance bonus paid if single peaks between #11–20 . . . . . . $ 6,000
Total performance bonus paid if single peaks between #5–10 . . . . $ 8,500
Total performance bonus paid if single peaks between #4–1 . . . . $12,500
For each week the single remains at #1 beyond the first week . . . . $ 5,000

For recordings and licenses obtained by the songplugger in genres of music other than pop, R&B, country, and adult contemporary, Writer shall pay a bonus equal to 20 percent of all income received.

Agreed and Accepted:

By: _____   **Date:** _____
       (insert writer's signature)

By: _____   **Date:** _____
       (insert songplugger's signature)

Using the Independent Songpluggers' Agreement and Bonus Schedule previously shown, a songplugger who secures a recording by a major artist that sells one million copies and reaches Number One on the *Billboard* Pop, Country, R&B, or Adult Contemporary charts would be due a total of $19,500:

- $ 1,000 for securing a release by a major artist

- $ 6,000 mechanical bonus (for more than 1 million units sold)

- $12,500 performance bonus (for reaching the #1 position).

This amount, which is in addition to the monthly retainer, may seem exorbitant at first glance, but it is only a fraction of the earnings split between the songwriters and publishers:

- $91,500 mechanical royalties (for 1 million units sold at the $0.091 statutory rate, in effect through December 31, 2007)

- $600,000 to $1,000,000 in performance royalties (estimated).

A songwriter who hires an independent plugger is solely responsible for paying the plugger's monthly retainer, as well as any bonuses incurred. In the event that the song was cowritten, or is published, in the absence of an agreement, the other writers and publisher(s) are not required to pay any portion of the songplugger's fees. However, one would hope that they would volunteer to do so.

Pitch Reports

Many songpluggers, especially those who represent unpublished songwriters, provide their clients with a *pitch report*. This is a listing of the writers' songs that were pitched, and the artists (or artists' representatives) to whom they were submitted. These reports are typically issued once a month, listing the pitches the plugger made in the previous month.

In most cases, pluggers don't specify whether these pitches were made at sit-down meetings, or if the songs were mailed or sent via the Internet. Songpluggers who represent top writers, and secure significant holds and cuts, do not typically provide pitch reports; they don't need to justify the money they are paid, or prove that they're doing their jobs.

Songwriters with material that matches or surpasses the songs being written by the current hit-makers may benefit greatly by the assistance of a well-connected songplugger. Aspiring writers who are not yet writing the caliber of songs that can compete with the top pros, and have not been able to attract the attention of music publishers, are advised to continue working on their craft.

Before spending money on independent pluggers, songwriters who are not certain their songs are at a competitive level are advised to seek feedback from professional song critiquing services, and qualified teachers, and at workshops. There are few, if any, instances of unpublished songwriters, or writers who have not previously had songwriting success, securing a major label recording as a result of paying an independent songplugger.

Avoiding the Scams

Companies and individuals that prey on songwriters are sometimes referred to as *song sharks*. The schemes they perpetuate are varied, but all share several common denominators: they appeal to writers' egos, providing flattery, encouragement, and hope; they promise quick, easy steps to success; and they are in business to make as much money as possible—not to help songwriters.

Many scams begin with an impressive, official-looking letter expressing interest in a writer's material. The correspondence typically originates from a company based in Los Angeles, Nashville, or New York, lending an element of glamour and implied credibility to the firm. Many of these letters begin with a phrase such as, "We know how difficult it can be for talented writers, such as yourself, to break into the exciting, lucrative world of songwriting. But there IS a solution."

In some cases, the letter insinuates that the company has already heard the writer's material—and was exceptionally impressed. Most often, the initial contact takes the form of an application—an opportunity for the writer to receive a free evaluation of his or her work for possible inclusion on an album, or for representation by the company. In some cases, a questionnaire is included, with questions crafted to fuel writers' hopes and dreams, such as:

- If these songs become hits, do you have more that you have written?

- How many songs, lyrics, or poems can you write in a typical month?

- If your songs become hits, would you consider moving to Hollywood or Nashville to accept full-time employment as a professional songwriter?

Soon after hopeful writers send in their poems, lyrics, or songs for consideration, they receive a letter that begins with "Congratulations!" It praises the writer's work profusely, and includes the offer of a contract. In some instances, the letters these companies send include statements such as, "Your talent is a precious gift from God, meant to be honored and shared with the world." Of course, the only talent required to be offered a contract by these con artists is the ability to write a check.

Compilation Albums

One of the most popular scams offers an opportunity to be included on a *compilation album*, a collection of recordings of songs from writers who fall for this scheme. Writers are promised that a specified number of albums (that include their song) will be distributed nationally to a long list of well-known record labels, radio stations, music publishers, and other music industry professionals who will, ostensibly, either broadcast the songs or have them recorded by famous artists. These albums are typically given an impressive sounding name, sometimes evoking a patriotic theme, such as *Songs from the Soul of America* or *The Sound of the U.S.A.*

The contracts the writers sign generally include provisions entitling the writers to receive the full statutory mechanical royalty rate for each album sold. The agreements also detail when payments are to be made (for instance, within ninety days of the end of each royalty accounting period), giving the appearance of being a legitimate agreement issued by a company that has every intention of issuing royalties. Songwriters are often ecstatic at their good fortune, sharing the news of their talent finally being recognized with family and friends.

In some cases, writers' demos are included on the compilation albums "as is," regardless of the quality of the recordings (or lack thereof). More often, the company offers to record the songs, providing "professional orchestrations, musical arrangements, and vocalists befitting the exceptional beauty of your words." Sometimes, these recordings are provided "at no cost to the writer," although the writer is required to pay an "administrative" or "processing" fee that might range from $600 to $1,500 or more.

In other cases, the writer is required to prepay for the purchase of a specified number of albums. Other variations of this scheme require writers to pay "only" for recording costs, with the company absorbing "100 percent of all marketing, promotional, and distribution expenses." These "recording costs" charged to the writers are typically at least $1,200, though in actuality, the song sharks may allot as little as $50 to $100 to record each song.

These albums are of the poorest quality, not even approaching professional standards. When albums are recorded by professional recording artists, they rarely finish more than two or three songs a day; recordings included on these compilations are typically churned out at a rate of forty or more a day. In many cases, the band and vocalist rehearses each song one time and then records it; inevitable mistakes remain on the recording.

In any case, the song shark will be sure to make a hefty profit from the twenty or more unsuspecting amateurs included on the compilations these companies produce. If twenty-five writers each purchase fifty copies of a compilation for $19.99 per copy, the scammer's gross receipts equal almost $25,000 for each compilation—and the song shark may produce fifty or more compilations a year, depending on how many writers fall for the scam.

In the event that only lyrics or poems are submitted, there will be an offer to have a professional composer add the music. When this occurs, it is handled as a work for hire and the lyricist retains 100 percent of the rights to the completed song. This sounds like a terrific offer, but as explained later in this chapter, the melodies these lyrics are paired with (as when writers pay to have their lyrics set to music) are not competitive in the commercial market.

These companies are permitted to continue bilking songwriters, because technically they provide all of the services contractually promised. They send copies of their compilation albums to radio stations and record labels—that promptly toss them in the trash, or laugh at them. They pay royalties on all copies sold—although, no copies are ever sold, except to the other unsuspecting songwriters who have fallen for the scheme.

When a copyright is registered, it becomes part of the *public record*, meaning the law provides that this information must be made available to anyone seeking it. By visiting the Copyright Office in person or online at www.copyright.gov, individuals and companies can easily access the names and contact information for copyright registrants. Using this information, unscrupulous companies send tens of thousands of letters to hopeful songwriters whose names and addresses they acquire from the Copyright Office.

Setting Song Poems, Poems, and Lyrics to Music

Advertisements for services that provide melodies for a fee often appear in the back of tabloids and magazines, and usually include phrases such as, "Lyrics and Song Poems Needed for Major Recording Artists," and "Free Evaluation of Songs and Poems." A *song poem* is a description apparently coined by these firms to attract customers who write poetry, and fail to understand the differences between poems and well-crafted lyrics. The use of this phrase should be an instant warning; song poems have no role in the music industry.

Although not exactly a scam, companies that set poems and lyrics to music for a fee are included in this chapter because many of these firms sell false hopes—not just melodies. The literature sent in response to inquiries implies that by paying to have your lyrics and poems set to music, recording artists and music publishers will be clamoring for the songs.

As previously mentioned, when a lyricist or poet engages one of these services to set his or her words to music, 100 percent of the resulting composition is owned by the lyricist or poet. The composers' contributions are considered works for hire, for which they are paid a flat fee, typically $25 to $50 for each melody they compose. The customer pays much more to the firm that employs the composers. In addition, there are usually additional fees imposed to provide customers with copies of demo recordings of the finished composition.

Melody is a crucial component to successful songs—not an afterthought. The ability to craft a hit melody, one that can compete with the songs that earn a coveted slot on recordings, is a rare gift and sometimes requires long hours of hard work and rewriting. Being paid on a per-song basis, composers employed by these services have an incentive to write as quickly as possible, sometimes churning out ten or more melodies a day.

Legitimate composers collaborate because they believe in the hit potential of the finished compositions. If composers employed to set poems and lyrics to music believed the stock melodies they attach to these amateur lyrics had the potential of earning hundreds of thousands of dollars, they would not be selling their rights to them for $25 to $50.

Paying to have a lyric or poem set to music is an acceptable option if the writer's sole purpose in doing so is personal enjoyment; sharing songs with family and friends can be fun. The scam element comes in when lyricists and poets are led to believe that by paying to have their work set to music, it will be able to compete with compositions written by professional songwriters. There has never been an instance of a song being published by a legitimate, major music publisher, or achieving significant commercial success, as a result of having a poem or lyric set to music by one of the firms that advertise these services. If this were the case, this information would certainly be included in their ads and literature.

Bogus Grammy Nominations

In an especially abhorrent scam, a firm, masquerading as a publishing company and record label, provides a list of their Grammy-nominated artists and songwriters. To understand this scam, one must be familiar with the Grammy voting process. In the first round of Grammy voting, members of the National Academy of Recording Arts and Sciences (NARAS) may nominate any recording, provided it was commercially released during a specified period of time. To be included on the list for Grammy consideration, the only requirements are the completion of paperwork and the submission of a specified number of copies of the recording by a voting member of NARAS.

Thousands of songs are submitted during this initial phase; the quality of the work is of no consideration whatsoever at this stage of the process. Next, NARAS publishes a booklet listing the titles of all the recordings submitted for Grammy consideration. Grammy voters vote for their favorites, and the top five recordings in each category receive actual Grammy nominations.

Some unscrupulous companies submit recordings that are, in actuality, poor-quality demos for Grammy consideration. By assigning the recordings a release number, they circumvent NARAS' requirement that the recordings be commercially released. They show their writers and artists a copy of the booklet, which includes their names and the titles of their works listed among superstar artists and top songwriters. The unsuspecting writers receive congratulatory letters from the scammers, and celebrate their "Grammy nominations"—despite the fact that their songs never receive any significant airplay or earn a dime.

Recording Studios Acting As Publishers

A commonly used scam is one in which, after a free evaluation, songwriters are informed that a company is eager to publish their material and pitch it to top recording artists. The excited writers are told that their songs could be huge hits—if only they were properly demoed. The so-called publishing company explains that it will gladly use its contacts and expertise to produce the necessary demo without taking any fee for itself—but the songwriter must pay for costs of hiring a studio, recording engineer, and musicians.

Of course, the "publishing company" owns the recording studio, knows that the songs will never be recorded by professional artists, and has no intention of pitching them. They are in business to produce overpriced demos—not to publish songs. Hopeful songwriters who balk may be admonished that if they are not willing to invest in their careers, then they must not be serious about wanting to have hit songs.

In a variation of this "demo-studio-acting-as-a-publisher" scheme, the "publisher" generously offers to pay half of the writer's demo-recording costs. In these instances, the demos are so overpriced that the 50 percent the writer pays is still typically higher than the going rate. Even if the demos were an acceptable price and up to professional standards, the writer has been scammed by being led to believe that his or her songs are being legitimately published.

Legitimate publishers typically advance 100 percent of the costs if they feel they need to record new demos of songs that they are interested in publishing.

How to Protect Yourself from the Scams

Writers should be able to assess whether a particular company falls into the category of "scam" by asking some specific questions:

- May I review samples of your previous albums? (Few songwriters would ever fall for the compilation album scheme if they heard how dreadful the albums are.)

- May I see sales figures for your previous releases? (The con artists will never make these available.)

- What successes have songwriters had as a result of your services? (Unless it's a brand new company, they should be able to provide verifiable credits.)

This final question can be tricky. It's easy for con artists to impress songwriters who lack knowledge about the workings of the music business. If these firms list companies that have published compositions as a result of their efforts, be certain that these are not affiliated companies. Writers should ask for a list of the publishing companies' credits; if the artists who have recorded songs from the company's catalog are all unknowns who released albums independently, the writers of their songs would likely have earned nothing.

Statements such as "We're located in the heart of the music business" and "Our offices are just down the hall from a top record label" should raise a red flag. Companies whose efforts have resulted in song placements with legitimate artists, song publishing deals, and other genuine successes do not need to advertise where they are located.

Likewise, the fact that songs have appeared, or even been Number One, on "the charts" may be meaningless. There are numerous obscure independent music charts created by dishonest individuals for the sole purpose of satisfying their clients' egos. These charts may have names that sound impressive, but they do not reflect significant airplay or sales. By using these charts, devious individuals and companies can promise "guaranteed chart success."

Legitimate publishing companies do not solicit songwriters through the mail, nor do they place advertisements in the back of tabloids and magazines. Companies that promise (or imply) that writers will become rich and famous are promoting only scams.

Some costs incurred by songwriters are typically necessary expenses. These include reasonably priced, professionally produced demos. Demo costs vary widely depending on musical style and writers' locations. As of this book's writing, songwriters did not need to spend more than $1,000 per song for demos, and the majority of excellent demos were recorded for considerably less than this amount.

Demos of ballads, which sometimes require only a professional vocalist and a guitar or keyboard accompaniment, can typically be produced for $300 or less. Writers should be extremely wary of demo production services charging considerably more than these figures. Additionally, writers may avail themselves of professional critiques. This is a legitimate expense if it is provided at a reasonable cost by teachers with professional credentials. Top songwriting teachers typically charge $30 to $50 per song for a thorough critique. (Prices listed were accurate in 2006 and should be adjusted for inflation. For a list of reasonably priced demo production services, visit www.jasonblume.com.)

By visiting the Better Business Bureau's national Web site at www.search.bbb.org, it is easy to check whether complaints have been lodged against a company located anywhere in the U.S. and, if so, whether the complaint was satisfactorily resolved. The best defense against being taken advantage of is education, coupled with a willingness to let go of the fantasy that writing a check can provide access to the fast lane to success.

PART IV

MAXIMIZING YOUR CHANCES FOR SUCCESS

CHAPTER EIGHTEEN

Collaborating

Collaboration, as it relates to the music business, refers to the process of two or more songwriters working together to create a composition; it is synonymous with cowriting. Some of the greatest songs ever written have been the result of collaborations such as those by George and Ira Gershwin, Rodgers and Hammerstein, Holland-Dozier-Holland of Motown fame, Sir Elton John and Bernie Taupin, Lennon/McCartney, and many more.

More recently, Max Martin's collaborations with writers, including Dennis Pop, Andreas Carlsson, and Rami Yacoub, resulted in some of the Backstreet Boys', Hilary Duff's, Celine Dion's, and Britney Spears' most memorable hits. Martin Sandberg and Lukasz Gottwald were responsible for a string of Kelly Clarkson successes; Babyface and Antonio "L.A." Reid penned a long list of hits for artists such as Usher, Toni Braxton, TLC, Boyz II Men, and Whitney Houston. In the country music genre, Toby Keith and Scott Emerick's collaborations resulted in numerous chart-topping singles for Toby Keith, and virtually all of Shania Twain's hits were written by Twain with her husband, Robert J. "Mutt" Lange.

The Rights Afforded Authors of Joint and Derivative Works

Copyright law defines a *joint work* as "a work prepared by two or more authors with the intention that their contributions be merged into inseparable or interdependent parts of a unitary whole." The vast majority of songs resulting from collaboration are included in this category.

The only cowritten songs not legally considered joint works are those that result from a composer adding to an original work that had not been intended for collaboration. For instance, if a melody is written by a composer who does not intend to have lyrics added, and then, at a later date, a lyricist sets words to the music, the resulting work is considered a *derivative work*, a new work based upon an existing composition.

If a lyricist were to write words to the instrumental theme from the movie "Chariots of Fire," the resulting song would be considered a derivative work. In this instance, the composer would still own the original melody, separate and apart from its contribution to the new derivative work. The composer has the right to license the use of his or her music to others, with no obligation to the lyricist. The same principle applies when an existing poem is set to music. However, when two songwriters write a song together, whether the collaboration takes place in person, over the telephone, or over the Internet, the resulting composition is considered a joint work and, as such, both writers' contributions are inextricable.

In the eyes of the law, once a joint work has been written, it cannot be "unwritten." The analogy most often used is that, like an egg that has been scrambled, the individual parts of a song written as a joint work cannot return to their respective forms after they have been combined. This means that collaborators do not have the legal right to withdraw their individual contributions from a song; a lyricist may not legally reclaim his or her words, and a composer may not take back his or her melody.

Cowriters sometimes protect themselves when beginning collaboration with a new partner by stating that they will each own their respective contributions to the joint work and, if either party is not pleased with the result, they may each take back their contribution. For this agreement to be enforceable, it must be in writing.

Establishing Percentages of Ownership

A look at the music charts reveals that the vast majority of hit songs are written by more than one writer. Theoretically, there is no limit to the number of writers who may contribute to a composition. Hit songs by artists such as Mariah Carey, Beyoncé, MercyMe, Jennifer Lopez, Faith Evans, and Fantasia have had as many as nine, ten, or eleven writers credited (as mentioned in Chapter 16, this is sometimes the result of using sampled compositions). In some instances, one or more writers compose only the music, while another writer, or writers, write the words. In many cases, collaborators all contribute to the melody and the lyric.

It is impossible to accurately assess and assign a value to a particular writer's contribution to a song. For instance, if one writer composes 80 percent of a song's verse melody and 100 percent of its lyric, and a second writer contributes only two short musical phrases that become the most memorable elements of the song, how much ownership does each writer deserve? To avoid this dilemma, percentages of ownership are not determined by keeping track of the number of notes or words written by each collaborator.

When collaborators begin a song, the assumption is that the writers' credits will be divided equally; for instance, with two writers the split would be 50/50; with three writers, each writer would own one third of the song. But in some instances (especially when writing with an established artist), percentages may not be assigned equally. A superstar recording artist might grant a 10 percent writer's credit to a member of his band who contributed a significant instrumental melodic figure, or 20 percent to a producer who rewrote lines of a verse lyric.

To avoid misunderstandings and potential lawsuits, it is always advisable for collaborators to discuss and agree upon the percentages of ownership during the writing process. Waiting to have this discussion until a song has already been recorded is a recipe for trouble.

When one writer contributes 100 percent of a song's lyric, while a second writer composes 100 percent of a song's music, splitting the song's ownership 50/50 is obvious. But in some instances, the contributions are not always so easily defined, and in some cases, it may be unclear whether a contribution constitutes collaboration at all.

What if a writer composes *a capella* (without using an instrument), providing 100 percent of the melody and lyric, and then engages a musician to add chords and provide accompaniment for a fee? Chords and harmonies play a significant role in expressing the feeling evoked by a melody, and they can contribute significantly to a song's success. Is the musician who provided the chords entitled to a percentage of the copyright?

To a large extent, the musical genre and, on a case-by-case basis, the song itself determines the significance of the chords that support the melody. In country and folk music, the chords typically found in successful songs are relatively straightforward, meaning those songs are likely to be harmonized primarily with major, minor, and seventh chords. With few exceptions, almost any skilled musician would suggest the same or similar chords.

This is not to imply that country and folk songs can't benefit from the exploration of various chord alternatives; finding the chords that best enhance and support the melody is important for any song. But for a composition to sound consistent with the music played in country and folk genres, there are a very limited number of reasonable options for each chord. A writer might ask to hear several suggestions and then make his or her choice. For instance, "I prefer the C in that measure, as opposed to the A minor."

The instance described above does not warrant granting the accompanist a writer's credit or a percentage of ownership in the song. He or she is simply providing the writer with one or two options of the chords that the melody clearly implies for the particular style of music. Nonetheless, it's crucial that this issue be discussed and agreed upon by both parties prior to the work being done.

For styles such as jazz, R&B, hip-hop, pop, and dance music, chords, musical figures, grooves, and bass lines often play an enormous role in the success of a song. The chords found in hits in these styles tend to be far more varied and distinctive than those generally used in country and folk music. A jazz or hip-hop song is likely to incorporate additional textures and flavors with the use of augmented, diminished, ninth, and other more complex accompaniments. Therefore, a contribution of chords and/or musical hooks in these genres may well merit a significant percentage of the writers' credit and partial ownership of the copyright.

In some collaborative efforts, one composer's contribution may consist solely of the musical track—the bass, drums, percussion, and keyboard parts, to which a second writer adds 100 percent of the melody and lyrics. This most often happens in the hip-hop, R&B, and dance genres, and in many of these instances the composer of the musical track earns a well-deserved 50 percent or more of the writer's credit, because the track itself may be a primary element of a song's success in these styles.

In many instances, musicians hired to perform on songwriters' demo recordings contribute identifiable, catchy musical licks (sometimes referred to as *signature licks*). These parts might be played during the songs' introductions or interspersed throughout the compositions. In the majority of cases, these melodic hooks are copied note for note when songs are recorded as masters for inclusion on albums by recording artists.

Do the musicians who create these musical phrases deserve a writer's credit and a percentage of ownership of the copyright? Again, the key is to have clear, up-front communication so there is no doubt of a musician's role (collaborator or performer), and whether he or she will be compensated with a flat fee, as a performer, or on a royalty basis as a cowriter.

When hiring demo performers as "hired guns," it should be clarified that a flat fee represents 100 percent of their compensation. Professional musicians, such as union members who regularly perform on demo recordings, usually understand this; they know they are hired to create the "radio-friendly" musical parts that contribute to a song's success. But it is always best to be sure that everyone has a clear understanding of the agreement.

Demo musicians and vocalists routinely contribute substantially to the success of hit recordings; they are often unsung heroes. It may seem unfair that their compensation can total as little as $100 to $300 when their work plays a significant role in the development of songs that might earn $1 million, should they top the charts. But remember, these musicians and singers get paid regardless of whether the songs they record ever earn a dime. Demo musicians and vocalists at the top of their fields can earn more than $200,000 a year—while the vast majority of the songs to which they contribute their talents never get recorded or generate any income.

In the event that a songwriter feels that a demo musician's or vocalist's contribution plays an exceptionally significant role in the success of a song, the writer certainly has the option to offer a writer's credit, although it is not required. But in these instances, if a song earns a substantial amount, a thank you note and a "bonus" check are probably appropriate.

Signing Collaborators' Agreements

The best way to avoid misunderstandings, and potential lawsuits, regarding writers' contributions and percentages of ownership of a song is to have all writers sign an agreement, such as the one that follows.

COLLABORATORS' AGREEMENT

(insert date)
This is to confirm that we, the sole writers of the song or musical composition listed below, hereby agree among ourselves to the following writers' divisions:

SONG TITLE: _____ "On Angels' Wings" _____

WRITERS (insert writer's full legal name)	CONTRIBUTION (insert "Lyrics Only," "Music Only," or "Music & Lyrics")	% OF OWNERSHIP (insert %)*
Jason Blume	Music & Lyrics	50%
Karen Taylor-Good	Music & Lyrics	50%

*Writers' percentages of ownership must total 100%.

If any samples are contained within this song, for which the sampled writers/publishers are to receive a copyright interest in and to the composition and/or payment of monies attributable to the composition, then we agree that our shares in the copyright and/or monies attributable to the composition shall be reduced proportionately.

The following represents all samples, known to date, embodied in the above composition:

SAMPLED SONG'S TITLE	ARTIST	LABEL	PUBLISHING CO.
No Samples			

WRITERS' PUBLISHING INFORMATION   **PRO AFFILIATION**

Jason Blume/Dreamer's Moon Music   BMI

Karen Taylor-Good/K.T. Good Music   SESAC

READ AND AGREED: DATE:
(writers each sign)   (the date form is signed)

_____   _____

_____   _____

Dividing the Publisher's Share

Each of a song's cowriters owns a portion of its publishing rights, equivalent to the percentage of his or her writer's share. If a song has two writers, each owns 50 percent of the writers' share, as well as 50 percent of the publisher's share. Likewise, if a song has ten writers who share equal ownership, each collaborator also owns one tenth of the publishers' share.

In some cases, the percentage of a song owned by each of its writers and publishers is not divided equally. This most often occurs when the cowriters are of unequal stature, for instance, when one of the writers is a multiplatinum recording artist, while the other has never had a song published or recorded. In a case such as this, the artist might request a larger percentage of ownership, or ask to retain his or her collaborator's share of the publishing rights and income. While this may seem unfair, a case can be made that, when a successful recording artist records a song resulting from collaboration, he or she is essentially fulfilling a publisher's primary function by securing a recording of the song.

A few top recording artists have reportedly demanded to receive a portion, or all, of the publisher's share of a song as a condition of recording it. In other cases, similar demands have been made by record producers. While not unheard of, these scenarios are by no means typical. There are also instances when artists demand to be credited as cowriters, despite the fact that their only contribution to songs is their name. At times, this may be financially motivated, while in other instances it may be based on an artist wanting to gain credibility by being listed as a songwriter.

These situations take unfair advantage of songwriters, but fortunately they are exceptions. Songwriting is a business, and it may be worth giving up a significant portion of a song if it is the only way to get it included on CD by a multiplatinum-selling artist; 100 percent of nothing is nothing. Still, each writer needs to assess circumstances such as these on a case-by-case basis to determine whether the benefit outweighs the negative aspects.

How to Find Collaborators—and Why

Music publishers and record labels accept only complete songs—melody and lyrics. It is never appropriate to submit only music, or only lyrics, unless specifically requested (for instance, if an artist is seeking to write lyrics to existing tracks). After a writer has established a relationship with a music publishing company, a publisher may suggest collaborations. But in order to reach that point, writers must have finished songs. For songwriters who compose only music, or only lyrics, finding collaborators is imperative.

Many writers capable of writing both music and lyrics choose to cowrite in the hopes that by collaborating, they will write songs that are different and better than those they write on their own. Additional benefits may include:

- *Increased contacts.* By cowriting, songwriters may be introduced to vocalists and musicians, studios and recording engineers, and additional collaborators. Collaborators who are published writers may also initiate introductions to their music publishers.

- *Additional pitches.* With two writers (and if applicable, their publishers) working to place a particular song, it may receive twice the number of pitches.

- *Discipline.* Having cowriting appointments scheduled in advance provides the impetus some songwriters need to work on their craft.

- *Inspiration.* When the "chemistry" is right, many writers feel that the quality of their songwriting far exceeds the work they do alone.

- *Political considerations.* Collaborating with recording artists, record producers, and successful writers may lead to increased opportunities to get songs recorded.

- *Feedback.* Sometimes it can be hard to assess whether an idea, melody, or lyric is effectively communicating what you intend. Collaborators provide instant feedback.

- *Writing Up.* An analogy often used to describe "writing up" is playing tennis. Similar to improving one's tennis game by playing with better players, songwriters may push themselves to do their best work by collaborating with writers who have more skills and experience.

Besides the business considerations, you can gain emotional support and encouragement from your collaborators. This can be especially important during the inevitable frustrations and disappointments that are part of the songwriting business.

The best way to find collaborators is by networking with other songwriters. Performing songwriters who play their original songs at local nightclubs, hotel lounges, restaurants, concerts, and coffeehouses may all be potential cowriters.

By attending events where songs are critiqued or pitched, writers can essentially audition each others' work. This typically occurs at songwriting workshops, camps, classes, and events such as Taxi's Road Rally (www.taxi.com), NSAI's Songposium and Spring Symposium (www.nashvillesongwriters.com), and a variety of events sponsored by the Songwriters Guild (www.songwritersguild.com), as well as at workshops presented by ASCAP (www.ascap.com) and BMI (www.bmi.com), the West Coast Songwriters Association's annual conference (www.westcoastsongwriters.org), and for writers of urban and gospel music, the Northwest Music Explosion (www.northwestmusicexplosion.com) and the Urban Network (www.urbannetwork.com).

Organizations such as NSAI and Just Plain Folks (www.jpfolks.com) have local chapters in cities throughout the U.S. Monthly meetings, as well as workshops and other events these associations sponsor, provide excellent opportunities for potential collaborators to meet.

With the advent of MP3s and e-mail, long-distance collaborations are easier than ever. Countless cowriting partnerships have been forged as the result of writers connecting at Internet sites where writers seeking collaborators can post listings. These sites include The Muse's Muse (www.musesmuse.com), Songwriters Resource Network (www.songwritersresourcenetwork.com), and Songwriters Directory (www.songwritersdirectory.com). Seeking collaborators online at sites such as those previously mentioned, and by networking by visiting songwriter chat rooms, can be especially helpful for songwriters who lack easy access to other writers.

Resolving Conflicts with Cowriters

Ideally, collaboration is a positive experience, providing an emotional environment in which writers can do their best work. But regardless of how well cowriters get along, there are likely to be instances when they disagree. Songwriting is an art, and as such, there are no "right" or "wrong" answers regarding how it should be done. Ideally, collaborators will share a common vision for their song and reach agreements.

Following are some problems that frequently occur among collaborators—and how to resolve them:

- *One of the writers wants to rewrite a particular line of their song's melody or lyric.* As in any relationship, communication is essential and, in order to do their best work, collaborators should feel free to express their concerns. By explaining the reasons why he or she feels the line isn't working, a writer may be able to persuade his or her collaborator to make the requested changes. If they are unable to reach an agreement, the team might seek feedback from objective sources, such as a professional song-critiquing service or a music publisher. If this does not lead to a consensus, another solution is to continue working on the problem spot until both parties are pleased.

- *One of the writers doesn't like the finished song and wants his or her contribution back.* If the composition is a "joint work," as explained earlier in this chapter, according to copyright law, in the absence of a signed agreement, it cannot be separated. The writers might rewrite the song until they are both satisfied, or simply move on, with the dissatisfied writer accepting that he or she will, hopefully, write many other songs.

- *A collaborator does not want to finish a song.* One member of a writing team may not want to complete a particular song because of other commitments— or because he or she simply doesn't like the song and doesn't choose to invest additional time in it. If the other writer feels strongly about finishing the song, he or she has the option of completing it alone, or bringing in an additional collaborator. As always, it's crucial to communicate, and to establish the original cowriter's percentage of the resulting song.

- *One of the writers wants to record a demo—the other doesn't, or can't afford to do so.* A discussion regarding how a song is to be demoed, and the amount allotted for the demo budget, should occur before the song is written. Although the style and tempo may dictate the type of demo required, the writers should agree in advance on issues such as whether the demo will be a home studio production or professionally produced; range of budgets; and, which one (or if both) of the writers will handle the production responsibilities. If one of the collaborators is unable to afford the cost of a demo, the other writer has the option of absorbing 100 percent of the expense. The writer advancing the money might specify that he or she be reimbursed out of any revenue the song generates. But if a writer does not choose to invest in a demo because he or she does not feel strongly about the song, the remaining writer(s) have the option of paying for the demo themselves, or not recording a demo of the song.

- *One of the writers is a recording artist, and wants to keep the song for his or her own artist project—the other wants to pitch the song to other artists.* As you learned in Chapter 9, each copyright owner retains the right to issue nonexclusive licenses (for instance, recording licenses and synchronization licenses for television and film), provided that all co-owners are paid. So, from a legal standpoint, a writer may not stop his or her cowriter from recording and releasing a particular song, or having another artist do so. Hopefully, the writers will reach an agreement based on what is best for both the writers—and the song.

Not all writers are well-matched collaborators; they may differ greatly in terms of their temperaments, approaches to the writing and demo processes, and their definitions of what constitutes a "great" song. Writers may have to collaborate with many individuals in order to find those with whom they "click," and those who bring out the best in them.

Even the best of cowriters occasionally disagree. When writers feel passionately about their songs and careers, it's inevitable that there will sometimes be conflicts. As in any relationship, communication and compromise are typically the keys to resolving problems.

CHAPTER NINETEEN

Organizing Your Business

Navigating the business of songwriting tends to be challenging, even for the most talented writers. In addition to working diligently to hone their craft, songwriters can improve the likelihood of attaining their goals by remembering that the music business is a business—and by treating it as such. By organizing recordings of their songs, keeping track of works in progress, monitoring royalty payments and demo expenses, and carefully managing their time, writers can maximize their chances for success. Additionally, they can ensure that they receive all the money to which they are entitled.

Managing Your Ideas and Finished Songs

For writers with multiple songs in progress, organizing their lyric ideas and keeping snippets of melodies easily accessible can be challenging. Some writers report frustrating scenarios such as the one that follows. They begin writing a song with a collaborator, but it doesn't get finished in one sitting, so the writers schedule a second writing appointment for four weeks later. In the interim, they each begin eight more songs, which also must be continued weeks later. In the weeks that follow the original writing session, each writer fills three or four notebooks with lyrics and ideas for the various songs.

When the collaborators arrive for their respective follow-up writing sessions, thirty minutes or more are spent riffling through notebooks, trying to find the right song. Then comes the challenge of tracking down where the melodic ideas were recorded and finding the right melodic fragments among the twenty other ideas stored on the cassettes, computer discs, or hard drive during the four weeks that have passed since the song was begun.

There are inevitable instances when an idea for a lyric pops into a writer's head at a time when the only paper handy is a napkin or an ATM receipt—both of which can be easily lost. An easy way to keep track of the assorted notebook pages, scraps of paper, and musical ideas is to allocate one manila folder or envelope for each song. The title of the song is written outside the envelope and all of the notes, recordings of melodic ideas, and other information (such as the name of each cowriter's publishing company, and his or her PRO affiliation) regarding the composition goes inside.

Similarly, titles, ideas, lyrics, and recordings of melodic ideas can be collected in a file titled, "Ideas," or for positive thinkers, "Future Hits." When using a cassette or computer disc to record multiple melodic ideas, writers can save time and avoid frustration by placing a blank label on it, and writing a brief description of the melodic excerpts, for instance: 1. Up-tempo R&B idea; 2. Country guitar lick; 3. Gwen Stefani–type dance groove; 4. Alternative rock chorus melody. Leaving at least ten seconds of space between recorded ideas makes it easier to locate the starts of the various snippets at a later date.

Many writers record melodic ideas onto their voicemail or answering machines when another recorder is not available. To keep track of these ideas it's best to rerecord the melodies onto a CD, hard drive, cassette, or other medium of permanent recording, label them, and place the recording in a file or envelope.

For technology-savvy songwriters, the solution is to store all of a particular song's lyric and melodic ideas in one folder within a computer (a laptop, for those who want to carry it to writing sessions). *MasterWriter* (www.masterwriter.com) is a popular computer software package that includes a program to keep track of lyrics, melodies, and information, such as cowriters' contact and publishing information. It also includes a collection of tools, such as rhyming dictionaries, an alliteration dictionary, a hard disc recorder for recording and storing melodic ideas, and more than two hundred fifty adjustable drum loops.

Some songwriters prefer the act of handwriting (as opposed to typing) their ideas. For them, jotting their thoughts into a notebook is more conducive to expressing their creativity than typing on a computer keyboard. These writers are advised to either use the "file folder" method previously described, or to transfer their notes into a computer on a regular basis.

The days of trying to keep track of master recordings stored on CDs, computer discs, DATs, or reel-to-reel tapes are gone. The advent of MP3, WAV, and other file-compression technology has made it easy to store entire song catalogs in a home computer or laptop, or on an MP3 player, such as an iPod. Many writers keep their songs in a separate computer drive from their documents, so all their music is in one easy-to-locate spot. This has the added benefit of not taking up space in the drive used to store documents and other computer programs. Finding particular songs and burning them onto CDs becomes as simple as the click of a few buttons, instead of searching for, and sorting through, piles of discs. When storing music in a computer or MP3 player, always retain a hard copy back-up (for instance, a CD).

Keeping Track of Your Money

Songwriters are essentially self-employed small business owners, responsible for both the creation and the marketing of their product. For any business to thrive, its owner must pay close attention to financial matters, but many songwriters and other creative individuals are notorious for failing to do so. There have been countless instances of superstar songwriters and recording artists filing for bankruptcy following periods of enormous earnings. In addition to failing to manage their money prudently, some writers neglect the bookkeeping, accounting, and other financial aspects of their business, letting potential income slip through the proverbial cracks.

Monitoring Performance Royalties

While the performing rights organizations typically do an excellent job, they enter information relating to hundreds of thousands of performances into their computer systems, and occasional errors are inevitable. By inspecting your performance royalty statements, you can ensure you are receiving appropriate payments.

It's impossible to determine whether all of the radio, television, Internet, and additional airplay and performances your songs receive are being accounted for. But if you are certain that a particular song has received significant airplay, and the title fails to appear on royalty statements, you need to check that the work has been properly registered.

Note that local radio airplay does not constitute "significant" airplay. While a song broadcast on a handful of stations may garner a hundred or more radio performances, as previously explained, most hit songs are broadcast more than a million times. If you are aware of instances in which your music was broadcast on television, you can check your royalty statements to ascertain whether your PRO has properly credited and paid for the television airplay.

When performance royalty statements are received, it's advisable to review them, checking to be certain that all performances have been listed properly. By using the information contained in Chapter 10 ("Understanding Performance Royalties"), writers should be able to assess the accuracy of various elements reflected on their performance royalty statements, paying close attention to the following issues that significantly impact earnings:

- Is the writer's percentage of ownership listed correctly (for instance, has a sole writer been credited with 100 percent of the writer's share of royalties, or only 50 percent)?

- Is the correct use attributed to the performance (for instance, for a television performance, was a full feature, theme song, end credit, visual vocal, or background use credited as such)?

- Is the length of the performance accurately reflected?

- Are works correctly credited with bonuses (if applicable)?

- If a song was performed as part of a major concert tour, does it appear on the statement? (As previously explained, ASCAP and BMI pay performance royalties for songs performed as part of the top two hundred grossing concert tours each year. SESAC pays royalties for performances in all of its licensed venues.)

Documenting and Verifying Demo Expenses

The cost of recording demos is a necessary part of doing business as a songwriter, and it is not uncommon for professional writers to incur $10,000 to $30,000 a year in demo expenses. While writers who own their own home recording studios save the costs of renting studios and hiring engineers (if they are able to serve this function themselves), they still must hire appropriate vocalists and musicians for each demo they record.

In most instances, music publishers pay for their writers' demos, either on a song-by-song basis or by factoring a demo budget into their annual advances. But, as noted in previous chapters, in virtually all cases, any money paid by a publisher for demo costs is treated as an advance, to be recouped from writers' future earnings.

In cases where music publishers advance their writers' demo costs, invoices are typically forwarded to the music publishers—who pay vendors, such as recording studios, engineers, musicians, and vocalists—directly. This money is deducted from writers' royalties as provided for by provisions of their song publishing agreements. Generally, the royalty statements that publishers issue their writers do not break down demo expenses for each individual song. They list only the total demo expenses paid during a given accounting period, for instance: "Demo expenses for the period of Jan. 1, 2006—June 30, 2006: $16,742."

It's essential that writers request and retain copies of all bills paid on their behalf; without them, they have no way to ascertain whether the amounts recouped from their royalties are correct. Writers earning substantial royalties, and spending $10,000 or more to record numerous demos during each accounting period, might easily fail to notice if additional demo expenses have been deducted.

Monitoring the invoices paid on one's behalf and comparing their totals to the amounts shown on royalty statements requires additional effort, and is not the creative work most songwriters prefer—but it is worth it. As in any situation requiring extensive numerical data entry, there is the risk of errors, and many songwriters have found they were inadvertently charged for other writers' expenses, or were overcharged for their own demo expenses.

Songwriters who are not signed to publishing agreements need to keep track of all demo recording expenses they incur, as well as other costs such as postage, printing, the cost of blank CDs, and the purchase of recording equipment. These expenses may be tax deductible, regardless of whether an individual is earning a living as a professional songwriter. A qualified accountant can assess whether a songwriter meets the criteria to deduct his or her songwriting expenses in any particular year.

Managing Your Income

There's an infamous story about a Nashville producer who received a $1 million royalty check. He bought a Cadillac, drove to Las Vegas—and returned to Nashville penniless. While this story is extreme, there are countless instances of songwriters and recording artists who failed to handle their money properly, with disastrous results.

For some individuals, problems arise because they spend extravagantly, buying the Mercedes, the boat, the wardrobe, or the jewelry they've always dreamed of owning. Others neglect to set aside enough money to pay Uncle Sam his sizable portion—and there may be state and local income taxes, as well.

It is important to point out that no taxes or Social Security payments are withheld from songwriters' mechanical or performance royalty payments; it is each individual's responsibility to set aside sufficient amounts to cover these costs. By seeking the assistance of an accountant skilled in the unique tax issues affecting music business clients, songwriters can learn the tax deductions to which they are entitled, potentially saving them substantial sums. They can also estimate the amount to be paid in taxes, and place the money allotted for this purpose into an interest-bearing account.

The Internal Revenue Service, under specified circumstances, formerly permitted taxpayers to calculate their taxes based on their average income over a period of several years. This process, known as *income averaging,* allowed songwriters (and others in similar financial circumstances) who earned an enormous amount some years, and relatively little in others, to average several years' earnings to determine their tax brackets. While the I.R.S. no longer offers this option, the PROs allow their members the alternative of having their income spread over multiple accounting periods (instead of being paid in a lump sum), essentially accomplishing the same result.

In most cases, songwriters wait many years before achieving their successes, and once they've seen one of their songs soar up the singles charts, appear on a hit album, or be performed on a television show, the wait continues. Six to nine months elapse following the end of the calendar quarter in which a song is played on the radio or television, and/or sold or downloaded, before any money arrives. It typically takes much longer before the bulk of the money generated is received, and if the airplay and sales occur outside the U.S., it may take twice as long for the money to begin flowing.

Writers eager to celebrate their successes are often able to secure bank loans with the help of the performance rights organization with which they are affiliated. The PROs work closely with banks in New York, Nashville, and Los Angeles that deal regularly with the unique situations applicable to songwriters and other music industry professionals. After a single has peaked on the charts, the PROs are able to estimate the performance royalties it will likely generate. Based on this information, in many cases banks will loan a songwriter a portion (usually up to 75 percent) of the money he or she has in the pipeline. When the royalties arrive, the writer's PRO pays back the bank (with interest), from the money due the songwriter. Until the loan is paid off, the songwriter does not receive any of his or her performance royalties.

An unpublished writer of a current successful song (or a song that is continuing to generate income), may choose to assign all, or a portion of, his or her publishing share to a company or individual in exchange for a sizable advance. Writers of a major, current hit are in an ideal negotiating position, and may be able to secure a nonrecoupable signing bonus or a substantial advance. They may also use the leverage gained by bringing a hit song to the proverbial table to garner a staff-writing deal with better terms than they might otherwise be able to obtain.

Songwriters signed to music publishing companies may be able to obtain an advance, a portion of the mechanical royalties and licensing fees their songs have generated—but there may be a price to pay. For instance, a publisher may say, "We'll advance you $25,000, but only if you grant us an additional one-year option period under the current terms." This may seem like a good thing on the surface, but it is to a successful writer's advantage not to be locked into a publishing contract any longer than is necessary. A writer who has hits during the term of his or her agreement should be able to have his or her attorney negotiate higher advances and better terms after his or her contract has expired.

It's extremely tough to get a hit song, and when it does happen, it opens doors, and provides incredible opportunities—but there is no guarantee that it will happen a second time. In some cases, struggling songwriters have lived hand to mouth for quite a while and that first big royalty check may represent more money than its recipient has earned over a period of years.

Songwriters whose publishers advance demo expenses and travel expenses (for instance, to collaborate in other cities or countries) may be lulled into forgetting that every penny advanced will be recouped (in most cases, from the writers' mechanical royalties). Fancy recording studios and top recording engineers, as well as the best musicians and vocalists, may contribute to a writer's future success—but are very expensive. Similarly, first class airline tickets, five-star hotels, and gourmet restaurants can quickly offset the earnings from even the biggest hit. It's important for writers to remember that even though they are not personally writing the checks, they are incurring these expenses—and will pay for them.

Some writers, dizzy with their "overnight success," spend wildly, lavishing gifts upon family, friends, and themselves. They assume that now that they've broken through, a string of hits will inevitably follow, and the money will continue flowing—but this does not always occur. Before the checks arrive, it's advisable for a writer to meet with a professional financial planner and/or investment counselor to develop a plan for how the money can be best put to use to accomplish his or her goals.

Making Time for Your Songwriting Business

Writing songs takes considerable time and energy, as does marketing them. Crafting exceptional songs, pursuing a publisher, negotiating contracts and licenses, recording demos, networking, and the additional tasks that are all part of the business of songwriting comprise a demanding, full-time job. The idea that songwriters live a life of leisure—writing an occasional song when the muse moves them and lying by the pool while awaiting royalty checks—is a fantasy.

Professional songwriters work hard, devoting long hours to their craft and to the noncreative aspects of their career. How can an aspiring songwriter who works a day job find the time and energy to compete with top writers who write songs and attend to the business of songwriting full time?

There's no easy answer to the question posed above. But virtually every individual currently earning a living as a songwriter has had to come up with the means of supporting him- or herself while still finding creative ways to pursue a songwriting career. For some writers, the solution is to wake up an hour early several days a week; others stop at a café on their way home from their jobs and work on lyrics uninterrupted; while for some writers it may work best to designate specific nights of the week, or weekends, for their songwriting. Some writers find that a nap and a shower after a long day of work leaves them refreshed and able to work on their music for several hours; others (with children) may find that having their spouse or a babysitter take the kids to a weekly night at the movies provides much-needed focused writing time.

There are only so many hours in each day, and, while we can't buy more of them, we can budget the time we have, choosing how best to use it. By turning off the television and computer one or more nights a week, writers may be amazed at how much creative work they are able to accomplish.

Another solution for songwriters with limited time for their creativity is to use vacation time to visit a music center or attend a music industry event. Options include sailing on a songwriting cruise, enrolling in a songwriting camp, visiting Los Angeles to participate in Taxi's Road Rally, or traveling to Northern California for the West Coast Songwriters Conference or to Nashville for NSAI's Songposium or a BMI workshop. Those who are unable to travel might structure all or part of their vacation as a "writer's retreat," a time to devote 100 percent of their energy to creative pursuits.

Everyone has responsibilities, and finding the energy and the time to devote to creative pursuits is a challenge. The bottom line is that each individual must find his or her own solutions. Writers for whom writing and marketing songs is a priority will find ways to make it work.

CHAPTER TWENTY

Developing Persistence and Realistic Expectations

Songwriting can be an extraordinary career, providing you with opportunities to express yourself, share your creativity with millions of people, and earn an excellent living. But validation and financial rewards are not guaranteed, regardless of how talented you might be, and the road to success can be long, arduous, and frustrating. By assessing the length of time it might reasonably take to achieve your goals, you can formulate a game plan for financial survival, and prepare yourself for the ups and downs that are likely to be a part of your journey.

Do You Need to Move to a Music Center?

Without the benefit of a crystal ball, it's impossible to know whether it's mandatory to relocate in order to achieve your career goals. There are a multitude of cities with vital, exciting music scenes. These cities have nightclubs and concert venues where audiences enthusiastically support live music; additionally, they may have one or more songwriter organizations. But there are only a handful of U.S. cities where the business of the music business regularly takes place—New York, Los Angeles, Nashville, and, to a lesser extent, Atlanta for R&B, rap, and hip-hop music. Austin is renowned for its exceptional live music scene and is the home to the annual South by Southwest (SXSW) music conference, but has few music publishers and record labels. With the exception of performing songwriters working in the folk/Americana genres, the majority of successful songwriters in the U.S. live in one of the aforementioned cities.

If you hope to write, publish, and market country or Christian hits, you will find more opportunities to do so in Nashville than anywhere else; if you aspire to a career writing pop, R&B, rock, rap, hip-hop, adult contemporary, or dance music you will increase your odds of achieving success by living (or spending considerable amounts of time) in Los Angeles or New York; and for R&B, rap, and hip-hop writers, in Atlanta as well.

If you reside in a major music business center you also have access to unsurpassed educational opportunities, such as the ongoing workshops offered by organizations such as BMI, ASCAP, NSAI, and the Songwriters Guild. These groups are often able to get their most successful members to teach workshops at events they sponsor. Likewise, the songwriting classes offered privately and at colleges and universities in these cities are likely to be taught by top songwriters and music industry professionals.

An additional benefit of living in a music business hub is access to a variety of recording studios. While most major cities are home to several recording studios, cities that are music meccas have hundreds, including some that specialize in recording various musical genres and those that offer the latest cutting-edge equipment and technology. Because of the "law of supply and demand," studios in music centers often charge lower rates than recording studios in smaller cities. Many songwriters find they can produce better demos at lower prices by recording them during periodic trips to one of the music centers.

Another advantage of living in New York, Los Angeles, or Nashville is the availability of exceptional musicians and vocalists to perform on demo recordings. Sheryl Crow, Gretchen Wilson, Garth Brooks, and James Ingram are among those who sang on songwriters' demos while awaiting their big breaks. Top musicians and vocalists who contribute their talent to superstar artists' albums tend to live in music business centers. Many of them supplement their income by performing on demos when they are not booked for master sessions. It's difficult, if not impossible, to find this caliber of talent in other cities.

And since many of the most talented, dedicated songwriters gravitate to New York, Los Angeles, and Nashville, if you are serious about your craft and your career, you will have the best chance of finding collaborators in these cities. With the prevalence of workshops, performance opportunities, and songwriter organizations in music centers, there are countless networking opportunities to meet potential cowriters, as well as other music industry professionals, in these locations.

Finally, virtually all major music publishing companies and record labels are located in music business centers, as are the majority of artists' managers and record producers. If you hope to develop business relationships and pitch your songs to music industry professionals, you will gain a distinct advantage by interacting with these individuals at industry events. Artist's showcases, seminars, parties, and other events hosted by songwriter organizations in music centers provide networking opportunities that cannot be found elsewhere.

Although there are instances of songwriters who forged successful careers prior to moving to a major music center and others who have sustained their successes while living in other locales, these cases are not typical. It's neither practical, nor advisable, for every aspiring songwriter to live in New York, Nashville, or Los Angeles. Writers who live elsewhere can still take positive actions, such as planning regular visits, attending song camps, and participating in music industry events to maximize their chances for success.

How Long Does It Take to Achieve Success?

Many writers wonder how long it will take them to secure publishing deals and watch their songs climb the charts. The answer is, "Much longer than you think." For most songwriters, even those with exceptional talent, honing their craft and developing music industry connections takes many years. Writers attending music industry events in one of the music centers are likely to hear comments such as, "L.A.'s a five-year town," or "L.A.'s a seven-year town." You can plug "New York" or "Nashville" into these phrases as well. They refer to the countless instances of songwriters pursuing their careers for five, seven, and even ten years or more before becoming "overnight successes." These cases are much more common than writers having hit songs in the first year or two of pitching their material.

Another often-quoted phrase is, "Your first one hundred songs are for practice." While the art of writing hit songs may seem effortless on the surface, for most writers the process includes years of sharpening their skills, getting feedback, and rewriting their melodies and lyrics. While every writer may not have to write a hundred songs before reaching a level of mastery of his or her craft, it is likely that many of the songs written along the way will fall short of the professional standard.

There are countless stories about songs (and recording artists) being repeatedly rejected before finding their way to the top of the charts. Celine Dion reportedly rejected "Unbreak My Heart," before Toni Braxton took it to the top of the pop, R&B, and adult contemporary charts. "I Hope You Dance," CMA's 2001 Song of the Year, was passed on by representatives of artists including Jessica Andrews and JoDee Messina before becoming a Number One single for Lee Ann Womack.

Among those recording artists repeatedly turned down by record labels and/or producers were the Beatles, Coldplay, Garth Brooks, and Whitney Houston.

Having a song recorded is no guarantee of it generating income. A song titled "Don't Tell My Heart" failed to garner significant sales or airplay for the Marcy Brothers. It was retitled, and when an artist named Billy Ray Cyrus released it as "Achy Breaky Heart" on his debut album, it made country music history. Similarly, when the legendary Kingston Trio recorded "The First Time Ever (I Saw Your Face)" it fell short of chart success. Several years elapsed before it became a career-breaking hit for Roberta Flack (and decades later topped the charts again, as recorded by the Fugees). "Bless the Broken Road" had an eleven-year journey, during which it was recorded four times, peaking at number forty-two on *Billboard*'s Country singles chart before Rascal Flatts' version attained the Number One spot and multiplatinum sales.

For all but the luckiest songwriters and recording artists, the journey to success is likely to take much longer, and be considerably more frustrating, than anticipated. Understanding and accepting this can help writers sustain their commitments through the unavoidable disappointments.

Developing Persistence

As pointed out in the previous section, even exceptional songs and recording artists may not necessarily attain commercial recognition quickly—and undoubtedly, some never do so. Rejection is to be expected; it is an integral part of the business of songwriting. It has been estimated that only one out of every twenty songs written by professional songwriters generates income. While recording artists writing for their own albums are likely to have much better odds, if this figure is accurate, it means that for most songwriters who earn a living from their music, 90 percent of what they write never achieves commercial success.

Songwriting is a business that comes with few guarantees, and only a small percentage of those writers who pursue a music business career will be rewarded with financial success. But if you give up, you can be assured you will have no chance of achieving your goals. In the face of such daunting odds it's essential to develop strategies for persevering and continuing to believe in yourself.

Establishing Realistic Goals

Regardless of how talented and lucky you may be, the realities of the music business are such that you will not be able to write a song today, and as a consequence, become rich and famous tomorrow. Let's examine a song's journey to success one last time.

After a song is written, a demo recording must be produced and then pitched to appropriate recording artists. This is most often accomplished by aligning with a reputable music publisher—which requires networking, and may take many years.

In many cases, publishers pitch songs for years, sometimes receiving more than a hundred rejections before a particular song skyrockets to the top of the charts.

When a song is being considered for recording by an artist it may go on hold until the artist is scheduled to work on his or her album; this may be months, or even a year or more away. In the event that the song is recorded, it has yet another hoop to jump through; more songs are recorded than are actually included on a given album. Presuming that the song is chosen to be among those comprising the album, many more months may elapse before the album is scheduled for release.

A song included on a hit album earns mechanical royalties, but these royalties pale in comparison to the performance royalties generated by a hit single. For instance, a gold album generates approximately $45,500 in mechanical royalties (based on the statutory rate in effect through December 31, 2007). This amount is divided among all the song's writers and publishers. If the song has two writers and two publishers, each writer and each publisher earns $11,375.

In contrast, if this same song is promoted as a single and reaches the Number One position on the pop, R&B, country, or adult contemporary charts, it may generate $1 million in performance royalties, yielding $250,000 for each of its writers. Keep in mind that it takes at least six to nine months before mechanical and performance royalties generated in the U.S. are paid to writers and publishers—and twice as long for foreign royalty income.

In most cases, the first single from an album is promoted to radio stations (and if applicable, video broadcasters) several months prior to the album's release; the single serves as a marketing tool to make listeners aware of the album and to encourage them to purchase it. If the song in our example is chosen as the second single, it will have to wait twenty weeks or more while the first single (hopefully) climbs the charts. A song chosen as the third or fourth single from a hit album may not be released to radio for a year or more after the release of the album on which it is included.

Overnight fame and fortune is a fantasy, but success, as a result of investing many years of effort, is attainable for many songwriters. It can be helpful to break down the process of songwriting success into manageable goals and to identify those areas that can benefit from additional attention. This applies equally to creative and business aspects. For instance, you might compile a list of short-term goals, followed by specific actions you can take to accomplish them, such as:

- *Produce a demo.* Research demo production services online; ask for referrals from writers at local songwriter organizations; call to check availability of local studios; get songs professionally critiqued (to be sure they're ready to be demoed)

- *Seek collaborators.* Plan to attend the Taxi Road Rally; attend local NSAI meetings; visit online sites that list collaborators

- *Work on developing melody skills.* Analyze the melodic techniques and chord structures in a favorite popular song; commit to devoting one hour twice a week to the melody exercises in the instructional CD, *Writing Hit Melodies with Jason Blume*; rewrite the chorus and verse melodies of your latest song at least three times.

- *Find a publisher.* Attend a BMI Nashville Workshop "publisher pitch"; ask for referrals from other writers; set a meeting with a PRO representative to request referrals; plan to attend the West Coast Songwriters Conference.

Writers make many decisions that directly impact their chances of achieving success. For instance, they decide how many hours to invest in writing, how much time to spend pursuing collaborators and publishers, the amount of money they are willing to spend on the production of demos, how many times a particular chorus melody is rewritten, and whether to attend songwriting camps, classes, and workshops. But there are many elements of both the creative and business sides of songwriting that are beyond a writer's control.

When they record demos, songwriters express how they envision their songs sounding. Once a song is chosen to be recorded by an artist, the producer rarely (if ever) consults with the songwriter about creative decisions. Crucial factors influencing a song's chances for success, such as the musical arrangement, the way the singer performs, and the musical parts created by the musicians, are all out of the songwriter's control. In some instances, the resulting recording is everything the songwriter could ever have imagined; in other cases, the results are devastating.

Similarly, there are factors in the business sector of songwriting that are out of writers' hands. For instance, after a demo is mailed, a writer is not in control of whether the song will ever be listened to, which employee at the record label (or publishing company) will actually listen, and the way a particular listener will react. An intern screening hundreds of submissions may fail to appreciate a particular song, but if this same song had been reviewed by someone else at the record label it might have been recorded, and gone on to become a huge hit.

The best strategy to circumvent the effects of "chance" is to write the strongest songs possible, songs that are undeniable hits; work hard to secure a publisher; and pitch the songs to the best of your ability. Writers who craft truly exceptional songs and take all the necessary actions to get them heard by decision makers tend to be those who get "lucky."

Identifying and working toward specific goals provides a sense of accomplishment and can help you remain motivated. While it may not be practical to set a goal of having a Number One hit in the next year, it is reasonable to say, "I will be writing better songs and will have taken actions to expand my network of music business contacts."

Finding Validation and Encouragement

Along the road to songwriting success, you are likely to hear comments such as "The chances are one in a million," "What makes you think you're so special?", and "How long are you going to waste your time on this pipedream?" Even if you have the strongest confidence and belief in your talent, you are sure to have times of self-doubt and fear that you may never attain your goals.

You can find support, encouragement, and camaraderie by joining local songwriter organizations, such as NSAI, Just Plain Folks, the Austin Songwriters Group, the Las Vegas Songwriters Association, or any of the hundreds of others located in cities throughout the U.S. and internationally. A comprehensive listing of songwriter organizations can be found in *6 Steps to Songwriting Success.*

While cowriters and friends can provide much-appreciated encouragement, ultimately, you need to find validation from within. If you look to external sources (such as sales figures and chart positions) to measure success, you will undoubtedly be disappointed. If you believe in yourself, honor your talent, and write from your heart, you are most likely to create works that touch your listeners. If you write songs because you truly love writing (as opposed to, as a means to becoming rich and famous), you'll find satisfaction and fulfillment along the way—and that is a true measure of success.

A Final Note from the Author

In the years that I've taught songwriting I've been privileged to watch some of my students attain their goals and live their dreams—but I've not seen it accomplished without dedication and hard work. I've shared the joy of writers celebrating their first recordings, congratulated students on winning first prize in the nation's biggest songwriting competitions, watched my students sign publishing contracts and major label recording deals, and watched as their songs climbed the charts. So I know that success is possible, despite how it might sometimes feel.

Take advantage of the educational and networking opportunities provided by classes, workshops, camps, and other music industry events; hone your skills by seeking professional feedback, studying the craft, and rewriting your work; learn about the business of songwriting; and most importantly, enjoy the ride. Information about receiving professional song critiques, purchasing books and instructional CDs, referrals to recording studios, and songwriting workshops is available at www.jasonblume.com. I hope I can help you achieve your songwriting goals.

Index